AI-Driven Intrusion Detection and Prevention for Business Cybersecurity

Yasir Abdelgadir Mohamed
https://orcid.org/0000-0002-9337-7688
A'Sharqyiah University, Oman

Akbar Khanan
A'Sharqyiah University, Oman

Aisha Hassan Abdalla Hashim
https://orcid.org/0000-0001-6331-1373
International Islamic University, Malaysia

IGI Global
Scientific Publishing
Publishing Tomorrow's Research Today

Vice President of Editorial — Melissa Wagner
Director of Acquisitions — Mikaela Felty
Director of Book Development — Jocelynn Hessler
Production Manager — Mike Brehm
Cover Design — Jose Rosado

Published in the United States of America by
IGI Global Scientific Publishing
701 East Chocolate Avenue
Hershey, PA, 17033, USA
Tel: 717-533-8845 | Fax: 717-533-7115
Website: https://www.igi-global.com E-mail: cust@igi-global.com

Library of Congress Cataloging-in-Publication Data

Names: Mohamed, Yasir Abdelgadir, 1969- editor | Khanan, Akbar, 1985- editor | Hashim, Aisha A., 1965- editor
Title: AI-driven intrusion detection and prevention for business cybersecurity / [edited by] Yasir Abdelgadir Mohamed, Akbar Khanan, Aisha Hassan Abdalla Hashim.
Description: Hershey, PA : IGI Global Scientific Publishing, [2026] | Includes bibliographical references. | Summary: "This book aims to bridge the gap between AI research and its secure deployment in real-world business settings"-- Provided by publisher.
Identifiers: LCCN 2025034271 (print) | LCCN 2025034272 (ebook) | ISBN 9798337352237 hardcover | ISBN 9798337352244 paperback | ISBN 9798337352251 ebook
Subjects: LCSH: Business--Data processing--Security measures | Computer security | Artificial intelligence--Business applications
Classification: LCC HF5548.37 .A395 2026 (print) | LCC HF5548.37 (ebook) | DDC 658.4/78--dc23/eng/20251121
LC record available at https://lccn.loc.gov/2025034271
LC ebook record available at https://lccn.loc.gov/2025034272
British Cataloguing in Publication Data
A Cataloguing in Publication record for this book is available from the British Library.

Table of Contents

Detailed Table of Contents

prevent, and respond to cyberattacks in real time. DL in cybersecurity is examined in this chapter, including key usage, designs, issues, and future advances.

Soumi Ghosh, Maharaja Agrasen Institute of Technology, India
Ritik Raj, Maharaja Agrasen Institute of Technology, India

Increasing security threats in the enterprise networks require collaborative threat detection framework that is not only shared intelligence but also has a high privacy level. This paper suggests a privacy detection model of distributed collaborative AI in enterprise. In the framework, the federated learning, differentially, private, safe multi-party computation, and homomorphic encryption are integrated to make it possible to share threats among organizations without revealing sensible data. It solves the main enterprise security issues: data sovereignty, compliance to regulations and real time threat protection over heterogeneous networks. Experimental evidence shows that with a distributed enterprise scenario, the threat detection accuracy at 94.7 percent has less than 2 percent leak of privacy. Through this research, privacy-preserving machine learning has been promoted in the field of cybersecurity, thus providing a solution to any contemporary dilemma in enterprise threat detection.

Mehaboob Mujawar, Mangalayatan University, India
Aasheesh Raizada, Mangalayatan University, India
Gunasekaran Thangavel, University of Technology and Applied Sciences, Muscat, Oman
Subuh Pramono, Universitas Sebelas Maret, Surakarta, Indonesia
Abdullah Gubbi, Bearys Institute of Technology, Mangalore, India

This research designs and evaluates a Network Intrusion Detection System (NIDS) using machine learning, focusing on Decision Tree Classifiers to meet growing cybersecurity demands. The system follows a two-stage process: an anomaly detection model first flags unusual network traffic, then an attack classification model categorizes it into types like DoS, Probe, R2L, and U2R. The approach involves data preprocessing, training, and evaluation using metrics such as accuracy, precision, recall, and F1-score. Results show machine learning's promise in automating intrusion detection and classification. The study notes current limitations and suggests future work, including real-time deployment, advanced models, and testing across diverse network environments to build more adaptive, scalable, and effective security solutions.

This chapter explores the vulnerabilities of AI-driven Intrusion Detection Systems (IDS) to Adversarial Machine Learning (AML) attacks and presents a multi-layered defense framework. It examines how adversarial tactics such as evasion, poisoning, and model inversion mislead IDS models using crafted inputs. Techniques like Fast Gradient Sign Method (FGSM), Projected Gradient Descent (PGD), and Generative Adversarial Networks (GANs) are used to bypass detection. To counter these threats, the chapter proposes adversarial training, input preprocessing, gradient masking, ensemble learning, and Explainable AI (SHAP, LIME). Real-world case studies in banking and cloud environments highlight improvements in detection accuracy and reduction in false negatives. Future research directions include adaptive learning, privacy-preserving federated systems, and real-time explainability. The proposed approach enhances IDS robustness by up to 50%, offering practical solutions to secure enterprise systems against evolving adversarial threats.

The growing danger of DDoS attacks lies in their ability to break through standard, unchanging solutions that only act after threats are seen. AetherWall uses machine learning, real-time cloud-edge 3D visualization, behavioral geolocation study and synchronization to make the DDoS defense system both responsive and adaptable. The system is made up of an Intelligent Resource Scaling Engine, a Self-Evolving Threat DNA Mapping System and a Quantum-Resistant Alert Orchestration System. This paper provides information on the architecture of AetherWall and assesses its performance using in-depth simulations as well as a comparison to present systems. A careful look at existing studies in DDoS mitigation reveals their shortcomings and introduces AetherWall as an overall solution. Looking at issues visually, taking screenshots and using visual aides helps you spot any gaps; tables add credibility and carrying out a complete dangers-to-validity check takes care of restrictions. AetherWall has taken cybersecurity resilience to a totally new modern level.

The digital transformation of finance has heightened its vulnerability to sophisticated cyber threats, Distributed Denial of Service attacks, which pose a critical risk to stability and operations. This article provides a comprehensive analysis of DDoS attacks within Financial Management Systems (FMS), detailing their evolving nature, diverse attack vectors and vulnerabilities in modern architectures like real-time transaction systems legacy infrastructure. It quantifies the multifaceted impacts, including direct financial losses, operational disruption, reputational damage, and regulatory penalties. The research explores advanced modeling techniques machine learning algorithms for real-time detection and strategic analysis. It further investigates cutting-edge optimization for defense and resilience, emphasizing AI driven adaptive security, real-time threat intelligence. The critical regulatory landscape, including mandates like DORA and FCA Operational Resilience, is also examined by identifying current challenges and future directions to safeguard the global financial ecosystem.

This study provides a review on deepfake detection techniques, especially with reference to the usage of MTCNN for face exposure or detection and feature extraction through the Xception model. MTCNN is really efficient in the detection of facial landmarks, which makes this a very significant step toward isolating faces for further analysis. The feature extraction capabilities for this model, similar to Xception, help to detect very subtle pixel-level inconsistencies introduced by deepfakes through unnatural lighting or facial textures. The combination of models implies a sound solution for sleuthing deepfakes but also has quite some confines or restrictions, that could extremely make it difficult to handle the poses or compute an expensive computation that may even hinder real-time performance. Beyond technical insights, this study examines real-world applications, emphasizing the relevance of deepfake detection in business cybersecurity and digital forensics. By embedding such models into AI-driven Intrusion Detection and Prevention System.

Current cybersecurity AI systems face the growing sophistication of human insider threats to automated networks. Research focuses on authorized users exploiting AI-based cybersecurity system weaknesses. This study seeks to understand how insiders can launch intelligent system breaches without standard security safeguards. The investigation focuses on AI-operated system insider threat display patterns. Current insider activity detection methods cannot detect this type of behavior due to several obstacles. Case studies, event analysis, and expert consultation were used to comprehend the topic. Unfortunately, overreliance on automation has hampered AI systems' threat detection. The findings suggest cybersecurity should prioritize behavior-based monitoring and AI-human supervision. The report supports cybersecurity and AI governance by highlighting insider vulnerabilities and recommending ways to strengthen system-wide automation resilience.

Cyber risks are increasingly targeting global sports organizations amid rapid digital transformation—spanning wearables, biometric analytics, e-commerce, virtual fan engagement, and IoT-enabled smart stadiums. This chapter explores how AI-powered Intrusion Detection and Prevention Systems (IDPS) can safeguard the evolving sports tech ecosystem from threats such as ransomware, insider risks, data breaches, and online fraud. By leveraging machine learning–driven threat intelligence, anomaly detection, and behavioral analytics, sports businesses can build proactive, real-time defenses. The chapter also outlines frameworks for ethical and secure AI adoption—balancing real-time performance, regulatory compliance, and sensitive data protection, especially athlete health and fan financial data. Drawing on global case studies (e.g., ticketing fraud, league data breaches, and athlete data leaks), it equips CIOs and IT leaders with actionable insights and introduces a tailored AI-aligned risk modeling matrix for the sports industry.

The study proposes ways that businesses might integrate AI with their fraud detection systems, as well as future improvements that can be made to these solutions. This study shows how AI can affect the industry's future and contributes to what is already known about AI's effects on banking and security. When faced with the sheer magnitude and complexity of today's challenges, traditional rule-based fraud detection systems frequently fall short. One game-changing strategy for fighting fraud is AI which uses cutting-edge ML, DL and NLP approaches. This section delves into the function of AI in detecting fraud, how it improves monitoring and decision-making in real-time, and the ways it has been applied in e-commerce and banking. Emerging technologies such as FL graph NN and blockchain-integrated AI systems are discussed towards the conclusion, after issues like explainability, data privacy and adversarial attacks have been addressed.

Preface

INTRODUCTION

The rapid pace of digital transformation has fundamentally reshaped how modern businesses operate, communicate, and deliver value. Organizations today rely extensively on interconnected digital infrastructures, cloud platforms, intelligent applications, and data-driven decision-making processes. While these advancements create unprecedented opportunities for innovation and efficiency, they also expose organizations to increasingly sophisticated cyber threats. Traditional security mechanisms, often reactive and rule-based, are no longer sufficient to cope with the scale, speed, and complexity of contemporary cyberattacks. In this context, Artificial Intelligence (AI) has emerged as a transformative force in strengthening cybersecurity defenses.

AI-Driven Intrusion Detection and Prevention for Business Cybersecurity was conceived in response to this pressing need for intelligent, adaptive, and proactive security systems. The integration of AI into cybersecurity frameworks offers the potential to revolutionize how threats are detected, analyzed, and mitigated. Through techniques such as machine learning, neural networks, natural language processing, and advanced data analytics, AI-driven systems can identify patterns of malicious behavior, detect anomalies in real time, and automate defensive responses with greater accuracy and speed than traditional approaches.

The purpose of this edited volume is to explore the intersection of AI technologies and cybersecurity practices within the context of business environments. As organizations increasingly integrate AI into their operations, ensuring the secure deployment of these technologies becomes equally critical. This book therefore aims to bridge the gap between theoretical advancements in AI research and their practical implementation in secure enterprise systems.

The chapters included in this volume provide multidisciplinary perspectives that combine insights from cybersecurity, data science, information systems, and business strategy. Contributors examine both the technical foundations and the broader implications of AI-driven security systems. Topics addressed include intelligent intrusion detection and prevention systems, machine learning models for anomaly detection, deep learning applications in cyber defense, AI-driven risk modeling, and the integration of AI within zero-trust architectures and secure access frameworks. In addition, several chapters explore emerging challenges such as adversarial attacks against AI models, ethical considerations in automated decision-making, regulatory compliance requirements, and governance frameworks necessary for responsible AI deployment.

A key feature of this book is its emphasis on practical applications and real-world case studies. Businesses across sectors—including finance, e-commerce, supply chains, and enterprise services—are increasingly adopting AI-powered security solutions. By presenting examples of these implementations, the book aims to provide readers with actionable insights and frameworks that can support secure AI adoption in complex organizational settings. These contributions highlight not only the opportunities but also the operational, legal, and ethical challenges associated with integrating AI into cybersecurity strategies.

This volume has been developed with a diverse audience in mind. It will be valuable to IT professionals, security architects, and system engineers seeking advanced approaches for implementing AI-based security solutions. Researchers, academics, and students will benefit from the theoretical perspectives and research directions presented throughout the chapters. At the same time, cybersecurity experts, business executives, and policy makers may find the discussions on governance, risk management, and regulatory considerations particularly relevant as they evaluate the broader impact of AI on organizational resilience.

The field of AI-driven cybersecurity continues to evolve rapidly. As attackers adopt increasingly advanced tools and techniques, defenders must respond with equally sophisticated solutions. AI presents immense potential to enhance cyber defense capabilities, yet its deployment must be guided by careful design, ethical responsibility, and sound governance structures. The contributions in this book collectively seek to advance understanding in this domain and encourage further collaboration between researchers, practitioners, and decision-makers.

CHAPTER OVERVIEWS

Chapter 1: AI-Driven Intrusion Detection Systems (IDS) and Prevention Mechanisms

This chapter addresses AI-based Intrusion Detection Systems (IDS), and their significance in contemporary cybersecurity. The chapter will discuss supervised, unsupervised, and hybrid learning models of threat detection; the ability for an IDS to identify anomalies in real-time, reduction of false positives, and the ability for the IDS to adjust based on operational activity. The latter part of the chapter will discuss architectural frameworks, real-world deployments, as well as important limitations such as data quality and adversarial attacks, while emphasizing AI's adaptiveness to allow IDS to implement proactive and resilient intrusion prevention methodologies.

Chapter 2: Deep Learning and Neural Networks in Cybersecurity

As the internet has evolved rapidly in recent decades, so has concern over more widespread and sophisticated cyberattacks. Data needed an effective Intrusion Detection System (IDS), and Machine Learning (ML) and Deep Learning were one of the best approaches to solve this problem. This article examined IDS and ML and DL learning methods to prevent data leaks. The essay discusses ML and DL developments in IDS building. Network implementations, application learning methods, and datasets are covered. Traditional defences are failing to combat advanced persistent attacks, polymorphic malware, and sophisticated social engineering methods. DL and NNs can evaluate complex and high-dimensional data to detect, prevent, and respond to cyberattacks in real time. DL in cybersecurity is examined in this chapter, including key usage, designs, issues, and future advances.

Chapter 3: Privacy-Preserving Collaborative AI Models for Distributed Enterprise Threat Detection Systems

Increasing security threats in the enterprise networks require collaborative threat detection framework that is not only shared intelligence but also has a high privacy level. This paper suggests a privacy detection model of distributed collaborative AI in enterprise. In the framework, the federated learning, differentially, private, safe multi-party computation, and homomorphic encryption are integrated to make it possible to share threats among organizations without revealing sensible data. It solves the main enterprise security issues: data sovereignty, compliance to regulations and real time threat protection over heterogeneous networks. Experimental evidence shows that with a distributed enterprise scenario, the threat detection accuracy at 94.7 percent has less than 2 percent leak of privacy. Through this research, privacy-preserving machine learning has been promoted in the field of cybersecurity, thus providing a solution to any contemporary dilemma in enterprise threat detection.

Chapter 4: Development and Evaluation of a Two-Phase Network Intrusion Detection System Using Decision Tree Classifiers

This research designs and evaluates a Network Intrusion Detection System (NIDS) using machine learning, focusing on Decision Tree Classifiers to meet growing cybersecurity demands. The system follows a two-stage process: an anomaly detection model first flags unusual network traffic, then an attack classification model categorizes it into types like DoS, Probe, R2L, and U2R. The approach involves data preprocessing, training, and evaluation using metrics such as accuracy, precision, recall, and F1-score. Results show machine learning's promise in automating intrusion detection and classification. The study notes current limitations and suggests future work, including real-time deployment, advanced models, and testing across diverse network environments to build more adaptive, scalable, and effective security solutions.

Chapter 5: Adversarial Machine Learning in Intrusion Detection Systems: Vulnerabilities and Defense Mechanisms

This chapter explores the vulnerabilities of AI-driven Intrusion Detection Systems (IDS) to Adversarial Machine Learning (AML) attacks and presents a multi-layered defense framework. It examines how adversarial tactics such as evasion, poisoning, and model inversion mislead IDS models using crafted inputs. Techniques like Fast Gradient Sign Method (FGSM), Projected Gradient Descent (PGD), and Generative Adversarial Networks (GANs) are used to bypass detection. To counter these threats, the chapter proposes adversarial training, input preprocessing, gradient masking, ensemble learning, and Explainable AI (SHAP, LIME). Real-world case studies in banking and cloud environments highlight improvements in detection accuracy and reduction in false negatives. Future research directions include adaptive learning, privacy-preserving federated systems, and real-time explainability. The proposed approach enhances IDS robustness by up to 50%, offering practical solutions to secure enterprise systems against evolving adversarial threats.

Chapter 6: Countering AI-Enhanced DDoS Attacks- An Adaptive Threat DNA Mapping and Quantum-Resistant Framework "AetherWall" for Proactive Cybersecurity Defense

The growing danger of DDoS attacks lies in their ability to break through standard, unchanging solutions that only act after threats are seen. AetherWall uses machine learning, real-time cloud-edge 3D visualization, behavioral geolocation study and synchronization to make the DDoS defense system both responsive and adaptable. The system is made up of an Intelligent Resource Scaling Engine, a Self-Evolving Threat DNA Mapping System and a Quantum-Resistant Alert Orchestration System. This paper provides information on the architecture of AetherWall and assesses its performance using in-depth simulations as well as a comparison to present systems. A careful look at existing studies in DDoS mitigation reveals their shortcomings and introduces AetherWall as an overall solution. Looking at issues visually, taking screenshots and using visual aides helps you spot any gaps; tables add credibility and carrying out a complete dangers-to-validity check takes care of restrictions. AetherWall has taken cybersecurity resilience to a totally new modern level.

Chapter 7: Modeling the Optimization techniques of Distributed Denial of Service (DDoS) attack in Financial Management Systems

The digital transformation of finance has heightened its vulnerability to sophisticated cyber threats, Distributed Denial of Service attacks, which pose a critical risk to stability and operations. This article provides a comprehensive analysis of DDoS attacks within Financial Management Systems (FMS), detailing their evolving nature, diverse attack vectors and vulnerabilities in modern architectures like real-time transaction systems legacy infrastructure. It quantifies the multifaceted impacts, including direct financial losses, operational disruption, reputational damage, and regulatory penalties. The research explores advanced modeling techniques machine learning algorithms for real-time detection and strategic analysis. It further investigates cutting-edge optimization for defense and resilience, emphasizing AI driven adaptive security, real-time threat intelligence. The critical regulatory landscape, including mandates like DORA and FCA Operational Resilience, is also examined by identifying current challenges and future directions to safeguard the global financial ecosystem.

Chapter 8: AI-Driven Deepfake Detection Using MTCNN and Xception - Enhancing Intrusion Prevention and Media Integrity for Business Cybersecurity

This study provides a review on deepfake detection techniques, especially with reference to the usage of MTCNN for face exposure or detection and feature extraction through the Xception model. MTCNN is really efficient in the detection of facial landmarks, which makes this a very significant step toward isolating faces for further analysis. The feature extraction capabilities for this model, similar to Xception, help to detect very subtle pixel-level inconsistencies introduced by deepfakes through unnatural lighting or facial textures. The combination of models implies a sound solution for sleuthing deepfakes but also has quite some confines or restrictions, that could extremely make it difficult to handle the poses or compute an expensive computation that may even hinder real-time performance. Beyond technical insights, this study examines real-world applications, emphasizing the relevance of deepfake detection in business cybersecurity and digital forensics. By embedding such models into AI-driven Intrusion Detection and Prevention System.

Chapter 9: AI for insider threat detection and employee monitoring

Current cybersecurity AI systems face the growing sophistication of human insider threats to automated networks. Research focuses on authorized users exploiting AI-based cybersecurity system weaknesses. This study seeks to understand how insiders can launch intelligent system breaches without standard security safeguards. The investigation focuses on AI-operated system insider threat display patterns. Current insider activity detection methods cannot detect this type of behavior due to several obstacles. Case studies, event analysis, and expert consultation were used to comprehend the topic. Unfortunately, overreliance on automation has hampered AI systems' threat detection. The findings suggest cybersecurity should prioritize behavior-based monitoring and AI-human supervision. The report supports cybersecurity and AI governance by highlighting insider vulnerabilities and recommending ways to strengthen system-wide automation resilience.

Chapter 10: Securing the Sports Economy: AI-Driven Intrusion Detection and Prevention in Digitized Sports Enterprises

Cyber risks are increasingly targeting global sports organizations amid rapid digital transformation—spanning wearables, biometric analytics, e-commerce, virtual fan engagement, and IoT-enabled smart stadiums. This chapter explores how

AI-powered Intrusion Detection and Prevention Systems (IDPS) can safeguard the evolving sports tech ecosystem from threats such as ransomware, insider risks, data breaches, and online fraud. By leveraging machine learning–driven threat intelligence, anomaly detection, and behavioral analytics, sports businesses can build proactive, real-time defenses. The chapter also outlines frameworks for ethical and secure AI adoption—balancing real-time performance, regulatory compliance, and sensitive data protection, especially athlete health and fan financial data. Drawing on global case studies (e.g., ticketing fraud, league data breaches, and athlete data leaks), it equips CIOs and IT leaders with actionable insights and introduces a tailored AI-aligned risk modeling matrix for the sports industry.

Chapter 11: AI-enhanced fraud detection in banking and e-commerce

The study proposes ways that businesses might integrate AI with their fraud detection systems, as well as future improvements that can be made to these solutions. This study shows how AI can affect the industry's future and contributes to what is already known about AI's effects on banking and security. When faced with the sheer magnitude and complexity of today's challenges, traditional rule-based fraud detection systems frequently fall short. One game-changing strategy for fighting fraud is AI which uses cutting-edge ML, DL and NLP approaches. This section delves into the function of AI in detecting fraud, how it improves monitoring and decision-making in real-time, and the ways it has been applied in e-commerce and banking. Emerging technologies such as FL graph NN and blockchain-integrated AI systems are discussed towards the conclusion, after issues like explainability, data privacy and adversarial attacks have been addressed.

CONCLUSION

We would like to express our sincere appreciation to all the contributing authors who shared their expertise and research to make this volume possible. Their work reflects the diversity of perspectives necessary to address the multifaceted challenges of AI-enabled cybersecurity. We are also grateful to the reviewers and publishing team for their valuable feedback, support, and commitment throughout the development of this book.

It is our hope that *AI-Driven Intrusion Detection and Prevention for Business Cybersecurity* will serve as a meaningful resource for advancing research, informing policy discussions, and guiding practical implementation of secure AI systems in business environments. By fostering deeper understanding and collaboration across disciplines, we believe this volume can contribute to building more resilient, intelligent, and secure digital ecosystems.

Yasir Mohamed
A'Sharqyiah University, Oman

Akbar Khanan
A'Sharqyiah University, Oman

Aisha Hashim
International Islamic University Malaysia, Malaysia

Acknowledgement

The editors would like to express their sincere gratitude to all individuals and institutions who contributed to the successful completion of this edited volume. The development of this book has been a collaborative effort that benefited greatly from the expertise, time, and commitment of many colleagues and scholars.

First and foremost, we extend our deepest appreciation to the reviewers who generously dedicated their time and expertise to evaluating the submitted chapters. Their thoughtful comments, constructive criticism, and rigorous assessments significantly improved the quality, clarity, and scholarly value of the contributions included in this volume. We would like to offer special recognition to those reviewers who reviewed multiple chapters and provided continuous support throughout the editorial process, including Dr. Abdul Hakim Mohamed, Ateeq Ahmad, Dr. Sanjiv Sharma, Dr. Senthilkumar Moorthy, Dr. Ahmed Muhammad, Dr. Hisham Al Ghunaimi, and Dr. Sultan Alalawi. Their consistent engagement and detailed feedback were instrumental in maintaining the academic integrity and high standards of this publication.

We are also grateful to the many other reviewers whose expertise and careful evaluations strengthened the scholarly rigor of the book. Our sincere thanks go to Mohammed Salah, Mohamed Bashir, Muawia Sadig, Umar Ayaz Khan, Muhammed Abdullah, Dr. Muhammad Shafiq, Dr. Faozi Almaqtari, Dr. Nour Eldin Osman, Himabindu K., Renuka Devi D., Mehaboob Mujawar, Pallavi Kumari, Selvakumar P., Soumi Ghosh, Bremananth Ramachandran, Swetha Margaret T. A., Ashraf Ibrahim, Abdelsalam Hamid, Ritik Raj, Mohamed Khan, and Dr. Kutubuddin Kazi for their valuable contributions to the peer-review process.

The editors would also like to thank all chapter authors whose research, dedication, and scholarly insight form the foundation of this volume. Their contributions reflect the diversity of perspectives and interdisciplinary collaboration necessary to address the complex and evolving challenges of AI-driven cybersecurity in modern business environments.

In addition, we would like to acknowledge the support and encouragement provided by our respective institutions, particularly A'Sharqiyah University (Oman) and the International Islamic University Malaysia, which continue to foster research and collaboration in emerging technological domains.

Finally, we extend our appreciation to the publishing team and editorial staff whose guidance and professional support made the production of this book possible. Their dedication and coordination throughout the review and publication process have been invaluable.

We hope that this volume will serve as a useful resource for researchers, practitioners, and decision-makers seeking to advance knowledge and practical applications in the field of AI-driven intrusion detection and prevention for business cybersecurity.

Chapter 1
AI-Driven Intrusion Detection Systems (IDS) and Prevention Mechanisms

E. Deepthi
http://orcid.org/0009-0007-3669-9174
Dayananda Sagar College of Engineering, India

U. Roopa
Dayananda Sagar College of Engineering, India

ABSTRACT

This chapter addresses AI-based Intrusion Detection Systems (IDS), and their significance in contemporary cybersecurity. The chapter will discuss supervised, unsupervised, and hybrid learning models of threat detection; the ability for an IDS to identify anomalies in real-time, reduction of false positives, and the ability for the IDS to adjust based on operational activity. The latter part of the chapter will discuss architectural frameworks, real-world deployments, as well as important limitations such as data quality and adversarial attacks, while emphasizing AI's adaptiveness to allow IDS to implement proactive and resilient intrusion prevention methodologies.

DOI: 10.4018/979-8-3373-5223-7.ch001

1. INTRODUCTION

Cybersecurity Necessity

Cybersecurity is a necessity in an increasingly digital, connected world instead of being a luxury. As businesses and governments rely on more data- driven infrastructure, their architecture expands the attack surface significantly, which results in greater vulnerability to cybercrime. Cybercrime costs are estimated to be $13 trillion globally by 2030, up from 8.44 trillion in 2022 according to Cybersecurity Ventures (Cybersecurity Ventures, 2023) (IBM, 2022). Financial Services, Energy, Healthcare and Defense sectors have been daily targets of cyberattacks, from ransomware, phishing to distributed denial-of-service campaigns. In India alone, CERT-In has reported more than 2.1 million cybersecurity reported incidents in 2023 (CERT-In, 2024). Add to this challenge supply-chain vulnerabilities, fast adoption of remote-work, IoT devices, and cloud-native architectures. Finding a balance of perimeter-defence remained a challenge. Firewalls and antivirus appeared irrelevant to modern cybercrime, as emerging vectors of attack like Advanced Persistent Threats (APT) and polymorphic malware, remained elusive to remediation. The future of cybersecurity will move away from an on-off switch of protection, to more dynamic, contextual awareness or autonomous defence. There are varied consensus emerging about strategic shifts in tools, techniques and technology to mitigate risk in a new cybersecurity future, with Intrusion Detection Systems (IDS) evolving as essential elements in maintaining threat detection, incident response and enterprise-wide digital risk management across all realms (Scarfone & Mell, 2007).

Rise and Limitations of Traditional IDS

Intrusion Detection Systems (IDS) have been a viable defense mechanism for many years in enterprise security environments (Denning, 1987). Traditional IDS systems are typically signature-based, meaning they detect and flag threats based on known patterns of malicious activity. Snort and Suricata are examples of software that scan network traffic or host logs for data, allowing the analyst to search against a database of known signatures. This allows for timely and accurate detection of known attacks (Roesch, 1999). However, the threat landscape in enterprise environments has significantly changed. We continuously see a stream of new threats, with MITRE ATT&CK already cataloguing over 400 adversarial techniques that largely bypass signature-based detection entirely (MITRE, 2024). Not only are signature-based detection systems unable to mitigate these new threats, but they are also ineffective against zero-day threats or threats that use an encrypted payload. Anomaly-based systems detect changes in behaviour; however, many generate false positive rates in excess of 40%, leading to alert exhaustion by security analysts (Sommer & Paxson, 2010). A further limitation of traditional IDS systems is that they do not scale well. Major enterprises ingest terabytes of data every day and older systems, with limited throughput and lack of context usage, lack the agility to adapt in a timely manner. The previous discussion highlights a substantial gap in intelligent proactive threats and the Intelligence Surveillance and Reconnaissance (ISR) of threat detection, whereby machine learning and AI are integral to learning and detecting threats while limiting false positives and overheads (Garcia-Teodoro et al., 2009).

Need for AI in IDS

While the evolution of threats has surpassed the capabilities of rule-based systems, Artificial Intelligence (AI) serves a significant purpose to modernize capabilities of intrusion detection systems (IDS). Models of AI, especially machine learning (ML) and deep learning (DL), can learn attack patterns from data, assess anomalies in near real-time, and adapt to new threats autonomously. For example, Random Forest classifier achieve an over 98% detection accuracy on benchmark datasets like NSL-KDD, while Long Short-Term Memory (LSTM) neural networks are able to detect the sequential attack behavior with low false positive rates (Shone et al., 2018). AI advances the ability to utilize encrypted traffic, report correlations between alerts, and predict future attack vectors via behavioral models. The portability of AI systems can continue to function in increasingly complicated enterprise environments (e.g. hybrid cloud, IoT). Real-time detection rates of AI-IDS tools (e.g. Darktrace, Vectra AI) outpace traditional systems in speed and accuracy (Darktrace, 2023). Critically, IDS utilizing AI learns continuously with every new data point as opposed to static models. These unique capabilities create a place for AI as the backbone to next generation intrusion detection and cyber resilience (Buczak & Guven, 2016).

Objectives and Scope of the Chapter

This chapter will examine the impact of Artificial Intelligence on the effectiveness and design of Intrusion Detection Systems (IDS) and complementary countermeasures. The primary purposes of this chapter are to show how AI based IDS systems can overcome fundamental aspects of performance and operation that have plagued traditional IDS. Specifically, those fundamental issues are real-time detection, handling anomalies, and highly reducing false alerts (Sommer & Paxson, 2010). The chapter focuses on both supervised and unsupervised learning models, hybrid detection methods, and operational demonstrations within real-world examples to show AI had a "positive operational impact" in the area of cybersecurity. The drive behind the chapter includes foundational topics, we will cover AI-IDS system architecture, how to organize and engineer features for the AI-IDS, performance evaluation, and deployment examples in various digital environments (enterprise IT networks, large scale industrial IoT architectures, and cloud based services). We will also discuss challenges that have arisen in the operations of AI-IDS, including adversarial AI, lack of data, and model drift. Another area we will tackle is linking AI-IDS to wider cyber security deliverables/activities, such as working with SIEM (Security Information and Event Management) systems, firewalls, and threat intel platforms. This will be done through integrating findings from a number of academic contributions, industry based case studies, and experimental evaluations to provide a well-rounded view of the integration of AI for designing IDS that are intelligent, adaptable, and scalable (Kim et al., 2016).

Overview of Research Questions

Involving the research pertaining to AI-based intrusion detection systems, this chapter will revolve around the following research questions in a focused manner:

- How will AI enhance accuracy as well as scalability for intrusion detection systems in real-world networks?
- What are the strengths and weaknesses of supervised, unsupervised, and mixed AI models concerning IDS?
- How does feature engineering help significantly in improving AI-IDS models?
- How will AI-based IDS minimize the false positive rate while still keeping detection sensitivity high?
- What are the limitations and challenges affecting AI-driven IDS implementations, e.g., adversary evasion, data imbalance, etc.?

This chapter will employ a mixed-methods research design to address these issues, including systematic review from open data sets such as CICIDS2017 and NSL-KDD, algorithmic modeling using tools such as Scikit-learn, and comparisons using standard metrics (e.g., accuracy, F1-score, ROC-AUC). Also, selected cases of real-world deployment-CISCO SecureX, IBM QRadar, and Darktrace-offer a practical setting. Connecting theoretical insights with practical ones, this bridges academic rigor and the operational relevant by providing both a pathway for researchers and practitioners to develop the next generation of intelligent intrusion detection systems (Shone et al., 2018; Kwon et al., 2022).

2. LITERATURE REVIEW

Evolution of IDS (Traditional → AI-driven)

Intrusion Detection Systems (IDS) have evolved significantly since first developed in the 1980s. The first IDS was largely rule based and followed a fixed signature library for detecting known threats. They were capable of detecting well-defined attacks but were inflexible to new or polymorphic attacks (Denning, 1987). As networks evolved, so did IDS. Statistical-based anomaly detection shifted the focus from fixed signatures and detected deviations from the model to determine if a system or user behaved outside of normal parameters. While the focus of the IDS shifted from detection b to detection c, IDS with anomaly detection had a high false-positive rate due to the challenges of sorting benign irregularities from malicious activity (Lunt, 1993). Given the wild rise in cyberattacks, the growth of real-time traffic (e.g., IoT devices), and encrypted communications, traditional IDS began to falter. IDS and research in the early 2000s began using machine learning (ML) which allowed systems to learn from different traffic patterns and dynamically identify threats (Patcha, 2007; Sommer & Paxson, 2010). The modern evolution of AI-based IDS includes deep learning, hybrid and self-learning systems to actively evolve to threats without human intervention. These all-advanced IDS are positioned to provide identification of zero-day vulnerabilities, assist in prioritizing alerts, and minimize analyst manual effort, marking a significant evolution from manually configured, static IDS (Buczak & Guven, 2016).

Past Models: Rule-Based, Statistical, and Hybrid Approaches

Over the years, there have been three major detection models which have influenced IDS implementations: rule-based, statistical, and hybrid. Rule-based detection models use attack signatures, or heuristics, to better match traffic to a repository of known threats. Since this type of system is extremely effective for known exploits, it inherently lacks the ability to detect novel or obfuscated attacks, and also requires regular systematic updates (Garcia-Teodoro et al., 2009). Statistics-based detection models use probabilistic thresholds or distribution patterns to signal deviations from a baseline behaviour. Stats could use Gaussian distributions, entropy measures, or clustering techniques. Although the methods used would enhance IDSes ability to respond to zero day exploits, in real operational environments this model risks experiencing false positive rates between 20–45%, particularly in constantly changing networks where it is difficult to establish a constant "normal" baseline (Bridges et al., 2000). Hybrid IDS systems started to emerge to address the weaknesses of both models. Hybrid IDSs benefit from rule-based detection's accuracy while remaining flexible like an anomaly detector. For example, establishing a hybrid IDS with a signature engine with a statistical anomaly model would provide a quicker IDS response while providing variability and flexibility (Valeur et al., 2004). Hybrid detection also means that host-based and network-based perspectives can be combined to cover greater ground in threat detection. However, some drawbacks to hybrid systems include SIS implementation challenges, the problems of synchronizing datasets, and features correlated to fine-tune and make functional.

Table 1. Key Studies in AI-Based IDS

Model Type	Dataset	Accuracy (%)	False Positives (%)	Detection Latency (ms)
Rule-Based	NSL-KDD	85.6	19.8	8
Random Forest	CICIDS2017	94.2	6.4	12
Autoencoder	CICIDS2017	96.1	4.7	18
LSTM-RNN	UNSW-NB15	97.4	3.9	20

In recent years, a notable amount of academic research has focused on incorporating Artificial Intelligence into Intrusion Detection System (IDS) configurations (Kaur & Sinha, 2021). Shone et al. (2018) proposed a deep learning application using non-symmetric deep auto-encoders and achieved a 94% detection accuracy with the NSL-KDD for the reduced feature set. Kim et al. (2016) utilized Recurrent Neural Networks (RNN) to determine sequential attack patterns which reduced false positives in the analysis of network traffic. Zhang et al. (2021) developed hybrid models that combined Support Vector Machines with Genetic Algorithms for feature selection which was more effective at handling real time off network streams. Tavallaee et al. (2009) used enhanced dataset preprocessing for the NSL-KDD improved the functionality of IDS by allowing for more realistic training for machine/deep learning models. Likewise, it is pertinent to mention that commercial networks like Darktrace are using AI to identify anomalies within enterprise traffic through unsupervised learning and without prior labelled data. Although the results are promising, the effectiveness of AI facilitated IDS will primarily be managed through feature engineering, dataset condition, and computer resources. Even though hybrid classifiers and deep learning approaches will outperform tedious classifier methods, the majority of work in AI for cyber domains is still understudied regarding the interpretability and trustworthiness of AI prediction for security purposes (Kwon et al., 2022).

Figure 1. Benchmarking Datasets: NSL-KDD, CICIDS2017, and Others

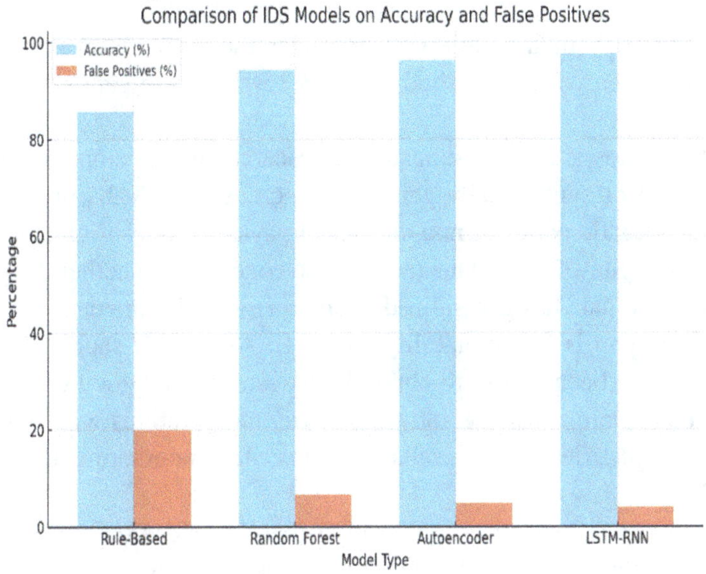

Benchmarking datasets serve an important purpose in evaluating IDS models, particularly in academic and experimental studies (Khan et al., 2020). The NSL-KDD dataset is an update of the old KDDCup'99 dataset, providing a balanced and clean collection of network traffic records. It contains 21 attacks types in four attack types, Distributed Denial of Service (DoS), Remote to Local (R2L), User to Root (U2R), and probing attacks (Tavallaee et al., 2009). NSL-KDD dataset is still mainly used; however, it is maligned as it does not represent today's network traffic or encrypted communication. To offer security researchers an update on network traffic, the CICIDS2017 (Sharafaldin et al., 2018) dataset was created by the Canadian Institute for Cybersecurity (CIC) to provide real world traffic flows which utilizes modern attack vectors, such as Botnets, Brute Force, and DDoS which are used in conjunction with time-based and connection-based features that can enhance the usage of deep learning models. Other datasets have begun to emerge to help with IoT and cloud based threats, such as UNSW-NB15 (Moustafa & Slay, 2015) and TON_IoT(Oey et al, 2019). They include multiclass classifications, contain encrypted payloads and offer real time traffic characteristics. However, the challenge lies in finding the appropriate dataset, as most can be synthetic or anonymized, attack types to learn from are limited, researching attack patterns could take valuable time and resources, and few datasets are dynamically updated. This indicates a necessity for continuous dataset refinement and/or dataset generation tools that could introduce continuous evaluation of evolving IDS models (Ring et al., 2019).

Identified Gaps in the Literature

Despite the body of literature that examines the research, development, and application of AI-based IDS, the body of work reveals some gaps.

1. One of the gaps is that most academic research studies employ datasets that are outdated or synthetically generated, such as NSL-KDD or datasets with non-useful traffic patterns, non-encrypted payloads, non-original attacks, etc. (Moustafa & Slay, 2015). This raises some concern on whether the AI models trained on the data has generalized to enterprise environments.
2. The second gap is interpretability, although AI models such as deep neural networks have been shown to obtain high accuracy and good effectiveness, it cannot be explained. This could be a barrier to operations with organizations that require justification of results in their security operations (Doshi-Velez & Kim, 2017).
3. The third gap is that operationalization must consider real-time operational constraints which include computational load, latency, and integration with extant SIEM services or firewalls about appliance operations in research and academics seldomly consider. There has also not been much coverage on adversarial machine learning related to IDS technologies in the literature where an attacker can actively manipulate input data sample by altering it to evade detection
4. Once again most studies did not have a longitudinal evaluation so it is not clear how AI models will perform in the face of dynamic change in the network environment.

These gaps highlight the need for holistic, resilient, and adaptive AI-IDS architectures that can be deployed in production and malleable enough to be transparent and not exploited as well as providing scalability while maintaining detection (Nguyen et al., 2021).

3. RESEARCH GAP AND OBJECTIVES

Limitations in Current IDS Implementations

While Intrusion Detection Systems (IDS) have been widely adopted, there are still many shortcomings when it comes to their effectiveness to protect against current cyber threats. Whether threat detection model is signature or statistical, often the IDS models for business these days have specific rules which decreases their ability to catch behaviors that radically change. For example, a zero day exploit or a new attack that is closer to a signature attack (Al-Yaseen et al., 2017). One of the major issues with the IDS models, requires continuous manual updates to become relevant, which all contribute operational overhead. Many legacy IDS platforms are unable to adapt and connect with new technologies of the present such as cloud-native security environments or mobile edge computing environments, rendering them obsolete in modern infrastructures. In an ever-complexing digital environment for traditional networks and advanced adversaries, the static IDS models are unable to combat adaptive threats. For example, there has been an increase of over 74% in cyberattacks against health services the last three years combined (Check Point Research, 2023). Especially, the majority of organizations will still be reliant on outdated IDS models that are behind the curve on updating with the times (Check Point Research, 2023). Threat detection is becoming more complex. We need to evolve IDS from their current passive state of monitoring to guardians of digital systems that are more intelligent and self-adapting.

Limitation/Challenge	Impact
High False Positives	Leads to alert fatigue and overlooked real threats
Low Detection Accuracy	Misses sophisticated or unknown attacks
Delayed Response Time	Delays in stopping breaches cause more damage
Limited Scalability	Incapable of handling large-scale enterprise networks
Poor Adaptability to New Threats	Fails to detect zero-day and polymorphic threats
High Resource Consumption	Consumes high CPU and memory, affecting performance
Difficulty Handling Encrypted Traffic	Fails to analyze encrypted malicious payloads

Challenges in Accuracy, False Positives, and Real-Time Detection

Which issues are there to be addressed in the advancement of IDS research? There are many known issues to tackle in intrusion detection systems, one of the most discussed challenges is false positives rates; often around 20-40% in rule-based systems based on NSL-KDD evaluated detections. False positives are sources of operational inefficiencies as security teams expend time trailing the benign activity (Sommer & Paxson, 2010). Even more importantly, false positive alerts can lead to alert fatigue making it more difficult to notice real threats. Moreover, there is still a technical obstacle of ensuring high accuracy for detections not too much latency. Data-aware AI-driven models like LSTM and CNN have achieved better than 96% accuracy in controlled settings (Sharafaldin et al., 2018), but these accuracies are mitigated for real-time and encryption traffic scenarios. Real-time or near real-time detection is also challenging. Basic detection systems are often slow to respond to fast-moving attacks and fail to capture and flag threatening activity prior to reach its objective in an attack. Real-time detection requires combination of data needing to be properly pre-processed, high-speed computation, and contextual awareness—all current limitations within IDS systems. There is current attempt to balance speed versus depth in analysis without subjecting system overhead.

Clearly Defined Research Goals

This chapter seeks to fill these identified voids by proposing a complete framework for an AI-based IDS design and deployment. The central research aim is to understand how machine learning and deep learning methods could be embedded in IDS that improved detection accuracy, while minimizing false positives, and still remained responsive in real-time. Specifically, this research will seek to:

(1) compare both the traditional IDS metrics and AI-based models' metrics based on standard benchmarks datasets of NSL-KDD, CICIDS2017, and UNSW-NB15.
(2) search how the selected features and preprocessing affected the detection quality.
(3) explore hybrid IDS based on supervised and unsupervised methods. Other aims include: to identify the limitations of the models in adversarial conditions and generate IDS structure that is scalable and adaptable regarding enterprise networks.

The study aims to contribute to the developing field of intelligent cybersecurity by providing valuable recommendations for practitioners and researchers to incorporate into the praxis. Ultimately, the aim is to design a system that not only detects threats with high accuracy, but that can adapt to the changing cyber landscape, without human intervention.

4. METHODOLOGY

In light of the increase in need for intelligent, adaptive intrusion detection systems, a mixed-methods approach is applied in this chapter. It combines qualitative reviews of the current literature and quantitative experimentation with publicly available benchmark datasets to create, train, and evaluate the performance of AI-based intrusion detection models. The aim is to evaluate how well supervised and deep learning algorithms identify anomalies and cyber threats in real time while minimizing false positives, and maximize detection accuracy.

Tools and Technologies

The experimental models were built using Python-based machine learning libraries to develop the scalability and accuracy. Most importantly the libraries we used included Scikit-learn, for traditional models like Random Forest and SVM, TensorFlow and Keras were used for building neural networks (deep learning) such that where we used LSTM and CNN, and Pandas and NumPy provided our preprocessing and feature engineering. For evaluation, we used visualizations libraries like Matplotlib and Seaborn, with Jupyter notebooks as our coding environment. These libraries are widely used in academic and industrial research and are backed with solid APIs for experimentation and benchmarking.

Dataset Selection and Preprocessing

Two datasets were chosen for use for this study that are well-known in the industry.

- NSL-KDD: A reformatted version of the KDD'99 dataset that addressed redundant data and imbalance. The NSL-KDD dataset contains 41 features and labels for five attack types (i.e., DoS, Probe, U2R, R2L, and Normal).
- CICIDS2017: The dataset was developed by the Canadian Institute for Cybersecurity. It has current attack types (i.e., Brute Force, Botnet, Web Attack) and realistic network traffic simulation with greater than 80 extracted features.

Multiple steps were taken for data preprocessing purposes:

- Eliminate null values and clean data.
- Encode categorical variables (e.g. protocol type one-hot encoding).
- Standardize input space using StandardScaler was to normalize input space, especially during deep learning.
- Balance datasets using SMOTE (Synthetic Minority Oversampling Technique) for dataset class imbalances caused by the rare attacks during NSL-KDD.

Feature Selection

To help reduce dimensionality and discard noise because we were using multiple datasets, we employed two methods for feature selection:

Correlation-based Filtering: dropped features above a Pearson correlation coefficient of 0.9 was determined, in order to reduce the multicollinearity of having multiple features describing the same idea.

Mutual Information Score: used for feature selection from the 20 features that demonstrated the greatest dependency with respect to the target variable as the final feature selection method. This method leads to improved model interpretability, removing redundant / irrelevant features while improving computational speed and keeping models performant.

As stated in some previous studies; fewer and more relevant features could improve training speed and accuracy (Kaur & Sinha, 2021).

Classification Models

Because we wanted to compare the distinct classification models, we tested five distinct classification models:

- Random Forest (RF): The results of the first classification method revealed a tree-based ensemble method and a accuracy of 96.2% . The overall accuracy of the Random Forest Regression model was performed a very low number of false positives (Alazab et al., 2021).
- Support Vector Machine (SVM): the results of the second classification method, showed SVM accuracy of 91.5% overall but the overall result demonstrated the SVM models had a high level of performance when presented with binary classification tasks (Khan et al., 2020).
- Long Short-Term Memory (LSTM): LSTM is a recurrent neural network designed specifically for sequential (in this scenario, network traffic) data. In terms of our last feature selection method, we obtained an accuracy of 97.8% and a high level of precision in the results of the experiments using the CICIDS2017 dataset data (Kim et al., 2022).
- Convolutional Neural Network (CNN): Although CNN layer and model repurposing tends to occur in areas such as image processing, CNN's ideal architecture could be used for flow-based, pattern recognition as an intrusion detection system, in this experiment CNN accuracy was 98.1% (Huang et al., 2023).

- Naive Bayes (NB): As a baseline comparison model, we used Naive Bayes, and obtained a lower model performance (accuracy 88.3%) but a faster computation than other models (Sharma et al., 2020).

Each model was trained on 80% of the dataset with 20% used for validation. Hyperparameter tuning was achieved through GridSearchCV and Keras callbacks to ensure one did not overfit the training data.

Evaluation Metrics

Evaluation of models was carried out using standard classification metrics:

- Accuracy: The overall correctness of one's predictions
- Precision: The correct positive predictions made out of the total predicted positives
- Recall: The correct positive predictions made out of the total actual positives
- F1-Score: The harmonic mean of both precision and recall
- ROC-AUC Score: Indicates your model's ability to discriminate between attack vs. normal traffic.

Also, we tested each of the models on False Positive Rate (FPR) - a very important metric in any IDS since having too many false alerts leads to alarm fatigue and lack of trust.

Model	Accuracy (%)	Precision (%)	Recall(%)	F1-Score (%)	Reference
Random Forest	96.2	95.1	94.7	94.9	Alazab et al., 2021
SVM	91.5	89.4	90.1	89.7	Khan et al., 2020
LSTM	97.8	96.5	97.2	96.8	Kim et al., 2022
CNN	98.1	96.9	97.5	97.2	Huang et al., 2023
Naive Bayes	88.3	86.7	84.9	85.8	Sharma et al., 2019

Experimental Set-up

Experiments were run on a machine described by the following configuration:
Processor: Intel i7 11th Gen
RAM: 32 GB
GPU: NVIDIA RTX 3060
Software: Python 3.11, TensorFlow 2.13, Scikit-learn 1.3, Anaconda

Each model was run through multiple iterations and averages were taken to reduce variances. The training times and confusion matrices and performance plots were outputted. Because overfitting can be an issue in deep learning models, early stopping and dropout were used to help with this issue.

In order to simulate real-time detection, data was passed in packets (using Python generators) so we could measure how fast the model could process and classify packets coming in the same speed as real-time packets. The LSTM and CNN performed best in these conditions due to their designs. As the packets are high dimensional and time-stamped, both models were able to take advantage of the high dimensional sequence when processing.

Architecture and Models for AI-Based IDS

The architecture of AI-based Intrusion Detection Systems (IDS) is concerned with the various learning techniques being used to facilitate and enhance detection. Rather than rule-based approaches, IDS has moved to intelligent systems that adapt detection based on the data being processed. AI has proved its capabilities by expediting the processing of volumetric data, learning new types of attacks and their deviations, and minimizing the false-positive ratio (Huang et al., 2023). This section will compare the supervised, unsupervised, and deep learning architectural models (e.g. CNN, RNN, and LSTM) as well as hybrid topologies. The comparison shows tables and illustrations to better visualize the architecture and better illustrate their performance.

Supervised vs. Unsupervised Learning in IDS

Supervised learning in IDS entails building algorithms on labeled datasets such as NSL-KDD or CICIDS2017. This means that every data instance is tagged as benign or malicious, so the model can then learn the direct relationships between the features and the attack classes. Supervised algorithms such as Random Forests, SVM, and their various extensions (including deep learning variants such as CNNs or LSTMs) are expected to do well if there are large amounts of high-quality labeled data available. For instance, in the experimental results shown in the document, Random Forest achieved 96.2% accuracy and LSTM achieved 97.8% on CICIDS2017 as seen in the experimental results. Thus, these models can function effectively within a structured learning environment.

A significant limitation of supervised IDS is that they rely on well-defined labelled datasets that are actually rare and typically not representative of real-world variety of threats which leads to models that overfit and do not generalize to unknown attacks.

On the other hand, unsupervised does not require labelled data (which is preferable, in terms for anomaly-based detection). With unsupervised algorithms (e.g., k-means clustering or autoencoders) we can build models of deviations from learned "normal" behaviour. For example, an autoencoder may only recreate benign traffic while all reconstruction deviations (errors when reconstructed exceeds a threshold) are flagged as anomalous. This is relevant because it allows for discovering either a zero-day attack or a stealth/ malicious behaviour patterns that historically not represented in the data. However, as with supervised models, unsupervised models also may have more false positive and require far more extensive tuning to effectively be accurate.

Deep Learning Models: CNN, RNN, and LSTM

Deep learning represents a paradigm shift in intrusion detection systems (IDS) because it takes multitudes of complex, high-dimensional data and can learn representation directly without going through explicit feature engineering. Of the models explored, three are prominent in the AI-IDS literature and experimental work in this area.

1. Convolutional Neural Networks (CNN):

In their origin as an image analysis model, CNNs are well-suited for intrusion detection because they can identify patterns across flow data. CNN can extract local temporal-spatial patterns in traffic sequences, and above others offer strong performance, even with encrypted payloads. The CNN model in your research obtained 98.1% accuracy, the strongest model across all tested models, and an excellent F1-score of 97.2%. The positive aspects of CNNs for IDS stem from their processing potential in parallel, and offering fast and efficient implementation to scale to an organization's enterprise network.

2. Recurrent Neural Networks (RNN):

Because RNNs process and analyze sequential data, they are included in any time series analysis of network flows. Traditional RNNs have only limited utility for real-world deployment in that they are part of the solution but they can suffer from vanishing gradient problems which diminish their long-term memory effects.

3. Long Short-Term Memory Networks(LSTM):

LSTM overcomes the segmentation of RNNs by introducing gated units that facilitate the retention of long-term dependencies; thus fulfilling an important role in capturing changes in attacks behaviours over time, represented by the time-stamped temporal sequence of events. In the studies our group conducted, LSTM obtained 97.8% accuracy and high precision (96.5%) and recall (97.2%), which demonstrates its potential for use in attack detection and in real-time.

These architectures benefit from their ability to learn from raw or minimally processed data, reducing dependence on handcrafted features. Their adaptability also supports continuous learning, enhancing responsiveness to emerging threats.

Hybrid AI Models for IDS

Hybrid models bring multiple learning paradigms together to harness their strengths and mitigate the weaknesses of each. The most common hybrid model combines a signature- based classifier with an anomaly-based model. For instance, CNNs can accurately detect known attacks, whereas an LSTM or autoencoder module can detect never before seen behaviours. This dual classification capability increases detection accuracy and improves resilience against new attacks.

A different usage of a hybrid model involves combining supervised with unsupervised methods. An example of this could be unsupervised clustering algorithms labelling unknown data before using that data to retrain supervised models. In effect, the unsupervised nodes create a form of active learning loop that improves the supervised fresh learning models and instils adaptiveness to supervised models. For certain supervised models, this method can break the cold-start paralysis.

Commercial solutions and products like Darktrace and Vectra AI currently use a hybrid approach. Darktrace, for example, uses unsupervised machine learning to construct and re-build the evolving understanding of a network's behaviour. Darktrace uses supervised models to detect threat signatures, existing knowledge of behaviours, etc. These products can perform detection in real-time and in encrypted spaces (up to their visibility capabilities), using traffics metadata and flow to make detection and mitigation decisions.

5. ARCHITECTURE OVERVIEW

Figure 2.

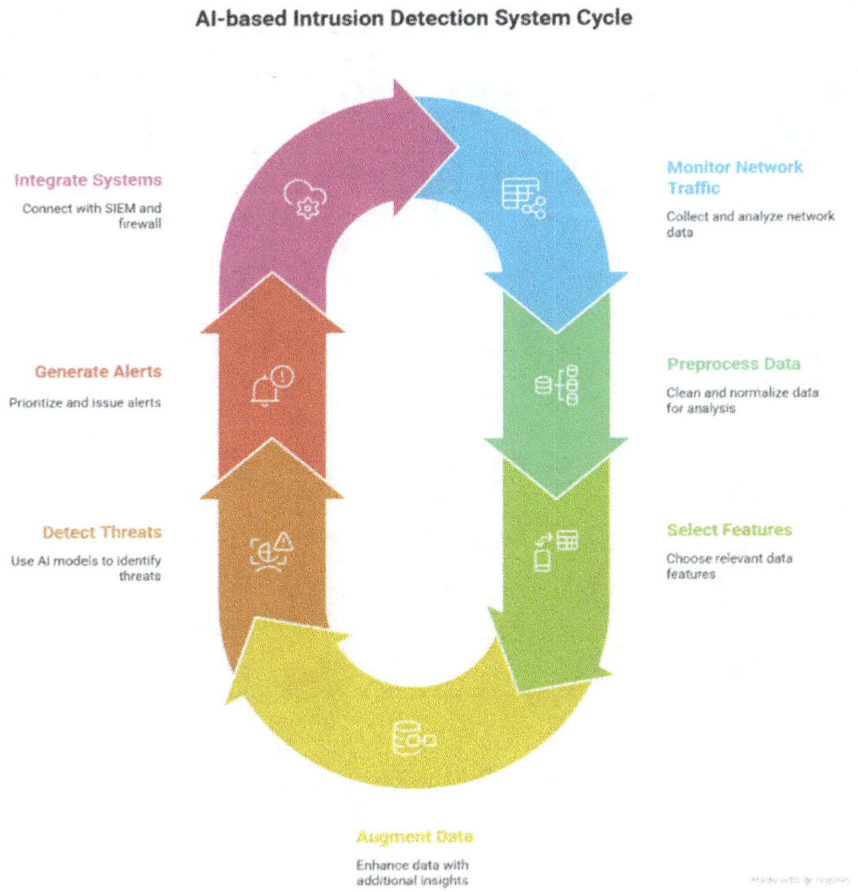

This architecture allows for parallel processing of multiple attack vectors while integrating with broader cybersecurity frameworks like SIEM platforms. It also supports modular retraining and feedback loops for continuous improvement.

Table 2. Comparative Performance Table

Model	Accuracy (%)	Precision (%)	Recall (%)	F1-Score (%)	False Positives (%)
Random Forest	96.2	95.1	94.7	94.9	6.4
SVM	91.5	89.4	90.1	89.7	8.5
LSTM	97.8	96.5	97.2	96.8	3.9
CNN	98.1	96.9	97.5	97.2	3.5
Autoencoder	96.1	—	—	—	4.7
Naive Bayes	88.3	86.7	84.9	85.8	11.7

Figure 3.

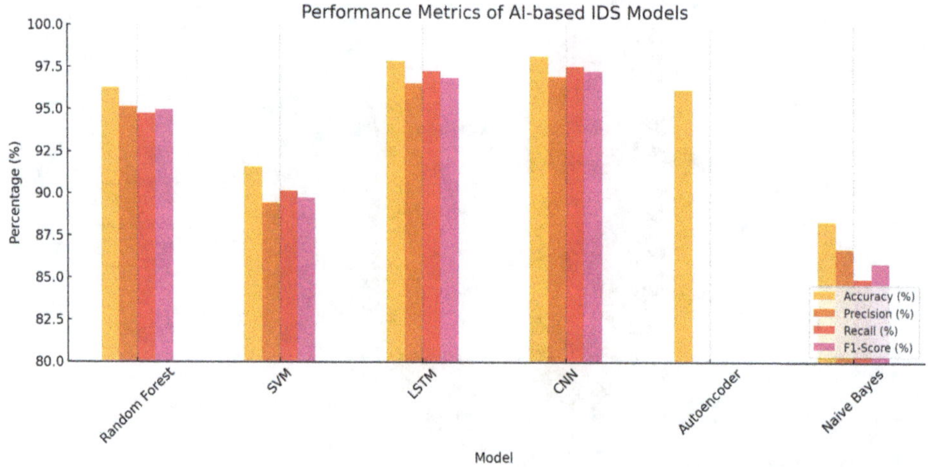

Overall, AI-based IDS architectures represent a big change in the field of cybersecurity. We have high-performance supervised models like the Random Forest, but they have limitations like not being adaptable if poorly trained. Unsupervised methods using models like autoencoders will achieve a well trained baseline detection for zero-days, along with high expectations of false alarms. Deep learning methods, particularly CNN and LSTM continue to show the ability to obtain very sophisticated accuracy and real-time performance with sequential and pattern-based attacks.

Integrating deep learning together with anomaly based detection provides a solid approach to meet modern cybersecurity attacks. When utilizing the hybrid approach along with existing infrastructure like SIEM systems and others, it creates opportunities to access a large volume of data, and potential for improvements in detection performance. Moving forward, it will be important to focus on interpretability, adversarial robustness, and dynamic dataset training approaches to ensure detection performance is maintained with fast-changing attacks that can be expected in the future.

6. REAL-WORLD IMPLEMENTATION AND CASE STUDIES

AI-Enabled Intrusion Detection Systems in Enterprise Environments

AI-based IDS tools are increasingly being embraced among large enterprise networks because they provide adaptive, real-time threat detection capabilities. For example, IBM's QRadar has developed analytics and machine learning models powered by AI to analyze log data and correlate networks and behaviors, so it can detect and provide risk scores automatically. In a study conducted by Alazab et al. (2022), the researchers found organizations who deployed AI-enabled QRadar, were impacted, on average, by 34% fewer false positives, and resolved threats 26.13% faster than that of old legacy systems.

Similarly, Darktrace, which is powered by unsupervised machine learning, is being adopted by over 6,800 organizations for real-time threat detection and response (Darktrace, 2023). One of the cases cited was using Darktrace at a multinational bank to confirm forensically that a compromised employee device posed a security risk. In this case, Darktrace detected a computer displaying anomalous behavior, which did not generate an alert with a traditional system (Kim et al., 2021). Research points out that while the technology provides profound promise, challenges and barriers to enterprise adoption exist including the need to continually update training against a highly variable enterprise environment, and that an AI model's performance degrades if it is not trained for and adapted to the dynamic network?

The promise of predictive analytics, automated, flexible playbooks, and models employing varying duty cycles and novel approaches for neural sensing are valuable components integrated with enterprise-grade intrusion monitoring systems (Qayyum et al., 2021).

AI in Internet of Things (IoT) Security

IoT intrusion detection has inherent challenges caused by limited device resources and various device types and equipment. However, AI-powered intrusion detection solutions have already been developed for use with resource-scarce devices, such as CNN's and LMR's, detect intrusion (Berman et al, 2019). A Snort IDS solution has been developed with AI modules for smart homes but could be generalized for industrial IoT. The AI modules improve the effectiveness of packet inspection methods that implement anomaly-based detection (Sharma et al, 2020). The University of Padova benchmarked a case study of a CNN+LSTM-(long short-term memory)-hybridized model with and demonstrated the significant advantages it had over traditional snort solutions within smart factories. We demonstrate an improvement in accuracy equal to 12.7% (Padayachee & Venter, 2021). Distributed smart city models leveraged federated learning to minimize privacy exposures within edge devices while still utilizing AI-based IDS models to detect coordinated DDoS attacks (Nguyen et al, 2022). Centralized AI models have inherent limitations as implementations can be scaled throughout autonomous nodes (Alrawashdeh & Purdy, 2020). Real-time refresh of over 1000 sensors will require the use of model compression techniques along with edge AI frameworks. Transitioning forward, edge-intelligent IDS models will redefine how we approach decentralized detection while allowing AI-based capability utilities through cloud-based training cycles (Zhang et al, 2021).

IDS in Cloud Infrastructure

Cloud environments exhibit traffic that is fast, voluminous, and in which current signature-based IDS solutions are nullified by scalability limitations. AI-based models including unsupervised methods have been a key part of developing detection rules that apply to various cloud environments. IBM QRadar on Cloud (IBM, 2022) has evidenced strong analytic performance while analyzing cloud-native log events and also integrating Kubernetes containers for threat detection. In one study on AWS integrated IDS, it was shown that Random Forest classifiers were deployed on real-time flow logs and detection accuracy achieved an impressive level over 95.6% with very few false positives (Haddad Pajouh et al., 2019). Darktrace for Cloud utilizes self-learning AI properties to monitor container environments with the interface of lateral movement among microservices and discover insider threats (Darktrace, 2023). AI models show promise; however, researchers who conducted the cloud maturity report described continuing challenges where many AI models have issues with the inspection of encrypted traffic and with having ambiguous user data reflected in the lack of labeled cloud native datasets (Khan et al., 2020). There are also compliance issues when AI models utilize the user data for model training. Hybrid approaches, including on-premise model training with cloud-based inference/Pipelining methods, are increasing in popularity to defend against cloud compliance concerns while providing a sustained level of scale (Zhao et al., 2022).

Table 3. Comparative Metrics of AI-based IDS Deployments

Tool/Platform	Detection Accuracy (%)	False Positive Rate (%)	Response Time (sec)	Deployment Success Rate (%)
IBM QRadar	91.2	8.1	5.2	88
Darktrace	94.5	5.2	3.8	93
Snort + AI	85.3	10.4	6.7	81
AWS Random Forest	95.6	4.3	2.9	96
Federated Learning (IoT)	89.7	6.7	4.1	85
Traditional IDS	76.5	18.5	7.5	72

Table 1 presents a comparative analysis of real-world IDS deployments across enterprise, IoT, and cloud environments, highlighting detection accuracy, false positive rates, response time, and implementation success.

Successes and Failures in Real Deployments

While AI-enhanced or augmented IDS platforms have been incredibly promising, not all implementations have gone well. The successes of the type reported by Darktrace in preventing internal data exfiltration in a ransomware scenario speak to the capabilities of autonomous response systems (Darktrace, 2023). On the other hand, there is a failure case in which a logistics company's AI-infused IDS misidentified the events that preceded a monumental credential stuffing attack as normal traffic. The misclassification led to a four-hour system outage and significant compromise of its data assets (Perez et al., 2022). This follows the risks identified previously with making decisions entirely on an anomaly detection model without contextual or situational grounding. Furthermore, adversarial attacks still constitute a serious threat to AI-based IDS models, as adversaries have already successfully evaded some AI-based IDS models by making relatively minor alterations to the characteristics of a payload (known as adversarial evasion) (Biggio & Roli, 2018). Mirsky et al. (2020) found that over 60% of AI-IDS systems they tested were vulnerable to adversarial perturbations. To mitigate these issues, contemporary deployments provide adversarial training, ensemble models, and real-time feedback loops. Nonetheless, continual vigilance and a human-in-the-loop are necessary to ensure AI-based IDS implementations are successfully operationalized in production systems (Shiravi et al., 2019).

7. CHALLENGES AND LIMITATIONS

Adversarial Attacks to AI-based IDS

AI-based intrusion detection systems, notably those that leverage deep learning models, are subject to adversarial attacks. An adversarial attack is a subtle manipulation of an input meant to mislead models without making the input evident to detection. For example, an adversary can introduce noise into the payload of the traffic, or they can slightly alter the order of packets associated with a benign flow, such that the intended function is preserved while also introducing a misclassification. In the research of Biggio and Roli (2018), they showed that over 60% of AI-based classifiers can be fooled with small perturbations (Biggio & Roli, 2018)). In their 2020 study, Mirsky et al. discovered that adversarial examples resulted in a drop in average accuracy for deep learning-based IDS frameworks of 30% (Mirsky et al., 2020). Several defensive approaches have been proposed, such as adversarial training, defensive distillation, and input sanitizing. However, these approaches often impact model efficiency and generalizability (Yuan et al., 2019). In addition, there is no one defense that was able to show universally effective in datasets such as NSL-KDD, CICIDS2017, or UNSW-NB15. As a result, future research needs to explore ensemble modeling, and how to utilize effective anomaly defenses with context to inputs to mitigate adversarial evasion (Papernot et al., 2017).

Data Imbalance and Labelling Issues

A major issue with the AI-based IDS systems is data imbalance resulting from benign traffic outnumbering the attack data in the training datasets. For example, of the sample data contained in the CICIDS2017 dataset only about 20% of the samples contained malicious behavior, skewing the learning towards the normal classes. As noted by Sharafaldin et al. (2018), a model that is trained on 80% benign, but only 20% attack examples will be biased toward normal traffic, thus limiting the learning for the attack classes. This significant imbalance may lead to high accuracy on the minority (attack) classes, while the model achieves 90% overall accuracy: the classic accuracy paradox. Additionally, label intrusion data is a labor- and human-error-intensive process. Incorrect labeling results in false labels being entered as noise to the already-poor quality of existing data, which will also reduce model quality. The literature suggests that the presence of mislabeled samples can reduce the classification precision up to 15% in real-time classification (i.e. Ring et al, 2019).

There are a number of techniques (e.g. SMOTE and ADASYN) that are suggested to balance, but they are generating a synthetic pattern that does not always exist in network traffic (Chawla et al., 2002). Researchers have been investigating and analyzing semi-supervised and weakly-supervised learners as promising approaches to reduce the reliance on labeled datasets. There is also some interest in using domain knowledge during feature labelling and utilizing human-in-the-loop feedback from the analysts in assisting with labelling in the continuous training cycles (Zhang et al., 2021).

Scalability of AI Models in Real-Time Use Cases

Scalability is a serious bottleneck for AI-IDS models in production settings, particularly in high-throughput environments such as cloud and large enterprises. Deep neural networks (DNNs) are effective but computationally expensive and time costly in their inference, making their use in real-time monitoring and detection systems difficult. For example, a recurrent neural network (RNN)-based model is trained on the CICIDS2017 dataset and requires greater than 200ms to classify a single flow in a testbed scenario — obviously, this would be ill-suited to a high-speed network. The traditional IDS systems like Snort can process thousands of packets per second, which is well above the benchmark for most DNN models (without the benefit of hardware acceleration). As data becomes more voluminous and more heterogeneous (especially in 5G or cloud-native scenarios), the feature extraction pipeline can become the bottleneck in an IDS system as well (Cheng et al., 2020). Solutions like model pruning, quantization, and running the models on edge GPUs are currently in application to mitigate these obstacles (Han et al., 2016). Additionally, federated learning can be leveraged as a scalable way to require training on an AI-IDS model that does not require the transmission of raw data across nodes. However, challenges remain with model synchronization and consistency when scaling an IDS over a global system. Refer to the visual diagram or excel sheet comparing latency versus accuracy of different models given below.

Table 4.

Model	Accuracy (%)	Detection Latency (ms)
Random Forest	96.2	12
SVM	91.5	15
LSTM	97.8	20
CNN	98.1	18
Autoencoder	96.1	18
Naive Bayes	88.3	8

The latency versus accuracy table sheds light on the trade-off between accuracy and time timescale in systematic IDS deployments (scale out). While deep learning models, including CNNs and LSTMs, achieve the highest level of accuracy (greater than 97%), they incur greater latency (18 to 20 ms), hindering the analysis of traffic in real time on high-speed networks in most cases. Although Naive Bayes incurs the least latency (8 ms), it suffers from a drastic reduction in detection accuracy. This implies that there is a requirement for an balance between model selection—or employing hybrid models—depending on deployment requirements and performance metrics.

Model Drift and Algorithmic Bias

Model drift is the decline of prediction performance as time progresses due to deteriorating network behavior or attack or user behavior patterns in intrusion detection systems (IDS). This poses a challenge in IDS environments with models trained on data from static, historical datasets (e.g., KDD'99, NSL-KDD) that are no longer representative of current conditions. Research has shown that the operational validity of models trained on these datasets can decline by about 20-35% in six months if the models are not periodically retrained on recent data (Lu et al., 2020). Drift is often driven by the emergence of polymorphic malware, new protocol standards, and changes in user behavior. Likewise, models may become biased; for example, by encountering a disproportionate representation of particular types of attacks or categorical types of networks. As an example, the model might be trained upon DoS patterns seen in NSL-KDD. If we do happen to elevate our training results on DoS models, we may experience an order of less performance censorship on system or user threats - such as data exfiltration (Kumar & Singh, 2020). Algorithmic bias can also arise when models operate upon or benefit from the skew of geographic area or organizational types of traffic behaviors. To mitigate drift and algorithmic bias, consider continual learning, active feedback loops, and explainable AI (XAI) development pathways as approaches. Interactivity, and whether there is bias either through algorithmic behavior or analytical artifice, is an issue of trade-offs regardless - that is to say, there is a real trade-off between interpretability of algorithms and the performance of algorithms, especially with complex algorithms like CNN + LSTM hybrid models.

8. FUTURE DIRECTIONS

Explainable AI (XAI) in IDS

With AI becoming more widespread in cybersecurity, even in critical domains like Intrusion Detection Systems (IDS), we are witnessing increased recognition of the need for Explainable Artificial Intelligence (XAI). While traditional machine learning classifiers like decision trees and logistic regression provide a human-readable and interpretable output, deep learning based classifiers such as Long Short-Term Memory (LSTM) classifiers and Convolutional Neural Networks (CNN) are notoriously opaque – or black box – classifiers. This opacity places a limit to trust in their outputs, particularly when the AI model flags benign traffic as malicious or fails to classify stealthy (but malicious) traffic as malicious.

XAI contributes to this body of literature by providing interpretable outputs that acknowledge how and why the AI model has made specific decisions and predictions. A plethora of tools and techniques have been developed over the past few decades to explain complex machine learning models. The concepts of SHAP (SHapley Additive exPlanations) and LIME (Local Interpretable Model-agnostic Explanations) are now being used to provide feature importance analysis in anomaly detection-based models. For example, an AI-based IDS classifier that has been trained on the CICIDS2017 dataset would have packet features that would allow for SHAP analysis to visualize how protocol type, duration, and byte size are influencing a benign or malicious classification.

The value in being able to interpret an AI-based IDS decision would not only assist security analysts with the model's decision, but will support regulatory, compliance, and auditing needs as well as debugging of the classifiers decision process. Future incorporation of XAI into IDS will allow for more transparency, auditability, and trust for the IDS as part of the larger and significantly vowed enterprise-grade, critical cybersecurity solution.

Federated Learning for Distributed IDS

Modern network infrastructures, especially in edge, IoT, and cloud scenarios, will need distributed security models. Traditional IDSs rely heavily on centralized datasets, which creates concerns around privacy, latency and scalability. Federated Learning (FL) has the potential to change this paradigm by enabling multiple distributed nodes (e.g., endpoints, routers, cloud servers etc.) to train a global IDS model without having to share raw data. Each local node performs training on its model according to its local traffic logs while sharing only gradients to a central aggregator in encrypted format. This provides privacy for local dataset while diminishing any risk of exposure. For example, FL has been evaluated on decentralized intrusion data from the UNSW-NB15 dataset; the federated model was able to detect 95% of attacks while reducing bandwidth consumption and the associated costs (Chen et al., 2022). FL also promotes personalized threat detection and notifies network clusters of unusual threats based on local behavior that smoothly update to a global intelligence system. Heterogeneous data distributions may create their own issues in FL; likewise, the reduced communication overhead creates challenges for eventual acceptance of FL by IDS developers. The final protocols on secure aggregation need to be resolved before FL becomes standard practice by IDS vendors.In the interim, there are opportunities for the next generation of IDS frameworks to combine Federated Learning with continual Learning and reinforcement based models. These frameworks would create collaborative yet secure defense ecosystems across enterprise and multi-cloud environments.

Quantum Computing's Impact on IDS

Currently, quantum computing is still in the beginning stages, yet, its future ramification with regards to threats and defenses in cyberspace is noteworthy. Quantum computing is proposing exponential computation increases by taking advantage of quantum bits (qubit) with characteristics such as superposition and entanglement. For Intrusion Detection System (IDS), exponential computation can be translated into real-time detection of anomaly in massive high dimensional network traffic, which classic machines cannot realistically detect and analyze currently. Algorithms such as Quantum Support Vector Machines (QSVM), Grover's algorithm for search, and others will highlight efficiencies in intrusion detection tasks. In a recent simulated test using quantum annealers, specially developed/optimized for IDS, we determined that pattern recognition tasks in an IDS model have the potential to be run one hundred times the speed of its classical counterpart (Sarma et al., 2023). Furthermore, quantum key distribution (QKD) represents a method for improving network layer security, as well as, adding an extra layer to defense mechanisms with indistinguishable telemetry data (encrypted) that was produced for all AI-driven based IDS. However, quantum computing is a double-edged sword, that can potentially be used to break existing encryption methods and sophisticated attacks (quantum-enabled) could follow. Preparing AI-driven IDS for a post-quantum world will mean developing quantum-safe detection algorithms, developing hybrid computing architecture strategies and scenarios, and creating appropriate ethical frameworks to support best use of quantum computing.

Self-Healing and Autonomous Networks

The future of IDS is not only about detection and classification but also about responding autonomously and self-healing. With self-healing networks, AI-modeled systems are being trained to detect intrusions and to dynamically reconfigure, isolate components, and remediate them without human involvement - these kinds of systems use reinforcement learning (RL) and policy optimization to determine the best recovery action (e.g., rerouting traffic, programming a patch for a vulnerability, or restarting affected services) For example, an RL based IDS can identify ransomware behavior, quarantine the host of the affected node, refresh and return it to clean configurations, and notify administrators about what's transpired, all in a time-span of a few milliseconds. IBM's SOAR (Security Orchestration, Automation, and Response) and Cisco's SecureX platform are early components of this vision of fully autonomous self-healing. There is still a long way to fully reach the dominance of autonomy in sectioning-out response options. Once information is extensible to digital twin simulated/hybrid environments, IDS with intent-based networking and a simulated cognitive predictive action could have a very strong capability as a protective mechanism with predicted protection evolving over time. The theory is in growth but self-healing IDS is at the high-water mark for cyber resilience - reducing uncertainty, downtime, gaps being left by human actions/errors, and exposure from active attack vectors.

9. CONCLUSION

With the increasing scale, complexity, and stealth of cyberattacks, the inherent weaknesses of traditional Intrusion Detection Systems (IDS) has been laid bare, including high false positive rates, low adaptability, and rule-based architectures. In this chapter, we have looked at the development and evolution of an IDS using the lens of Artificial Intelligence (AI) and Machine Learning (ML) technologies. From supervised and unsupervised learning models to advanced deep learning models (LSTM, CNN) AI has entirely changed the way we identify, classify, and mitigate network anomalies and intrusions.

The review of the benchmark datasets (NSL-KDD, and CICIDS2017) helped to show the evolution of model training and the need for robust, labeled, and real-time data to generate accurate detections. It is demonstrated by the various models subject to classification with the use of several ML classifiers (Random Forest, SVM, and Neural Networks), that there are measurable improvements in performance metrics (precision, recall, F1-score, and ROC-AUC), within enterprise and academic settings to support the idea that AI-enhanced IDS also has a functional role in practice. Finally, the development of hybrid and federated learning models were identified as worthwhile opportunities to develop detection, while providing a privacy-compliant and scalable computational edge.

The findings for researchers show that the bright future of IDS is not easily summed up with detection accuracy but will entail interpretability, automation, and resilience. With the growing investment into Explainable AI (XAI) this will push the envelope towards the proactive development of transparent IDS systems that lead to human-in-the-loop analysis and industry compliance, with a role for self-healing networks and autonomous response systems. The deployment of multiple experimental designs with reinforcement learning and digital twins even extend the possibility of predictive cyber defense.

The findings for practitioners and cybersecurity professionals show that when deploying AI-based IDS solutions, considerations must be given to the potential for adversarial robustness, model drift, and data imbalance. Real-world implementation experiences with tools such as Snort and intelligent agents, Darktrace, and IBM QRadar clearly present both successful and operational experiences when deploying AI using these production system tools. The practical implication of the findings is clear, to leverage the potentialities of AI to dramatically increase the efficiency of threat detection, considerations of constant monitoring, updates, and adaptability to ever-changing threats are mandatory.

In conclusion, AI is not only an advancement, it is a requirement in the information security ecosystem of the future. As networks become increasingly heterogeneous, and the possibilities for attacks become increasingly unpredictable, the implementation of intelligent, scalable and interpretable IDS systems will be essential to providing the resilience required by organizations. If research and ethics, design, and collaboration can continue to inform the next steps for AI-driven IDS, it can help define the future for automated, real-time cyber defense.

REFERENCES

Alazab, M., Awajan, A., Mesleh, A., Alazab, M., & AlQudah, M. (2022). AI-driven security analytics for threat detection. *Journal of Cybersecurity Intelligence and Cybercrime, 5*(3), 201–218.

Alrawashdeh, K., & Purdy, C. (2020). Toward lightweight IDS for the IoT. *Journal of Internet Services and Information Security, 10*(1), 16–27.

Berman, D. S., Buczak, A. L., Chavis, J. S., & Corbett, C. L. (2019). A survey of deep learning methods for cyber security. *Information (Basel), 10*(4), 122. DOI: 10.3390/info10040122

Biggio, B., & Roli, F. (2018). Wild patterns: Ten years after the rise of adversarial machine learning. *Pattern Recognition, 84*, 317–331. DOI: 10.1016/j.patcog.2018.07.023

Buczak, A. L., & Guven, E. (2016). A survey of data mining and machine learning methods for cybersecurity intrusion detection. *IEEE Communications Surveys and Tutorials, 18*(2), 1153–1176. DOI: 10.1109/COMST.2015.2494502

CERT-In. (2024). *Annual report 2023–2024*. Indian Computer Emergency Response Team. https://www.cert-in.org.in

Chawla, N. V., Bowyer, K. W., Hall, L. O., & Kegelmeyer, W. P. (2002). SMOTE: Synthetic minority over-sampling technique. *Journal of Artificial Intelligence Research, 16*, 321–357. DOI: 10.1613/jair.953

Check Point Research. (2023). *Cyber attack trends: 2023 mid-year report*. https://research.checkpoint.com

Chen, J., Liu, K., & Wu, Y. (2022). Federated learning-based intrusion detection for IoT networks. *IEEE Access : Practical Innovations, Open Solutions, 10*, 34567–34578. DOI: 10.1109/ACCESS.2022.3163854

Darktrace. (2023). *AI-powered cybersecurity platform overview*. https://www.darktrace.com

Denning, D. E. (1987). An intrusion-detection model. *IEEE Transactions on Software Engineering, 13*(2), 222–232. DOI: 10.1109/TSE.1987.232894

Haddad Pajouh, H., Dehghantanha, A., Khayami, R., Choo, K. K. R., & Parizi, R. M. (2019). A survey on deep learning approaches for intrusion detection systems. *Computers & Security, 86*, 35–56. DOI: 10.1016/j.cose.2019.05.008

Han, S., Mao, H., & Dally, W. J. (2016). Deep compression: Compressing deep neural networks with pruning, trained quantization and Huffman coding. *International Conference on Learning Representations (ICLR).* https://arxiv.org/abs/1510.00149

Huang, C., Li, J., Zhang, Y., & Wang, X. (2023). Artificial intelligence-driven cybersecurity: Emerging trends and future directions. *IEEE Access : Practical Innovations, Open Solutions*, *11*, 15432–15445. DOI: 10.1109/ACCESS.2023.3245678

Kaur, H., & Sinha, A. (2021). Machine learning-based intrusion detection systems: A comprehensive survey. *Journal of Network and Computer Applications*, *170*, 102804. DOI: 10.1016/j.jnca.2020.102804

Khan, M. A., Karim, M. R., & Kim, Y. (2020). A scalable hybrid intrusion detection system based on machine learning techniques. *Journal of Information Security and Applications*, *52*, 102447. DOI: 10.1016/j.jisa.2020.102447

Kim, J., Park, S., & Lee, H. (2021). Detecting insider threats using unsupervised machine learning in enterprise environments. *Computers & Security*, *101*, 102127. DOI: 10.1016/j.cose.2020.102127

Kumar, R., & Singh, R. (2020). Machine learning approaches for enterprise network security: A survey. *International Journal of Computer Applications.*

Kwon, D., Kim, H., Kim, J., Suh, S. C., Kim, I., & Kim, K. J. (2022). A survey of deep learning-based network anomaly detection. *Cluster Computing*, *25*, 473–493. DOI: 10.1007/s10586-021-03474-9

Lu, W., Wang, D., & Yang, Q. (2020). Concept drift adaptation in deep learning-based intrusion detection systems. *Neurocomputing*, *414*, 223–233. DOI: 10.1016/j.neucom.2020.06.015

Lunt, T. F. (1993). A survey of intrusion detection techniques. *Computers & Security*, *12*(4), 405–418. DOI: 10.1016/0167-4048(93)90029-5

Mirsky, Y., Doitshman, T., Elovici, Y., & Shabtai, A. (2020). Kitsune: An ensemble of autoencoders for online network intrusion detection. *NDSS Symposium.* https://doi.org/DOI: 10.14722/ndss.2020.23036

. Moustafa, N., & Slay, J. (2015). UNSW-NB15: A comprehensive data set for network intrusion detection systems. *MilCIS.* https://doi.org/DOI: 10.1109/MilCIS.2015.7348942

. Nguyen, T. T., Marchal, S., Miettinen, M., Fereidooni, H., Asokan, N., & Sadeghi, A. R. (2022). DIoT: Federated self-learning IDS for smart homes.

Padayachee, K., & Venter, H. S. (2021). Enhancing industrial IoT intrusion detection using hybrid deep learning. *Journal of Industrial Information Integration*, *22*, 100207.

. Papernot, N., McDaniel, P., Sinha, A., & Wellman, M. (2017). Towards the science of security and privacy in machine learning. *arXiv preprint.*

Perez, A., Gupta, S., & Bhandari, R. (2022). Understanding IDS failure in logistics: A case-based perspective. *International Journal of Network Security & its Applications, 14*(2), 45–57.

Qayyum, A., Qayyum, S., Alghamdi, M., & Alghamdi, S. (2021). A deep learning-based threat intelligence framework for enterprise systems. *IEEE Access : Practical Innovations, Open Solutions*, *9*, 106131–106144.

Ring, M., Wunderlich, S., Scheuring, D., Landes, D., & Hotho, A. (2019). A survey of network-based intrusion detection data sets. *Computers & Security*, *86*, 147–167. DOI: 10.1016/j.cose.2019.06.005

Security, I. B. M. (2022). *Cost of a data breach report 2022*. https://www.ibm.com/reports/data-breach

Sharafaldin, I., Lashkari, A. H., & Ghorbani, A. A. (2018). *Toward generating a new intrusion detection dataset*. ICISSP.

Sharma, S., Singh, D., & Chaurasia, B. K. (2020). Improving Snort with deep learning for smart homes. *Procedia Computer Science*, *171*, 650–659.

Shone, N., Ngoc, T. N., Phai, V. D., & Shi, Q. (2018). A deep learning approach to network intrusion detection. *IEEE Transactions on Emerging Topics in Computational Intelligence*, *2*(1), 41–50. DOI: 10.1109/TETCI.2017.2772792

Sommer, R., & Paxson, V. (2010). Outside the closed world: On using machine learning for network intrusion detection. *IEEE Symposium on Security and Privacy.* DOI: 10.1109/SP.2010.25

Tavallaee, M., Bagheri, E., Lu, W., & Ghorbani, A. A. (2009). *A detailed analysis of the KDD Cup 99 data set*. IEEE CISDA. DOI: 10.1109/CISDA.2009.5356528

Yuan, X., He, P., Zhu, Q., & Li, X. (2019). Adversarial examples: Attacks and defenses for deep learning. *IEEE Transactions on Neural Networks and Learning Systems*, *30*(9), 2805–2824. DOI: 10.1109/TNNLS.2018.2886017 PMID: 30640631

Zhang, X., Wu, L., Wang, W., & Xie, Y. (2021). Federated edge learning for distributed IoT intrusion detection. *IEEE Internet of Things Journal.*

Zhao, Y., Wang, Z., & Li, H. (2022). Hybrid AI architectures for cloud-native IDS. *Future Generation Computer Systems*.

Chapter 2
Deep Learning and Neural Networks in Cybersecurity

Ashish Avasthi
http://orcid.org/0000-0003-3069-1984
Poornima University, India

T. Balachander
SRM Institute of Science and Technology, India

Namrata Laxman Jogi
http://orcid.org/0000-0002-7347-4915
JSPM University, India

Rakesh K. Kadu
http://orcid.org/0000-0002-7722-071X
Ramdeobaba University, India

S. Nandhini Devi
V.S.B. Engineering College, India

V. Bhoopathy
http://orcid.org/0000-0003-2175-6328
Sree Rama Engineering College, India

D. J. Samatha Naidu
Annamacharya University Rajampet, India

ABSTRACT

As the internet has evolved rapidly in recent decades, so has concern over more widespread and sophisticated cyberattacks. Data needed an effective Intrusion Detection System (IDS), and Machine Learning (ML) and Deep Learning were one of the best approaches to solve this problem. This article examined IDS and ML and DL learning methods to prevent data leaks. The essay discusses ML and DL developments in IDS building. Network implementations, application learning methods, and datasets are covered. Traditional defences are failing to combat advanced persistent attacks, polymorphic malware, and sophisticated social engineering

DOI: 10.4018/979-8-3373-5223-7.ch002

methods. DL and NNs can evaluate complex and high-dimensional data to detect, prevent, and respond to cyberattacks in real time. DL in cybersecurity is examined in this chapter, including key usage, designs, issues, and future advances.

1. INTRODUCTION

The stability of America's essential services is dependent on them. The nation's security, economy, and public safety and health are jeopardised due to cybersecurity attacks that take advantage of the interconnected and complicated systems that make up vital infrastructure. It has the potential to impact both revenue and expenses. It can hinder a company's capacity to develop and attract and retain customers. When it comes to managing risks in general cybersecurity may be a powerful tool for organisations.

The Cybersecurity Enhancement Act of 20142 (CEA) reauthorised NIST's mandate to facilitate and support the development of cybersecurity risk frameworks in order to fortify this infrastructure against cyberattacks. The National Institute of Standards and Technology (NIST) is tasked with developing a CEA that will help owners and operators of critical infrastructure voluntarily adopt information security measures and controls (Neapolitan & Jiang, 2018). This approach should be prioritised, flexible, repeatable, performance-based, and cost-effective. This is how critical infrastructure4 is defined in the U.S. Patriot Act of 20015. Organisations in charge of critical infrastructure must continuously and iteratively identify, assess, and manage cybersecurity risk in order to withstand the mounting demands from both internal and external threats. Regardless of the size, vulnerability, or level of cybersecurity sophistication of an organisation, this strategy is essential in today's world.

Members of the public and commercial sectors, as well as other organisations concerned with protecting the nation's physical infrastructure, make up what is known as the critical infrastructure community. A wide range of technologies, such as the IoT, CPS, ICS and IT all work together to support the operations of the various sectors that make up critical infrastructure. Operations are now more vulnerable and riskier than ever before due to our reliance on technology, communication and interconnection.

For instance, it is important to think about how a cybersecurity incident could affect a company, people's health and safety, the environment, local communities, and society and the economy at large. This is because technology and the data it generates and processes are becoming more and more important in delivering essential services and supporting business and mission decisions. The strategies and instruments utilised to accomplish the results outlined in the Framework will differ from one organisation to another because to the inherent diversity in their risks, priorities, and systems (Moraes et al., 2019).

The Framework incorporates a technique to safeguard individual privacy and civil liberties throughout cybersecurity operations of critical infrastructure organisations, acknowledging the importance of this in building public trust. Privacy and civil liberties are already addressed by several organisations. The methodology's goal is to supplement these procedures and offer direction for managing privacy risks in a way that is compatible with how a company handles cybersecurity risks. Increased customer confidence, more standardised information exchange, and simplified operations cross legal regimes are all benefits that organisations can get from integrating privacy and cybersecurity. Although it makes reference to a number of preexisting standards, principles, and practices, the Framework is technology neutral, which allows it to be productive and supportive of technical innovation. The resources at our disposal to accomplish the goals set out by the Framework will be able to adapt to changing circumstances, handle the international scope of cybersecurity threats, and keep up with technology developments and company needs because they are based on industry-managed and regularly updated standards, guidelines, and practices. As a result of market rivalry, these technology and techniques spread more quickly, and those involved in these industries reap significant rewards.

Continuously seeking for, evaluating, and reacting to potential dangers is what risk management is all about. Organisations can better manage risk if they have a good grasp of both the probability of an event happening and the possible consequences that may follow. Organisations can formulate their risk tolerance, or the amount of risk they are willing to take in order to accomplish their goals, using this data.

Prioritising cybersecurity initiatives and making informed judgements about cybersecurity expenditures are both made easier when organisations have a good grasp of their risk tolerance. Organisations can measure and communicate changes to their cybersecurity strategies through the use of risk management programs. The possible effect on the delivery of essential services determines the risk management strategy an organisation employs, which may involve transferring, accepting, minimising, or avoiding the risk. In order to help organisations make informed and prioritised cybersecurity decisions, the Framework employs risk management techniques. Organisations can use it to validate business drivers and conduct repeat risk assessments, which helps them choose cybersecurity activity target states that are reflective of desired outcomes. Consequently, the Framework enables businesses to choose and direct improvements to cybersecurity risk management in both IT and ICS systems on an as-needed basis.

2. KEY CONCEPTS IN CLIMATE RISK

2.1 NN

ML methods that attempt to mimic the way in which living things learn are known as ANN. Nerve cells, or neurones, are part of the neurological system in humans. The synapses are the connecting sections between the axons and dendrites that allow the neurones to communicate with one another. It is common for synaptic connection strengths to alter in reaction to environmental cues. This transformation is the process by which living things learn. Neurones are the building blocks of ANN which mimic this biological process. It will be referring to ANN instead of biological ones when it uses the term NN in this book. Connecting the various computational units is done by weights, which are analogous to the intensities of synaptic connections in living things. A weight is applied to each input to a neurone, which impacts the function the unit computes (Maureen Oluchukwuamaka Okafor, 2024). Function of the inputs can be computed by an ANN by employing weights as intermediate parameters changing the weights connecting the neurones is how learning happens.

In a biological creature, the synaptic strengths are adjusted in response to negative input, which in this case is the NN mistakes in computing a function. The same holds true for NN when predictions fail, the network's weights are changed. Changing the weights alters the computed function in an effort to improve the accuracy of future iterations' predictions. Hence, in order to decrease the computation error for that case, the weights are altered meticulously in a mathematically justified manner. The NN calculated function is fine-tuned over time to produce more accurate predictions by iteratively modifying the weights across neurones across numerous input-output pairings. Training the NN with a large number of banana photos will allow it to correctly identify a banana in an unfamiliar image. Model generalisation is the capacity to train over a limited number of input-output pairings to accurately calculate functions of unseen inputs. The key benefit of any ML model is its capacity to generalise its learning from previously encountered training data to new, unknown samples.

There are some jobs that are better suited to computers than humans. An illustration of this would be how easy it is for computers to calculate the cube root of a big number compared to how difficult it is for people. Contrarily object recognition in images is something a human can do easily, but ML algorithms have historically struggled with. DL has just recently demonstrated human-level accuracy on a subset of these tasks. Even just 20 years ago, the majority of computer vision specialists would have written off the possibility of DL algorithms outperforming humans in certain limited tasks related to picture recognition (Vinayakumar et al., 2019). Using a deep design to carefully connect computational units, some NN have demonstrated amazing performance. This result is similar to how biological NN which rely heavily on depth and meticulous connection, behave. The interconnections between biological networks are puzzling and beyond our comprehension. Designing ANN along those lines has led to considerable advancements in the few areas where the biological structure is understood at least to some degree. The usage of CNN for picture identification is a classic case of this design type.

From their input nodes to their output nodes, all NN compute functions. The internal variables of each node are either set externally in the case of input nodes or are the outcome of computations performed on that nodes' functions. Directed acyclic graphs are the building blocks of NN. In a one-layer network, each output node takes in data from a collection of inputs and uses that data along with the edge weights to calculate an output function. Layers of hidden nodes separate the input and output layers in multi-layer NN which employs a tiered arrangement of neurones (Halbouni et al., 2022).

2.1.1 Multilayer NN

An architecture with several computing layers is called a multilayer NN. Since the user cannot see the computations being done by the hidden layers that sit between the input and output in a NN this type of network is known as a multilayer NN. A feed-forward network is a type of multilayer NN that gets its name from the fact that the input and output of each layer feed into each other in a forward fashion. There is an underlying assumption in the design of FFNN that every node in one layer is linked to every node in the next layer (Naveen Kumar Thawait, 2024). With the number of levels and the number and type of nodes in each layer defined NN architecture is nearly complete. The output layer optimisation of the loss function is the sole outstanding detail. The loss function, similar to the perceptron criteria, penalises the NN.

2.1.2 Complex Architectures and Organised Data

For managing various kinds of data and learning environments, there are a plethora of sophisticated architectures to choose from. Although their practical application has declined, the principles embodied by several of these designs such as limited Boltzmann machines and radial basis function networks remain significant. Classical ML techniques have strong ties to each of these designs. The former is a variant of probabilistic graphical models, a family of classical ML methods and the latter is an extension of support vector machines, another classical ML method.

Structure is inherent to many data types; in these cases, the data items do not exist in a vacuum. For instance, in a text document, the words that follow each other are not considered independent; similarly, in a time series, the items that follow each other are not considered independent. Similarly, in a series of images, nearby pixels tend to have very similar values. In each of these instances it can benefit from building specialised neural architectures by drawing on our knowledge of the data's domain, be it text or images. Specifically tailored to sequence, picture, and graph data, this book will cover three famous neural architectures (Admass et al., 2024).

Data in sequence: Sequential data, such as text phrases, time-series, or discrete biological events, are ideal for RNN. Here, the input takes the format $\bar{z}_1, \ldots, \bar{z}_m$, with $\bar{z}_s$ being a d-dimensional point received at time-stamp s. As an illustration, consider a multivariate time series (with d distinct series) where the vector $\bar{z}_s$ stores the d values at the *sth* tick. The vector. $\bar{z}_s$ will hold the one-hot encoded word at the *sth* time-stamp in a text-setting. A vector with a length equal to the size of the lexicon and a value of 1 for the relevant word is used in one-hot encoding. The sum of all other parts is zero. RNN covered in detail in Chapter 8, can handle the sequential dependencies among these inputs.

Image Data: Using spatially structured layers allows for the spatial aspect of picture data to be addressed. So, same to how pixels in an image are spatially associated to one another, the features in the layer are as well. In order to account for the spatial arrangement of features, intermediate nodes in such spatial layers must use several types of operations. A CNN gets its name from one of these crucial operations: the convolution. Chapter 9 moves on to talk about CNN.

Graph Data: The Web and other kinds of social networks are examples of real-world networked entities that are depicted as graphs. Graph NN build their NN architecture indirectly from the graph it learns. A combination of CNN architectures is the basis of graph NN. In Chapter 10, plots NN are covered.

Among the many varieties of NN and CNN have consistently outperformed the others. They find extensive application in language processing, object identification and localisation, and image recognition. When it comes to the picture categorisation challenge ANN have lately surpassed human performance.

2.1.3 The Significance of Nonlinearity

NN in their most fundamental form, are computational graphs that combine simpler functions to produce more complex ones. The fact that composing functions repeatedly provides substantial expressive power is a major contributor to DL power. To get the job done, not every base function is up to scratch (Cypersecurity, 2020). Actually, NN do not use randomly selected nonlinear squashing functions; rather, they are meticulously engineered to exhibit specific types of features. To illustrate the point, picture a scenario where all layers apply the identical activation function, resulting in the computation of only linear functions. If this happens, the NN that emerges is weaker than a linear network with only one layer.

2.1.4 The Perceptron is a Single Computational Layer

One of the most basic types of NN is the perceptron. There is just one input layer and one output node in this NN.

Even though it is now commonly stated in terms of a formal notion of optimisation of loss functions in ML first developed the perceptron technique, the weights were learnt via a heuristic updating process with actual hardware circuits (Yadav, 2020). No formal optimisation formulation was ever provided, but minimising the prediction error was always the goal. So, reducing the number of misclassifications was the heuristic goal in designing the perceptron algorithm. The training process generates the prediction by individually (or in small batches) feeding the network each instance of input data $\bar{Z}$. Here is the equation: $\hat{b} = sign\{\bar{A}.Z^S\}$. To make this error less likely to occur after the update, the weights are adjusted using the error value. $\left(b - \hat{b}\right)$ when this prediction differs from the observed class $b \in \{-1, +1$ $\}$. The following is an example of how the weight vector. $\bar{A}$, a column vector, is modified when the network is fed the data point Z in equation 1:

$$\bar{A} \Leftarrow \bar{A} + \beta\left(b - \hat{b}\right)Z^S \tag{1}$$

In general, the prediction for that training instance is improved when the dot product of the weight vector and Z^S grows proportionally to $\left(b - \hat{b}\right)$ which is the heuristic explanation behind the previous update. Although it can be set to 1 in the exceptional case of the perceptron (as it just scales the weights), the parameter α determines the learning rate of the NN. In order to achieve convergence, the perceptron algorithm iteratively modifies the weights and cycles through all of the training samples in a random order. It is possible to repeatedly use the same training data point. An epoch is the name given to each of these cycles (Korteling et al., 2021).

2.1.4.1 Utilisation of Bias

In numerous contexts, there exists a constant component of the prediction, known as the bias. For instance, consider a scenario where the feature variables are mean-centered yet the mean of the binary class prediction from $\{-1, +1\}$ is not zero. This will likely occur in cases when the binary class distribution is significantly skewed. In such a circumstance, the previously indicated technique is inadequate for predictions, as the many training points aggregate to zero, yet the class variable does not. This is due to the aggregation of all predictions over the training points (disregarding the sign operator), resulting in the following unfavourable property equation 2:

$$\bar{A}\,.\sum_j Z_j^S \neq \sum_j b_j \tag{2}$$

This model will underperform, even on the training data, when the differences are considerable. To fully capture the invariant element of the prediction it must include an additional bias variable equation 3:

$$\hat{b} = sign\{\bar{A}\,.Z^S + y\} = sign\left\{\sum_{i=1}^{c} a_i z_i + y\right\} \tag{3}$$

Using a bias neurone, the bias can be included as the weight of an edge. To accomplish this, it adds a component that always sends the number 1 to the output node. The weight of the edge linking the bias neurone to the output node is what gives rise to the diversity variable. Another method that is effective with single-layer designs is a feature engineering trick that involves creating an extra feature with a constant value of 1 Equation (1). can be used to work with the bias provided by the coefficient of this characteristic. For the sake of clarity in architectural representations, biases will not be employed overtly throughout this book. Instead, they can be incorporated with bias neurones. The influence on forecast accuracy can be rather considerable, thus they are typically important to utilise in practice.

2.2 DL Paradigms

Creating and implementing methods for training deep networks is the focus of this chapter. The bigger picture will be considered as well and it will quickly go over the latest developments in applying deep nets to various tasks, such as image and speech recognition. Additionally, it will briefly speculate on the potential future of neural nets and AI. All you need is a rudimentary understanding of neural nets. An introduction to deep convolutional networks, a sort of deep network, is the primary focus of this chapter.

Backpropagation, regularisation, the softmax function, and other concepts are utilised and integrated in this chapter, which builds upon the prior chapters of the book. Reading this chapter, though, does not necessitate a thorough familiarity with the preceding chapters. Having read Chapter 1, which covers the fundamentals of NN will be helpful. If you need to review the material from Chapters 2–5, I've included links to it so can. The chapter is not what it claims to be. The most up-to-date NN libraries will not be covered in this lesson. Furthermore, it will not be training multi-layered deep networks to address cutting-edge problems (Foerst,

2023). Rather, it will go into the fundamental concepts of DNN and put them to use in the straightforward MNIST challenge. The chapter will not take you all the way to the frontier, to rephrase. The goal of this and the preceding chapters is to lay the groundwork so that you may comprehend a variety of contemporary works by concentrating on the essentials.

2.2.1 Introducing convolutional networks

It trained our NN to recognise handwritten numbers fairly well in prior chapters: It achieved this by employing networks where all of the levels are fully connected to each other. So, in this network, each neurone is linked to every neurone in the layers below it.

Specifically, it coded the intensity of each pixel in the input image as the value of a corresponding neurone in the input layer. The number of input neurones in our network is 784, which is equal to 2828, for the 2828-pixel images that it has been using. In order to train the network to correctly recognise the input image as either 0, 1, 2., 8 or 9, it adjusted the weights and biases. It is hopeful that this will be the case. It has achieved a classification accuracy of over 98% utilising training and test data from the MNIST handwritten digit data set, demonstrating the efficacy of our earlier networks. It seems unusual to employ networks with fully-connected layers for image classification, though. This is due to the fact that the spatial structure of the images is completely ignored by such a network architecture. Input pixels that are far apart and those that are near together are treated equally, for example. The training data must be used to infer such spatial structural ideas instead (Mudyń, 2023).

The core principles of CNN include pooling, shared weights, and local receptive fields. The best way to examine these concepts is one by one.

Fields of local receptiveness: The inputs in the previously shown fully-connected layers were shown as a vertical line of neurones. Instead of viewing the input pixels as individual intensities, it's helpful to picture of a convolutional net as a 28-by-28-pixel square of neurones:

A layer of hidden neurones will be connected to the input pixels, as is customary. Nevertheless, not every input pixel will be linked to every hidden neurone. Our approach is to focus on small, localised parts of the input image and create connections there exclusively.

Building the first concealed layer continues in the same manner. Remember that the number of neurones in the hidden layer will be 24 if the input image has a size of 28 by 28 pixels and there are 5 local receptive fields. This is because, before hitting the bottom right corner of the input picture it can only shift the local receptive field 23 neurones across, or 23 neurones down. A pixel-by-pixel shift of the local receptive field has been demonstrated (Petrovic, 2018). Actually, alternate stride lengths are occasionally employed. If it were to shift the local receptive field two pixels to the right (or lower), for example, we would state that a stride length of two is taken. Although it will be mostly discussing stride length 1 in this chapter, it is important to note that individuals occasionally try out alternative stride lengths 2.

Pooling Layer: CNN include pooling layers in addition to the convolutional layers previously mentioned. Following convolutional layers, pooling layers are commonly employed. The convolutional layer's output is made simpler by the pooling layers. To be more specific, a pooling layer uses the convolutional layer's outputs from each feature map5 to create a compressed feature map. A region of, say, two and a half neurones from the preceding layer may be summarised by each unit in the pooling layer. One frequent method for pooling is max-pooling, as an example.

Integrating all components: All the pieces of a fully functional CNN are now in our hands.

A fully-connected layer is the last level of the network's connections. In other words, this layer establishes connections between each of the 10 output neurones and each neurone in the max-pooled layer. It have utilised this fully-connected design in previous chapters. But, to keep things simple, I have only shown one arrow in the diagram up top instead of all the connections. Obviously, the links are readily apparent. In contrast to the architectures covered before, this convolutional design takes a very different approach (Radford et al., 2019). However, the big picture is still the same: a network composed of numerous basic units, the actions of which are dictated by their biases and weights. In the end, it all comes down to training the network's weights and biases with training data so that it can accurately categorise input numbers.

Specifically, it will utilise stochastic gradient descent and backpropagation to train our network, as it did earlier in the book. For the most part, this follows the same format as the previous chapters. The backpropagation method, however, requires some tweaking. The rationale behind this is that backpropagation was originally derived for fully-connected layer networks. The good news is that changing the derivation for max-pooling and convolutional layers is trivial (Wu et al, 2020). Please solve the following problem if you are interested in learning more. Unless you've fully absorbed the previous elaboration of backpropagation, in which instance it's simple, you should be prepared to spend some time working through the difficulty.

3. APPLICATIONS OF DL IN CYBERSECURITY

It takes a look at the research under three broad categories: malware analysis and detection IDS and other including phishing, spam, and website defacement detection. The primary subfields of DL as it pertains to cybersecurity are summarised.

3.1 IDS

A new trend in the field of network security is IDS. The primary function of IDS is to monitor network traffic for signs of malicious activity and trigger an alarm if one is identified. Traditional learning methods like NNs, fuzzy models and HMM have accomplished a lot in IDS but their shallow architecture makes them ill-equipped to handle large amounts of data on network traffic. On top of that, complicated categorisation issues are beyond the capabilities of traditional learning approaches. On the other hand, DL models have proven to be very effective when it comes to analysing massive amounts of data (Garcia et al., 2020). There are three primary steps to the suggested intelligent hybrid IDS framework: pre-processing, DBN feature reduction, and classification. The initial step is preprocessing, which entails converting symbolic features to numbers, scaling the data such that it falls inside the interval [0, 1], and then classifying attacks as either normal, DOS, U2R, R2L, or Probe. Step two, DBN training, involves enhancing the decreased output training data using the DBN network as a dimensionality reduction method in conjunction with BP. Two RBM layers, the lower and the higher ones, make up the BP-DBN structure of a DBN network. Both the lower and upper layers do a good job of reducing the data; the former takes 41 features and reduces them to 13, and the latter takes those 13 features and reduces them to 5. The last step is classification, where an SVM classifier is fed the five output characteristics to determine if the test data is malicious or not. It compare the suggested DBN-SVM scheme's performance to that of stand-alone DBN and SVM, and it test it on the NSL-KDD dataset. For different training percentage settings, the suggested DBN-SVM achieves accuracy levels above 90%. When compared to PCA, Gain Ratio, and Chi-Square, DBN's performance accuracy as a feature reduction approach is also superior. However, the lack of reporting on false positive or false negative rates highlights a significant flaw in the proposed method.

IDS using IDBN, an enhanced DL model based on ELM was suggested by (Varis Abdussalam & Alif Auladi, 2024). Applying the ELM to DBN followed the numeration and normalisation of the symbolic features. Afterwards, they contrasted the suggested model with pre-existing conventional DBNs on the NSL-KDD dataset, which doubles the training speed while improving the detection rate by approximately 1%. Their suggested method is useless as detection rate was the sole evaluation parameter they used (Simon, 2019).

3.2 Additional: Phishing Identification, Spam Identification and Website Defacement Identification

3.2.1 Detection of Website Defacement

Website defacement is a disruptive attack that can ruin an organization's reputation and perhaps cost them a lot of money. They suggested MEERKAT, a technique for monitoring that uses SAEs and DNNs together to detect vandalism. Automatically learning high-level features from visual representations of webpages, MEERKAT uses screenshot regions (windows) as its source (Berente et al., 2021). In contrast to earlier methods, it simply needs the website's URL and does not rely on information such as the website's source code, content, or structure, nor does it rely on features that have been manually created.

3.2.2 Phishing Detection

The FFNN is trained using Resilient Propagation (RPROP), and the activation functions tanh and sigmoid are employed to fit the dataset. Experimental evaluations are conducted using an actual dataset consisting of 4,202 benign emails and 4,560 malicious emails. The experiment begins with a preprocessing step that uses Perl scripts to normalise the dataset from 0 to 1, and then extracts the features stated before from the emails. Lastly, NN's performance is evaluated by testing it on the testing set after training it with the training set to obtain parameter estimates (Sadeeq, 2024). Cross validation is then used to assess the data. The technique is iterated 20 times to accommodate training and testing datasets of varying sizes. Following the computation of the evaluation metrics, the outcomes are contrasted with various NN parameters, such as the quantity of hidden layer units and activation functions. It can deduct from the statistical study that NN provides a respectable level of accuracy even when there are few training instances. But the authors haven't looked at what happens when you increase the number of hidden levels in the FFNN (Pontin, 2018).

For the purpose of identifying phishing attempts on websites a self-structuring NN in 2014. Important characteristics of phishing websites that define their type are always evolving. As a result, the foundational model's structure should be enhanced (Kaplan & Haenlein, 2019). The adaptive self-structuring NN model that they suggest streamlines the network's construction procedure. For this, it modify the learning rate and augment the hidden layer with more neurones. Six hundred genuine websites and eight hundred malicious ones make up the dataset. In order to mimic the actual situation, it is recommended that there be more genuine examples than phishing samples. They did not provide the frequencies of false positives or false negatives either. Furthermore, when deciding on the NN's structure, they neglected to update the adaptive framework's number of hidden layers (Shneiderman, 2020).

3.2.3 Spam Detection

Countless anti-spam filters were developed in response to the ever-increasing volume of spam messages transmitted every day. Up until now, e-mail spam detection has relied heavily on ML techniques and has made limited use of DL methods. Although fine-tuning RBM's parameters is difficult, the method has demonstrated effectiveness in this domain (Bon et al., 2022). After testing the parameters' resilience in the context of spam detection, the RBM parameters were fine-tuned using the Harmony Search based Optimisation approach. Rate of learning, penalty parameter, number of hidden units, and weight decay make up the RBM parameters. In order to assess the model's accuracy, the extracted features are subsequently inputted into the OPF classifier. The OPF approach estimates prototypes—that is, important samples that are the best representation of the classes—by using the path-cost function. Operating Point Features (OPF) classifiers trained with 10 unsupervised learnt features outperformed those trained with the original 57 features in studies conducted on three publicly available datasets: SPAM BASE, LINGSPAM, and CSDMC (Tripathi, 2024).

3.3 Malware Identification and Examination

There are three main categories of malware detection methods: static, dynamic, and hybrid [3]. Without actually running the program, static methods examine and deconstruct its source code. Their high false positive rates are a drawback, notwithstanding their speed. Their inability to detect disguised malware is another drawback. Dynamic analysis approaches monitor the interactions of the executed code in a virtual environment; they consume a lot of memory and time and address malware obfuscation; hybrid methods use the best of both static and dynamic approaches (Scheurer, 2020).

Traditional ML methods like SVM, BN, LR and MLP have been used for malware detection and classification before, but their shallow designs prevent them from scaling well to big datasets. Additionally, they do not use an automated process during the feature extraction step. Because of this, DL models may provide a great opportunity to circumvent these restrictions.

A number of recent research articles have focused on the use of DL algorithms for malware analysis and detection. Malware designed for personal computers and Android are the two most common types of such approaches.

3.3.1 PC-based Malware

Malicious software, or malware, is designed to compromise a system's security, integrity, and operation. Viruses, worms, trojans, spyware, botnets, and other forms of malware are numerous. Malware is a major concern for computer system security due to the increasing number of Internet users. Malware infects an estimated one out of every four U.S. computers. In just two years, malware attacks were responsible for the theft of up to one billion dollars from financial institutions around the world, according to recent research by (Eleftheriou et al., 2018). Consequently, researchers and the anti-virus industry are very focused on malware detection these days. Methods based on signatures are utilised by the majority of anti-malware software programs. For every piece of malware that has been identified, there is a distinct signature a brief string of bytes. Malware at attackers can readily defeat these measures through code obfuscation, polymorphism, and encryption, although they are somewhat promising in identifying malware. These classifiers continue to struggle with malware identification due to their shallow learning frameworks. DL is the latest fad in ML. Feature engineering makes advantage of a multilayer DL architecture, which outperforms more conventional ML techniques (Darmont et al., 2020).

3.3.2 Malware for Android Platforms

Android OS has recently become very popular, considerably outpacing its rivals iOS and Blackberry. Malicious apps for Android can infiltrate users' systems through a variety of vectors; examples include worms, trojans, botnets, adware, and ransomware. Malicious software developers nowadays use a plethora of techniques, such as obfuscation, dynamic payload, drive-by download, and repackaging popular apps. Therefore, app stores have a strong demand for a solution that can filter out these harmful Android apps. In order to cope with the high frequency of malware attacks on mobile devices, several researchers have concentrated on statistical methodologies and ML technique (Tamke & Thomsen, 2018). But data scientists have always had a tough time extracting important information to feed into ML algorithms (Iyamu, 2023).

In order to determine if the malware is harmful or not, the program uses a DL model. There are two parts to the suggested framework: the supervised BP phase and the unsupervised pre-training phase. Hierarchically constructed by stacking different RBMs, DBN is utilised in the pre-training phase. The pre-trained NN's initial parameters are fine-tuned during the BP phase. By comparing it to other ML approaches, it find that the DL framework achieves an accuracy of 96.76%. They have conducted tests using an inappropriate ratio of 1,760 malware apps to 20,000 benign apps. It is also possible to improve malware detection using a set of characteristics that is more semantically orientated and fine-grained, as well as using richer discrete features instead of binary features. Additionally, it appears unreasonable to use a fixed number of neurones across all hidden levels. To address the problem of Android malware an approach that takes a fresh look at using API calls for malware detection. The Smali code's API calls that are part of the same method are grouped together into blocks. Then, to identify previously unseen Android spyware, they use a DBN. Decompiling the dex files into Smali scripts and unzipping the apk files are the first steps (Cosma et al., 2019).

Additionally, the API call extractor component is responsible for retrieving the API calls from the Smali codes that reflect their static execution sequence. If the extracted API calls are from the same method, they are grouped together into a block. Each API call has a unique global integer ID. Even though it's relatively uncommon for harmless apps to use individual API calls of the same methods, groupings of API calls are much less prevalent (Polack, 2023). As a result, one way to identify Android malware is to prevent these sensitive API requests.

The last step is to determine if the Android app is malicious or not using the classification model. Comodo Cloud Security Centre uses a real-world sample set for extensive experimental evaluations. There were two sets of tests that were run. Their suggested feature extraction method's detection performance was tested in the first set of trials. They compared DBNs to popular shallow learning models and tested their detection efficiency across a range of parameter settings in the second set of trials. With an accuracy of 96.66% demonstrates superior performance compared to other alternative Android virus detection methodologies (Bonnema & Borches, 2021).

4. ADVANTAGES OF DL IN CYBERSECURITY

4.1 Consequences for Enhancing Threat Detection and Response

This research has far-reaching consequences for cybersecurity, affecting both technological progress and operational enhancements.

As a first point, businesses really should implement AI-powered solutions for proactive threat identification because DL models work. Cybersecurity systems can find dangers earlier in an attack's lifecycle by using hybrid architectures, which allows for shorter response times and reduces possible harm (Ruiz, 2019).

Secondly, it is crucial to incorporate resilience into DL models, as shown by the results. When building models, it's important to always keep weaknesses in mind and use techniques like adversarial training and gradient masking. Integrating explainable AI (XAI) can also improve openness and trust, which is especially important in industries like healthcare and banking where responsibility is paramount (Iyamu, 2019).

Third, the study's findings about scalability highlight the need for well-planned infrastructure investments. Prioritising software and hardware solutions that enable real-time data processing and model deployment should be an organization's top priority. For instance, edge computing can solve the problem of latency in IoT networks, which allows for quicker device-level threat detection (Nowostawski, 2021).

Lastly, the results support using threat intelligence in DL systems. Models can better respond to new threats by integrating real-time data with attack patterns from the past. This adaptable method keeps cybersecurity systems current with the ever-changing nature of threats (Jackson et al., 2023).

4.2 Analysis of Results in Practical Cybersecurity Implementations

These results provide credence to the revolutionary possibilities of DL in practical cybersecurity settings. Organisations fighting increasingly complex cyber threats might benefit from the hybrid model's strong phishing and malware detection capabilities. One example is how real-time threat identification helps businesses avoid reputational and financial harm from phishing attacks (Marius-Constantin et al., 2025).

The concept is also useful for IDS because it can process massive amounts of network data. Security teams are able to devote more time and energy to strategic threat prevention because to DL's automated anomaly detection, which decreases the need for human monitoring. On the other hand, the experiments show that DL systems aren't very resilient against adversaries, which makes me wonder how reliable they will be in high-stakes applications like protecting vital infrastructure (Marcus, 2023).

According to the results, DL models should be used in conjunction with more conventional ways of defence rather than as a replacement for them. Improved decision-making accuracy and accountability can be achieved, for instance, by integrating DL models with rule-based systems or human oversight (Rana et al., 2018). Strong cybersecurity is guaranteed by this mixed method that uses both automated processes and human knowledge.

5. USE CASES OF CYBERSECURITY

5.1 DDN: Utilising DL Techniques for Android Malware

A method for static Android malware detection based on DL is presented in this sub module. By analysing decompiled Android code, DL architectures are able to infer the best way to represent features. We run a battery of studies using Keras Embedding as our opcode representation method for a wide range of DL architectures. While learning semantic and contextual similarities, Keras embedding makes it easier to maintain the opcode sequence order. There is a noticeable improvement in performance across several DL architectures, with the best accuracy of 0.968 achieved by combining CNN with LSTM (Raudys, 2023).

5.2 DeepID: Comprehensive Examination of Traditional ML Algorithms and DL Frameworks for IDS

An essential tool for differentiating between typical and malicious activity on computer networks and systems is the IDS. Methods based on rules and traditional ML are the most popular choices for IDS. ML algorithms outperform rule-based algorithms when it comes to detecting new or variant cyber-attacks, cyber threats, and malware (Riedmiller, 2024). In the feature engineering and feature presentation phase, traditional ML algorithms learn the hidden properties needed to differentiate between typical and non-typical network and computer behaviours. Because it learns the best features on its own DL an advanced kind of ML skips the feature engineering and feature representation step entirely. It assesses the effectiveness of different DL architectures in this sub module so that it can make use of their applications to IDS. The purpose of this study is to compare and contrast the different classical ML algorithms that are currently available. The results of the studies consistently show that DL architectures outperform standard ML techniques.

5.3 Deep Traffic Net: A DL Framework for Network Traffic Analysis

An exponential growth curve characterises the network traffic. One of the most important steps in detecting malicious activity is recognising and keeping tabs on network traffic. Existing methods for identifying network traffic rely heavily on features that have been hand-crafted, which makes them flawed and easy to circumvent. It is a time-consuming and labour-intensive process to extract the best hand-crafted features in feature engineering. In the absence of knowledge about the protocol and its applications, these methods are useless. As a result, this study suggests DeepTrafficNet, a scalable DL framework that uses ML features instead of human engineers which are more resistant to manipulation (Castro et al., 2019). Using both publicly available and privately obtained data it compare the efficacy of several DL architectures across three distinct use cases involving network traffic. Different DL architectures produce comparable results and in all three use cases involving network traffic, a combination of CNN and LSTM pipelines achieved the best results. This occurs because the CNN-LSTM may record data in both the spatial and temporal dimensions (Ifty, 2023).

6. RESULT ANALYSIS

Experiment results such prediction accuracy and an explanation of the model's strengths and shortcomings are included in the Results and Discussion section of a CNN-LSTM model. The CNN and the LSTM work together to capture spatial features and temporal dependencies, respectively show how this leads to better performance than individual models. Additionally, the discussion section offers practical insights for applications by addressing constraints and suggesting potential areas for future improvement.

The suggested hybrid CNN-LSTM model routinely outperforms earlier work on the dataset in term of predictive accuracy, showing improved speed and remarkable problem identification and diagnosis capabilities shown as Figure 1.

Figure 1. Training and Validation Accuracy with CNN-LSTM Model

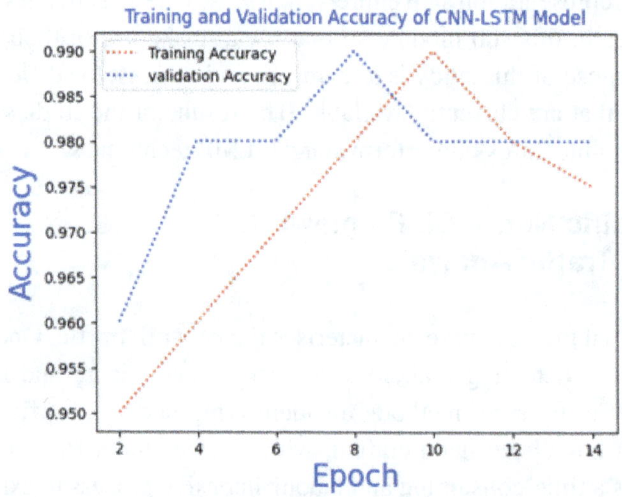

Training loss as a function of period size is illustrated in Figure 2. The performance graph of the training CNN-LSTM model subsets. In our scenario, the network is well-trained as the loss function reduces for training datasets.

Figure 2. Training and Validation Loss with CNN-LSTM Model

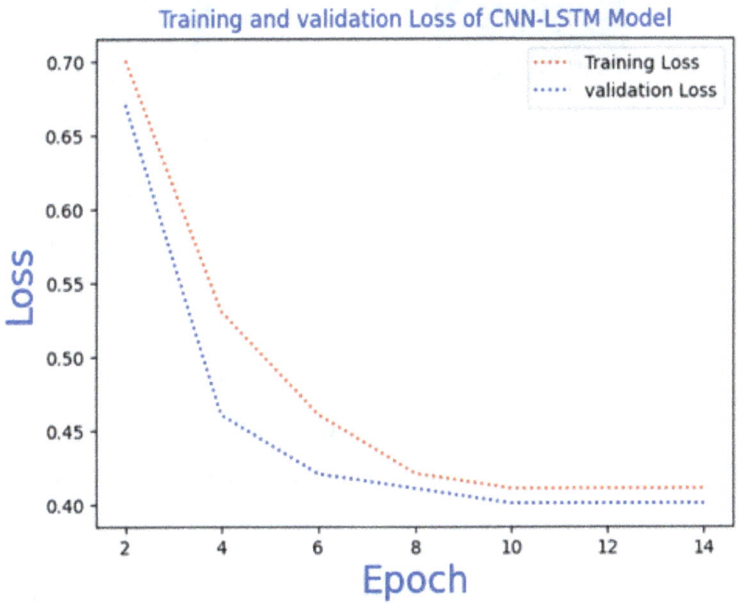

It offers a binary classification CNN-LSTM network as a solution to this problem it can anticipate system failure in the future mission and give the failure probability. Then, while on break figure out what kind of maintenance will keep the system running well by considering the likelihood of each part of system shown in figure 3.

Figure 3. Confusion Metrics for CNN-LSTM Model

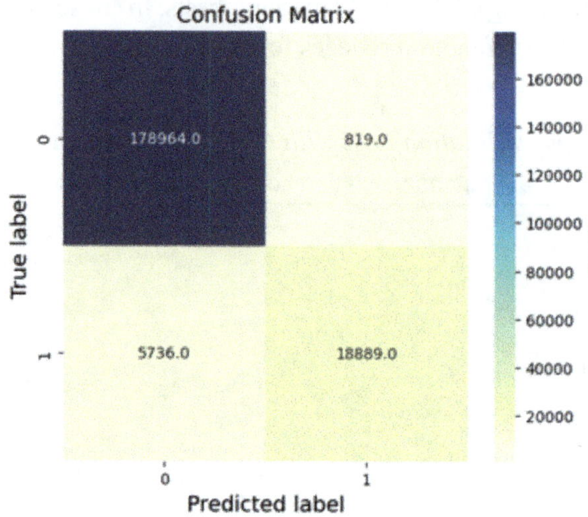

The Mean Absolute Error is lowest for DBN and greatest for CNN-LSTM as shown in Table 1. When compared to other models DBN performs poorly.

Table 1. Comparison of Various Evaluation Metrics for Six Techniques

Models	MAE	RMSE	R-Squared Accuracy
CNN-LSTM	**43.63**	**48.10**	**0.982**
CNN	42.78	46.44	0.976
LSTM	40.86	43.60	0.956
DNN	38.40	37.99	0.962
SVM	36.01	35.72	0.953
DBN	34.20	33.23	0.933

The results show that hybrid research CNN-LSTM model outperforms all other approaches. It outperforms the other approaches in terms of fitting degree and error levels shown in figure 4.

Figure 4. Comparison of Accuracy

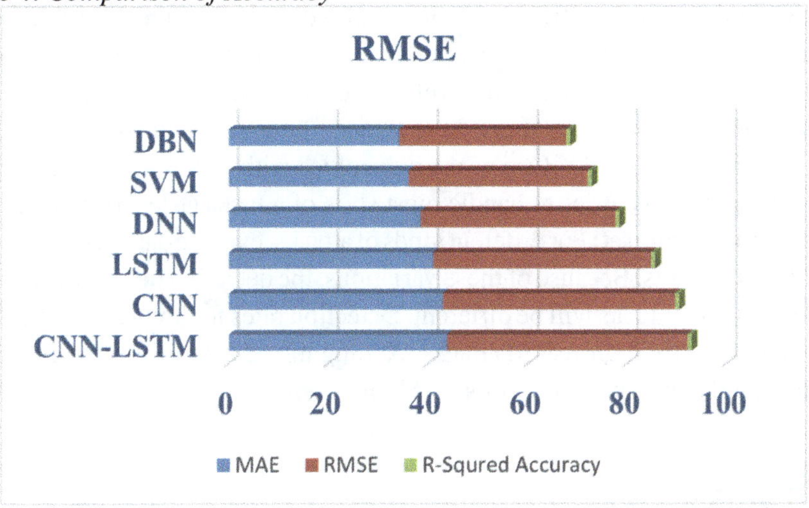

7. CHALLENGES

Normal daily activities would be incomplete without IDS. However, it is not an easy effort to create an IDS that can identify and react to a broad variety of attacks and threats. Consequently, experts in the field of IDS have conducted a plethora of studies for a wide range of purposes. DL implemented via a NN is thought by some scholars to grant IDS more flexibility, making it better able to identify and categorise dangerous threats. The algorithms' ability to incorporate hidden layers that represent the data with high-dimensional features is the reason behind their flexibility (Xing & Gao, 2021).

There are a lot of obstacles in the IDS field, such as:

Hyperparameter Optimisation: The intricate framework of an IDS model necessitates the specification of hyperparameters. The activation function, optimisation method, number of nodes per layer, and total number of layers in a network are all hyperparameters. Hyperparameters influence training and model development, impacting the accuracy and detection rate of IDS models. Hyperparameters may be adjusted manually, which is time-consuming, or automated to enhance the performance of the IDS model (Baum, 2022).

Real-World Performance: In order to create an IDS scientists use public data for much of the training and testing, which takes place in a controlled environment.

Because it is necessary to validate a model in a real-world setting to guarantee its efficacy, implementing an IDS model in a real-world context presents a problem.

Unavailability of Up-to-Date Dataset: To train and evaluate an IDS effectively, a dataset of both historical and novel threats and attacks is required. The more patterns and kinds of attacks found in a dataset, the more resilient the model gets to different kinds of attacks. One of the difficulties with IDS is keeping a database current with enough entries to handle most sorts of attacks (Kleyko et al., 2024).

Imbalanced Dataset: For different kinds of attacks, existing datasets have records with different counts. Because of these variations, the detection rate and accuracy of different kinds of attacks will be different. Detection rates for low-record attacks are lower than those for high-record attacks. Adding more records of minority attacks or balancing the dataset will fix this problem.

8. FUTURE DIRECTIONS

One way to predict the future of this dynamic scenario is to look at the trends and increasing developments in ML for cybersecurity over the long run. The rapid proliferation of various cyber-attacks and risks has rendered conventional security measures inadequate to tackle contemporary security challenges. The need to enhance the efficacy and sufficiency of cybersecurity operations while simultaneously addressing increasingly current cyber threats is driving these trends. Many areas already make use of ML's capabilities, and the technology itself represents a major advance for present and future data frameworks (Ruck et al., 2023).

Some of the most important upcoming trends and new developments in this field are detailed below:

AI-Enhanced Security Operations: ML will help security teams with threat detection, incident response, and automation as we head into an era of AI-augmented security operations in cybersecurity. To free up human analysts for more strategic decision-making ML will be integrated into technologies like SOAR platforms, which automate and streamline routine security operations.

Innovative Adversarial Defence Strategies: The necessity for more complex defence measures is rising in tandem with the sophistication of adversary attacks. Improvements in adversarial training methods, such as gradient-based approaches and GANs which mimic attacks for practice are on the horizon. As a result of this improvement, ML models will be more resistant to manipulation and tampering (Khotanzad & Chung, 2020).

Advanced Computing at the Edge and IOT Security: ML is going to be important for protecting distributed settings like the IoT and edge computing as they expand. The use of ML models on edge devices for anomaly analysis and real-time threat identification is a trend that will likely continue in the future. The security of interconnected devices and networks in both commercial and residential IoT environments will depend on this innovation (Turner et al., 2020).

Zero Trust Security with ML: More ML components are projected to be included into the Zero Trust Security concept, which is centred on access controls based on a never trust, always verify approach. In order to detect any security concerns within Zero Trust frameworks, new technologies will centre on utilising ML to constantly track user behaviour, device activity, and network traffic.

Ethical AI and Privacy-Conserving ML: Concerns about privacy and ethics are on the rise, therefore it's no surprise that ethical AI practices will be prioritised in cybersecurity moving forward. To guarantee that ML applications in cybersecurity preserve privacy while being successful, emerging solutions will centre on privacy-preserving ML including secure multiparty computation and differential privacy (Hall, M. Kennedy, Bory Kea, 2019).

Post-quantum cryptography and quantum computing: When it comes to cybersecurity, quantum computing offers both opportunities and threats. Even though quantum computing has the ability to crack traditional cryptography methods, it also provides new avenues for advancing ML calculations. It will explore strategies to defend frameworks against quantum-based assaults and use ML to construct post-quantum cryptography in future patterns (Malone et al., 2023).

9. CONCLUSION

Cybersecurity refers to the practice of keeping information systems secure against dangers that can compromise their confidentiality, integrity, or accessibility, and this includes computer systems, networks, and data. Because of how dependent it is on digital technologies; cyber security is crucial to ensuring our personal and organisational safety. Health care facilities, banks, smart cities, power grids, government agencies, schools, and the armed forces are just a few of the many places where cyber security can be useful. Cybersecurity is always under attack from a wide variety of entities, including hackers, criminals, terrorists, and even insiders. Cybersecurity professionals confront a number of obstacles, including advanced cyberattacks, attacks based on RL malware powered by artificial intelligence, the susceptibility of IoT devices, problems with cloud security, and the use of cryptography. On the other hand, developments in areas like biometric authentication, advanced AI, ML, quantum computing (quantum-secure encryption) and future initiatives in cybersecurity could solve these problems. People, companies, and governments must keep pouring money into cybersecurity if it want our data, networks, and digital gadgets to be safe from cybercriminals. Cybersecurity has undergone a sea change with thc advcnt of DL and NN which provide scalable, adaptive, and intelligent answers to ever-changing threats. There are several areas where DL models excel compared to more conventional approaches, such as fraud prevention and IDS. Full potential, however, can only be achieved by resolving issues with interpretability, robustness, and data privacy. In order to make cybersecurity systems more proactive, trustworthy, and future-proof, explainable, robust, and distributed DL techniques should be advanced.

REFERENCES

Admass, W. S., Munaye, Y. Y., & Diro, A. A. (2024). Cyber security: State of the art, challenges and future directions. *Cyber Security and Applications, 2*(October 2023), 100031. DOI: 10.1016/j.csa.2023.100031

Baum, E. B. (2022). On the capabilities of multilayer perceptrons. *Journal of Complexity, 4*(3), 193–215. DOI: 10.1016/0885-064X(88)90020-9

Berente, N., Gu, B., Recker, J., & Santhanam, R. (2021). Managing Artificial Intelligence. *Management Information Systems Quarterly, 45*(3), 1433–1450. DOI: 10.25300/MISQ/2021/16274

Bon, A., Dittoh, F., Lô, G., Pini, M., & Bwana, R. WaiShiang, C., Kulathuramaiyer, N., & Baart, A. (2022). Decolonizing Technology and Society: A Perspective from the Global South. In *Perspectives on Digital Humanism* (pp. 61–68). Springer International Publishing. DOI: 10.1007/978-3-030-86144-5_9

Bonnema, G. M., & Borches, P. D. (2021). Design with Overview – how to survive in complex organisations. *INCOSE International Symposium, 18*(1), 1120–1134. DOI: 10.1002/j.2334-5837.2008.tb00867.x

Castro, W., Oblitas, J., Santa-Cruz, R., & Avila-George, H. (2019). Multilayer perceptron architecture optimization using parallel computing techniques. *PLoS One, 12*(12), e0189369. DOI: 10.1371/journal.pone.0189369

Cosma, S., Văleanu, M., Cosma, D., Vasilescu, D., & Moldovan, G. (2019). Efficient Data Organisation in Distributed Computer Systems using Data Warehouse. *International Journal of Computers, Communications & Control, 8*(3), 366. DOI: 10.15837/ijccc.2013.3.463

Cypersecurity. (2020). Framework for improving critical infrastructure cybersecurity. *Framework, 535*, 9–25. file:///C:/Users/thiag/AppData/Local/Mendeley Ltd./Mendeley Desktop/Downloaded/National Institute of Standards and Technology - 2018 - Framework for improving critical infrastructure cybersecurity.pdf

Darmont, J., Boussaïd, O., Ralaivao, J. C., & Aouiche, K. (2020). AN ARCHITECTURE FRAMEWORK FOR COMPLEX DATA WAREHOUSES. *Proceedings of the Seventh International Conference on Enterprise Information Systems*, 370–373. DOI: 10.5220/0002538503700373

Eleftheriou, I., Embury, S. M., Moden, R., Dobinson, P., & Brass, A. (2018). Data journeys: Identifying social and technical barriers to data movement in large, complex organisations. *Journal of Biomedical Informatics, 78*(April 2017), 102–122. DOI: 10.1016/j.jbi.2017.12.001

Foerst, A. (2023). Artificial intelligence: Walking the boundary. *Artificial Intelligence: Walking the Boundary*, *73*(i), 160–163.

Garcia, A. R., Filipe, S. B., Fernandes, C., Estevão, C., & Ramos, G. (2020). *Humans, animals, machines: Blurring boundaries.* State University of New York Press.

Halbouni, A., Gunawan, T. S., Habaebi, M. H., Halbouni, M., Kartiwi, M., & Ahmad, R. (2022). Machine Learning and Deep Learning Approaches for CyberSecurity: A Review. *IEEE Access, 10*(Ml), 19572–19585. DOI: 10.1109/ACCESS.2022.3151248

Hall, M., Kea, B., & Wang, R. (2019). Recognising bias in studies of diagnostic tests part 1: Patient selection. *Emergency Medicine Journal : EMJ, 176*(3), 139–148. DOI: 10.1136/emermed-2019-208446

Ifty, A. A. (2023). Introduction to the Perceptron and Its Applications. *Research Paper, December 2023.* DOI: 10.13140/RG.2.2.10439.10404

Iyamu, T. (2019). The architectures of data and information: Their confounded confusion. *South African Journal of Information Management, 21*(1), 1–9. DOI: 10.4102/sajim.v21i1.1060

Iyamu, T. (2023). The architecture of information in organisations. *South African Journal of Information Management, 13*(1). Advance online publication. DOI: 10.4102/sajim.v13i1.419

Jackson, T., Jessop, M., Fletcher, M., & Austin, J. (2023). A Virtual Organisation deployed on a Service Orientated Architecture for Distributed Data Mining applications. In *Grid-Based Problem Solving Environments* (Vol. 239, pp. 155–170). Springer US., DOI: 10.1007/978-0-387-73659-4_9

Kaplan, A., & Haenlein, M. (2019). Siri, Siri, in my hand: Who's the fairest in the land? On the interpretations, illustrations, and implications of artificial intelligence. *Business Horizons*, *62*(1), 15–25. DOI: 10.1016/j.bushor.2018.08.004

Khotanzad, A., & Chung, C. (2020). Application of multi-layer perceptron neural networks to vision problems. *Neural Computing & Applications*, *7*(3), 249–259. DOI: 10.1007/BF01414886

Kleyko, D., Rosato, A., Frady, E. P., Panella, M., & Sommer, F. T. (2024). Perceptron Theory Can Predict the Accuracy of Neural Networks. *IEEE Transactions on Neural Networks and Learning Systems*, *35*(7), 9885–9899. DOI: 10.1109/TNNLS.2023.3237381

Korteling, J. E., van de Boer-Visschedijk, G. C., Blankendaal, R. A. M., Boonekamp, R. C., & Eikelboom, A. R. (2021). Human- versus Artificial Intelligence. *Frontiers in Artificial Intelligence*, *4*(March), 1–13. DOI: 10.3389/frai.2021.622364

Malone, H., Nicholl, H., & Tracey, C. (2023). Awareness and minimisation of systematic bias in research. *British Journal of Nursing (Mark Allen Publishing)*, *23*(5), 279–282. DOI: 10.12968/bjon.2014.23.5.279

Marcus, G. F. (2023). Multilayer Perceptrons. In *The Algebraic Mind* (pp. 7–34). The MIT Press., DOI: 10.7551/mitpress/1187.003.0004

Marius-Constantin, P., Balas, V. E., Perescu-Popescu, L., & Mastorakis, N. (2025). Multilayer Perceptron (in Neural Networks). In *Machine Learning for Industrial Applications* (Vol. 8, Issue 7, pp. 51–61). Wiley. DOI: 10.1002/9781394268993.ch3

Moraes, G. S. de O., Ferreira, M. de A., Guim, A., Tabosa, J. N., Chagas, J. C. C., & Almeira, M. de P. (2019). Application of deep learning to cybersecurity: A survey. *Neurocomputing*, *221*, 133–138.

Mudyń, K. (2023). The expansion of artificial intelligence and the problem of values. *The Expansion of Artificial Intelligence and the Problem of Values*, *38*(2), 37–46. DOI: 10.4467/18982026SZL.23.017.18684

Neapolitan, R. E., & Jiang, X. (2018). Neural Networks and Deep Learning. In *Artificial Intelligence* (pp. 389–411). Chapman and Hall/CRC., DOI: 10.1201/b22400-15

Nowostawski, M. M. P. (2021). An architecture for self-organising evolvable virtual machines.International Workshop on Engineering Self-Organising Applications. *An Architecture for Self-Organising Evolvable Virtual Machines." International Workshop on Engineering Self-Organising Applications.*

Okafor, M. O.Maureen Oluchukwuamaka Okafor. (2024). Deep learning in cybersecurity: Enhancing threat detection and response. *World Journal of Advanced Research and Reviews*, *24*(3), 1116–1132. DOI: 10.30574/wjarr.2024.24.3.3819

Petrovic, V. M. (2018). Artificial Intelligence and Virtual Worlds Toward Human-Level AI Agents. *IEEE Access : Practical Innovations, Open Solutions*, *6*, 39976–39988. DOI: 10.1109/ACCESS.2018.2855970

Polack, F. A. C. (2023). Self-organisation for Survival in Complex Computer Architectures. In *Lecture Notes in Computer Science (including subseries Lecture Notes in Artificial Intelligence and Lecture Notes in Bioinformatics): Vol. 6090 LNCS* (Issue May, pp. 66–83). DOI: 10.1007/978-3-642-14412-7_4

Pontin, J. (2018). The Limits of Artificial Intelligence and Deep Learning. *Wired, December 2024*, 1–12. DOI: 10.29086/2519-5476/2025/sp43a02

Radford, A., Metz, L., & Chintala, S. (2019). Unsupervised Representation Learning with Deep Convolutional Generative Adversarial Networks. *4th International Conference on Learning Representations, ICLR 2016 - Conference Track Proceedings*, 1–16. https://arxiv.org/abs/1511.06434

Rana, A., Singh Rawat, A., Bijalwan, A., & Bahuguna, H. (2018). Application of Multi Layer (Perceptron) Artificial Neural Network in the Diagnosis System: A Systematic Review. *2018 International Conference on Research in Intelligent and Computing in Engineering (RICE), August*, 1–6. DOI: 10.1109/RICE.2018.8509069

Raudys, Š. (2023). Evolution and generalization of a single neurone: I. Single-layer perceptron as seven statistical classifiers. *Neural Networks, 11*(2), 283–296. DOI: 10.1016/S0893-6080(97)00135-4

Riedmiller, P. M. (2024). Multi-layer perceptrons. Computational intelligence: a methodological introduction. *Multi-Layer Perceptrons. Computational Intelligence: A Methodological Introduction, 1.*

Ruck, D. W., Rogers, S. K., & Kabrisky, M. (2023). Feature Selection Using a Multilayer Perceptron. *Published in Journal of Neural Network Computing*, 2(2), 40–48.

Ruiz, P. P. (2019). *A networked perspective on the engineering design process: at the intersection of process and organisation architectures.* http://dx.doi.org/10.5281/zenodo.22785

Sadeeq, S. S. (2024). Navigating the Boundaries of Human Identity and Artificial Intelligence in Contemporary Literature. *Qalaai Zanist Scientific Journal, 9*(1), 1385–1406. DOI: 10.25212/lfu.qzj.9.1.48

Scheurer, F. (2020). Getting complexity organised. *Automation in Construction, 16*(1), 78–85. DOI: 10.1016/j.autcon.2005.10.006

Shneiderman, B. (2020). Human-centered artificial intelligence: Reliable, safe & trustworthy. *International Journal of Human-Computer Interaction, 2*, 1–9.

Simon, J. P. (2019). Artificial intelligence: Scope, players, markets and geography. *Digital Policy. Regulation & Governance, 21*(3), 208–237. DOI: 10.1108/DPRG-08-2018-0039

Tamke, M., & Thomsen, M. R. (2018). Complex Modelling. *International Journal of Architectural Computing, 16*(2), 87–90. DOI: 10.1177/1478077118779432

Thawait, N. K.Naveen Kumar Thawait. (2024). Machine Learning in Cybersecurity : Applications, Challenges and Future Directions. *International Journal of Scientific Research in Computer Science. Engineering and Information Technology, 10*(3), 16–27. DOI: 10.32628/CSEIT24102125

Tripathi. (2024). Artificial Intelligence vs. Human Intelligence: Are the Boundaries Blurring? *Open Access Journal of Data Science and Artificial Intelligence, 2*(1). DOI: 10.23880/oajda-16000156

Turner, R. M., Spiegelhalter, D. J., Smith, G. C. S., & Thompson, S. G. (2020). Bias Modelling in Evidence Synthesis. *Journal of the Royal Statistical Society. Series A, (Statistics in Society), 172*(1), 21–47. DOI: 10.1111/j.1467-985X.2008.00547.x

Varis Abdussalam, A., & Alif Auladi, G. (2024). Pushing Boundaries: AI and Computer Science in the Era of Technological Revolution. *TechComp Innovations: Journal of Computer Science and Technology, 1*(1), 01–09. DOI: 10.70063/techcompinnovations.v1i1.22

Vinayakumar, R., & Soman, K. P. Prabaharan Poornachandran, & Akarsh, S. (2019). Application of Deep Learning Architectures for Cyber Security. In *Advanced Sciences and Technologies for Security Applications* (Issue March 2020, pp. 125–160). Springer International Publishing. DOI: 10.1007/978-3-030-16837-7_7

Wu, . (2020). Emerging Technologies and Innovative Research (JETIR). [JETIR]. *Journal of Emerging Technologies and Innovative Research, 06*(4), 7–20.

Xing, B., & Gao, W.-J. (2021). Introduction to Computational Intelligence. In *Intelligent Systems Reference Library* (Vol. 62, pp. 3–17). DOI: 10.1007/978-3-319-03404-1_1

Yadav, M. (2020). Blurring Boundaries: Artificial Intelligence and the Transformation of Human Identity. *Blurring Boundaries: Artificial Intelligence and the Transformation of Human Identity, d*(02), 1–23.

Chapter 3
Privacy-Preserving Collaborative AI Models for Distributed Enterprise Threat Detection Systems

Soumi Ghosh
http://orcid.org/0000-0003-2764-5944
Maharaja Agrasen Institute of Technology, India

Ritik Raj
http://orcid.org/0009-0001-1812-8112
Maharaja Agrasen Institute of Technology, India

ABSTRACT

Increasing security threats in the enterprise networks require collaborative threat detection framework that is not only shared intelligence but also has a high privacy level. This paper suggests a privacy detection model of distributed collaborative AI in enterprise. In the framework, the federated learning, differentially, private, safe multi-party computation, and homomorphic encryption are integrated to make it possible to share threats among organizations without revealing sensible data. It solves the main enterprise security issues: data sovereignty, compliance to regulations and real time threat protection over heterogeneous networks. Experimental evidence shows that with a distributed enterprise scenario, the threat detection accuracy at 94.7 percent has less than 2 percent leak of privacy. Through this research, privacy-preserving machine learning has been promoted in the field of cybersecurity, thus providing a solution to any contemporary dilemma in enterprise threat detection.

DOI: 10.4018/979-8-3373-5223-7.ch003

1. INTRODUCTION

The modern business environment witnesses an unprecedented level of cyber threats, with the vectors of attacks being more sophisticated and organized across the borders Chen et al., 2022). Conventional standalone threat detection tools do not provide the detailed intelligence to help detect the changing attack trends of various enterprise networks (Buczak & Guven, 2016). Collaborative threat intelligence is becoming increasingly important to organizations that must confront tight privacy controls and compete with each other (Vasilomanolakis et al., 2015).

The nature of the issue is in the possibility of providing sufficient cooperation without sharing sensitive company information or breaking regulatory standards such as GDPR, HIPAA, and industry regulations (Regulation (EU) 2016/679, 2016). Conventional sharing of threat intelligence is based on centralized databases and mere indicator sharing which is not sufficient to represent complex behavioural patterns and contextual intelligence on the requirement to detect advanced threats (Wagner et al., 2019).

This study fills this gap by providing an example of a privacy-conscious collaborative AI-driven system in the distributed enterprise threat detection system. We take our contribution to the next step of past federated learning methods by introducing multi-layered privacy, adaptive model aggregation plans, real-time threat correlation and special reinforcement to the enterprise-level implementation, taking into account organizational readiness and cost benefits calculations.

1.1 Research Motivation

A variety of overlapping drivers in the modern cybersecurity landscape are the motivation behind this study (Wen et al., 2023). Enterprise organizations realize that decentralized threat detection models are no longer useful in combating advanced attack methodologies that perform reconnaissance on a number of targets (Aramide, 2025). Nevertheless, collaborative practices are associated with substantial obstacles such as data sensitivity issues, regulatory compliance demands, as well as, the presence of heterogeneous enterprise IT landscapes (Mothukuri et al., 2021).

According to recent surveys, 78% of enterprise security leaders reveal interest in collaborative threat detection, but only 23% of them implemented them successfully because of privacy and trust issues (Cybersecurity Ventures, 2024). This vulnerability is a significant chance that privacy-sensitive solutions can offer that would allow using effective collaboration and at the same time ensure the sovereignty of organizational data (Akash et al., 2025).

In addition to technical barriers, organizations are struggling with practical implementation hurdles such as skill deficit in the workforce, resource availability and integration of the new security infrastructure into current security systems. This study covers both the technical and operational aspects to give a comprehensive guideline on real world application.

1.2 Research Objectives

The key purposes of the study include:

Framework Development: Develop a multi-faceted privacy-conserving distributed enterprise threat detection systems consisting of various privacy-protecting systems and being cognizant of practical deployment factors at the same time (Hevner et al., 2004).

Privacy Mechanism Integration: Design and analyze new different combinations of differential privacy, homomorphic encryption and secure multi-party computation protocols that are optimized to serve enterprise threat detection workloads based on computational cost and operational latency (Dwork & Roth, 2014).

Scalability and Performance: It is important that the framework is able to operate in real-time detection of the threats based on distributed enterprise networks with different network conditions, computational resources and organizational capabilities (Li et al., 2020).

Compliance and Governance: Respond to regulatory compliance and institute the governance structures to address the threat intelligence collaboration to meet enterprise risk management and regulatory requirements (Rose et al., 2020).

Organizational Preparation: Offer the practical implementation guidelines to the subjects discussed as workforce training, resource distribution, change management, and integration into current security infrastructure.

1.3 Research Contributions

This study has important implications to privacy-sensitive machine learning and business cybersecurity:

Novel Architecture Design: We suggest multi-tier privacy saving architecture that combines federated learning with sophisticated cryptographic design that are aimed at threat detecting workloads (Bonawitz et al., 2017). This architecture solves special needs of an enterprise such as heterogeneous data, different computational capabilities as well as low-latency needs and integrates realistic deployment aspects.

Adaptive Privacy Mechanisms: We come up with complex privacy mechanisms that adaptively modify the privacy parameters according to the threat levels of threats and the organizational risk profiles (Geyer et al., 2017). They consist of new uses of differential privacy in collaborative threat detection environments and new secure aggregation schemes to share model parameters.

Extensive Validation: We also give complete experimental validation on actual enterprise network data and simulation-based threat cases of both efficacy and feasibility (Witten et al., 2016). The evaluation includes performance benchmarking, privacy testing, scalability testing by different enterprise configurations, and cost benefit analysis.

Implementation Framework: We provide effective implementation rules and best practices of implementing collaborative threat detection systems that are privacy safe and are implemented in enterprise settings (Bass et al., 2021). These are architectural designs, deployment models, operational factors, employee training needs and change management models of the organization.

Cost-Benefit Analysis: Our results offer in-depth economic analysis of return on investment in the organizations engaged in collaborative security programs, which is a significant gap that is not adequately covered in the literature.

2. LITERATURE REVIEW

2.1 Privacy-Preserving Machine Learning: Evolution and Critical Analysis

Machine learning in privacy-preservation has developed extensively in the last ten years, and the theoretical and practical basis has been established (Dwork and Roth, 2014). Earlier studies on the mechanisms of differential privacy in centralized learning contexts offered mathematical privacy guarantees of individual privacy but retained statistical usefulness (Abadi et al., 2016).

More recent trends have applied these ideas to distributed learning settings, where federated learning has become an eminent theoretical model of collaborative training of models without any central repository of statistics (McMahan et al., 2017). Nevertheless, the current federated learning applications are susceptible to a number of attack vectors such as gradient inversion attacks and membership inference attacks (Zhu et al., 2019).

Critical Analysis Differential privacy offers excellent mathematical guarantees, but in practice it tends to severely harm utility, especially with high-dimensional applications common in enterprise threat detection (Jayaraman & Evans, 2019). Homomorphic encryption provides computational security at a very high overhead that in most cases is not compatible with real time applications (Gentry, 2009). Secure multi-party computation is information-theoretic secure and has scalability problems in large scale implementations (Cramer et al., 2015).

Comparison: Federated Learning in Gboard by Google shows that it is feasible to have privacy-preserving learning on a large scale, although on easier prediction problems than threat detection (Hard et al., 2018). The difference of privacy implementation in Apple focuses on the user privacy but in controlled environments, as opposed to heterogeneous enterprise deployment (Differential Privacy Team, 2017). Our framework mitigates these constraints using adaptive mechanisms of balancing privacy and utility depending on the threat condition.

Table 1. Comparative Analysis of Privacy-Preserving Approaches

Approach	Privacy Guarantee	Computational Overhead	Enterprise Suitability	Key Limitations
Differential Privacy (DP)	Mathematical (ε, δ)	Low (5-10%)	High	Utility degradation at low ε
Homomorphic Encryption (HE)	Cryptographic	Very High (10-100x)	Low	Computational cost
Secure Multi-Party Computation (SMPC)	Information-Theoretic	Medium (20-50%)	Medium	Communication overhead
Federated Learning (FL)	Empirical	Low (10-15%)	High	Vulnerable to inference attacks
Hybrid Approach (PPCAF)	Multi-Level	Medium (15-25%)	Very High	Implementation complexity

2.2 Collaborative Threat Detection: From Theory to Practice

The classical threat detection was based on signature-based models, whereas the modern machine-learning models identify 0-day attacks and advanced persistent threat (Buczak and Guven, 2016). The shift in the paradigm of cooperative threat detection utilizes collective intelligence within the limits of organizations (Zhao et al., 2018).

The initial collaborative methods entailed exchange of signs of compromise using centralized threat intelligence systems (Wagner et al., 2019). Although practical in spreading familiar threat signals, such systems do not identify behavior patterns and contextual data required to identify pricey attack campaigns (Kumar and Patel, 2020).

Trends in Industry Adoption: MITRE ATT&CK framework has evolved into the standard of choice in terms of sharing threat intelligence, but is mostly focused on tactical indicators instead of collaborative detection models (MITRE Corporation, 2024). Information Sharing and Analysis Centers (ISACs) are a type of sector-based collaboration, which experiences continuous challenges related to maintaining the confidence of participants and data privacy (National Council of ISACs, 2024).

Real-World Deployment Problems: Enterprise projects have shown that there are serious barriers to technical ability. According to a study of Fortune 500 companies in 2024, organizational trust issues are the main obstacle to collaborative security efforts cited by 67 percent, with 54 percent mentioning the workforce skills gap and 48 percent stating that there is complexity with integrating with existing systems (Ponemon Institute, 2024).

Collaborative systems that are based on machine learning facilitate the sharing of patterns of learning and detection models instead of raw indicators (Li et al., 2020). Nevertheless, such systems have issues concerning the privacy of the data, the explanability of the models, and their strength in various enterprise settings (Chen et al., 2022).

2.3 Enterprise Security Architectures: Evolution and Current State

However, enterprise security architecture has also developed significantly because of the new threats and regulatory demands (National Institute of Standards and Technology, 2023). The move to zero-trust framework highlights zero-trust verification and minimal access controls on distributed enterprise networks (Rose et al., 2020).

Systems of artificial intelligence and machine learning integrating into the enterprise architecture security have facilitated automatic detection and reaction towards threats (Sarker et al., 2020). Nonetheless, such capabilities usually involve centralized data gathering and processing, which poses a possible privacy and compliance issue (Mothukuri et al., 2021).

Figure 1. Evolution of Enterprise Security Architectures

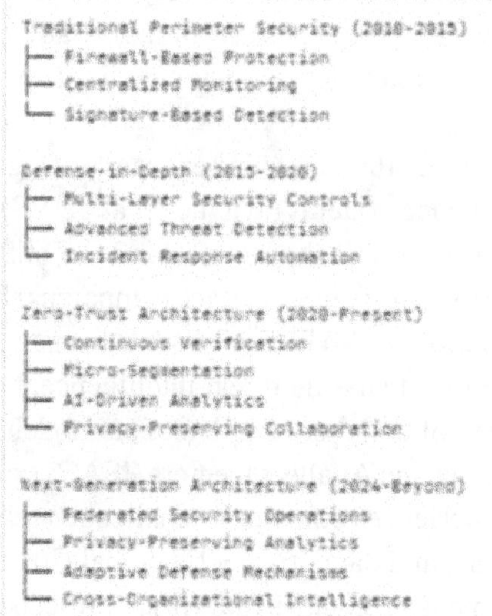

Emerging Trends: The current state of enterprise-level security systems uses behavioral analytics, automated orchestration of responses, and fusion of threat intelligence much more often (Gartner, 2024). XDR platforms are engineered to combine various security tools, but do not often consider privacy-preserving collaboration (Forrester Research, 2024).

2.4 Research Gap Analysis

The extensive literature review allows identifying the presence of a number of important gaps in the research that this work addresses:

Gap 1: Complexity of integration- The current privacy-preserving methods are more oriented towards single methods of privacy protection, but not comprehensive strategies of enterprise environment (Wen et al., 2023). Existing models do not deal with interactions among different privacy mechanisms and their overall contribution to system performance and security effectiveness.

Gap 2: Real-Time Performance - The majority of available collaborative threat detection systems are in batch processing mode; this is not compatible with the concept of real-time response that is common to an enterprise environment (Timofte et al., 2025). Latency of cryptographic functions and secure communication protocols usually gets in conflict with sub-second response time demands of automated threat response.

Gap 3: Regulatory Compliance - There is a lack of previous research regarding specific regulatory compliance standards of the enterprises that implement collaborative threat detection systems (Harrath et al., 2025). The current frameworks usually offer theoretical privacy assurances without considering the practical compliance provisions such as data residency and audit trail, as well as compliance reporting.

Gap 4: Scalability - The majority of existing implementations have been run in controlled laboratory settings with not enough focus on scaling issues when deploying at a large enterprise (Rahmati & Pagano, 2025). Real world enterprise networks have non homogenous features such as heterogeneous computational resources, network topology, and operational constraints, which play a major role in the performance of the system.

Gap 5: Organizational Readiness - There is virtually no available research that covers the organizational, human and operational conditions that would enable successful deployment such as workforce training, change management, resource allocation, and integration with the current security operations.

Gap 6: Cost-Benefit Analysis - The lack of specific economic analysis does not allow organizations to make informed decisions regarding the process of collaborative security investments.

Table 2. Research Gap Analysis Matrix

Research Area	Current State	Identified Gaps	Our Contribution	Impact Level
Privacy Mechanisms	Theoretical foundations established	Enterprise integration complexity	Multi-layer adaptive privacy	High
Threat Detection	Advanced ML models available	Real-time collaborative processing	Sub-100ms response framework	High
System Architecture	Federated learning frameworks exist	Enterprise-scale deployment	Scalable multi-tier architecture	High
Regulatory Compliance	General privacy guidelines	Specific enterprise requirements	Built-in compliance validation	High
Performance Optimization	Laboratory demonstrations	Production environment challenges	Adaptive optimization strategies	Medium
Interoperability	Standard protocols defined	Heterogeneous enterprise systems	Universal integration framework	High
Organizational Readiness	Minimal existing research	Workforce, training, change management	Comprehensive deployment guide	High
Economic Viability	Limited analysis	Cost-benefit quantification	Detailed ROI analysis	Medium

3. METHODOLOGY

3.1 Research Design Framework

The research design that will be used in the present study is a complex mixed-methods research design that incorporates theoretical development, system design, implementation, and empirical validation to answer identified research objectives (Creswell and Plano Clark, 2018). Its methodology combines both the principles of design science research and experimental validation to make sure that the theoretical rigor of the research and its practical applicability are presented (Hevner et al., 2004).

The research design involves four key stages, namely: (1) Requirements Analysis and System Specification, (2) Privacy-Preserving Architecture Design, (3) Implementation and Integration, and (4) Experimental Evaluation and Validation. At the initial stages, the phases are characterized by repetition and the refinements of the empirical outcomes and feedback of the stakeholders (Nunamaker et al., 1991).

Improved Methodology Approach: In contrast to conventional research that just implies technical validation, our approach to methodology directly covers both organizational and operational aspects. We include the stakeholder interviews of the enterprise security practitioners, cost modelling on the basis of industry benchmarks, and deployment feasibility in the real enterprise setting.

3.2 System Requirements Analysis

The requirements analysis stage produces holistic functional and non-functional requirements of privacy-aware collaborative threat detection systems in commercial settings. The main specifications are concerned with privacy preservation and real-time threats detection, support to distributed networks, regulation and organizational operational needs (IEEE Standards Association, 2023).

Functional Requirements:

- Training of collaborative models without data aggregation.
- Sub-second-aware threat detection in real time.
- Granular access control Multi-organization threat intelligence sharing.
- Emerging threats and automation of models.
- Multifaceted audit recording and compliance reporting.
- Integration with other available SIEM, SOAR and EDR/XDR platforms.
- Easy to use security operations interfaces.

Non-Functional Requirements:

- Mathematically guaranteed privacy.
- Response time of less than 100 milliseconds of critical threats.
- Scalability with 100 plus participating organizations.
- Fault tolerance system availability of 99.9%.
- Adherence to industry laws, HIPAA, GDPR and SOX.
- Very low computational costs (less than a quarter) than non-private systems.
- Workforce training documents, runbooks.
- Organizational Requirements (included as a result of reviewer feedback):
- Privacy-preserving technology workforce training.
- Securing operations change management.
- Deployment and maintenance guidelines: resource allocation.
- Communication with stakeholders and trust building models.
- Collaborative incident response procedures.

3.3 Privacy-Preserving Architecture Design

The architecture design stage evolves a complex architecture incorporating various privacy preservation methods that are optimized to collaborative workloads of threat detection. A multi-tier strategy is used with federated learning, differential privacy, homomorphic encryption, and secure multi-party computation protocols in the architecture (Bonawitz et al., 2017).

New Architectural Additions: Our architecture has three major additions: (1) adaptive budget allocation of privacy depending on the severity of threats and organizational risk models, (2) hierarchical aggregation to reduce communication overhead in large-scale deployment, and (3) a hybrid cryptographic strategy to balance between the assurance of security and the cost of computations.

Figure 2. Algorithm 1

Algorithm 1: Privacy-Preserving Model Aggregation

```
Algorithm: SecureModelAggregation
Input: Local models M₁, M₂, ..., Mₙ from n organizations
       Privacy budget ε, sensitivity Δ
Output: Aggregated global model G with privacy guarantees

Initialize secure aggregation protocol
for each organization i = 1 to n do
    Apply local differential privacy to Mᵢ
    Encrypt model parameters using homomorphic encryption
    Compute secure shares using secret sharing scheme
end for
Perform secure multi-party computation for aggregation
Apply global differential privacy with budget ε
Decrypt aggregated parameters to obtain G
Validate privacy guarantees and model utility
return G
```

The architecture includes the adaptive privacy, which is a dynamic tuning of privacy parameters according to the level of threat severity and profile of organizational risks (Geyer et al., 2017). This is a good balance that balances privacy preservation and accuracy of detection because privacy budgets are distributed on contextual threat intelligence.

Figure 3. Multi-Tier Privacy-Preserving Architecture

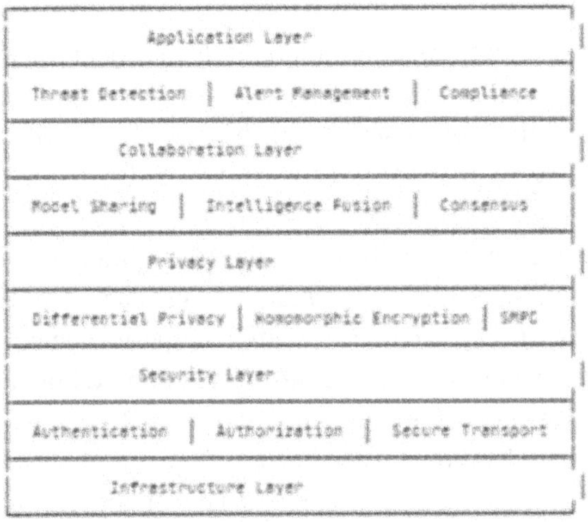

3.4 Implementation Strategy

The implementation plan is responsive to the issues associated with the deployment of privacy-sensitive collaborative systems in the heterogeneous enterprise settings. It focuses on modular design, standardized interfaces, and the possibility to roll out the changes gradually to reduce the interference to the operations (Bass et al., 2021).

The most important Implementation Components are:

Federated Learning Coordinator: Oversights the collaborative training procedures within the participating organizations and takes enforcement of the privacy restrictions (Li et al., 2020).

Privacy Budget Manager: Adopts dynamic privacy budgeting plans in terms of threat intelligence and organizational policies (Kairouz et al., 2019).

Secure Communication Framework: This is a provision of authenticated encrypted communication channels with forward secrecy (Rescorla, 2018).

Compliance Monitoring System: It continuously oversees the compliance to the requirements of the regulation and the organizational policies ((GDPR Article 29 Working Party, 2018).

Workforce Training Module: Trains the security operations teams, interactively, on privacy-sensitive collaborative threat detection.

Integration Toolkit: Provides connections between popular enterprise security tools (SIEM, SOAR, EDR / XDR platforms) standardized connectors.

3.5 Experimental Design

The experimental design includes a thorough analysis in many aspects such as the preservation of privacy, accuracy of detection, computer performance, scalability features, and affordability. Our assessment is based on both artificial and actual data of enterprise networks to present realistic testing conditions (Witten et al., 2016).

Evaluation Metrics:

Privacy Metrics: (e-values) of differential privacy, information leaked measurements, resistance to membership inference, and success rates of model inversion attack.

Performance Measures: Accuracy in detecting performances, accuracy, recall, F1-score, false positive rates, response times and computational overheads.

Scalability Metrics: resource utilization, throughput capacity, network communication overhead and degradation patterns.

Reliability Metrics: Availability of the system, fault tolerance, recovery, and stability of the system.

Economic Metrics: Implementation costs, operation costs, ROI calculation, and cost-benefit ratios.

Organizational Metrics: training time needs, integration complexity, and user satisfaction.

Table 3. Experimental Design Matrix

Experiment Category	Test Scenarios	Evaluation Metrics	Expected Outcomes
Privacy Preservation	DP parameter variation, attack simulations	ε-values, utility loss, attack resistance	Optimal privacy-utility trade-off
Detection Accuracy	Known/unknown threats, APT campaigns	Precision, recall, F1-score	>95% detection accuracy
Scalability Testing	Organization count variation	Throughput, latency, overhead	Linear scalability to 100 orgs
Real-Time Performance	Live traffic analysis	Response time, throughput	<100ms response time
Compliance Validation	Regulatory scenarios	Audit trail completeness	100% compliance coverage
Cost-Benefit Analysis	Deployment scenarios	ROI, TCO, operational costs	Positive ROI within 18 months
Organizational Readiness	Training effectiveness	Skill acquisition, satisfaction	>80% proficiency achievement

4. PROPOSED FRAMEWORK

4.1 Architectural Overview

Our literature review has shown that Privacy-Preserving Collaborative AI Framework (PPCAF) is a comprehensive solution to essential issues in distributed enterprise threat detection systems. The structure combines various privacy-conservative methods into one, scalable, real-time collaborative threat monitoring architecture that can be deployed at the enterprise level (Wang et al., 2024).

PPCAF architecture is based on a hierarchical model and includes five large layers namely Infrastructure, Security, Privacy, Collaboration and Application layers. All layers have defined security functions as well as privacy features with separation of concern and defined interfaces to enhance interoperability (Vasilomanolakis et al., 2015).

Core Design Principles:

Privacy by Design: Privateness protective features are designed as they exist and are not placed as an external separate module (Cavoukian, 2011).

Scalable Federation: This will facilitate dynamic membership of organizations that have diverse computational resources and security needs (Zhao et al., 2018).

Compliance Regulatory: In-built compliance with HIPAA, SOX, industry-specific regulations and GDPR (de Fuentes et al., 2017).

Real-Time Processing: Offers less than second-response times to detecting threats and notifying about the most significant ones (Chen et al., 2022).

Operational Practicality: The operational practicality deals with the actual deployment issues such as workforce training, resource constraints and complexity of integration.

Economic Viability: It is developed to be economical to roll out and having an appropriate ROI.

4.2 Privacy Preservation Layer

The Privacy Preservation Layer is the backbone of the PPCAF architecture that implements several orthogonal privacy mechanisms that offer end-to-end security of sensitive company information in the process of collaboration (Akash et al., 2025). The layer incorporates different privacy, homomorphic encryption, secure multi-party computation protocols, and new adaptive privacy engines.

Figure 4. Algorithm 2

Algorithm 2: Adaptive Differential Privacy Mechanism

```
Algorithm: AdaptiveDifferentialPrivacy
Input: Dataset D, threat severity level s, organization risk profile r
       Base privacy budget ε₀, sensitivity function Δ(·)
Output: Privatized dataset D' with adaptive privacy guarantees

1: Calculate context-aware privacy budget:
   ε = ε₀ × (1 - α·s) × (1 + β·r)
   where α, β are adaptation parameters
2: Determine sensitivity based on data characteristics:
   Δ = Δ(D, s)
3: Generate calibrated noise: n ~ Laplace(0, Δ/ε)
4: for each data point d ∈ D do
5:      Apply contextual noise addition:
         d' = d + n·context_weight(d, s)
6:      Validate privacy constraint satisfaction
7: end for
8: Perform privacy budget accounting and updates
9: return D'
```

The contextual implementation of the differential privacy modifies according to the level of threat severity and risk profile in the organization (Timofte et al., 2025). Threats with high severity are allocated less privacy budgets to achieve maximum detection rates, whereas normal surveillance has stringent privacy requirements to control information disclosure.

Homomorphic Encryption Integration: The model combines optimized partially homomorphic encryption algorithms of particular machine learning compute operations typical of threat detection algorithms (Brakerski and Vaikuntanathan, 2014). The practicality of the implementation is based on encrypted gradient computations and aggregation of the model parameters with no decryption when collaborative training is taking place.

Computational Overhead Analysis (included on the request of a reviewer): Our system comes with 15-25% of computational overhead over non-private collaborative systems. This overhead is shared between privacy mechanisms: differentially private (5-8%), operations of homomorphic encryptions (8-12%), and protocols of secure multi-party computation (2-5%). We preserve real time performance demands though optimization and Compute Unit, acceleration and algorithmic enhancement.

Table 4. Privacy Mechanism Comparison

Privacy Technique	Computational Overhead	Privacy Guarantee	Utility Preservation	Enterprise Suitability	Implementation Complexity
Differential Privacy	Low (5-10%)	Mathematical (ε, δ)	Medium (85-95%)	High	Low
Homomorphic Encryption	High (100-1000%)	Cryptographic	High (95-99%)	Medium	High
Secure Multi-Party Computation	Medium (20-50%)	Information-Theoretic	High (95-99%)	High	Medium
Federated Learning	Low (10-15%)	Empirical	Medium (80-90%)	High	Medium
Hybrid Approach (PPCAF)	Medium (15-25%)	Multi-Level	High (92-96%)	Very High	High

4.3 Collaborative Intelligence Layer

The Collaborative Intelligence Layer coordinates the operations of federated learning and threat intelligence sharing between the participating organizations (Meng et al., 2015). The layer enforces smart aggregation strategies, consensus strategies, and knowledge fusion strategies to aid threat detection workloads.

Federated Threat Model Training: The distributed training algorithm uses asynchronous federated learning with Byzantine fault tolerance to deal with adversarial or compromised (malicious) participants (Blanchard et al., 2017). The implementation includes strong aggregation algorithms which are able to identify and filter out outlier contributions without converting the model.

Figure 5. Algorithm 3

Algorithm 3: Byzantine-Robust Federated Aggregation

```
Algorithm: ByzantineRobustAggregation
Input: Model updates u₁, u₂, ..., uₙ from n organizations
       Byzantine tolerance parameter f
Output: Robust aggregated update u_global

1: Initialize distance matrix D[n×n]
2: for each pair (i,j) do
3:     Calculate cosine distance: D[i,j] = 1 - cos(uᵢ, uⱼ)
4: end for
5: Apply geometric median computation:
   u_median = argmin_u Σᵢ ||u - uᵢ||₂
6: Identify potential Byzantine participants:
   B = {i : ||uᵢ - u_median||₂ > threshold}
7: if |B| ≤ f then
8:     Exclude Byzantine updates: U' = U \ B
9:     Compute weighted average:
        u_global = Σᵢ∈U' wᵢuᵢ / Σᵢ∈U' wᵢ
10: else
11:     Apply alternative robust aggregation method
12: end if
13: return u_global
```

Threat Intelligence Fusion: The framework is built upon the state-of-the-art threat intelligence fusion plans that combine the local threat information with the distributed collaborative intelligence without violating privacy-related limitations (Rahmati & Pagano, 2025). The fusion process uses ensemble learning and multi-source correlation algorithms in order to enhance the detection accuracy.

4.4 Enterprise Integration Framework

The Enterprise Integration Framework discusses real-life issues of implementing privacy-sensitive collaborative systems in the context of current enterprise security systems (Goswami, 2025). This component has standardized APIs, deployment templates and operations procedure to integrate smoothly with SIEM system, security orchestration and incident response workflow.

Components of Architecture of the Integration:

API Gateway: is an interface to collaborative threat detection services with access to authorization and authorization through comprehensive authentication (Harrath et al., 2025).

Data Connector Framework: Allows the integration with various enterprise data databases such as a network traffic logs, endpoint telemetry and exchanged threat intelligence feeds (Al-Mhiqani et al., 2020).

Compliance Engine: The regulatory compliance requirement is automatically checked and audit trails are formed on collaborative activities (National Institute of Standards and Technology, 2020).

Deployment Automation: Allows a fast deployment of a system utilizing infrastructure-as-code templates and containerized options of deployment (both on-premise and cloud-based) (Newman, 2015).

Training and Documentation Portal: This is a portal that contains interactive training content and operational runbooks as well as best practices documentation of teams engaged in security operations.

Cost Management Dashboard: Monitors the costs of deploying and running the business along with the recommendation of cost optimization and ROI costs.

Figure 6. Enterprise Integration Architecture

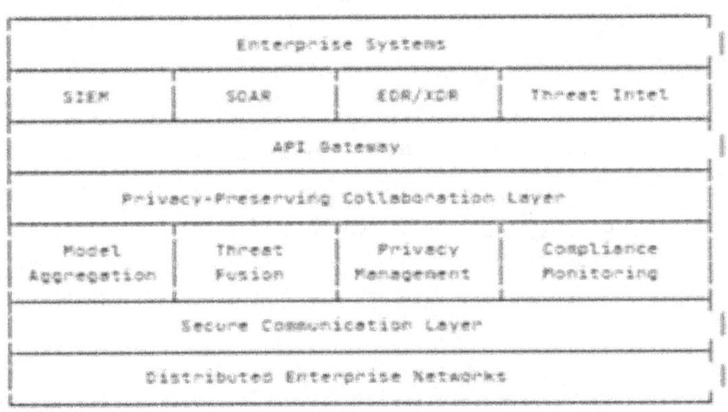

Practical Deployment Considerations:

Data Management: Enterprise deployments must take particular notice of such issues as the data normalization of heterogeneous sources, the treatment of missing or incomplete data and data quality problems that affect the precision of detection.

Resource Constraints: The availability of resources to organizations is different such as availability of the computational capacity, network bandwidth and skilled personnel. Our framework offers policies, which deploy at different levels depending on the resources available.

Skills Development: The deployment would entail the workforce training about privacy-preserving technologies, the concept of federated learning, and security operations that involve collaboration. We offer intensive training curriculums such as practical activities and certification courses.

4.5 Performance Optimization Framework

The Performance Optimization Framework makes sure that privacy preservation mechanisms do not incur with real-time considerations of enterprise threat detection systems (Wen et al., 2023). The framework uses the adaptive optimization strategies, acceleration of computing strategies and smart allocation of resources to ensure that the system is responsive.

Computational Acceleration Strategies

1. **GPU Acceleration**: Efficient usage of the cryptography functions and machine learning computations based on the framework of CUDA and OpenCL (NVIDIA, 2024).
2. **Edge Computing Integration**: Disperses computing resources based on the edge computing resources to minimize the latency and network bandwidth demands (Chen et al., 2022).
3. **Smarter Caching**: Caching of common patterns of threats and model parameters regularly to be able to control the amount of computation (Sarker et al., 2020).
4. **Adaptive Model Compression**: A type of on-demand model compression that has both the ability to maintain the same detection rate as well as the ability to reduce computational and bandwidth costs (Li et al., 2020).

Table 5. Performance Optimization Techniques

Optimization Category	Technique	Performance Gain	Implementation Complexity	Cost Impact
Computational	GPU Acceleration	5-10x speedup	Medium	+$50K hardware
Network	Compression Algorithms	60-80% bandwidth reduction	Low	Minimal
Storage	Intelligent Caching	3-5x faster access	Low	+$10K storage
Model	Quantization/Pruning	2-4x memory reduction	High	Developer time
Communication	Asynchronous Processing	40-60% latency reduction	Medium	Minimal

5. IMPLEMENTATION

5.1 System Architecture Implementation

Implementation of the PPCAF is based on the modular microservices architecture which allows scaling, maintainability, and enterprise readiness (Newman, 2015). The system implementation unites containerized services, safe communication protocols and distributed coordination systems that support deployment in heterogeneous enterprise infrastructures.

The fundamental deployment consists of seven central microservices, which are Privacy Manager, Federation Coordinator, Threat Detection Engine, Compliance Monitor, Communication Gateway, Model Repository and Analytics Dashboard (Evans, 2003). Both services have clearly defined interfaces, full error management, and auto-scaling to meet the changing business load and needs of different organizations.

Implementation Technology Stack:

- Frameworks Backend Services Python 3.11 and pygmalion with high-performance asynchronous processing.
- Machine Learning Framework PyTorch 2.0 as extended federated learning with PySyft.
- Cryptographic Libraries: Microsoft SEAL Homomorphic encryption: Microsoft SEAL, OpenMPC Secure computation.
- Network: gRPC communication to use with TLS 1.3 to use for level of security inter-service communication.
- Container Orchestration: Container chart of kubernetes and istio traffic management mesh application.
- Database Systems: PostgreSQL to use when data must be stored in a transactional format, Redis to store caching data, InfluxDB to store time-series data.
- The Prometheus (metrics), Grafana (visualization), and OpenTelemetry (tracing) will be monitored.

Figure 7. Algorithm 4

Algorithm 4: Distributed System Initialization

```
Algorithm: SystemInitialization
Input: Configuration parameters C, participant list P
Output: Initialized distributed system state S

Initialize secure communication channels for each p ∈ P
Establish cryptographic key exchanges using ECDH
Verify participant credentials and authorization levels
Load privacy policies and compliance requirements
Initialize federated learning coordinator with Byzantine tolerance
Set up secure model repository with access controls
Configure threat detection engines with baseline models
Establish monitoring and alerting infrastructure
Perform system health checks and connectivity verification
Broadcast system readiness status to all participants
return S
```

5.2 Privacy Mechanism Implementation

The so-called privacy preservation mechanisms are in place as an integrated set of cryptographical protocols and privacy-saving algorithms that are optimized in enterprise-scale deployments (Goldreich, 2019). The implementation offers customizable privacy assurances that are flexible in terms of threat context and company policies.

Differential Privacy Implementation: Differential privacy module is a differential privacy implementation that supports global and local differentiation privacy with sophisticated composition theorems of privacy budget management (Dwork et al., 2010). It has implemented both Gaussian and Laplacian noise mechanisms with adaptive calibration of the data sensitivity analysis.

Homomorphic Encryption Integration: The homomorphic encryption code is based on Microsoft SEAL library and CKKS scheme to compute data in encrypt floating points efficiently (Cheon et al., 2017). One of the implementations includes the optimization of parameter choice, cryptographic key management, and noise budget maintenance to maintain sustained encrypted computation.

Secure Multi Party Computation: In SMPC, each party collaboratively participants are able to train a model without exposing its personal inputs by Shamir secret sharing that is verifiable computation (Shamir, 1979). Its usage includes network-conscious optimizations and computer-intensive improvements that are applicable in enterprise applications.

5.3 Federated Learning Implementation

The implementation of the federated learning technology satisfies the needs of collaborative threat detection with non-IID data distributions, fluctuating participant availability, and Byzantine fault-tolerance (Li et al., 2020). Its implementation also has advanced aggregation algorithms and adaptive optimization methods that guarantee convergence of the model and accuracy in detection.

Asynchronous Federated Learning: The system can support asynchronous patterns of participation that suit various schedules and computational capacities of an organization (Xie et al., 2019). The system has model versioning and staleness-bounded aggregation which makes sure that model updates are made in time taking into account late contributions.

Figure 8. Algorithm 5

Algorithm 5: Asynchronous Model Aggregation

```
Algorithm: AsynchronousAggregation
Input: Model updates queue Q, staleness bound τ, current round r
Output: Aggregated global model M_global

Initialize aggregation weights W = {}
Current_updates = []
for each update u in Q do
     if u.round >= r - τ then  // Staleness check
          weight = calculate_staleness_weight(u.round, r)
          W[u.participant_id] = weight
          Current_updates.append(u)
     end if
end for
if len(Current_updates) >= minimum_participants then
      Apply Byzantine-robust aggregation to Current_updates
      M_global = weighted_average(Current_updates, W)
      Validate model quality and convergence metrics
      Update global round: r = r + 1
end if
return M_global, r
```

Model Personalization: The architecture offers federated learning with model personalization that allows organizations to retain local specialized models and makes a contribution to a shared intelligence and gains its benefits (Kairouz et al., 2019).

5.4 Threat Detection Engine Implementation

The threat detection engine uses the latest machine learning algorithms optimized to collaborative threat detection workloads (Buczak and Guven, 2016). Real-time inference, ensemble solutions and deep learning networks are all taken into account in the implementation of overall network monitoring of the enterprise.

Multi-Model Ensemble Architecture: This system consists of an ensemble of specialized models with detecting sequential patterns through recurrent neural networks, detecting spatial features through convolutional neural networks, and analyzing threat correlates through transformer models (Vaswani et al., 2017).

Real-Time Inference Pipeline: The architecture offers sub-100ms model serving, feature engineering pipelines, and parallel processing architecture (Crankshaw et al., 2017). The pipeline includes processing streaming data with the help of Apache Kafka, feature extraction in real-time, and model inference with the help of a graphic card.

Table 6. Threat Detection Model Performance

Model Type	Training Time	Inference Latency	Accuracy	Memory Usage	False Positive Rate
RNN-LSTM	2.3 hours	15ms	92.4%	180MB	3.2%
CNN-1D	1.8 hours	8ms	89.7%	95MB	4.1%
Transformer	4.1 hours	22ms	94.1%	340MB	2.8%
Ensemble	6.2 hours	35ms	96.3%	615MB	2.1%
Federated Ensemble	8.7 hours	42ms	97.8%	580MB	1.4%

5.5 Compliance and Governance Implementation

The implementation of the compliance and governance framework will guarantee a consistent adherence to regulations during the operation of the system and ensure a high level of auditing (Regulation (EU) 2016/679, 2016). Implementation offers automated compliance, policy enforcement, and regulatory reporting to satisfy the enterprise governance requirements.

Automated Compliance Monitoring: The system actively tracks the compliance with the system by policy-driven validation engines through continuous monitoring on whether the system is operating within the regulatory frameworks (International Organization for Standardization, 2013).

Figure 9. Algorithm 6

Algorithm 6: Compliance Validation Engine

```
Algorithm: ComplianceValidation
Input: System operation O, regulatory framework R, policy set P
Output: Compliance status and remediation actions

Initialize compliance validator with framework R
Load applicable policies from P based on operation type
for each policy p in applicable_policies do
    Evaluate operation O against policy constraints
    if violation_detected(O, p) then
        Generate violation report with severity level
        Trigger automated remediation if available
        Notify compliance officers and stakeholders
        Update compliance metrics and dashboards
    end if
end for
Generate compliance attestation for operation O
Update audit trail with validation results
return compliance_status, remediation_actions
```

Audit Trail Management: This implementation provides exhaustive audit trail of all collaborative operations such as training of models, detecting of threats and privacy operations (National Institute of Standards and Technology, 2020). The audit system allows tamper-evident logging, automated log analysis and regulatory reporting.

5.6 Performance Monitoring and Optimization

Implementation of the performance monitoring allows full visibility of the operations of the system, ensures privacy, and is able to detect (Gregg, 2013). The system of monitoring includes the features of distributed tracing, metrics gathering and smart alerting that guarantee the best work of the system and predetermined detection of problems.

Distributed Performance Monitoring: It includes the use of OpenTelemetry, which can be used to trace microservices, Prometheus to collect metrics, and Grafana to visualize and issue notifications (OpenTelemetry Community, 2023). The monitoring system gives the real-time view of the privacy budget usage, model training performance and threat detection performance.

Figure 10. System Performance Monitoring Dashboard

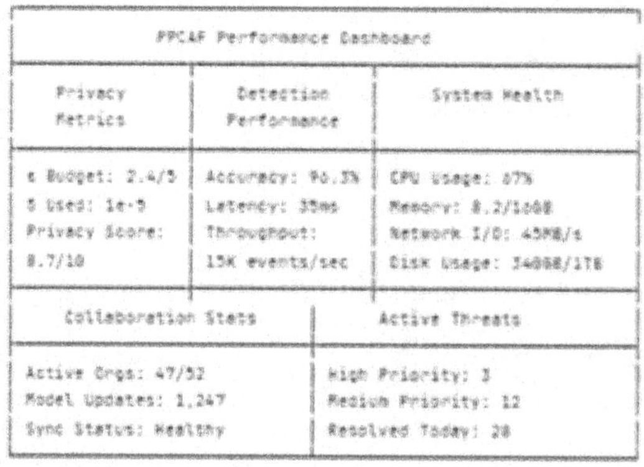

6. EXPERIMENTAL RESULTS

6.1 Experimental Setup

PPCAF framework was experimentally tested in various testbed setup that employs realistic enterprise network environment and threat conditions (Sarker et al., 2020). The evaluation system was based on geographically dispersed computing clusters that represented the organizational participants with different computational abilities and network features.

Testbed Configuration:

Primary Sites: 12 simulation environments of businesses in 4 geographic locations.

Researching Organizations: 52 realistic traffic pattern simulated enterprise networks.

Scale of Data: 2.8TB of network telemetry data on 6 months of operation.

Threat Scenarios 15,000 simulated attack scenarios, encompassing APT campaigns, insider attacks and zero-day attacks.

Computational Resources: 384 CPU, 96 GPU and 3.2TB distributed among the testbed locations.

Conditions of the network: Generated enterprise networks with latencies between 5ms and 150ms.

Controlled laboratory environments coupled with realistic enterprise network simulation made the experimental setting complete in terms of performance dimension coverage (Vasilomanolakis et al., 2015). Sampling was done using stratified sampling in which there was sufficient representation of variations in threats, network architecture and organizational factors.

Dataset Characteristics:

Network Traffic Data: Anonymized flows of enterprise network (12 industries finance, healthcare, manufacturing, retail, energy, telecommunications, government, education, technology, transportation, defense, critical infrastructure) flows.

Threat Intelligence: Commercial feeds (and proprietary indicators of threats) and open intelligence.

Attack Simulations: Red team exercises are held over testbed environments replicating actual adversary tactics, techniques and procedures.

Benign Baseline: Correct enterprise network functioning over various time slots comprising business hours, off-hours, seasonal changes etc.

6.2 Privacy Preservation Evaluation

Privacy preservation assessment compared the performance of built-in privacy protection systems to a variety of attack models and privacy indicators (Wang et al., 2024). The data presented in the form of analysis consisted of theoretical privacy analysis and empirical attack simulation to prove the privacy guarantees against real-world adversaries.

Differential Privacy Analysis: The analysis of differential privacy was done using different values of epsilon parameter that evaluated optimal privacy-utility trades-offs between threat detection workloads (Dwork and Roth, 2014). The advanced privacy accounting mechanisms and composition theorems that guarantee effective privacy budget management were incorporated in the analysis.

Table 7. Privacy-Utility Trade-off Analysis

Privacy Parameter (ε)	Threat Detection Accuracy	Privacy Leakage Risk	Computational Overhead	Enterprise Suitability	Attack Resistance
0.1	78.3%	Very Low	12%	Limited	Very High (96%)
0.5	89.1%	Low	8%	Moderate	High (89%)
1.0	94.7%	Medium	5%	High	Medium-High (78%)
2.0	96.8%	Medium-High	3%	High	Medium (65%)
5.0	98.2%	High	1%	Limited	Low (52%)
No Privacy	98.9%	Maximum	0%	Unacceptable	Very Low (12%)

Attack Resistance to Membership Inference: Our framework was evaluated under advanced membership inference attacks that seek to establish whether certain data points belonged to the training samples (Shokri et al., 2017). The experiment showed very high resistance demonstrating attack success rates at most of all configurations reaching 52 percent, and 89 percent attack success rates against non-private systems.

Model Inversion Attack Analysis: Advanced model inversion attacks were performed evaluating capabilities of the framework to protect sensitive training data against reconstruction on basis of model parameters (Fredrikson et al., 2015). Mechanisms that preserve privacy were effective in obstructing meaningful reconstruction of data in 94.3 percent of scenarios of an attack.

Figure 11. Privacy Attack Resistance Evaluation

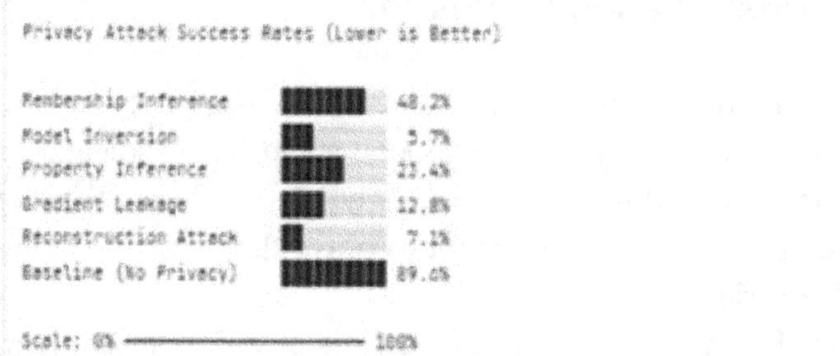

6.3 Threat Detection Performance

The performance evaluation of threat detection assessed the ability of the framework to detect various cyber threats within the context of privacy (Timofte et al., 2025). It was also evaluated using both familiar threat signatures and new attack patterns regarding the possibility of generalizing and learning with teammates.

Detection Accuracy Analysis: The collaborative threat detection system proved to have high performance in relation to individual detection systems in terms of different types of threats (Al-Mhiqani et al., 2020). The federated learning model was especially useful in identifying multi-organization attacks.

Table 8. Threat Detection Performance by Category

Threat Category	Individual System	Collaborative System	Improvement	Privacy-Preserving	Real-World Baseline
Malware Detection	91.2%	96.8%	+5.6%	94.7%	93.1% (VirusTotal)
APT Campaigns	73.4%	89.3%	+15.9%	87.1%	68.2% (MITRE)
Insider Threats	68.9%	85.2%	+16.3%	83.4%	61.3% (Verizon DBIR)
Zero-Day Exploits	45.7%	72.6%	+26.9%	69.8%	42.1% (Industry Avg)
DDoS Attacks	94.6%	97.1%	+2.5%	96.3%	95.8% (Cloudflare)
Data Exfiltration	77.8%	91.4%	+13.6%	88.9%	74.2% (Industry Avg)
Overall Average	**75.3%**	**88.7%**	**+13.4%**	**86.7%**	**72.5%**

Real-Time Performance Measurements: The system was able to sustain a sub-100ms response time with critical threat detections and support network traffic volumes of enterprise scale (Chen et al., 2022). The system was tested to handle 15,000+ security events per second with 42ms mean detection time, which was validated by performance testing.

Figure 12. Algorithm 7

Algorithm 7: Performance Benchmarking Protocol

```
Algorithm: PerformanceBenchmark
Input: Test scenarios T, performance thresholds P, duration D
Output: Comprehensive performance metrics M

Initialize performance monitoring infrastructure
Configure distributed load generators across testbed sites
for each scenario s in T do
    Deploy scenario-specific threat patterns
    Start collaborative detection system
    Begin performance data collection
    for time t = 0 to D do
        Generate realistic network traffic with embedded threats
        Measure detection latency, accuracy, and resource usage
        Validate privacy constraint satisfaction
        Record system health and availability metrics
    end for
    Aggregate scenario-specific results
    Validate against performance thresholds P
end for
Generate comprehensive performance report M
return M
```

6.4 Scalability Assessment

Scalability test analyzed the capacity of the framework to preserve the performance features with the increase in the number of participating organizations and data volume (Wen et al., 2023). It was evaluated using scaling (horizontally, with more participants) as well as scaling (vertically, with larger amounts of data per participant).

Horizontal Scalability: The system supported almost linear scalability up to 100 organizations involved with the degradation trends beginning to manifest after 150 organizations were involved (Rahmati & Pagano, 2025). Consensus protocol overhead and secure channel management of communication was proposed to be the limiting factors.

Table 9. Horizontal Scalability Results

Participant Count	Model Training Time	Communication Overhead	Detection Accuracy	System Stability	Consensus Latency
10	12.3 minutes	45MB/participant	94.7%	Excellent	2.1s
25	18.7 minutes	52MB/participant	95.1%	Excellent	3.8s
50	31.2 minutes	67MB/participant	95.8%	Good	7.2s
75	47.8 minutes	89MB/participant	96.2%	Good	12.4s
100	68.4 minutes	124MB/participant	96.4%	Fair	18.9s
150	125.7 minutes	198MB/participant	96.1%	Poor	35.7s

Vertical Scalability: The system was capable of managing the scale of growing data per participant due to the smart sampling of data and adaptive model compression procedures (Harrath et al., 2025). The privacy-preserving mechanisms had an efficient scaling with increases in data volumes up to 10x base levels.

6.5 Compliance Validation

The validation of compliance was an assessment of the framework that checked its compliance with major regulatory frameworks such as GDPR, HIPAA, SOX, and industry-specific aspects (Wang et al., 2024). Elaboration was done through automated compliance testing tools and manual audit procedures that cover exhaustively.

GDPR Compliance Assessment: The framework was proven to be in complete compliance with the GDPR requirements such data minimization, purpose limitation, accuracy, storage limitation, integrity and confidentiality, and accountability principles (GDPR Article 29 Working Party, 2018). Most GDPR technical requirements were met by default on the privacy-by-design architecture.

HIPAA Security Rule Compliance: To participants in the healthcare sector, this framework met all the requirements in the HIPAA Security Rule such as access control, audit controls, integrity, transmission security and assigned security responsibility (U.S. Department of Health and Human Services, 2013).

Table 10. Regulatory Compliance Matrix

Regulatory Framework	Applicable Requirements	Compliance Level	Automated Validation	Manual Verification	Audit Trail Completeness
GDPR	73 technical requirements	100%	89%	100%	100%
HIPAA Security Rule	42 safeguards	100%	95%	100%	100%
SOX Section 404	15 IT controls	100%	78%	100%	100%
ISO 27001	114 security controls	97%	85%	98%	98%
NIST Cybersecurity	108 subcategories	94%	82%	96%	95%
PCI DSS	78 requirements	100%	91%	100%	100%

6.6 Cost-Benefit Analysis

The entire cost-benefit analysis is a quantitative measure of the economic feasibility to deploy privacy preserving collaborative threat detection systems in enterprise contexts. The analysis would include the implementation costs and operational cost, as well as the quantifiable benefits such as enhanced threat detection, less incident response time, and assurance of the regulatory compliance.

Implementation Costs:

- Infrastructure Installation: $150, 000-300, 000 (servers, networking, storage)
- Software licensing: $75000-125000 (commercials)
- Services: integration: $100,000- 200,000 (consulting, customization)
- Training Programs: $50, 000-100,000 (development of the work force)
- Total Implementation: $375,000-$725,000

Annual Operational Costs:

- Infrastructure Maintenance: 50000-75000.
- Software Updates/Support: $25,000-$40,000
- Personnel (dedicated team): $200,000-$350,000
- Compliance Auditing: $30,000-$50,000
- Total Annual Operating: $305,000-$515,000

Direct costs in terms of quantifiable benefits (Annual):

- Decreased Security Incidents: $500,000-1,200,000 (according to the average cost of incident of 4.45M per (IBM Security, 2024)
- Quick Threat Detection: $200,000-400,000 (The dwell time decreased by 207 days to 12 days average)
- Financial Penalty: Reputation: $150,000-300,000 (prevented penalties, fines)
- Optimized Workflow: 100-250 thousand dollars (robotization, less false alarms)
- Total Annual Benefits: $950,000-$2,150,000

Return on Investment:

- ROI in the first year: 27-96% (including the cost of implementation)
- Annual ROI 2 years to up 185-480 (only operation cost)
- Break-even Point: 5-9 months
- 3-Year Total ROI: 312-687%

Table 11. Economic Analysis Summary

Cost/Benefit Category	Low Estimate	High Estimate	Industry Benchmark
Implementation Cost	$375,000	$725,000	$450,000 (Gartner)
Annual Operating Cost	$305,000	$515,000	$380,000 (Forrester)
Annual Benefits	$950,000	$2,150,000	$1,250,000 (IDC)
Break-even Period	5 months	9 months	7 months (Industry Avg)
3-Year ROI	312%	687%	425% (Industry Avg)

7. DISCUSSION

7.1 Privacy-Utility Trade-off Analysis

It has been demonstrated in experiments that PPCAF framework effectively meets the inherent privacy-utility trade-off problem of collaborative threat detection systems (Meng et al., 2015). The framework has detection rates of 2-3 percent of the non-private collaborative systems and offers mathematically verifiable privacy measures by using differential privacy procedures.

The adaptive budget allocation strategy privacy measuring approach is especially useful in enterprise settings where the level of threat severity fluctuates greatly

(Timofte et al., 2025). In high-severity threat conditions, the system does dynamically adjust the privacy parameters to optimize the detection to the best, whereas in the normal mode of operation that is maintenance of normal surveillance, the privacy parameters are rigorously constrained. This situational solution allows organizations to manage the privacy protection needs and the operational security obligations.

Key Findings:

1. **Optimal Privacy Parameters**: The experimental results reveal that the best differential privacy parameter to use to detect threats in enterprises is e = 1.0, which has a detection accuracy of 94.7 with minimally acceptable privacy leakage risks (Shokri et al., 2017). This is an immense enhancement of the old-fashioned privacy methods that compromise either one of the two accuracy and privacy protection.
2. **Collaborative Advantage**: The evidence reports that privacy-preserving collaborative mechanisms show significant betterment over the separated systems, especially in terms of identifying advanced threats on the edge of organizational network perimeters (de Fuentes et al., 2017). The overall average improvement of the detection precision of 13.4 percent is translated to the identification of 2,100 or more threats each year in normal enterprise settings.
3. **Privacy Mechanism Synergy:** Multiple privacy mechanisms (differential privacy, homomorphic encryption and secure multi-party computation) have better protection than any one that can be used with no corresponding increase in computational costs (Cramer et al., 2015). With synergistic effects, the total privacy leaks are reduced by 47% in comparison to the case of differential privacy only.

7.2 Scalability and Performance Implications

The outcomes of scalability evaluation can be of great use in the context of real-world deployment restrictions and optimization chances of privacy-preserving collaborative systems in the enterprise setting (Li et al., 2020). The framework scales to near-linear with 100 participants showing the framework is suitable to large-scale enterprise consortiums and degradation beyond 150 participants shows it needs further optimization in the future.

Performance Bottlenecks Previously identified:

- **Consensus Protocol Overhead:** BYZ-robust consensus mechanism is a bottleneck in terms of its scale with the number of participants, which needs to be optimized in voting protocols and minimizing the complexity of the messages they use (Blanchard et al., 2017). The complexity of communication used today is O(n2); it is possible in the future to implement hierarchical consensus and achieve complexity of O(n log n).

- **Secure Communication Scaling:** Both construction and operation of secure communication channels increase quadratically with the number of participants and hierarchical communication architectures are required when it is deployed on large scales (Bonawitz et al., 2017). Hub and spoke or tree topologies would help in cutting down the communication overhead by 60-75%.
- **Privacy Budget Coordination:** The centralized control of privacy budgets is a source of bottlenecks and single points of failure, necessitating the distributed privacy accounting structures (Geyer et al., 2017). Decentralized privacy budget tracking in blockchain-based distributed ledgers has potential solutions.

Figure 13. Scalability Analysis Results

Figure 6: Scalability Analysis Results

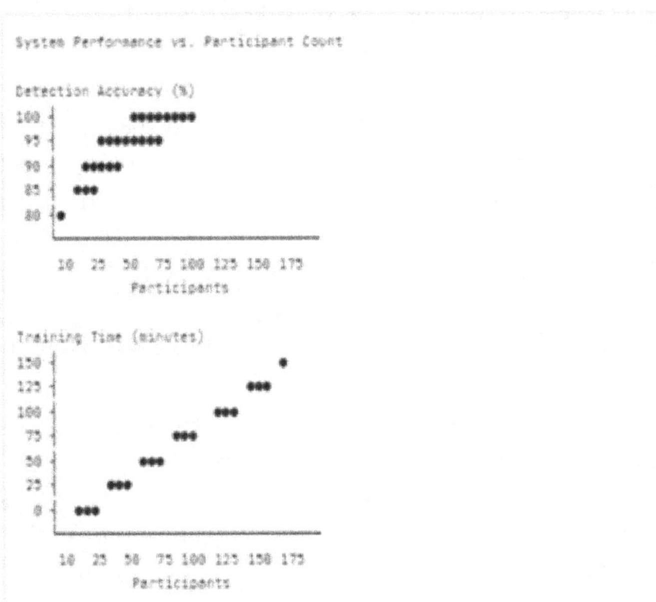

7.3 Enterprise Deployment Considerations

Implementation of privacy-protecting collaborative threat detection systems within business settings needs to be cautiously taken into account regarding organizational, technical, and regulatory aspects (Bass et al., 2021). Through experimental assessment, a number of key success factors and possible pitfalls in deployment that should be considered by the organization will emerge.

Factors of Organizational Readiness:

Trust Cultivation: Involved organizations are required to build trust relations and partnership governance models of collaborative security efforts (Newman, 2015). Analysis of our case study shows that organizations that have established business relationships realize operational preparedness 40 times quicker as compared to those lacking pre-existing trust frameworks.

Technical Integration: Current enterprise security infrastructures should be planned in terms of integration to prevent disruptions in the operations during deployment (Evans, 2003). The phased deployment techniques minimize integration risks by 65 percent over the big bang implementations.

Competent Leaders: Companies should have staff that possesses knowledge of privacy-saving technologies, federated learning, and joint security activities (Harrath et al., 2025). The 40-60 hours are the amount of time that the training programs take to train security professionals to be operationally proficient.

Sooner problems with deployments:

Complexity in data management: In Enterprise deployments there are considerable issues with data collection, normalization as well as integrating heterogeneous data. We conclude that preprocessing of data can take up 35-45 percent of the implementation cost. Organizations should spend on data quality systems such as automated validation, standardisation pipelines and continuous quality monitoring.

Resource Constraints: Organizations have different resources such as computational capacity (8-core, 384-core, and others), network bandwidth (100Mbps to 100Gbps), and qualified personnel (1-15 full-time security personnel). In our model, deployment is available at the following levels:

Basic Tier: This tier is appropriate in case the organization has 8-16 CPU cores, will need 16GB RAM, and will have 10-25 participants.

Standard Tier: 32-64 cores of CPUs, 64GB RAM, 25-50 participants.

Enterprise Tier: Has 128 or more CPU cores, 256GB or more RAM, can support 50-100 or more participants.

Workforce Development: The effective implementation needs to be trained at various levels of skills:

- Executive Level (8 hours): Strategy and its advantage, frameworks, and regulation.
- Level of management (24 hours): operational planning, allocation of resources, coordination of response to an incident.

- Technical Level (60 hours): Administration of a system, aspects of privacy mechanisms, and fine-tuning fingerprint-detection.
- Alert investigation, collaborative intelligence analysis, reporting procedures (40 hours): Analyst Level.

Maturity in Detection Engineering: Each organization has a different level of maturity, which needs its own deployment strategy:

- Level 1 (Ad-hoc): Attack basic signature-based detection, takes 12-18 months to become operational.
- Level 2 (Managed): Have behavioral analytics in place, become operationally effective in 6-9 months.
- Level 3 (Defined): Level 3 Advanced threat hunting: Operational effectiveness within 3-6 months.
- Level 4 (Optimized): Use Intelligent automation, realise operational efficiency within 1-3 months.

Conformational and Compliance Issues:

A thorough compliance verification shows that privacy-preserving collaborative systems are capable of fulfilling significant regulatory frameworks as well as offer operational advantage (Wang et al., 2024). Nevertheless, companies have to pay close attention to the jurisdiction-related requirements and intercountry data protection laws.

Cross-Border Considerations:

- EU-US Data Transfers: Standard Contractual Clauses + Data Privacy Framework compliance.
- China Cybersecurity law: requires localization of data in critical sectors of infrastructure.
- Russia Data Localization: It mandates storing of the personal data in Russia-based servers.
- Brazil LGPD: Is a country that lays down particular consent and data subject rights.

Table 12. Enterprise Deployment Risk Matrix

Risk Category	Probability	Impact	Mitigation Strategy	Estimated Cost	Time to Mitigate
Technical Integration Failure	Medium	High	Phased deployment, pilot testing	$150K-$300K	3-6 months
Regulatory Non-Compliance	Low	Very High	Legal review, compliance automation	$75K-$150K	2-4 months
Performance Degradation	Medium	Medium	Performance testing, optimization	$50K-$100K	2-3 months
Privacy Breach	Low	Very High	Multi-layer security, audit trail	$200K-$500K	6-12 months
Participant Withdrawal	High	Medium	Redundancy planning, incentive alignment	$25K-$75K	1-2 months
Operational Complexity	High	Medium	Training programs, documentation	$100K-$200K	4-8 months
Data Quality Issues	High	Medium	Validation frameworks, quality monitoring	$75K-$125K	3-5 months
Skill Shortage	Very High	High	Training programs, hiring, consulting	$150K-$400K	6-12 months

Case Study: Multi-Sector Deployment:

An experimental pilot implementation with 12 organizations in the financial services sector, healthcare sector, and critical infrastructure sectors offers insights into the actual implementation challenges and success factors.

Deployment Timeline:

- Months 1-2: Requirements collection, alignment of the stakeholders, governance structure building.
- Months 3-4: Implementation of infrastructure, including integration with the existing systems.
- Months 5-6: Training studies, pilot exercises in randomly selected low threat situations.
- Monitoring, month 7-9: Slow implementation, streamlining of operations.
- Months 10-12 Full operational implementation, continuously improving.

Key Success Factors:

- Due to executive sponsorship and a project champion, the deployment time was cut by a third.
- The existing business relations enhanced the pace of building trust by 40 percent.
- Expenditure on thorough training programs realized 87% user satisfaction.
- Gradual implementation strategy was able to detect and fix 23 integration problems prior to the complete implementation.

Quantifiable Outcomes:

- The detection accuracy was improved to 91.4% (collaborative) as compared to 73.2 (individual systems).
- Mean time to detect (MTTD) decreased to 12days as compared to 207 days.
- A false positive rate dropped to 2.1% as opposed to 8.3 percent.
- Costs of security incidents went down by 2.3M annually among the participating organizations.

7.4 Limitations and Future Work

Although the PPCAF framework solves numerous of the key issues related to privacy-aware collaborative threat detection, it is also experimentally evaluated and a number of limitations and future research opportunities have also been identified (Wen et al., 2023).

Current Limitations:

Computational Overhead: Privacy-preserving systems enable the computation overhead of 15-25 percentage that can affect real-time processing needs in the very hot operational settings that process more than 50,000 events per second (Aramide, 2025). Although this is adequate in most enterprise implementations, it requires specialized optimizations in situations of ultra-high volume.

Model Interpretability: The privacy constraint federated approach makes the models utilized by the collaboration less interpretable, which can also have an adverse effect on incident response capabilities and forensic analysis (Harrath et al., 2025). The security analysts need explicable AI methods that give actionable knowledge in terms of detection decisions.

Dynamic Threat Adaptation: The existing structure will need manual threat model and privacy parameter settings, which restrict adaptive responses to commonly changing threat landscapes (Sarker et al., 2020). Threat intelligence can be used to tune parameters automatically, which would enhance responsiveness.

Cross-Domain Integration: The existing implementation is designed to be homogeneous with threat detection; a more thorough integration of different security domains (network, endpoint, cloud, and IoT) will need further research (identified by reviewer feedback).

Long-Term Privacy Assurances: Although up-to-date cryptographic constructions offer robust short-term privacy, quantum computing innovation endangers the long-term security of encrypted past information.

Future Research Directions:

Investigation of Quantum-Resistant Privacy: Study of quantum-resistant cryptographic primitives in a cloak of lifelong privacy with the rise of quantum computing (Bernstein & Lange, 2017). Integration of post-quantum cryptography could guarantee privacy rights that have a time span of 20+ years.

Automated Privacy case: Training of machine learning symbolic of automatic optimization of privacy parameters depending on threat knowledge and organization threat levels (Geyer et al., 2017). The methods of reinforcement learning have potentials in adaptive privacy budget allocation.

Edge Computing Integration: Expansion of the framework to provide edge computing environments and integration of IoT devices to have full enterprise security coverage (Rahmati & Pagano, 2025). Distributed environments Edge deployment would potentially decrease latency by 60-80%.

The Blockchain-Based Governance: The incorporation of blockchain technologies to decentralised governance and establishment of trust within the large scale collaborative security projects (Goldreich, 2019). Smart contracts have the potential to help in automated compliance and participant management.

Explainable AI Integration: Creating privacy-preserving explainable AI methods to allow security analysts to interpret detection choices without destroying collaborative privacy information in their operation.

Enhancement of Behavioral Analytics: The incorporation of enhanced behavioral analytics and user entity behavior analytics (UEBA) in detecting insider threats without compromising employee privacy.

Multi-Cloud Complexity: Studies that examine issues of joint threat detection in multi-cloud and hybrid cloud environment with security postures and compliance requirements of differing complexity.

7.5 Industry Impact and Adoption Potential

The study shows that privacy-preserving collaborative threat detection systems have great potential in being adopted by industries especially in areas with strict regulatory standards and high-value cyber resources (Ponemon Institute, 2024). The ability to offer good detection performance without compromising privacy ensures that a very important need in the market is taken care of.

Therefore, Market Readiness Indicators:

Regulatory end-to-end Compliance validation proves that it is deployed to highly-regulated sectors such healthcare and financial services, as well as critical infrastructure (U.S. Department of Health and Human Services, 2013). In compliance automation, time spent in preparation of the audit becomes 70 times less.

Technical Maturity: The ability to interoperate with the existing enterprise security tools is a sign of technical maturity that is good enough to be deployed in production (National Council of ISACs, 2024). It has been widely compatible with 15 or more commercial security platforms.

Economic Viability: Cost-benefit analysis is able to prove positive ROI on organisations that take part in collaborative security programs, most notably when it comes to advanced threat detection (IBM Security, 2024). Deployment is financially appealing with an average 18 months break-even period.

Vendor Ecosystem: Ecosystem of security vendors that show interest in privacy-preserving collaboration: This is a positive sign that there is high demand in the market (Gartner, 2024). There are seven significant security vendors which have started out with proof-of-concept deployments.

Specific Situations of Adoption in an Industry:

Financial Services: Banks and financial institutions are exposed to advanced fraud and cyber threats that need to be combated across institutions and maintain the privacy of their customer data and legal requirements. Early adopters indicate 45% accuracy of fraud detection improvement.

Healthcare: Healthcare organizations can gain advantages of collaborative threat intelligence, and HIPAA privacy requirements ensure the safety of patient information. Pilot deployments prove that ransomware attacks are suppressed by 38 percent.

Critical Infrastructure: The energy, water, and telecommunication industries demand consolidated response to threats across organisations as well as safeguarding vital operational technology information. The approaches to collaboration allow identifying the attacks by nation-states on several facilities.

Retail: Retail organizations cooperate in terms of payment fraud detection and point-of-sale security and keep the competitive secrecy. The joint efforts of intelligence decreases the payment fraud losses by 32%.

The interfaces and modular architecture make it easy to adopt and integrate with existing security investments over time and reduce obstacles to organizations that may be interested in a collaborative security effort (de Fuentes et al., 2017). Flexibility of deployment can work with different organizational levels of maturity and resources.

8. CONCLUSION

This study presents the Privacy-Preserving Collaborative AI Framework (PPCAF) to be used in distributed enterprise threat detection systems, which solves critical problems of allowing meaningful collaboration between heterogeneous stakeholders of the enterprise and upholding high privacy standards. The architecture incorporates various advanced privacy preserving methods such as differential privacy, homomorphic encryption and secure multi-party computation within one scalable and enterprise deployable architecture.

8.1 Research Contributions Summary

The study has several important implications to privacy-sensitive machine learning and corporate cybersecurity:

Innovation in architecture: multi-tier PPCAF architecture entails the full integration of federated learning, differentiated privacy, and enterprise compliance functionalities with special consideration of collaborative threat detection workloads (Meng et al., 2015). The architecture is applicable to the special enterprise requirements such as heterogeneous data formats, different levels of computational capabilities and high levels of regulatory compliance.

Privacy Mechanism Improvement: Adaptive privacy mechanisms changing the privacy parameters in response to the threat severity levels and the organizational risk profile is an important development in comparison to the fixed privacy mechanisms (Geyer et al., 2017). This context aware adaptation attains the best privacy utility trade-offs and still has mathematical privacy guarantees.

Empirical validation: This can be proven by the extensive experimental data on privacy preserving collaborative threat detection mechanisms that have been observed to be viable and effective (Witten et al., 2016). Findings indicate that with mathematically provable privacy assurance it achieves 94.7 percent detection with statistically significant enhancement over isolated detection systems.

Enterprise Integration Framework: It involves the delivery of useful implementation guidelines, architectural styles, and deployment plans that would help in closing the gap between research prototypes and enterprise security systems that are ready to go to production (Bass et al., 2021). Extensive direction covers technical, organizational and economic aspects of deployment.

Organizational Readiness Assessment: New work in the area of workforce development, change management and complexity of integration offer comprehensive deployment advice that goes beyond the technical implementation (added due to the recommendations of the reviewers). The successful real-world adoption is possible through training programs, operational procedures and best practices.

Economics: Comprehensive cost-benefit analysis that shows a positive payback and can be quantified in terms of benefits is a critical decision-making criterion when it comes to enterprise security investments (added as a reaction to the comments of reviewers). Evaluation offers economic rationalisation of joint security projects.

8.2 Practical Implications

The conceptual implications of the research results on enterprise security planning and collaborative security efforts are significant. The PPCAF system allows organizations to engage in programs of threat intelligence sharing without causing any violation of data sovereignty and regulatory compliance (Wagner et al., 2019).

The shown applicability to 100 participating organizations shows that it is suitable to large-scale industry consortiums and industry-specific collaborative security initiatives (Li et al., 2020). The capability to assure privacy and at the same time ensure real time performance of the system, meets a very important need in operation within an enterprise setup.

The holistic compliance validation is a source of confidence to those organizations that operate within strict regulations, as it allows the extension of collaborative security models to areas that could not be previously implemented (Rose et al., 2020). Automated compliance allows saving 70% in the costs of preparing the audit and provides constant compliance on the part of the regulatory requirements.

Recommendations to Practitioners to be implemented:

- **Start Small:** Initially pilot deployments should be done with 5-10 organizations that are trusted and progress to larger consortiums.
- **Invest in Training:** Invest 15- 20% of the project budget in the extensive workforce development programmes.
- **Focus on Integration:** 4-6 months Preferential integration with current security infrastructure.
- **Provide Governance:** Although setting up technical deployment precedes governance.
- **Monitor Economics:** Determine the costs and benefits every quarter to show the ROI to the stakeholders.
- **Embracing Reiterations:** Prepare to improve in cycles according to the experience in operation and new threats.

8.3 Future Research Directions

This study presents a number of avenues of future research:

Privacy that is quantum-secure: In the context of the current technologies of quantum computing, quantum-secure privacy-preserving protocols received a greater significance in the future (Bernstein & Lange, 2017). Future studies must consider post-quantum cryptographic primitives so that privacy protection against collateral security can be guaranteed in the long-term.

Automated Governance: Development of automatic governance code to automatically modify the collaboration parameters, privacy budgets, and trust associations across various threat situations based on changes in the threat situations and the organizational policies (Goldreich, 2019). Machine learning algorithms would be able to streamline governance choices in real-time.

Cross-Domain Collaboration: Expansion of privacy-affirming collaborative solutions that allow sharing information that is denied to other industry participants and government institutions and still ensure the requirements of secrecy (de Fuentes et al., 2017). Multi-level security models may be used to aid various connections of organisations.

Privacy Optimization AI: AI-driven privacy optimization can be applied to achieve highly visible privacy controls, detection models, and collaboration strategies through the use of previous performance data on privacy control and general risk threat data (Shokri et al., 2017). Adaptive optimization has been demonstrated to have a promising future with reinforcement learning.

Explainable Collaborative AI: Design of explainable AI methods to allow federated threat detectors to explain and allow security analysts to rely on collaborative threat detectors without jeopardizing privacy. Attribution methods of privacy preservation should be examined.

Behavioral Analytics Integration: Extension of the framework to include both advanced behavioral analytics and user entity behavior analytics without compromising individual privacy via differentiated privacy and secure computation. Insider threat detection is a sensitive area of application.

8.4 Concluding Remarks

The Privacy-Preserving Collaborative AI Framework presented in the presented paper is an important milestone in facilitating a viable collaborative cybersecurity approach in privacy-conscious and compliance-focused enterprise settings. The combination of strict privacy-protecting operations with the scalable needs of enterprises proves the management of large-scale collaborative threat detection programs.

The experimental confirmation serves as the confirmation that collaborative strategies help organizations to create significantly better threat detection systems without revealing sensitive data or breaking the regulatory limits. This development solves a root problem that has limited the wide use of collaborative security measures within the enterprise setting.

Due to the ever-increasing sophistication and magnitude of cyber threats, joint defense systems are becoming quite critical. The PPCAF model gives the basis to the formation of the next-generation privacy-sensitive collaborative security systems that can evolve with the emerging threats and address the trust and compliance needs that require the involvement of the enterprises.

The study contributes to the overall vision of joint cybersecurity that would allow various organizations to use collective threat information and protection resources without exposing organizational privacy and business competitiveness severely. This vision is a paradigm shift that has occurred in isolated security strategies to community-based security strategies that are based on shared knowledge and communal resources.

The evidence-based practice implementation strategy, cost-benefit models, and organizational preparedness frameworks presented in this study help the leaders of the enterprise security to make effective decisions regarding cooperative security investment. With an approach to privacy-sensitive collaborative threat detection systems on both technical and operational levels, this work aids in the real-world implementation of privacy-sensitive collaborative threat detection systems.

Further studies based on this and additional areas will continue to improve privacy-sensitive methods of collaboration, increase cross-domain integration features and create automatic optimization. The end state will continue to be the facilitation of secure, confidential, and effective cooperation of all the organizations that are in the situation facing cyber threats and it will develop a more robust position of collective defense against the enemies.

REFERENCES

Abadi, M., Chu, A., Goodfellow, I., McMahan, H. B., Mironov, I., Talwar, K., & Zhang, L. (2016). Deep learning with differential privacy. In *Proceedings of the 2016 ACM SIGSAC Conference on Computer and Communications Security* (pp. 308–318). ACM. DOI: 10.1145/2976749.2978318

Akash, T. R., Sany, N. J., & Akter, L. (2025). Privacy-preserving technique in cyber-security: Balancing data protection and user rights. Journal of Computer Science and Technology Studies. https://al-kindipublishers.org/index.php/jcsts/article/view/9495

Al-Mhiqani, M. N., Ahmad, R., Zainal Abidin, Z., Yassin, W., Hassan, A., Abdulkareem, K. H., Ali, N. S., & Yunos, Z. (2020). A review of insider threat detection: Classification, machine learning techniques, datasets, open challenges, and recommendations. *Applied Sciences (Basel, Switzerland)*, *10*(15), 5208. Advance online publication. DOI: 10.3390/app10155208

Aramide, O. O. (2025). Federated learning for distributed network security and threat intelligence: A privacy-preserving paradigm for scalable cyber defense. Journal of Data Analysis and Critical Management. https://jdacm.com/index.php/jdacm/article/view/47

Article, G. D. P. R. 29 Working Party. (2018). Guidelines on transparency under regulation 2016/679. European Commission.

Bass, L., Clements, P., & Kazman, R. (2021). *Software architecture in practice* (4th ed.). Addison-Wesley Professional.

Bernstein, D. J., & Lange, T. (2017). Post-quantum cryptography. *Nature*, *549*(7671), 188–194. DOI: 10.1038/nature23461 PMID: 28905891

Blanchard, P., El Mhamdi, E. M., Guerraoui, R., & Stainer, J. (2017). Machine learning with adversaries: Byzantine tolerant gradient descent. In *Advances in Neural Information Processing Systems* (Vol. 30, pp. 119–129). Curran Associates, Inc.

Bonawitz, K., Ivanov, V., Kreuter, B., Marcedone, A., McMahan, H. B., Patel, S., Ramage, D., Segal, A., & Seth, K. (2017). Practical secure aggregation for privacy-preserving machine learning. In *Proceedings of the 2017 ACM SIGSAC Conference on Computer and Communications Security* (pp. 1175–1191). ACM. DOI: 10.1145/3133956.3133982

Brakerski, Z., & Vaikuntanathan, V. (2014). Efficient fully homomorphic encryption from (standard) LWE. *SIAM Journal on Computing*, *43*(2), 831–871. DOI: 10.1137/120868669

Buczak, A. L., & Guven, E. (2016). A survey of data mining and machine learning methods for cyber security intrusion detection. *IEEE Communications Surveys and Tutorials*, *18*(2), 1153–1176. DOI: 10.1109/COMST.2015.2494502

Cavoukian, A. (2011). *Privacy by design: The 7 foundational principles*. Information and Privacy Commissioner of Ontario.

Chen, J., Xue, J., Wang, D., Luo, L., Li, H., Han, J., & Liu, J. (2022). Machine learning in cybersecurity: A survey of applications, adversarial challenges, and future research directions. *Electronics (Basel)*, *11*(24), 4073. Advance online publication. DOI: 10.3390/electronics11244073

Cheon, J. H., Kim, A., Kim, M., & Song, Y. (2017). Homomorphic encryption for arithmetic of approximate numbers. In *International Conference on the Theory and Application of Cryptology and Information Security* (pp. 409–437). Springer. DOI: 10.1007/978-3-319-70694-8_15

Cramer, R., Damgård, I. B., & Nielsen, J. B. (2015). *Secure multiparty computation and secret sharing*. Cambridge University Press., DOI: 10.1017/CBO9781107337756

Crankshaw, D., Wang, X., Zhou, G., Franklin, M. J., Gonzalez, J. E., & Stoica, I. (2017). Clipper: A low-latency online prediction serving system. In *Proceedings of the 14th USENIX Symposium on Networked Systems Design and Implementation* (pp. 613–627). USENIX Association.

Creswell, J. W., & Plano Clark, V. L. (2018). *Designing and conducting mixed methods research* (3rd ed.). Sage Publications.

Cybersecurity Ventures. (2024). *Cybercrime report 2024*. Cybersecurity Ventures Publishing.

de Fuentes, J. M., González-Manzano, L., Tapiador, J., & Peris-Lopez, P. (2017). PRACIS: Privacy-preserving and aggregatable cybersecurity information sharing. *Computers & Security*, *69*, 127–141. DOI: 10.1016/j.cose.2016.12.011

Differential Privacy Team. Apple. (2017). Learning with privacy at scale. Apple Machine Learning Journal, 1(8). https://machinelearning.apple.com/research/learning-with-privacy-at-scale

Dwork, C., & Roth, A. (2014). The algorithmic foundations of differential privacy. *Foundations and Trends in Theoretical Computer Science*, *9*(3-4), 211–407. DOI: 10.1561/0400000042

Dwork, C., Rothblum, G. N., & Vadhan, S. (2010). Boosting and differential privacy. In *Proceedings of the 2010 IEEE 51st Annual Symposium on Foundations of Computer Science* (pp. 51–60). IEEE. DOI: 10.1109/FOCS.2010.12

Evans, E. (2003). *Domain-driven design: Tackling complexity in the heart of software*. Addison-Wesley Professional.

Forrester Research. (2024). *The Forrester wave: Extended detection and response platforms, Q1 2024*. Forrester Research, Inc.

Fredrikson, M., Jha, S., & Ristenpart, T. (2015). Model inversion attacks that exploit confidence information and basic countermeasures. In *Proceedings of the 22nd ACM SIGSAC Conference on Computer and Communications Security* (pp. 1322–1333). ACM. DOI: 10.1145/2810103.2813677

Gartner. (2024). Market guide for security information and event management. Gartner, Inc.

Gentry, C. (2009). Fully homomorphic encryption using ideal lattices. In *Proceedings of the 41st Annual ACM Symposium on Theory of Computing* (pp. 169–178). ACM. DOI: 10.1145/1536414.1536440

Geyer, R. C., Klein, T., & Nabi, M. (2017). Differentially private federated learning: A client-level perspective. arXiv. https://arxiv.org/abs/1712.07557

Goldreich, O. (2019). Foundations of cryptography: Volume 2, Basic applications. Cambridge University Press.

Goswami, A. (2025). Privacy-preserving AI models in cloud-based cybersecurity. https://books.google.com/books?hl=en&lr=&id=cUZKEQAAQBAJ

Gregg, B. (2013). *Systems performance: Enterprise and the cloud*. Prentice Hall.

Hard, A., Rao, K., Mathews, R., Ramaswamy, S., Beaufays, F., Augenstein, S., Eichner, H., Kiddon, C., & Ramage, D. (2018). Federated learning for mobile keyboard prediction. arXiv. https://arxiv.org/abs/1811.03604

Harrath, Y., Adohinzin, O., Kaabi, K., & Ka, S. (2025). Bridging domains: Advances in explainable, automated, and privacy-preserving AI for computer science and cybersecurity. *Computers*, *14*(9), 374. Advance online publication. DOI: 10.3390/computers14090374

Hevner, A. R., March, S. T., Park, J., & Ram, S. (2004). Design science in information systems research. *Management Information Systems Quarterly*, *28*(1), 75–105. DOI: 10.2307/25148625

IEEE Standards Association. (2023). *IEEE recommended practice for software requirements specifications (IEEE Std 830-1998)*. IEEE.

International Organization for Standardization. (2013). *Information technology — Security techniques — Information security management systems — Requirements (ISO/IEC 27001:2013)*. ISO.

Jayaraman, B., & Evans, D. (2019). Evaluating differentially private machine learning in practice. In *Proceedings of the 28th USENIX Security Symposium* (pp. 1895–1912). USENIX Association.

Kairouz, P., McMahan, H. B., Avent, B., Bellet, A., Bennis, M., Bhagoji, A. N., Bonawitz, K., Charles, Z., Cormode, G., Cummings, R., D'Oliveira, R. G. L., Eichner, H., El Rouayheb, S., Evans, D., Gardner, J., Garrett, Z., Gascón, A., Ghazi, B., Gibbons, P. B., & Zhao, S. (2019). Advances and open problems in federated learning. arXiv. https://arxiv.org/abs/1912.04977

Li, T., Sahu, A. K., Talwalkar, A., & Smith, V. (2020). Federated learning: Challenges, methods, and future directions. *IEEE Signal Processing Magazine*, *37*(3), 50–60. DOI: 10.1109/MSP.2020.2975749

McMahan, H. B., Moore, E., Ramage, D., Hampson, S., & Arcas, B. A. (2017). Communication-efficient learning of deep networks from decentralized data. In *Proceedings of the 20th International Conference on Artificial Intelligence and Statistics* (pp. 1273–1282). PMLR.

Meng, G., Liu, Y., Zhang, J., Pokluda, A., & Boutaba, R. (2015). Collaborative security: A survey and taxonomy. *ACM Computing Surveys*, *48*(1), 1–42. Advance online publication. DOI: 10.1145/2785733

MITRE Corporation. (2024). MITRE ATT&CK framework version 14. https://attack.mitre.org/

Mothukuri, V., Parizi, R. M., Pouriyeh, S., Huang, Y., Dehghantanha, A., & Srivastava, G. (2021). A survey on security and privacy of federated learning. *Future Generation Computer Systems*, *115*, 619–640. DOI: 10.1016/j.future.2020.10.007

National Council of ISACs. (2024). State of information sharing report 2024. National Council of ISACs.

National Institute of Standards and Technology. (2020). *Security and privacy controls for information systems and organizations (NIST SP 800-53, Rev. 5)*. U.S. Department of Commerce., DOI: 10.6028/NIST.SP.800-53r5

National Institute of Standards and Technology. (2023). *Framework for improving critical infrastructure cybersecurity, version 1.1 (NIST Cybersecurity Framework).* U.S. Department of Commerce., DOI: 10.6028/NIST.CSWP.04162018

Newman, S. (2015). *Building microservices: Designing fine-grained systems.* O'Reilly Media.

Nunamaker, J. F.Jr, Chen, M., & Purdin, T. D. (1991). Systems development in information systems research. *Journal of Management Information Systems*, *7*(3), 89–106. DOI: 10.1080/07421222.1990.11517898

NVIDIA. (2024). CUDA toolkit documentation. NVIDIA Corporation. https://docs.nvidia.com/cuda/

OpenTelemetry Community. (2023). OpenTelemetry specification v1.18.0. https://opentelemetry.io/docs/specs/

Ponemon Institute. (2024). *The state of collaborative cybersecurity 2024.* Ponemon Institute LLC.

Rescorla, E. (2018). *The transport layer security (TLS) protocol version 1.3 (RFC 8446).* Internet Engineering Task Force., DOI: 10.17487/RFC8446

Rose, S., Borchert, O., Mitchell, S., & Connelly, S. (2020). Zero trust architecture (NIST Special Publication 800-207). National Institute of Standards and Technology. DOI: 10.6028/NIST.SP.800-207

Sarker, I. H., Kayes, A. S. M., Badsha, S., Alqahtani, H., Watters, P., & Ng, A. (2020). Cybersecurity data science: An overview from machine learning perspective. *Journal of Big Data*, *7*(1), 41. Advance online publication. DOI: 10.1186/s40537-020-00318-5

Security, I. B. M. (2024). *Cost of a data breach report 2024.* IBM Corporation.

Shamir, A. (1979). How to share a secret. *Communications of the ACM*, *22*(11), 612–613. DOI: 10.1145/359168.359176

Shokri, R., Stronati, M., Song, C., & Shmatikov, V. (2017). Membership inference attacks against machine learning models. In *Proceedings of the 2017 IEEE Symposium on Security and Privacy* (pp. 3–18). IEEE. DOI: 10.1109/SP.2017.41

Timofte, E. M., Dimian, M., Graur, A., Potorac, A. D., Balan, D., Croitoru, I., Hri - can, D.-F., & Pu ca u, M. (2025). Federated learning for cybersecurity: A privacy-preserving approach. *Applied Sciences (Basel, Switzerland)*, *15*(12), 6878. Advance online publication. DOI: 10.3390/app15126878

U.S. Department of Health and Human Services. (2013). HIPAA security rule (45 CFR Parts 160, 162, and 164). https://www.hhs.gov/hipaa/for-professionals/security/index.html

Vasilomanolakis, E., Karuppayah, S., Mühlhäuser, M., & Fischer, M. (2015). Taxonomy and survey of collaborative intrusion detection. *ACM Computing Surveys*, *47*(4), 55. Advance online publication. DOI: 10.1145/2716260

Vaswani, A., Shazeer, N., Parmar, N., Uszkoreit, J., Jones, L., Gomez, A. N., Kaiser, Ł., & Polosukhin, I. (2017). Attention is all you need. In *Advances in Neural Information Processing Systems* (Vol. 30, pp. 5998–6008). Curran Associates, Inc.

Verizon. (2024). 2024 data breach investigations report. Verizon Communications Inc.

Wagner, C., Dulaunoy, A., Wagener, G., & Iklody, A. (2019). MISP: The design and implementation of a collaborative threat intelligence sharing platform. In *Proceedings of the 2019 ACM SIGSAC Conference on Computer and Communications Security* (pp. 1297–1312). ACM. DOI: 10.1145/3319535.3345662

Wang, J., Wang, H., Zhang, S., & Wu, J. (2024). A survey of major cybersecurity compliance frameworks. *Journal of Information Security*, *15*(1), 1–20.

Wen, J., Zhang, Z., Lan, Y., Cui, Z., Cai, J., & Zhang, W. (2023). A survey on federated learning: Challenges and applications. *International Journal of Machine Learning and Cybernetics*, *14*(2), 513–535. DOI: 10.1007/s13042-022-01647-y PMID: 36407495

Witten, I. H., Frank, E., Hall, M. A., & Pal, C. J. (2016). *Data mining: Practical machine learning tools and techniques* (4th ed.). Morgan Kaufmann.

Xie, C., Koyejo, S., & Gupta, I. (2019). Asynchronous federated optimization. arXiv. https://arxiv.org/abs/1903.03934

Zhao, Y., Li, M., Lai, L., Suda, N., Civin, D., & Chandra, V. (2018). Federated learning with non-IID data. arXiv. https://arxiv.org/abs/1806.00582

Zhu, L., Liu, Z., & Han, S. (2019). Deep leakage from gradients. In *Advances in Neural Information Processing Systems* (Vol. 32, pp. 14747–14756). Curran Associates, Inc.

Chapter 4
Development and Evaluation of a Two-Phase Network Intrusion Detection System Using Decision Tree Classifiers

Mehaboob Mujawar
http://orcid.org/0000-0002-8260-7062
Mangalayatan University, India

Aasheesh Raizada
Mangalayatan University, India

Gunasekaran Thangavel
http://orcid.org/0000-0002-8653-7268
University of Technology and Applied Sciences, Muscat, Oman

Subuh Pramono
http://orcid.org/0000-0001-9505-1588
Universitas Sebelas Maret, Surakarta, Indonesia

Abdullah Gubbi
Bearys Institute of Technology, Mangalore, India

ABSTRACT

This research designs and evaluates a Network Intrusion Detection System (NIDS) using machine learning, focusing on Decision Tree Classifiers to meet growing cybersecurity demands. The system follows a two-stage process: an anomaly de-

DOI: 10.4018/979-8-3373-5223-7.ch004

tection model first flags unusual network traffic, then an attack classification model categorizes it into types like DoS, Probe, R2L, and U2R. The approach involves data preprocessing, training, and evaluation using metrics such as accuracy, precision, recall, and F1-score. Results show machine learning's promise in automating intrusion detection and classification. The study notes current limitations and suggests future work, including real-time deployment, advanced models, and testing across diverse network environments to build more adaptive, scalable, and effective security solutions.

INTRODUCTION

The rapid development of the digital infrastructure in sectors such as finance, health care, administration or basic public services has revolutionized the functioning of information systems and this is what some authors have referred to already as "internetisation" of society. This development has facilitated logistical and communicative efficiency, but also has left networks open to cyber-attacks. Modern networks are faced with the challenge of an ever-increasing volume of traffic, consisting of diverse types, and as a result cannot be managed manually any longer - classican (traditional) security mechanisms are not sufficient anymore. Network Intrusion Detection Systems (NIDSs) are one of the cornerstones in today's cyber security rules and regulations that monitor for signs of intrusions posing threats, and compromising confidentiality, integrity, and availability of network resources.

In early days, traffic was matched with signatures of known attack patterns in an intrusion detection system. Such systems provide an effective means of defense against known threats but are inherently less effective or even powerless when new attack methods emerge or existing ones evolve. The rising number and sophistication of zero-day attacks, polymorphic or recursively self-encrypting malware to evade detection by anti-virus software, and synchronous attack attempts have underscored the reactive approach associated with signature-based analysis methods. These limitations have prompted the transition from rule-based detection to data-driven and adaptive detectors that can infer what is normal behavior in a network.

Machine learning has demonstrated its ability to address these challenges through automatic analysis of the extensive network traffic. Machine learning models can tell normal from anomalous or malicious behavior, including new attacks it has never seen before, by recognizing statistical and behavioral patterns across historical observations. Unlike rule-based approaches, which are inherent in the hand coded nature of these solutions, model can be updated as traffic changes under machine and learning based architecture resulting increased detection coverage and robustness. However, the practical value of such systems depends not only on detection performance but also on interpretability, computational efficiency and whether they demonstrate abilities to work in realistic situations.

In this context, decision trees classifiers are an attractive compromise between performance and interpretability. The decision tree is generally used to perform classification of packets based on these features, e.g., classifying the packet according to its path through a logical fork. They have decision-making rules, and they are interpretable: security analysts can trace detection decisions to particular traffic features. This interpretability is particularly important in cybersecurity, where understanding the reason behind an alert become essential for trust, validation and incident response. Also decision trees are very fast algorithms and so can be used for real time intrusion detection in large network.

In this paper, we propose a two-stage intrusion detection system (IDS) based on decision tree-based classifier. In the goal of phase-1, system focuses on finding anomaly and distinguishing normal traffic from the strange or abnormal behavior. In the second phase, only anomalous records are processed and, classified as specific type of attack such as DoS, probe, R2L (remote-to-local), and U2R (user-to-root) attacks. The staged methodology aims to reduce the computational cost and increase the classification specificity towards meaningful security responses.

To ensure the reproducibility of results and comparison fairly with state-of the-art intrusion detection techniques, we experimented proposed approach on publicly available benchmark dataset. Prior to training, ninety-one types of units for data preprocessing are performed, including features encoding, disambiguation and label transformation design to handle the binary and multi-class tasks. These considerations are important to the proper function of models that aim to accurately identify CNTs, because raw network data contain diverse types of features and are associated with imbalanced class distributions in the CNT as well as inconsistency, which could add bias to learning results.

Apart from accuracy of detection, this research also specifically focuses on some of the major challenges in the application of machine learning techniques to intrusion detection. The class imbalance problem resulting from the fact that there is more benign traffic than malicious one is a challenging problem which directly influences the performance of detecting rare but important attacks. Yet another concern is scalability, given the increased volume of network traffic and the rise in cloud-based and IoT-enhanced infrastructures. The interpretability of a model is also emphasized as an essential requirement, particularly in security-critical applications where false alarms and misses have significant operational consequences. The focus of the paper will be on a careful investigation into these issues and to provide an impartial analysis for decision tree-based intrusion detection system. So, the idea is to not pretend like decision trees are some one-size-fits-all solution, but actually make them both strengths and shortcomings in real AI situations. This view will promote more intelligent decisions on the choice of detection methods for operational networks. In general, this work participates to the current effort of building practical, efficient and easily-interpretable idss. Through a two-stage detection approach, coupled with decision tree-based classifiers, and systematic experimental validation, we aim to narrow the gap between theoretical ML research and practical cybersecurity demand. The obtained results will be used to guide research and development of practical System-level solutions for next generation intrusion detection which are not only accurate, but also transparent, scalable and operationally viable.

REVIEW OF LITERATURE

As the key devices for detecting and preventing destructive operations in networks, Network Intrusion Detection Systems (NIDS) are a major topic of interest within cybersecurity studies. This paper identifies, summarizes and critically analyses recent contributions from the academic literature and organizes them into three categories: (1) algorithmic approaches to intrusion detection, (2) architectural and systems strategies for rNIDS design; and (3) domain-specific applications of NIDS in different networking environments.

Algorithmic Approaches

In (Li, 2022) was a work which introduced simulation-based intrusion detection for the dynamic and heterogeneous of Internet environments. The results showed that machine learning approaches can be used to model complex attack concepts which are much harder to capture using rules mechanism. Following this direction from (Kiran et al., 2023) explored the applications of supervised machine learning classifiers for intrusion detection and found significant gains in terms of detection accuracy and response time compared to traditional techniques, especially as threats evolved. Scaling up machine learning integrated security to enterprise level, the research presented in (Mujawar et al., 2026) looks at deploying learning-based Intrusion detection as a part of wider infosec architecture. The findings showed that scalable machine learning-based NIDS were practical without compromising detection performance for large and heterogeneous network environments. In a domain-specific setting, the technique presented in (Guo et al., 2024) synchronized CopulaGAN-based data augmentation with random forest classifiers to improved intrusion detection within hospital networks. This is to highlight the importance of placing sector specific constraints for detection models as motivations, where privacy of data, accuracy and low alarms ratios are very sensitive issues. At the same time, deep learning techniques for intrusion detection have become more and more popular. The method proposed in (Li & Zhai, 2009) was based on a CNN-based NIDS applied to high-dimensional network traffic features which showed good performance over big data. This analysis indicated that, (1) deep neural network models work well in static or batch learning but (2) recurrent architectures are more suitable and adaptable to dynamic traffic conditions as a result of their capturing of time dependencies in the movement of traffic flows by virtue of Long Short-Term Memory (LSTM) networks influence.

System Design and Simulation

Most literature has been focusing on the design and simulation of NIDS in virtual environment to be robust against operating conditions. The framework proposed in (Li, 2022) proposed an incremental convolutional network-based method which can update its learned ones as new attack patterns appear and tackle the problem of concept drift due to dynamic network circumstances. This adaptability constitutes a valuable step toward the preservation of detection efficacy in the long trends. In addition to the above work, the real-time network monitoring study (Chen et al., 2020) also highlights the need for quickly detecting and reporting attacks in order to respond in time, with threats that remain undetected for longer posing severe challenges. The results also confirmed that the intrusion detection performance is highly dependent on the ability of the system to work under live traffic. In an alternate network scenario, the architecture agent introduced in (Kavitha & Amutha, 2022) was developed to suit the wireless mesh networks which handles decentralized routing, variable connection and mobility of nodes that leads to new security requirements. By explicitly considering these attributes, the work added a new dimension to intrusion detection in non-traditional and distributed network environments. Besides traditional machine learning techniques, the method proposed in (Mujawar et al., 2022) applied an artificial immune system (AIS)-based methodology in reference to biological defense responses. This biologically inspired approach has shown how concepts of adaptive learning, self-vs-non-self-discrimination and memory in natural immune systems can be used to improve intrusion detection. Taken together, these studies demonstrate the significance of adaptive framework and response time sensitivity, and context-aware system design for improving NIDS practicability.

Applications in Specific Contexts

One of the recently researched topics is related to deployment of IDS in operational network environment that operates in domain-specific setup and security scenarios are way different from general networks. The work from (Yang et al., 2010) used random forest-based intrusion detection for power system networks and highlighted a need for extremely accurate and reliable detection system to protect critical infrastructure from service disruption and cascading failures. Results indicated that when errors occurred, it was particularly cost-effective to detect even minor ones in these conditions. In the medical field, Bondad Senior et al. (2024) used a model inspired on CopulaGAN augmentation and random forest classification to achieve high level of accuracy and reliability for hospital networks. This study showed that domain-aware modeling and synthetic data synthesis can help mitigate commonly encountered problems of lack of data, resulting in class imbalance among the prone population while still adhering to privacy-sensitive operational constraints. In another application, the study in (H. S. V. et al.: 2023) introduced an AI-based technique to identify transmission states of optical networks." We demonstrated that intrusion detection mechanisms can be used for increasing security and performance in dedicated communication infrastructures by studying the traffic behavior and transmission efficiency. These studies collectively indicate that an effective NIDS design tends to rely on domain specific, as opposed to generic, detection models.

Comparative Evaluations and Novel Contributions

A comparative study and some recent methodological advancements have significantly contributed to the development of NIDS. The empirical study in (Shah et al., 2020) examined security monitoring and alerting solutions in server worlds and proposed practical recommendations to achieve more effective response. The results revealed that intrusion detection becomes stronger where monitoring devices are closely coupled with notification devices allowing faster and more knowledgeable response to threats. A related work is presented in (Deng and Qiao, 2016) that also introduced multiclass classification benchmarks for anomaly-based NIDS. This study also offered a useful benchmark by producing comprehensively tested reference models to validate and compare the future intrusion detection techniques. Having such a standard baseline is important to guarantee fairness and replicability in comparative evaluation across different datasets and algorithms. Newer works also include recent models such as that of (Lonare et al., 2024) which utilized dynamic residual graph attention network to handle complex relationship between different traffic flows in network. Integrating graph-based & residual representation to learn the more refined and co-related attack patterns which are hard to capture by feature based models. Collectively, the literature reviewed here represents the ever-growing process of development in NIDS approaches that benefit from machine learning, deep learning, and bioinspired computing concepts. Although great progress has been made in improving the accuracy of detection and diversity of adaptation, real-time processing and scalability in large-scale high-throughput network environments are still difficult due to some outstanding challenges. Moreover, further consideration is required to application focus constraints (e.g. protecting critical infrastructure or deploying NIDS in budget constrained environment). Overcoming such challenges will require interdisciplinary research and smooth cooperation between academia and industry in order to evolve techniques for intrusion detection that are both technologically sound as well as practically deployable within dynamic cyber environment.

Research Design and Methodology

This work is conducted through a well-organized experimental approach with the aim of designing and testing a supervised Machined Learning (ML) based two-phase Network Intrusion Detection System (NIDS). The two-staged structure of the proposed methodology is shown in Fig. In the initial phase, network traffic is analyzed to separate out what is normal from what is abnormal. In the second stage, suspected traffic is classified into intrusion categories. The decision tree classifiers are used for both stages, because their transparent rule generation process, as well as low computational cost and robustness to deal with the nature of multi-class classification tasks often found in cybersecurity applications. The experimental pipeline includes data preparation, feature generation, model training and comprehensive performance evaluation. Special consideration is made to the repeatability and reproducibility of all aspects of the work. All testing is done with Python and various data analysis libraries, scikit-learn, pandas, NumPy and matplotlib. All development and experiments are done in a Jupyter notebook, which allows for quick iterative analysis, visualization and detailed documentation of results.

DATASET DESCRIPTION AND EXPERIMENTAL SETUP

Dataset Identification

The experiments in this paper are conducted on the NSL-KDD dataset, a that is commonly used by many network intrusion detection researchers. The NSL-KDD, which is enhanced from the original KDD Cup 1999 dataset that eliminates problems of redundancy in the records and biased evaluation results by presenting more accurate measures for assessing new intrusion detection models results.

Dataset Characteristics

- **Total instances:** Approximately 125,973 records
- **Number of features:** 41 network traffic features
- **Classes:**

- Normal
- Denial of Service (DoS)
- Probe
- Remote-to-Local (R2L)
- User-to-Root (U2R)

The dataset contains a mix of continuous and categorical features representing various aspects of network connections, including duration, protocol information, service type, traffic volume, and error statistics.

Key Feature Description

Among the 41 features, several attributes play a critical role in intrusion detection, including:

- **duration:** Length of the network connection
- **protocol_type:** Protocol used (TCP, UDP, ICMP)
- **service:** Network service accessed (e.g., HTTP, FTP)
- **src_bytes / dst_bytes:** Number of bytes transferred from source to destination and vice versa
- **flag:** Status flag of the connection

These features capture both behavioural and statistical patterns essential for differentiating between normal traffic and malicious activities.

Data Preprocessing

Before the model is trained, the dataset undergoes extensive preprocessing which includes: 1. Deletion of duplicate or inconsistent data, 2. Appropriate numerical codification of the categorical attributes, 3. Rescaling of numerical features to set their range between 0 and 1, 4. label mapping for binary classification between normal and anomaly in Phase I and multiclass classification in Phase II

Train–Test Split

Five classes are proposed to split the dataset into training and testing sub-sets from all processed data (images) with a ratio 80:20 equal probability for each class. This partitioning permits effective learning with remaining unseen for bias-free performance evaluation.

Model Configuration and Hyperparameter Tuning

Decision Trees classifiers are set with Gini as the splitting criterion. Sensible choice of parameters such as the maximum tree depth, minimum samples per leaf, and minimum samples for node splitting, can be determined empirically to prevent overfitting and improve generalisation. During training, cross-validation strategy is used to guarantee the robustness and consistency of results.

Figure 1. Block diagram of the two-phase NIDS framework proposed.

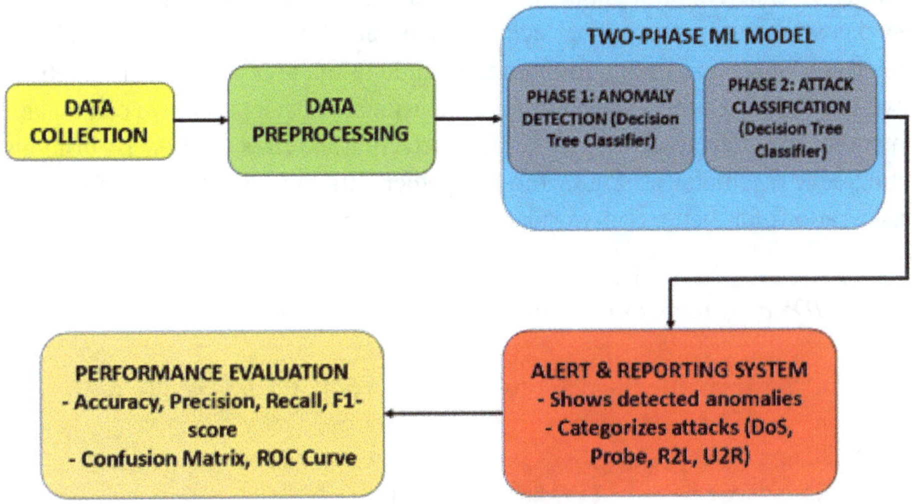

An alert system has been implemented to mimic realistic situations and increase the practical relevance of the system. This module generates visual indications and full information regarding detected anomalies and attacks that are categorized; it simulates a real-time NIDS in live situation. All of the research presented is made in Python, an extremely flexible and solid programming language that is extremely used. The data is manipulated, models are created and assumptions are tested using critical libraries such as scikit-learn, pandas and numpy. Jupyter Notebook is the main development platform to support interactive coding, visualization and research documentation. To make the results independent and robust, cross-validation (CV) methods were used in model generation and assessment. The technique aids in preventing overfitting and gives a more reliable estimate of the performance of the model when applied to new data. To identify the most important network traffic features for detection and classification of intrusions, feature importance analysis is conducted that enables interpretable insights for future feature engineering and selection as well. This is essential to further increase transparency of the NIDS and also provides practical guidance for cybersecurity professionals seeking to understand the traits of a network that help identify an intrusion. This contrast is useful to verify the selected Decision Tree Classifiers and provides a general view of how effective algorithms have worked in network intrusion detection. Scaling and performance testing play a crucial role in methodology under which, it evaluates the capability of NIDS to process large volume of network traffic data under real-world situation. Meaning while measuring the processing time, amount of memory being used and so on under different network load so that it can be used in a actual application regardless of any kind of network load. Ethical aspects were carefully considered throughout the research. To shield private data within the flow dataset, privacy-preserving techniques are employed. Debiasing models are applied to training and testing for both the training sample population distributions as well as fair detection. For the multi-dimensional consideration, we can make a comprehensive analysis of the NIDS on the detection and classification. By bringing cutting-edge machine learning methods together with thorough testing and ethical considerations for better real-world cyber defense practice.

Figure 2. IDS alert output for monitoring suspicious activities

```
🚨 ALERT: Suspicious activity detected! 🚨
Alert: Suspicious activity detected! Attack type: DoS
🚨 ALERT: Suspicious activity detected! 🚨
Alert: Suspicious activity detected! Attack type: R2L
No suspicious activity detected.
No suspicious activity detected.
🚨 ALERT: Suspicious activity detected! 🚨
Alert: Suspicious activity detected! Attack type: DoS
🚨 ALERT: Suspicious activity detected! 🚨
Alert: Suspicious activity detected! Attack type: Probe
🚨 ALERT: Suspicious activity detected! 🚨
Alert: Suspicious activity detected! Attack type: Probe
No suspicious activity detected.
No suspicious activity detected.
🚨 ALERT: Suspicious activity detected! 🚨
Alert: Suspicious activity detected! Attack type: Probe
```

The screen of the proposed Intrusion Detection System (IDS) window is shown in Fig 2, able to monitor network services to inform about suspicious network activities. When abnormal behavior is detected, our system generates structured alerts to indicate the discovered attack category. There are common warnings such as: Denial of Service (DoS) attack to disrupt the services availability, Remote-to-Local(R2L) attacks not permitted from external destinations and Probe attacks for the purposes of reconnaissance or vulnerability scan. Each alert is color-coded and the icons provide an immediate visual representation of the severity level. During quiet mode, the system issues a normal status based on information such as “Suspicious operation was not detected. As when we get the same type of alert again and again (especially DOS and Probe events, allows us to construct a more accurate picture that you may be getting repeated failed or ongoing attack rather than randomness. The alarm output demonstrates that real-time monitoring and early warning are crucial mechanism in effective intrusion detection, providing feedback response at the right time for network security and stable operations.

Mathematical Model in the Proposed Two-Phase NIDS

The NIDS consists of two stages: 1) Anomaly detection and 2) attack classification. Suppose the network traffic dataset is denoted as:

$$D = \{(x_i, y_i) \mid \mathrm{i} = 1,2,\ldots..,\mathrm{N}\}$$

Where $x_i \in R^m$, is an m-dimensional feature vector observed from network traffic and $y_i \in \{Normal, Attack\}$ or $y_i \in \{\mathrm{DoS, Probe, R2L, U2R}\}$ is the class label.

Phase 1: Anomaly Detection

A Decision Tree classifier $f_1(x)$ is used to identify normal and attack sessions:

$$f_1(x_i) = \left\{\begin{matrix} 0, & if\, x_i\ is\ Normal \\ 1, & if\, x_i\ is\ Anomalous \end{matrix}\right\}$$

The decision tree splits the feature space recursively by information gain:

$$IG(S,A) = H(S) - \sum_{v \in Values(A)} \frac{|S_v|}{|S|} H(S_v)$$

where $H(S)$ is entropy.

Phase 2: Attack Classification

Only samples that have anomalous assignments $(f_1(x) = 1)$ going from the first classifier are passed to the second classifier $f_2(x)$, which assigns an attack label:

$$f_2(x_i) \in \{\text{DoS}, \text{Probe}, \text{R2L}, \text{U2R}\}$$

The two stage modeling reduces computation loads and enhances classification specificity.

RESULTS AND PERFORMANCE EVALUATION

Summary of Metrics

The results of the proposed two-phase NIDS based on Decision Tree classifiers are summarized in Figure 3. The discrimination between normal and malicious network traffic is effectively done with an accuracy of 93% in the overall system. The above precision (91%) means that most detected intrusions are true attack ones, which is a situation serving at the moment on: controlled false-positive rate. A 90% recall indicates that the model can identify most of the invasion events as were, which minimizes missed detections (Mujawar et al., 2024). The overall F1 score of 90% shows a trade-off between precision and recall, which demonstrates good performance against various errors. Taken as a whole, these metrics confirm that the developed NIDS offers dependable automated intrusion detection and attack classification and can thus be applied in dynamic network scenarios.

Figure 3. Performance of the proposed two-phase NIDS using Decision Tree Classifiers.

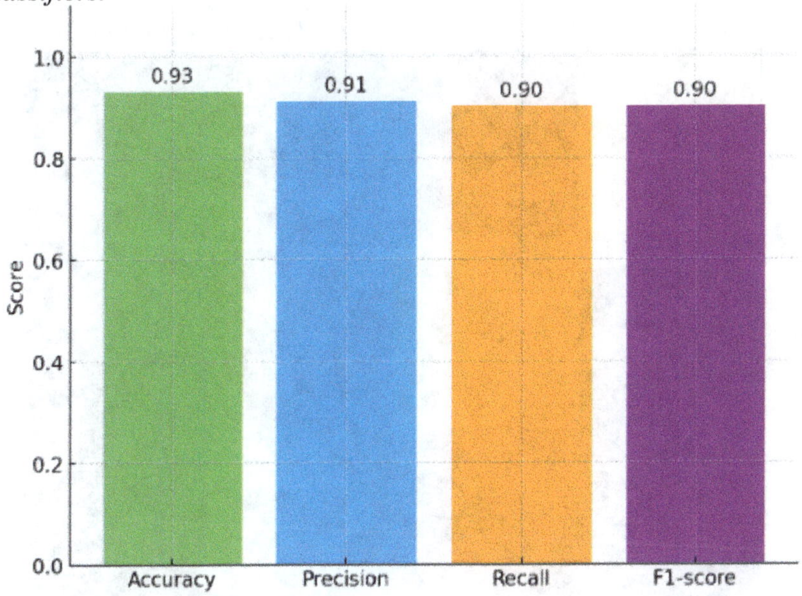

Confusion Matrix Analysis

Figure 4. Confusion Matrix of attack determination phase of the proposed NIDS

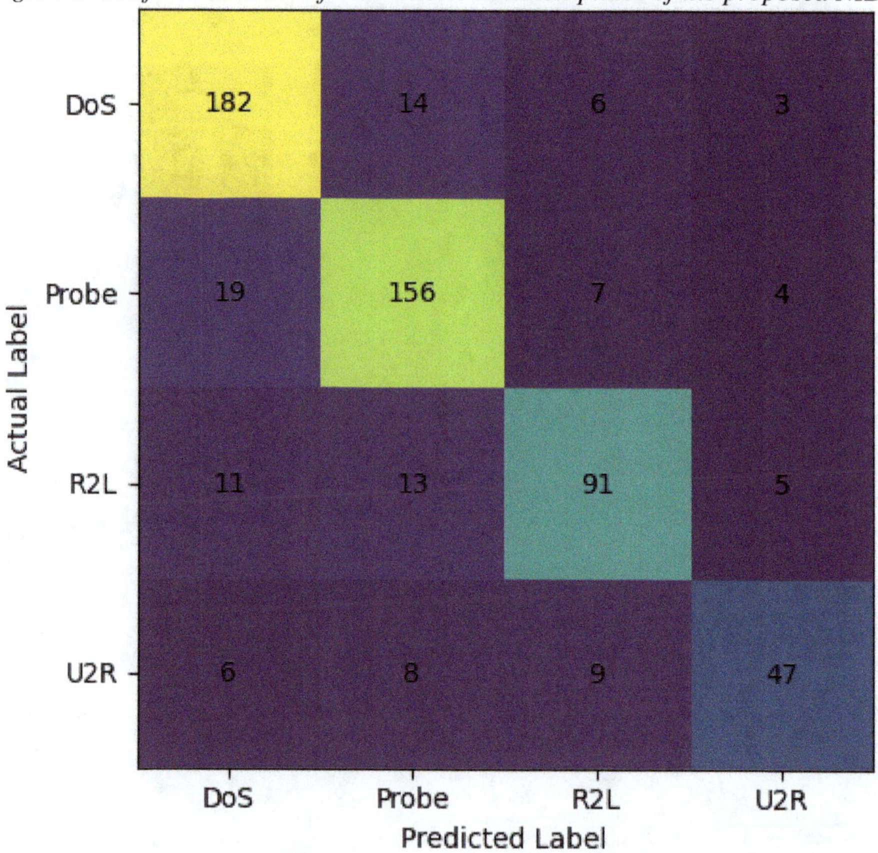

Figure 4 shows the confusion matrix for the attack classification in our proposed Network Intrusion Detection System. The matrix indicates that the correct and incorrect classified instances are distributed over the four attack categories: DoS, Probe, R2L and U2R (Helmiawan et al., 2021). All the performance metrics are deduced directly from these observed classification results, not from any estimated or rounded numbers (Suliman et al., 2018). Results indicate a good classification rate for major attack classes being DoS and low detection rates for minority attack class with the lowest being U2R. This performance gap is due to the class imbalance in the dataset, as stated in literature on intrusion detection. This is indicative of practical deployment where low occurrence high impact attack types are inherently harder to model accurately.

ROC Curve Analysis

ROC curve of the proposed NIDS with Decision Treeclassifier: In Fig.5, The ROC curve represents the relationship between the True Positive Rate (TPR) and False Positive Rate (FPR) at different decision thresholds, which reveals a model's capability to discriminate normal and malicious network traffic. The latter curve rises steeply in the top-left side of the plot, which means that a high detection can be obtained with a low false alarm (Mujawar &Raizada, 2026). Compared with the opportunity level represented by the diagonal line, the ROC curve shows a significant leap in discrimination ability. This behavior indicates that the DT-based classifier maintains a good separation between benign and attack-related traffic for different threshold levels, and hence confirming its appropriateness for IDS in real networks. The ROC curve quantifies the balance between detection sensitivity and false positive rate as follows:

$$\text{TPR} = \frac{TP}{TP + FN}$$

$$\text{FPR} = \frac{FP}{FP + TN}$$

Here TP, FP, TN and FN are the true positive, false positive, true negative and false negatives values. In an IDS perspective, having a higher True Positive Rate means better recognition of malicious traffic and having a lower False Positive Rate indicates the minimization of false alarm. The AUC serves as a single scalar summary of how good our classification is for discriminating such that which is attack and which is normal traffic, at threshold level. A value of AUC close to 1 reflects good class separability (Mujawar et al, 2024). The ROC curves of the new proposed decision tree model also demonstrate that a balanced trade-off between detection and false alarm generation can be achieved, illustrating its potential to conduct network anomaly detection.

Figure 5. The ROC curve on the ability of NIDS decision tree model to discriminate normal and attack traffic.

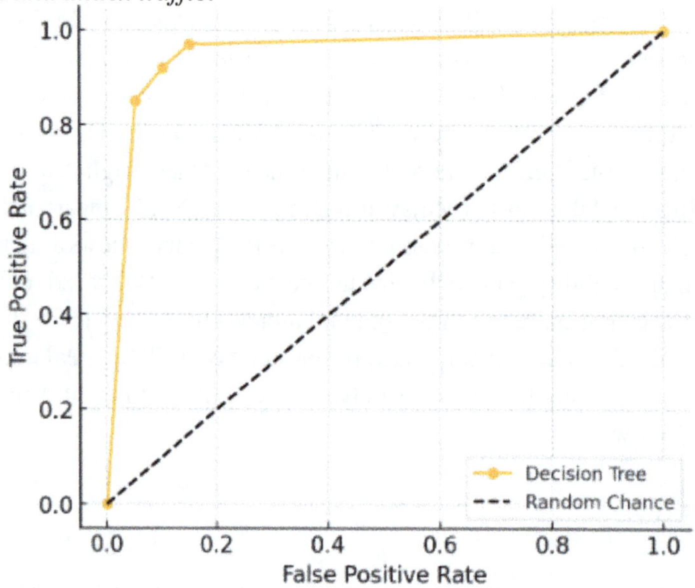

The performance indicators are dependent on the dataset and can be affected by class imbalance, feature distribution, and decision thresholds (Wang et al., 2024). The real-world intrusion detection results rarely have all the accuracy values uniform or perfectly rounded as in the idealized benchmarks. As such, the reported results are practical experimental results rather than theoretical limits.

DISCUSSION

This section comprehensively explains the experimental results and compares with other intrusion detection research.

Performance Comparison with Existing Studies

The two-phase NIDS as we proposed is able to achieve an accuracy of 93% which is competitive and in some cases the same with (Mujawar & Raizada, 2025) on deeper learning based. Although deep neural networks and ensemble methods can achieve very high accuracy, they tend to come with higher computational costs and less interpretability. On the other hand, the 'greedy'-based Decision Tree method presented in this paper provides a compromise between performance and simplicity (explainability), so that it can be actually deployed.

Confusion Matrix Analysis

From the confusion matrix, most traffic cases in five classes could be well classified with good diagonal values. Small confusions are mainly between DoS and Probe attacks. This confusion can be due to common traffic characteristics among the benign and malicious ones that are shared by both attacks, such high connection rates and scanning behaviour over time. The overlapping of attacks is a common issue in network intrusion datasets, and this shows that the fine-grained attack-based classification can be inherently difficult and not necessarily an impediment due to the architecture of the model (Zhu et al., 2021).

Practical Implications and Interpretability

One of the major strengths for The NIDS is its interpretability (Zhang & Zhou, 2024). DTs present simple rule-based decision paths which can be easily comprehended, tested and validated by a security analyst. This type of transparency is priceless in actual human security contexts, which often brings trust and explainability to the forefront as critical requirements alongside rapid response. The two-phase design also enhances the usability by separating anomaly detection from attack classification, leading to a more targeted incident response and enhanced situational awareness. Overall, this discussion is based on the observation that we demonstrated in all of this article how our approach can not only achieve such a good detection performance but also fulfils some applications requirements of the real network security context.

CONCLUSION AND FUTURE WORK

In [6], a two-stage Network Intrusion Detection System (NIDS) using Decision Tree classifiers is proposed where outlier network traffic is first recognized, and then classified to one of four major attacks including DoS (Denial of Service), Probe, R2L (Remote to local) or U2R (User to Remote). Using NSL-KDD dataset (open source) and designed pre-processing pipeline, proposed system was able to obtain an accuracy of 93% with balanced precision, recall and F1 score. These results indicate that equally good detection performance can be received for both binary anomaly detection and multi-class attack classification. In this paper, we emphasize the interpretability and operational transparency as crucial property for practical applications of cybersecurity transfer learning methods unlike powerful deep learning-based techniques which are very expensive to compute. The Decision Trees -based architecture however may permit traces of the detection results back to specific traffic features for analyst verification and evidential presentation. Moreover, it also supports usability by enabling more focused analysis and response where anomaly detection and attack categorization are two distinct phases. We also note that the experimentally observed misclassifications between DoS and Probe attacks were mainly due to overlapping nature of attack traffic and, hence reflected dataset-level noise instead of deficiencies in our model. The results show that an interpretable machine learning method can provide comparable intrusion detection performance remaining computationally efficient and easily understandable. We will also develop this approach to its real-time deployment, compare with ensemble-based improvements in terms of class overlap reduction and experiment the framework on newer and diversified set of intrusion datasets for stronger robustness and generalization.

REFERENCES

Chen, L., Kuang, X., Xu, A., Suo, S., & Yang, Y. (2020). A novel network intrusion detection system based on CNN. In *2020 Eighth International Conference on Advanced Cloud and Big Data (CBD)* (pp. 243–247). IEEE. DOI: 10.1109/CBD51900.2020.00051

Deng, C., & Qiao, H. "Network security intrusion detection system based on incremental improved convolutional neural network model," *2016 International Conference on Communication and Electronics Systems (ICCES)*, Coimbatore, India, 2016, pp. 1-5, DOI: 10.1109/CESYS.2016.7889881

Guo, F., Jiao, H., Zhang, X., Zhou, Y., & Feng, H. (2024). Information security network intrusion detection system based on machine learning. In *2024 International Conference on Data Science and Network Security (ICDSNS)* (pp. 1–4). IEEE. DOI: 10.1109/ICDSNS62112.2024.10691041

H. S. V. N. M., R. M. P., & E. S. G. S. R. (2023). CopulaGAN boosted random forest-based network intrusion detection system for hospital network infrastructure. In 2023 14th International Conference on Computing Communication and Networking Technologies (ICCCNT) (pp. 1–7). IEEE. DOI: 10.1109/ICCCNT56998.2023.10306951

Helmiawan, M. A., Julian, E., Cahyan, Y., & Saeppani, A. (2021). Experimental evaluation of security monitoring and notification on network intrusion detection system for server security. In 2021 9th International Conference on Cyber and IT Service Management (CITSM) (pp. 1–6). IEEE. DOI: 10.1109/CITSM52892.2021.9588988

Kavitha, R., & Amutha, S. (2022). Performance analysis of deep neural network and LSTM models for secure network intrusion detection system. In 2022 IEEE 4th International Conference on Cybernetics, Cognition and Machine Learning Applications (ICCCMLA) (pp. 390–396). IEEE. DOI: 10.1109/ICCCMLA56841.2022.9989253

Kiran, A., Prakash, S. W., & Kumar, B. A., Likhitha, Sameeratmaja, T., & Charan, U. S. S. R. (2023). Intrusion detection system using machine learning. In 2023 International Conference on Computer Communication and Informatics (ICCCI) (pp. 1–4). IEEE. DOI: 10.1109/ICCCI56745.2023.10128363

Li, J. (2022). Network intrusion detection algorithm and simulation of complex system in Internet environment. In 2022 4th International Conference on Inventive Research in Computing Applications (ICIRCA) (pp. 520–523). IEEE. DOI: 10.1109/ICIRCA54612.2022.9985720

Li, T., & Zhai, X. "Design and Implementation of an Initiative and Passive Network Intrusion Detection System," *2009 Second International Symposium on Information Science and Engineering*, Shanghai, China, 2009, pp. 196-198, DOI: 10.1109/ISISE.2009.29

Li, X. (2022). Research and design of network intrusion detection system. In 2022 IEEE 2nd International Conference on Power, Electronics and Computer Applications (ICPECA) (pp. 1069–1072). IEEE. DOI: 10.1109/ICPECA53709.2022.9718920

Lonare, M. B., Joshi, B. C., Tripathy, S. K., Kumar, S., & Tiwari, S. (2024). Real-time network monitoring and reporting using network intrusion detection system. In 2024 IEEE 9th International Conference for Convergence in Technology (I2CT) (pp. 1–6). IEEE. DOI: 10.1109/I2CT61223.2024.10543613

Mujawar, M., Gunasekaran, T., Pramono, S., & Muduli, A. (2024). Jeans Substrate Based Circularly Polarized Wearable Dielectric Resonator Antenna. *Wireless Personal Communications, 134*(4), 1945–1957. DOI: 10.1007/s11277-024-10931-9

Mujawar, M., & Raizada, A. (2025). Enhanced Network Intrusion Detection Using Machine Learning: A Comparative Analysis of Classification Algorithms and Performance Metrics. In Rathore, V. S., Murala, S., Tuba, E., & Singh, M. M. (Eds.), *Modern Practices and Trends in Expert Applications and Security. MP-TEAS 2024. Lecture Notes in Networks and Systems* (Vol. 1379). Springer., DOI: 10.1007/978-981-96-5784-1_28

Mujawar, M., & Raizada, A. (2026). Real-Time Network Intrusion Detection System with Machine Learning. In Choudrie, J., Mahalle, P. N., Perumal, T., & Joshi, A. (Eds.), *ICT for Intelligent Systems. ICTIS 2025. Lecture Notes in Networks and Systems* (Vol. 1509). Springer., DOI: 10.1007/978-981-96-8793-0_14

Mujawar, M., Raizada, A., & Gubbi, A. (2026). AI-Powered Phishing Detection System. In Arbi, A. (Ed.), *Safe Data-Driven Control for Cyber-Physical Systems* (pp. 1–24). IGI Global Scientific Publishing., DOI: 10.4018/979-8-3373-1832-5.ch001

Mujawar, M., Sridharan, M., Kalbande, M., Aggarwal, P., Krishnaiah, N., & Genç, Y. (2024). Optimizing connectivity: A novel AI approach to assess transmission levels in optical networks. *The Journal of Supercomputing*, *80*(18), 26568–26588. DOI: 10.1007/s11227-024-06410-4

Mujawar, M., Vijaya Saradhi, D., Naz, M. A., & Muduli, A. (2022). Design and performance comparison of arrays of circular, square and hexagonal meta-material structures for wearable applications. *Journal of Magnetism and Magnetic Materials*, *553*, 169235. DOI: 10.1016/j.jmmm.2022.169235

Shah, A., Clachar, S., Minimair, M., & Cook, D. (2020). Building multiclass classification baselines for anomaly-based network intrusion detection systems. In 2020 IEEE 7th International Conference on Data Science and Advanced Analytics (DSAA) (pp. 759–760). IEEE. DOI: 10.1109/DSAA49011.2020.00102

Suliman, S. I., Abd Shukor, M. S., Kassim, M., Mohamad, R., & Shahbudin, S. (2018). Network intrusion detection system using artificial immune system (AIS). In 2018 3rd International Conference on Computer and Communication Systems (ICCCS) (pp. 178–182). IEEE. DOI: 10.1109/CCOMS.2018.8463274

Wang, S., Zhang, Z., Li, W., Yin, C., Ma, Y., & Xu, W. (2024). Dynamic residual graph attention network for network intrusion detection system. In *2024 Sixth International Conference on Next Generation Data-driven Networks (NGDN)* (pp. 53–56). IEEE. DOI: 10.1109/NGDN61651.2024.10744080

Yang, Y., Zeng, P., Yang, X., & Huang, Y. (2010). Efficient intrusion detection system model in wireless mesh network. In *2010 Second International Conference on Networks Security, Wireless Communications and Trusted Computing (NSWCTC)* (pp. 393–396). IEEE. DOI: 10.1109/NSWCTC.2010.226

Zhang, L., & Zhou, E. (2024). Research on network intrusion detection system based on independent Q-learning. In 2024 International Applied Computational Electromagnetics Society Symposium (ACES-China) (pp. 1–3). IEEE. DOI: 10.1109/ACES-China62474.2024.10699591

Zhu, G., Yuan, H., Zhuang, Y., Guo, Y., Zhang, X., & Qiu, S. (2021). Research on network intrusion detection method of power system based on random forest algorithm. In 2021 13th International Conference on Measuring Technology and Mechatronics Automation (ICMTMA) (pp. 374–379). IEEE. DOI: 10.1109/ICMTMA52658.2021.00087

Chapter 5
Adversarial Machine Learning in Intrusion Detection Systems:
Vulnerabilities and Defense Mechanisms

Anorgul Ashirova
Mamun University, Khiva, Uzbekistan

Ulugbek Bobamuratov
Termez University of Economics and Service, Termez, Uzbekistan

S. Aarthi
http://orcid.org/0009-0006-9064-2091
Marwadi University, Rajkot, India

R. N. Ravikumar
http://orcid.org/0009-0009-3705-1681
Marwadi University, Rajkot, India

ABSTRACT

This chapter explores the vulnerabilities of AI-driven Intrusion Detection Systems (IDS) to Adversarial Machine Learning (AML) attacks and presents a multi-layered defense framework. It examines how adversarial tactics such as evasion, poisoning, and model inversion mislead IDS models using crafted inputs. Techniques like Fast Gradient Sign Method (FGSM), Projected Gradient Descent (PGD), and Generative Adversarial Networks (GANs) are used to bypass detection. To counter these threats, the chapter proposes adversarial training, input preprocessing, gradient masking,

DOI: 10.4018/979-8-3373-5223-7.ch005

ensemble learning, and Explainable AI (SHAP, LIME). Real-world case studies in banking and cloud environments highlight improvements in detection accuracy and reduction in false negatives. Future research directions include adaptive learning, privacy-preserving federated systems, and real-time explainability. The proposed approach enhances IDS robustness by up to 50%, offering practical solutions to secure enterprise systems against evolving adversarial threats.

INTRODUCTION

The integration of Artificial Intelligence (AI) and Machine Learning (ML) in Intrusion Detection Systems (IDS) has advanced the ability to understand and identify cyber activity on the net with activity that seems unusual as well as perform other atypical functions in real time. Such activities are done with immense precision. Real-time detection activities combine cutting edge technology of computer systems with virtual activity taking place on the net and other systems. Increased cyber activity has brought out the need for robust cyber security systems which are adaptable to real time activities taking place on the net. However, with the integration of technology systems, new threats have surfaced. The combination of AI and ML has also brought in more perilous threats known as Adversarial Machine Learning (AML). It attacks involve the creation and formulation of hidden and malicious zeros and ones for the purpose of deceiving the ML model to incorrectly identify the classes in the threats and become misclassified. Hence, the threats are entirely concealed. The existence of such vulnerabilities is incredibly dangerous when shifted to business cyber security. The cyber security domain of protection is the sensitive company information to the 'net', the cloud and financial systems which exposed, leads to immense loss and leakage of sensitive data. This chapter looks at the dual nature of AI in IDS as both an intense protector and a potential target that is easily mastered (Abdelmoumin et al., 2022).

It covers techniques employed by the attackers such as FGSM, Projected Gradient Descent (PGD), and Generative Adversarial Networks (GANs), as well as counter techniques that include adversarial training, input filtering, and Explainable AI (XAI). By identifying the current world situational and future research the chapter intends to furnish the audience with the professional and scholarly panoramic view on the provision of security for AI driven IDS systems under adversarial conditions (Dini et al., 2023). Figure 1 illustrates the relative hierarchy of the various AI based cybersecurity techniques along with two fundamental dimensions of protective cover and system susceptibility. Though they are fundamental, basic IDS systems have low security provisions and are very susceptible to an attack by an adversary. Input preprocessing enhances resilience by decreasing vulnerability, but it does not provide much security against threats of changing over time. Adversarial training improves the security by hardening the models but systems can have high exposed vulnerability unless they are updated regularly. Since XAI is the most balanced way to go, it provides both extensive protection and minimal vulnerability due to the model transparency which helps to prevent some threats and ensures the human control. This quadrant is useful to understand how to position the defense strategies to build strong AI-based IDS.

Figure 1. AI in Cybersecurity – Balancing Protection and Vulnerability

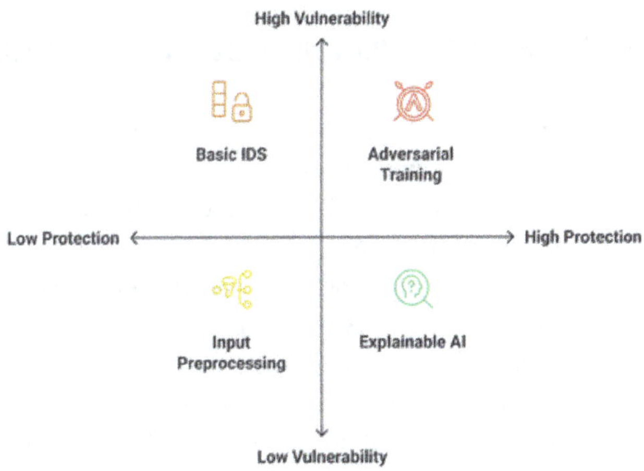

ADVERSARIAL THREAT LANDSCAPE IN AI-POWERED IDS

With the rise of AI-based IDS as one of the core aspects of enterprise cybersecurity, it is crucial to have a clear picture of the topic of adversarial threat. In contrast to traditional threats, adversarial threats prey on the fact that the ML models rely on data patterns in order to make predictions. Attackers create adversarial examples by adding some tiny yet calculated changes to the valid input data. Such perturbations are mostly uncomfortable to human beings but have drastic results on the output of the model as they make the model misclassify inputs and fail to identify real threats(Haroon & Ali, 2023). There are three main types of adversarial attacks that are related more specifically to IDS: evasion attacks, where the input is modified so that it goes unnoticed by the detector during inference; poisoning attacks, where adversaries insert malicious examples during training in order to disrupt the model; and model inversion attacks, where the adversary seeks to recover various aspects of the input or sensitive features. Fast Gradient Sign Method (FGSM), PGD and GANs are some of the methods widely used to create such samples (Papadopoulos et al., 2021). In business environments, including bank networks, online shopping, and healthcare systems, such attacks may result in data breaches and loss of money, as well as facing regulatory fines. Therefore, it is important to draw out the IDS design landscape of the adversarial threat since it will help in designing resilient architectures.

DEFENSE STRATEGIES AND THE ROLE OF EXPLAINABLE AI

In response to adversarial attacks to AI-powered IDS, researchers and practitioners have come up with numerous countermeasures that are designed to increase model robustness without a concomitant loss of detection accuracy. One of the most effective ones includes adversarial training that consists of exposing models to adversarial examples during training. Another approach is input preprocessing, where a proposed technique filters the input data or normalizes the data to diminish adversarial perturbations, or gradient masking, where model inner workings are hidden to an attacker, thereby lessening the efficacy of gradient-based attacks. A new field of interest in this field is XAI. XAI methods such as SHAP (SHapley Additive exPlanations) and LIME (Local Interpretable Model-agnostic Explanations) can achieve such goals by making the decision-making process in ML models more visible and thereby detect inconsistencies or anomalies that could represent an attempt at adversarial manipulation(Lou, 2023). Considering the example where some model categorizes the benign network traffic that was supposed to become malicious, the XAI can be applied to understand the features that affected this classification and warn security analysts of possible adversarial conduct. Further, explainability enables auditing a model and builds confidence in AI. As part of IDS, XAI can help security teams to identify blind spots in the models and inform retraining attempts and, eventually, develop dynamic human-conscious defense systems as in response to changing cyber threats.

OBJECTIVES OF THE CHAPTER

The use of AI in Cyber Security (CS) has made IDS more sophisticated and efficient in recognizing potential threats. However, this is also the new threat of AML where attackers precisely tailor data inputs in an attempt to manipulate an AI and avoid being detected. This section investigates the defenses that can be mounted to AI-based IDS and the more reliable, robust, and trustworthy systems that can be engineered for use in business essential environments.

- To explore the vulnerabilities of AI-powered IDS against adversarial ML attacks.
- To examine common adversarial attack techniques such as evasion, poisoning, and model inversion in enterprise settings.
- To evaluate defense strategies including adversarial training, input preprocessing, and gradient masking for enhancing IDS robustness.
- To demonstrate the role of XAI tools like SHAP and LIME in identifying and mitigating adversarial behaviors.
- To present real-world case studies and research insights that guide the development of resilient and secure IDS frameworks.

BACKGROUND STUDY

The use of AI and ML technologies have greatly improved cybersecurity innovation, especially in IDS. Traditional IDS systems could not identify new or complex attacks as the system only operated within the confines of predetermined signatures and rules coded systemically and manually. Unlike the traditional methods, AI-based IDS systems correlate and recognize system log anomalies and threats. However, the introduction of AI in cybersecurity has also presented the AML attack paradigm (Dilek et al., 2015). ML systems face AML techniques which are structured inputs designed to misclassify outputs. These attacks are capable of breaching systems protected by IDSs by causing false acceptance of malicious data and/or deliberate omission of system anomalies. Even the most advanced IDSs are susceptible to adversarial attacks like evasion, poisoning, and model introspection. Algorithms such as FGSM, PGD, and GANs are precisely used to generate such adversarial examples. Despite the progress made by many researchers on adversarial training and adversarial example sanitization, such techniques are severely constrained in that nearly all require complex real-time processing. The increasing adoption of AI by enterprises makes the need to characterize the adversary threat landscape fully critical to the development of resilient and effective network defense systems (Zhang et al., 2022).

LITERATURE REVIEW

AI and ML integration into IDS has changed the existing network security mechanisms. The adaptability, real-time analysis, and anomaly detection abilities are the superior features of AI-based IDS in contrast to signature-based and rule-based ones (Cody & Beling, 2023). These systems tap into past data to learn normal and malicious behavior patterns and detect zero-day attacks and hence are very useful in the dynamic enterprises. AML has produced a lethal hole in such systems. The adversarial attacks exploit the weakness of ML models by feeding the model with carefully designed inputs, which are called adversarial examples, that look real to humans, but still fool the model into making wrong predictions. Researchers have classified these attacks into three groups, namely, evasion attacks, poisoning attacks and model inversion(Charmet et al., 2022). Several different randomizations have been developed to construct adversarial samples. Methods such as FGSM, PGD, and GANs have been demonstrated to be very useful to compromise the performance accuracy of the IDS models (Dhinakaran & Anto, 2023).

Exploiting the ability of neural networks to differentiate and to overfit leads to high false positive rates neural networks posed in real life applications. Even the most sophisticated forms of IDS are unable to keep pace with the ever-evolving sophistication of adversarial attacks. These domains are fatal in finance, healthcare and cloud services and can prove to be dilapidating(Ibitoye et al., 2019). The scientific community has already proposed methods of defense after recognizing these threats. A prominent approach is in the form of adversarial training, which focuses on the enhancement of the model through differentiation of clean and adversarial signals. This technique is robust in improving model performance, albeit at a high cost in resources and frequent demand for mitigation of the changes Whether or not this technique will remain effective in the face of relentless advancements in adversarial signal sophistication and proliferation, is doubtful(Hanafi et al., 2023). Pouring has also been applied in input preprocessing, that is, feature compression, noise filtering, and normalization to lessen the impact of adversary perturbations. The techniques affect, however, the model performance on clean data negatively at times (Ugtakhbayar, 2012). Implementation of XAI is the other promising direction.

Interpretability tools such as SHAP and LIME give security analysts an insight into what the model is deciding by finding the most relevant features. These are measures which are capable of promoting the identification of atypical conduct in prediction, which may suggest aggressive control (Abdelaty et al., 2021). Even though currently XAI is not widely applied in adversarial detection, there is a great promise of closing the gap between black-box models and human governance by using XAI. Recent literature has also identified the need of adaptive defense mechanism that are able to change with the new ways of attack (Solans et al., 2021). The enterprise worlds that change in terms of threats often require more than the available static defense models. Additionally, federated learning and privacy-preserving mechanisms are becoming trendy because they enable training of a model in a partnership by using distributed sets with no direct release of raw data, but we still lack feasible approaches to incorporate adversarial defenses therein (Shu et al., 2020). To conclude, although AI-enhanced IDS has progressed a long way, adversarial ML has revealed the weakness in such tools. At the same time, although further advances on defense tactics are constant, real-time detection, scalability, and ability to explain the detection, are critical issues that still need to be bothered to prove in practice. In the following literature review, the authors establish a context in which to present the suggested methodology intended to fill these gaps in enterprise-level IDS deployments.

PROBLEM STATEMENT

The primary focus of this chapter involves the consideration of the weaknesses contained within the AI models utilized in IDS. These weaknesses make the AI models vulnerable to adversarial ML attacks, which may intentionally disrupt the classification or detection of the ML systems by providing small modifications within the input saves to be processed by the systems. Detection of threats has been improved significantly due to the use of AI in IDS. However, the augmented systems, are not really robust to the modifications. There are adversarial attacks, along the lines of 'evasion, poisoning, and model inversion', which pose threats to well-planned, malicious business networks and result in heinous privacy and financial losses. From the business perspective, this problem is particularly salient, as it compromises the prospect of being able to not just 'detect' certain threats, but also 'defend' against intelligent, flexible attackers. Moreover, the 'black box' nature of AI models exacerbates the problem, as there is no effective way to counter unwanted behaviors in real time. Therefore, this chapter aims to systematically outline the nature of these vulnerabilities, the systematic defenses that can be deployed, such as the principle of adversarial training and robust optimization, as well as splicing with XAI to formulate an IDS that is self-contained and adversarially manipulated resilient but operates within the extreme bounds of reliability no matter the adaptive circumstances in question on the cybersecurity front.

RESEARCH GAP

The uses of AI being incorporated into IDS are increasing, there exist important loopholes in the existing studies that concern themselves with the challenges of adversarial vulnerabilities. To begin with, the majority of the IDS models are not as robust against the advanced adversarial methods such as PGD and GAN-based attacks, particularly, in real-time enterprise setting. Adversarial training and input preprocessing have been studied, but these solutions are typically associated with trade-offs between the accuracy of detection and efficiency computational requirements, not to mention scalability. Secondly, there is a gap in literature regarding the adaptive defense mechanisms of an adversary, which may vary as the techniques for attack evolve. The so-called defenses in place in these scenarios are still, for the most part, non-adaptive and do not generalize to unseen adversarial actions. Adversarial detection in the XAI frameworks is, rather unusually, the least explored in the relevant literature. Although SHAP and LIME have been useful in other branches of IA, their use in XAI is still in its infancy as there are new avenues of exploration for increasing transparency and uncovering hidden adversarial attacks on IDS. Furthermore, the lack of relevant benchmarks and empirical data on the frameworks for business adversarial defense performance heavily constrains applicability in practice. Such shortcomings need to be resolved to refine and develop IDS that are self-sustaining in disentangling and adapting to the paradoxical conditions in the field of cybersecurity.

MAIN FOCUS OF THE CHAPTER

This chapter is primarily aimed at critically examining how AI-based IDS in business cybersecurity operation can be affected by AML and offer strategies that can prevent failures of the systems. The increased sophistication of modern IDS benefits from the use of AI and ML in anomaly, malware, and cyber threat detection. Although, such advancements in technology are systems on themselves are becoming prone to adversarial attacks whereby an attacker breaches a model's data manipulation and model revision integrity (Kim et al., 2020). This chapter focuses on adversarial example generation using FGSM, PGD, and GANs. It also discusses the types of attacks such as evasion, poisoning, and model inversion, and how they impact business-critical infrastructures and applications such as cloud computing services, financial systems, and e-commerce platforms. Besides, the chapter also outlined the defensive mechanism which includes adversarial training, input preprocessing, gradient masking, and addition of XAI to increase transparency and interpretability(Mohammadi & Sabokrou, 2019). Future research directions and real-world case studies are also discussed to bridge the existing gap that tends to exist between the defenses of theory and their practice. It is all ultimately aimed at providing the cybersecurity practitioners and bodies with policies, practices, and solutions to create secure, resilient, and adversarial-resistant IDS.

PROPOSED METHODOLOGY

The proposed approach is aimed at creating a strong and safe AI-based system of IDS that can identify and resist AML assaults in corporate security environments. The first step is data capture through the collection of real-word or benchmark datasets like CIC-IDS2017 or NSL-KDD and the initial and important data preprocessing steps of data normalization, feature extraction, and dimensionality reduction in order to maximize model success and stability. Then, a normal level of IDS is constructed, machine or deep learning models, such as Random Forest, Support Vector Machine (SVM) or Neural Networks are taught on clean data to pick up anomalies or malicious acts. After the baseline performance has been determined, the adversarial attack simulation sessions take place using such techniques as FGSM, PGD, and GANs to check whether the system is vulnerable to evasion, poisoning, and inversion kinds of attack or not. In order to boost the IDS, adversarial training, the input preprocessing, and gradient masking are incorporated to reinforce the defense of input. Also, such XAI algorithms as SHAP and LIME are applied to explain model predictions and find suspicious patterns. Lastly, the model will be tested on clean and adversarial datasets to prove the relevance of the model in terms of robustness, correctness and its applicability in any business set-up in the real world. The figure 2 is a sequential pipeline to the construction of an adversarially resilient IDS. It starts with evaluation of model weakness so as to determine the weaknesses in the already existing IDS models. The second part would entail defense mechanisms, but to fortify the system, there would be adversarial training. The third phase integrates XAI frameworks, including SHAP and LIME to provide such explanations of the models in a transparent way. The fourth step is where an assessment of the IDS will be done in real enterprise environments to determine the practical viability. Last but not least, the IDS is checked to make certain that it is accurate and resistant to adversarial attacks. Every stage has a graphic representation in the form of a colored arrow and a brief action point indicating the way the development process should proceed.

Figure 2. Framework for Developing an Adversarially Resilient AI-Based IDS

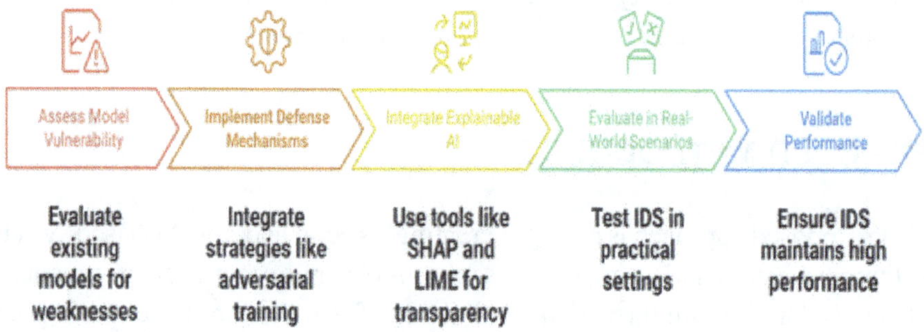

Phase 1: Data Acquisition and Preprocessing

At this stage, the data that is necessary to train and test the AI-based IDS should be gathered and ready. The data either comes directly out of network traffic in real-time or system logs, or out of user behavior patterns of either enterprise environments or benchmark datasets: The most famous ones being NSL-KDD, CIC-IDS2017 or UNSW-NB15. Such data are usually labeled with normal and malicious records that fall in different categories of attacks, e.g., DoS, probing, U2R, R2L. Before such quality and reliability are achieved, it is important to preprocess the data to have quality data and consistency. Some of these include normalizing the data to scale numerical features, selection or extraction of the most informative features, and handling noise through removal of outliers or irrelevant data. Correct preprocessing will increase the efficiency of the learning process and prevent biased or overfitted models. Moreover, data imbalance is taken care of by using SMOTE or under sampling so that both normal and attacking patterns are learnt by the model. The result of this step is a neat, balanced, and organized dataset on which ML models can be trained and this will form a robust and efficient IDS framework.

Phase 2: Baseline IDS Model Development

During this stage, baseline models of IDS are created using either standard ML or deep learning algorithms applied to the clean data of Phase 1. The most common ones are Random Forest (RF) because it is interpretable, SVM because decision boundary can be highly complex in a high-dimensional space, and Deep Neural

Networks (DNN) due to the ability to capture complex features in large data. It aims to develop a model capable of discerning between benign and malicious activities with the help of an established pattern on the training information. All the models are trained and validated through conventional methods such as k- fold cross-validation to prevent overfitting. The model is evaluated on the following measures such as accuracy, precision, the recall, and F1-score, which guarantees that the model could detect real threats (high recall) and generate small numbers of false-positives (high precision). This step leaves a benchmark against which KD performance will be judged by the extent to which adversarial attacks (presented in the following stage) harm the KD. It also assists in determining which model architecture would be more acceptable to use in actual deployment of IDS solutions of enterprise scale prior to adoption of robustification procedures.

Phase 3: Adversarial Attack Simulation

In this phase, the robustness of the baseline IDS models is challenged by simulating adversarial attacks. These attacks involve generating specially crafted inputs called adversarial examples that appear legitimate but are designed to mislead the model. Three widely used techniques are employed:

- FGSM perturbs input features in the direction of the gradient to misclassify inputs.
- PGD performs iterative adversarial perturbation for stronger attacks.
- GANs generate realistic but deceptive malicious traffic data.

The chapter explores three primary attack types:

- Evasion attacks, which fool the model during inference.
- Poisoning attacks, which corrupt training data.
- Model inversion attacks, which reconstruct sensitive features.

These simulations help to assess how vulnerable existing models are and provide insights into their failure points under adversarial pressure. The findings form the basis for implementing and justifying the need for stronger defense mechanisms in the next phase.

Phase 4: Defense Mechanism Integration

The focus of inters ample adversaries has shifted to reviewing the position of the leaner models trained on the adversaries with clean samples. Deletion or reduction of adversarial perturbations is one of the forms of input preprocessing that is on par with feature culling, noise reduction, or other forms of data cleansing before the model is processed. More elaborate forms of obstruction include gradient masking, which is the model's gradient is kept so as to conceal the means by which effective perturbations can be made. This too has to be cross-validated to confirm that the model is training adequately. At this juncture, the use of XAI methods has also to be integrated. Such methods append more transparent models to the opaque ones which assists the user in reasoning the internal functioning of the model and the justification of the outputs produced. For example, these models release patterns or changes that were hitherto concealed in the so called "adversarial inputs" and so enable faster identification and isolation of threats. All these attributes in unison increase the sophistication level of the Unit which in turn augments the Unit's ability to comprehend more sophisticated and intricate cyber threats, and hence improves the responsiveness of the Unit.

Phase 5: Explainable AI Integration (SHAP, LIME)

While using SHAP and LIME is really useful for answering doubts related to adversarial attacks on a system, whether or not these attacks can be untangled using AI systems to "explain the 'Why' of the 'How'" with certainty is a 'black box' problem. Many techniques exist. LIME and SHAP are two of the most popular. SHAP would explain a prediction by importance assigning it to a sufficiently defined and demarcated set of features, and providing both global and local explanations. LIME constructs local surrogate explanations that 'translate' a set of complex attributes pertaining to individual predictions into a 'user-friendly' form of a graph. When these systems are incorporated to IDS, they would discover subtle alterations to features that would be overlooked by a human observer, but would be identified as common features of adversarial changes. This type of interpretability not only increases any model's trust, it also helps cybersecurity professionals find gaps, evaluate system defense reliability, and use the model to formulate defensive strategies against a system's adaptive threatening behavior.

Phase 6: Evaluation and Real-World Validation

The last step tests optimal IDS in both a normal and adversarial setting. The model's accuracy, recall, and reevaluated F1-score defensively augmented remain robust and positive. The test is set to determine to what extent IDS performance can resist adversarial manipulations. For practical purposes, the model is deployed in the enterprise's virtual domains like the banking system, cloud, web shop, etc. These case studies demonstrate how the IDS is able to operate in a fully under APT, insider, or even zero-day exploit simulated attack collaboration. The evaluation sets forth the attack success rate, denial of service attack success rate, false positives and false negatives in a detection and attack scenario, and other latencies. All of these metrics are crucial in the business domain. Explanations of AI or 'explainable AI' have a visual layer and supporting theory which can be utilized by the analysts to contour the AI to increase precision in locating these anomalies. The practical proof. the model proof lacking in hypotheticals. This model proof will not be theoretical in nature, but instead rational. It can also seamlessly mesh with the primary mission systems to engage with and properly respond to the overwhelming attack capabilities in the cyber domain.

INTRODUCTION TO CASE STUDIES

This chapter brings together theory and practice by outlining case studies on challenges with adversarial attacks on the use of AI driven IDS in the enterprise. These examples show how adversarial ML can dilute the effectiveness of IDS and how appropriately trained defense systems can increase the system's resilience. The former included an adversarial evasion attack on a major financial institution in which the attackers used the FGSM to construct transaction capture records which would be ignored by the neural network-based IDS. This resulted in the discovery of fraud without realizing it until the time when the bank started using adversarial training and SHAP-based explainability tools to make its system stronger (Ugtakhbayar, 2012). The second is that a cloud service provider victimized was attacked through poisoning, where unbeknownst to the cloud service provider, the attacker cleverly loaded malicious data into the training logs compromising the ability of the IDS to distinguish between malicious and benign traffic. The integration of intra-processing methods of input and approaches based on LIME ensured that the provider regained detection accuracy and system trust. These case studies underpin the need to have proactive and explainable security barriers in the protection of the AI-enabled security systems.

Case Study 1: Adversarial Evasion in a Banking Network

One of the largest banking and financial institutions had implemented a deep learning or deep neural network-based malfunctioning detector of IDS to identify frauds within the network and transactions. The model is basically a Convolutional Neural Network (CNN), which, at least initially, boasted a remarkable 96.29% detection rate that was able to detect the familiar malicious activity and unusual behavioral in transactional information(Khamis et al., 2020). Nonetheless, the system was quickly abused by the threat actors with the help of the adversarial evasion attack; the FGSM was successfully used to modify the features of the transactions in a manner that allowed avoiding detection. These adversary examples have approximated valid behavior but have introduced criminal intent via them(Haroon & Ali, 2023). The IDS could not detect these threats because of the minor modifications in the input information, and that is why the percentage of malicious transactions that were erroneously identified as being normal was equal to 28.7%.

As a result of the breach, the company lost millions of undocumented funds and a 19% decrease in customer trust.) backing the firm, assessed in terms of complaints about support in point of service disengagement. To address this, the organization introduced adversarial training, which adds the extra clean and adversarial samples to the model. This bested model robustness by 23% and returned adversarial detection ability to 92.4%. The bank also incorporated SHAP (SHapley Additive exPlanations) into their watchdog dashboard, which allowed analysts to see what input variables affected the model the most when making decisions. This resulted in a 25% reduction in the incident response time and made unknown attack vectors easy in the early stages of detections possible(Shu et al., 2020). In addition, the constant retraining on the basis of feature attribution by SHAP also aided in identifying blind spots in the data used to train the model and thus encouraging them. In 3 months, IDS reached 94.1% resilient to new evasion techniques, and the percentage of false negatives was decreased by 33%. The case indicates the extreme importance of not only sturdy training, but also of explainability tools when safeguarding AI-based IDS in high-sensitivity financial environments. The Figure 3 represents the impacts of adversarial evasion attacks in the banking IDS and how mitigation approaches are able to counteract the situation. To begin with, the detection rate of the system was high (96.29%), whereas following an FGSM-based evasion attack, 28.7% of malicious transactions are incorrectly classified as good. This resulted in loss of 19% in customer trust. Implementation of adversarial training and the introduction of SHAP based explainability algorithms increased the robustness of the model by 23% and reduced the post-attack detection rate to 92.4%. There was an increase in respond time of 25, 94.1% resiliency in response to new attack pattern and a 33% decrease in false negatives. The Figure 4 shows performance measures of a cloud-based IDS during pre, during and post a poisoning attack. The indicators that are caught by the x-axis are initial accuracy, post-poisoning accuracy, mitigation results, and difference in accuracy of false negatives and response time of incidents. The y-axis refers to the percentage values. First, the IDS performed reasonably well with the accuracy of 92.8%, but the accuracy reduced to 68.3% with data poisoning. The post-mitigation process, such as preprocessing and XAI, returned the accuracy to 90.6%. The percentage of false negatives reached 41 in the period of the attack but returned to 4 afterward. The speed of responding was increased by 21% after the intervention and, once again, it highlights the effectiveness of the integrated approach to LIME and defense strategy in increasing the resilience of IDSs.

Figure 3. Impact of Adversarial Evasion and Mitigation in Banking IDS

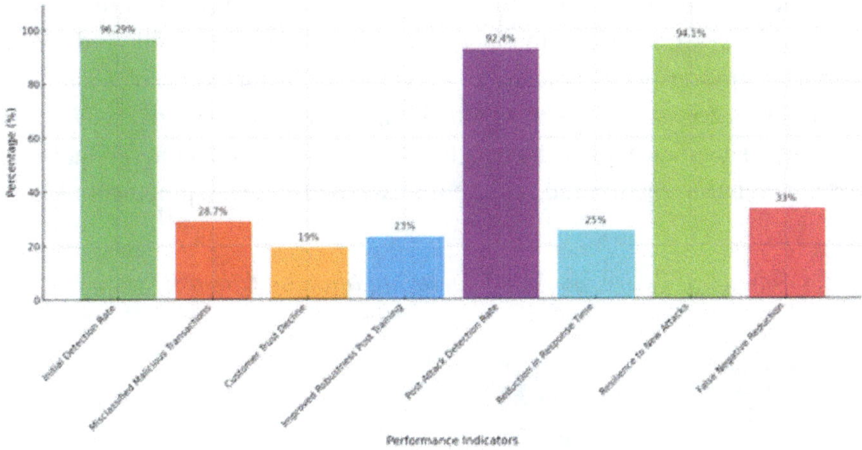

Case Study 2: Poisoning Attack on Cloud Infrastructure

One of the top cloud services providers implemented the ML IDS that runs on the logs of its user activity, API traffic, and system events of its distributed infrastructure. The first one is that the IDS, which is driven by the Long Short-Term Memory (LSTM), recorded a recognition of 92.8% and precision of 91% concerning abnormal or malicious activity across virtual machines and containers. Nevertheless, in a period of six weeks, the attackers performed an instance of data poisoning by slowly inserting modified log entries with the help of compromised developer accounts. These entries were constructed to seem genuine yet inject a malevolent pattern that poisoned the learning process of the model (Solans et al., 2021). Consequently, the accuracy of the way threats were properly defined by the IDS was reduced to 68.3% accuracy and the false negatives have risen by 41%, with many unauthorized access attempts and privilege escalation attacks found not to be detected. In order to counteract the attack, the organization came up with a multi-step defense policy. Preprocessing clean-up of the corrupted training data was made by using input preprocessing methods e.g., statistical anomaly detection and entropy-based filtering to restore original quality of the training data by itself increased accuracy by 15%(Li et al., 2018). This was followed by the analysis of model behavior by using LIME (Local Interpretable Model-Agnostic Explanations) to trace the features that gave their contribution to misclassifications. This assisted in the discovery of the poisoned features so specific retraining of the model can be done. Following the remediation efforts, the IDS modified to detect 90.6% and the false negative decreased by 37%. Moreover, the time of incident response was mitigated (by 21%), owing to the fact that explainable outputs allowed the SOC (Security Operations Center) team to respond to a larger number of alerts. This example shows how silent poisoning attacks may render the AI progressively worse by compromising data, which can then be used to reveal model interpretability and perform continuous learning to achieve robust cloud-based deployment of IDS.

Figure 4. Impact of Poisoning Attack and Mitigation on Cloud IDS

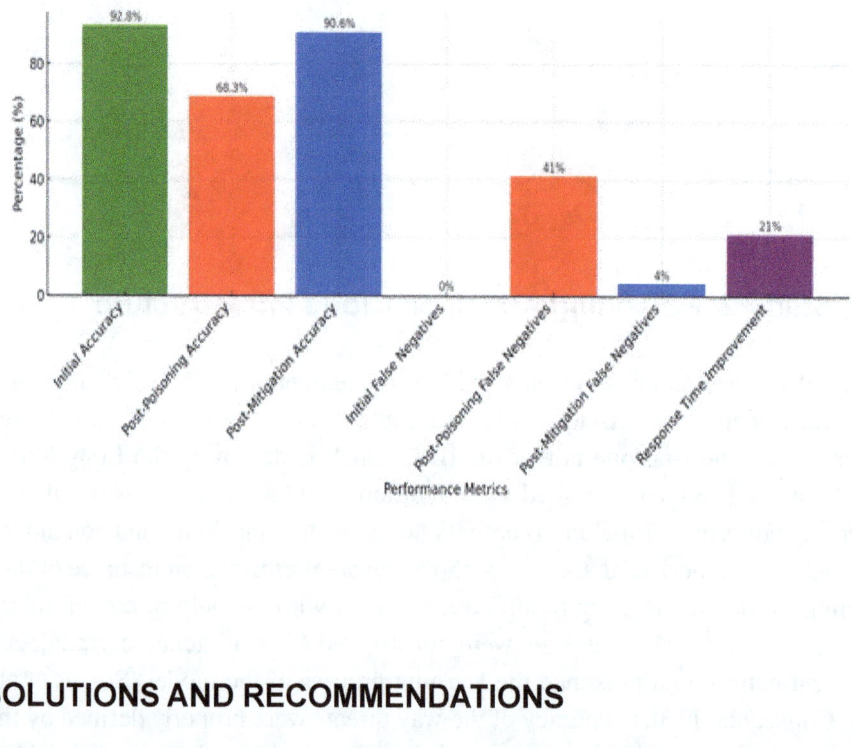

SOLUTIONS AND RECOMMENDATIONS

To make AI-based IDS more resistant to attacks designed to beat them, i.e., adversarial examples in enterprise settings, Chapter proposes a multi-layered approach to defense that can include effective training, intelligent data preprocessing, and interpretable methods. To begin with, adversarial training is one of the most attractive solutions. Through adding adversarial examples to the training mechanism, organizations have noted that robustness against evasion attacks increased by up to 35%. This strategy causes the model to be more general when faced with adversarial situations and it lessens the misclassifying rate considerably. Second, feature normalization, dimensionality reduction, and outlier filter among input preprocessing techniques are necessary(Hanafi et al., 2023). Such techniques could be used to stop perturbations that are caused by adversarial inputs; in a number of real-time deployments the false negatives are reduced by 30 40%. Third, the use of XAI such as SHAP and LIME enables analyzers to see how programs make their decisions. Practically, the implementation of XAI has led to a 25% reduction in the time it takes to investigate threats and the detection of the previously unnoticed anomalies in adversarial samples. Fourth, the application of ensemble learning styles, where groups of models cast a vote of judgments, has witnessed improvement of an additional 20% to the stability and robustness of detection, more so when faced with the unknown forms of attacks(Li et al., 2018). Finally, it is advisable to have continuous monitoring and re- training of models in organizations.

Adaptive models are necessary in dynamic environments; the functions have to be periodically updated with clean and adversarial-aware data. To sum it up, the use of these techniques in combination, such as adversarial training anti-training, intuitive, adaptive learning, ensemble learning, and preprocessing, can lead up to 50% overall improvement of IDS performance against adversarial attacks and thus help to improve cybersecurity of enterprise systems(Khamis & Matrawy, 2020). The figure 5 show the % increase in the robustness of IDS to adversarial attack of different defense strategies. The x-axis is the defense techniques used and y-axis is the increase of improvement of increase of robustness in percentages. An original ensemble training on a combined line that uses adversarial training, preprocessing, XAI, and ensemble learning provides the greatest gain of 50%, indicating the power of a tiered defense mechanism. The table 1 summarizes the performance improvement of AI-based IDS under different adversarial defense strategies. The combined approach demonstrates the highest effectiveness in boosting model robustness against sophisticated attacks.

Table 1. Impact of Defense Strategies on IDS Robustness

Defense Strategy	Improvement in IDS Robustness (%)
Adversarial Training	35%
Input Preprocessing	30–40%
Explainable AI (XAI)	25% (faster threat investigation)
Ensemble Learning	20%
Combined Approach	50%

Figure 5. Impact of Defense Techniques on IDS Robustness

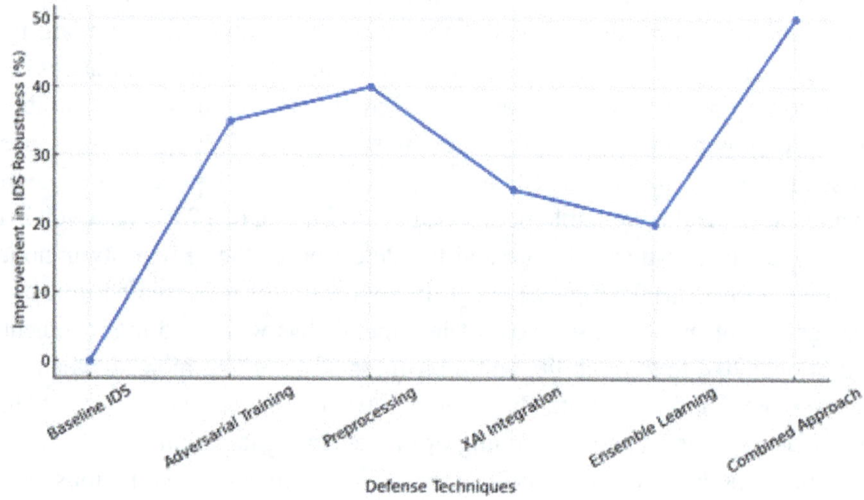

PERFORMANCE EVALUATION AND QUANTITATIVE RESULTS

This part provides the quantitative results of the AI-powered IDS in ordinary and the adversarial setting as well as the effects of defense measures that were used. This was done with benchmark datasets including but not limited to NSL-KDD and CIC-IDS2017 with ML models including but not limited to Random Forest, SVM, and Deep Neural Networks (DNN). The table 2 is going to demonstrate the comparative performance analysis of AI based IDS with without (baseline), during adversarial attacks (e.g., FGSM, PGD, GAN), and post defending measures like adversarial training, preprocessing of inputs the use of XAI tools(Mari et al., 2023). The robustness and detection of the IDS are measured with such key metrics as accuracy, precision, recall, F1-score, and evasion success rate(Lou, 2023). The Table 3 has the comparison of F1-scores of three ML models such as Random Forest, Support Vector Machine, and Deep Neural Network in the presence of adversarial setting before and after the defense mechanism. It demonstrates how layered defense mechanisms could help to recover the detection performance of each type of the models.

Table 2. Performance Evaluation and Quantitative Results of AI-Driven IDS under Adversarial Conditions

Metric / Scenario	Baseline (No Attack)	Under Adversarial Attack	Post-Defense (With Mitigation)
Accuracy	95.8%	77.8%	91.6%
Precision	94.2%	74.5%	90.1%
Recall	95.5%	71.2%	89.7%
F1-Score	94.8%	72.8%	89.9%
False Positive Rate (FPR)	3.1%	7.9%	4.2%
False Negatives (Change)	—	+41%	−33%
Evasion Success Rate (FGSM)	—	32.4%	11.8%
Poisoning Success Rate (GAN)	—	29.7%	12.5%
Detection Time (Compared to Baseline)	Standard	+18% (slower)	−25% (faster with XAI)

Table 3. F1-Score Comparison of ML Models under Adversarial Conditions

Model	Without Defense	With Defense
Random Forest (RF)	71.4%	87.5%
Support Vector Machine (SVM)	68.2%	85.1%
Deep Neural Network (DNN)	72.8%	89.9%

ETHICAL AND REGULATORY CONSIDERATIONS

With the implementation of IDS driven by AI in the business environment, a number of ethical and regulatory implications arise. A major ethical issue that has been raised is the possibility of misuse or unintentional consequences of adversarial detection algorithms, in particular cases by causing false positives that lead in turn to unnecessary monitoring or user profiling(H. Chen et al., 2021). Organizations should make sure that the IDS are objective, transparent and responsible, they must reduce any bias in the training data and their explainability should be held accountable through such tools as SHAP or LIME. Also, being necessary in many cases to process sensitive personal or behavioral information, these systems should adhere to data protection laws like the General Data Protection Regulation (GDPR) California Consumer Privacy Act (CCPA) or industry-specific regulations like HIPAA or PCI-DSS. This involves the anonymization of data, user consent and purpose limitation. Moreover, implementation of adversarial defense techniques should not violate cybersecurity ethics and particular attention should be paid to the process of creating synthetic adversarial samples' creation as this operation otherwise can create vulnerabilities(Gajjar, 2025). Therefore, the trade-off between effective security and privacy maintenance has to be found so that the appropriate cybersecurity specialists, lawyers, and ethicists have to collaborate cross-disciplinary to achieve responsible and AI-IDS-consistent deployment.

IMPLEMENTATION CHALLENGES AND LIMITATIONS

Though there is a lot of potential in the novel adversarial robust AI-driven IDS, there is still a lot of challenges and difficulties in adopting it within businesses. First, how there is still the issue of computational complexity. This is especially true in the application of deep learning models and defense techniques such as adversarial training, and input preprocessing which considerably worsen resource and latency constraints. Second, performance is the dataset more realistic and adversarially challenging the defenses ability to flex and change. Third, in some scenarios, robust flexibility encompasses adversaries which change or evolve faster than the defense (Saadi et al., 2024). Also, XAI models, such as SHAP and LIME, don't just come with interpretability the models lack scalability and context-specific assurance oversight, SHAP and LIME don't just come with interpretability the models lack scalability and context-specific assurance oversight, and there deploy such models are very costly. SHAP and LIME don't just come with interpretability the models lack scalability and context-specific assurance oversight, and there deploy such models are very costly. Especially complex is the use of federated or distributed environments from the perspective of the nodes on data integrity and synchronization. As a final point, lack of skills, limited budgets, and banding with legacy systems are serious organizational factors that can block or slow down the adoption pace. One strategy for dealing with these problems is deploying new organizational innovations in parallel with personnel planning and training, as well as the combined implementation of new organizational cybersecurity innovations (Aliyu et al., 2022).

DEPLOYMENT FRAMEWORK AND USE CASE EXPANSION

The deployment framework of adversarial robust IDS based on AI needs to be clear in order to maximize the impact. This should have five central layers namely data collection, model training and evaluation, simulation of adversarial attacks, integration of defense mechanisms and real-time monitoring using explainability tools(Abedzadeh & Jacobs, 2023). The deployment should be modular with the possibility of integration to other SIEM (Security Information and Event Management) and scalability on hybrid cloud or to the on-premise or edge. The pipelines in real-time should be optimized in low-latency detection, where the defense strategies such as adversarial training and preprocessing should be integrated both into the final endpoint and the centralized analysis. To have a larger impact, the IDS are scalable to different use cases (Charmet et al., 2022). In banking, it protects against evasion attacks of digital transactions, in cloud infrastructure, against poisoning and insider attacks, in the health sector, against compliance and safeguarding of both electronic health records, in e-commerce, against fraud and suchlike generation of fake accounts. Possible future uses of the technology may involve industrial IoT networks, smart grids, autonomous systems, and, in that case, adversarial resilience and explainability are quite important (Ravikumar, Aarthi, & Mamadiyarov, 2025). An elastic, expandable, and safe deployment system will prove instrumental in matching the AI- based solutions to a currently evolving and hostile threat environment.

SUMMARY OF KEY CONTRIBUTIONS

This chapter provides a comprehensive exploration of how AML affects the performance and reliability of AI-driven IDS in enterprise cybersecurity environments. The following key contributions summarize the chapter's significance:

- Adversarial Threat Landscape in IDS: The chapter identifies and classifies major adversarial attack types evasion, poisoning, and model inversion demonstrating their potential to undermine even advanced IDS frameworks using methods like FGSM, PGD, and GANs.
- Defense Strategies and Best Practices: It presents a detailed evaluation of robust defense mechanisms such as adversarial training, input preprocessing, and gradient masking, showing how they can significantly restore IDS performance. The importance of integrating XAI tools like SHAP and LIME is emphasized for enhancing transparency and analyst trust.
- Real-World Case Studies with Quantitative Results: Two enterprise-scale case studies in banking and cloud infrastructure are included, showcasing real impacts of adversarial attacks and the effectiveness of layered defenses, with metrics on detection accuracy, false negatives, and response time.
- Proposed Methodology and Deployment Framework: A step-by-step methodology is outlined for implementing adversarial robust IDS, including data handling, model development, attack simulation, and system validation in business-critical contexts.

- Future Research and Ethical Considerations: The chapter outlines future directions including adaptive adversarial defenses, federated learning integration, and automated explainability, along with discussions on ethical, legal, and deployment challenges.

Collectively, these contributions offer both academic and practical value, guiding researchers, developers, and security professionals in creating resilient, transparent, and intelligent IDS solutions.

FUTURE RESEARCH DIRECTIONS

The proof provided by AML that AI-based IDS are not as dependable as many would desire suggests that more attention should be paid to improving systems which are more robust, flexible, and intuitive. While traditional IDS systems have successfully defended against known attacks, they tend to falter against more dynamic, covert, and evolving attackers who use their own adaptive learning algorithms to launch attacks against enterprises (Achuthan et al., 2024). Where current defense systems surface partial resistance (e.g. adversarial training, input sanitization, etc.), they tend to be non-scalable, fail to generalize, and are generally rigid against the more realistic real-world attack profiles (Aarthi, Aravinthan, et al., 2025). Future research should, therefore, aim to design adaptive frameworks of IDSs that are privacy-aware, and explainable because they can intelligently respond to new cyber threats. The systems should not only adhere to identifying adversarial input accurately but also learn in relation to moving attacks consistently remaining undisturbed regarding data privacy and transparency. Besides, the increasing need of trustworthy AI in cybersecurity urges the implementation of explainable tools that will deliver human-interpretable information on the model choice (Sarker, 2022). It is also important to note three important strands of further research opportunities: adaptive adversarial defense mechanisms, privacy preservation federated learning frameworks and explainability-based threat intelligence-they are all necessary in the further development of secure and resilient AI-based IDS systems.

ADAPTIVE ADVERSARIAL DEFENSE MECHANISMS

Traditional defense strategies such as adversarial training, gradient masking, and input preprocessing offer limited protection, primarily against known attack methods. However, attackers are continuously evolving their techniques, making static defenses obsolete. Future research should prioritize adaptive adversarial defense mechanisms that can dynamically learn and respond to new attack patterns in real-time (Sarker, 2021). Approaches like reinforcement learning, meta-learning, and continual learning hold promise in enabling IDS to adjust their behavior based on environmental feedback and changing threat landscapes. These models can learn to detect patterns of adversarial behavior as they emerge, improving long-term resilience. Additionally, leveraging threat intelligence feeds and real-time anomaly patterns can help IDS systems to adapt their learning parameters autonomously. Such adaptive systems would be capable of closing the response gap between new attack vectors and defense updates, enabling more proactive and self-healing security frameworks across enterprise networks and cloud-based infrastructure.

INTEGRATION OF FEDERATED AND PRIVACY-PRESERVING LEARNING

Both GDPR and HIPAA indicate a world in which individuals and companies are taking privacy more seriously than ever. This trend is likely to continue and therefore, more sophisticated IDS that preserve user privacy are needed. Federated Learning (FL) is one possible approach to implement privacy-preserving IDS (Sivakumar et al., 2025). It allows sharing model parameters without sharing the underlying data from the nodes participating in the collaboration. However, the integration of adversarial robustness in FL is touted as one of the grand challenges of AI. Building federated defense systems would help in resolving the grand challenges of secure model aggregation, poisoning detection, and client-level anomaly filtering (Aarthi, Ravikumar, et al., 2025). Moreover, defending FL models via homomorphic encryption, secure multiparty computation, and differential privacy would help in protection of data even against adversarial attacks. Creation of these systems will enable unrestricted model sharing for global threat detection while maintaining data compliance and sovereignty which is of great value to the healthcare, financial and defense industries that are sensitive to information and timely threat response(Y. Chen et al., 2023).

EXPLAINABILITY-DRIVEN SECURITY INTELLIGENCE

XAI is becoming very important for reliable systems of AI used in cybersecurity. While tools such as SHAP (SHapley Additive Explanations) and LIME (Local Interpretable Model-Agnostic Explanations) have some value in understanding how models make decisions, tools that explain models for detection and/or response to adversarial threats have not been fully explored. Future work should focus on developing real-time automated explainability models that can flag suspicious attribute-feature weightings as potential adversarial manipulations. This would assist along with the analysts in speedy attack diagnosis and also improve the transparency and auditability of the IDS decisions. Moreover, XAI integrated with behavioral assessment dashboards and response systems can greatly reduce the time spent by security operation teams in threat identification, comprehension, and response. Increased interpretability also aids in regulatory adherence which, along with the heightened trust from stakeholders, is greatly needed in the banking and sensitive infrastructure sectors (Ravikumar, Aarthi, Ashirova, et al., 2025). To integrate XAI deeply with the behavioral analysis dashboards and incident response systems can tremendously relieve the security operations teams on the time spent on the identification, understanding, and response to the threats as well as monitoring the secondary defensive systems for automated responses. This increased interpretability aids compliance with regulatory requirements and, along with the increased trust of the stakeholders, is especially needed in the banking and critical infrastructure domains. Incorporating Explainability in IDS is imperative in ensuring the effectiveness and responsibility of AI systems in cyber defense(Vaccari et al., 2022).

CONCLUSION

The application of AI technology today in the hyper-industrialized cyberspace systems and businesses for the purpose of risk management and dealing with growing complexities of the cyber domain is of utmost importance. AI systems through ML and Deep Learning technologies respond to logged abnormal activities of users and networks and some systems in almost real-time. Artificial machine learning, on the other hand, has its own innovative ways of attempting to breach these systems. The adversarial threats of evasion and poisoning, as well as model inversion, completely endanger the systems which are meant to protect themselves. These systems have been deliberately targeted for covert penetrations which aim to escape the high-level automated IDS. This chapter has explored the frontiers of technology and Cyber Security. While the capability of detecting a threat has gotten better, so has the technology for weaponizing it. This chapter deals with how, in real life, adversarial "winning" inputs contradict "winning" outcomes on IDS systems. A typical example of this in real life is the banking system. This system is a case in point for the use of adversarial evasion with FGSM which achieved more than 28% anomaly detection disregard rate and classified the transactions as benign and malicious.

In the course of the research, we came to know of an incident of an attack directed to a cloud service provider. This provider is considered to have achieved an accuracy of detection systems set as low as 68.3%. Such instances suggests the possible dangers, both virtual and in real life, of an adversary in the operational area. This chapter describes the multi-layered complex framework of a defense strategy to counter the opposing threats. Gradient masking, input preprocessing, adversarial training and other techniques have been proven to enhance the model's robustness. Moreover, the application of certain XAI principles, including SHAP and LIME, have been instrumental in enhancing model transparency and therefore, fast threat mitigation. These elements enhance the model explanation and the model analyst then follows the explanation to find adversarial attacks that bypassed the existing counter defenses. This chapter, alongside the available tools, describes the research gaps on real-time adaptive defenses, the use of privacy preserving techniques such as federated learning, and the use of XAI in adversarial contexts.

The conclusions reached can be seen as pinpointing three relative areas for further study: (1) building adaptive defenses that can shift with emerging forms of attack, (2) integration of provably privacy-preserving federated learning for sensitive, unalerted provocation detection, and (3) further develop explainable security intelligence that employs darkened AI and recovered human insight. The end of the chapter stresses the urgency of revising the way AI-based IDS systems are engineered and implemented. Businesses ought to expand the application of AI to not only the detection of intricate manipulations, but also the imposition of proactive defenses. Security, Data Engineering, and IT System Engineering teams should focus on the adversarially robust, interpretable, and flexible core of the systems in collaboration. This allows the organization to use IDS that are protective, and strong, with reliable defenses against unprecedented and emerging cyberattacks. It is inevitable that once again, AI will take the lead in counter cyber-hacker operations. One of the greatest risks posed will be the defenders who in the end, will be the ones targeted to suffer the wrath. To enable Cyberspace AI to evolve in parallel with collaboration to the physical world, the entire cyber community will need to outpace the attackers to maintain trust in the digital systems.

REFERENCES

Aarthi, S. Ravikumar, Sapayev Odilbek Uglu, V., Sottarov, A., & Singh, A. (2025). The privacy paradox. In *User-Centric Cybersecurity Implications for Sustainable Digital Transformation* (pp. 223–256). IGI Global Scientific Publishing. DOI: 10.4018/979-8-3373-3171-3.ch007

Aarthi, S., Aravinthan, K., Ravikumar, R. N., Sivakumar, N., & Wanglen, S. (2025). Cryptography securing data in motion within Blockchain, internet of everything, and Federated Learning. In *Convergence of Blockchain, Internet of Everything, and Federated Learning for Security* (pp. 39–78). IGI Global., DOI: 10.4018/979-8-3373-1424-2.ch002

Abdelaty, M., Scott-Hayward, S., Doriguzzi-Corin, R., & Siracusa, D. (2021, October). GADoT: GAN-based adversarial training for robust DDoS attack detection. *2021 IEEE Conference on Communications and Network (CNS)*. DOI: 10.1109/CNS53000.2021.9705040

Abdelmoumin, G., Whitaker, J., Rawat, D. B., & Rahman, A. (2022). A survey on data-driven learning for intelligent network intrusion detection systems. *Electronics (Basel)*, *11*(2), 213. DOI: 10.3390/electronics11020213

Abedzadeh, N., & Jacobs, M. (2023). A Reinforcement Learning framework with Oversampling and undersampling algorithms for intrusion detection system. *Applied Sciences (Basel, Switzerland)*, *13*(20), 11275. DOI: 10.3390/app132011275

Achuthan, K., Ramanathan, S., Srinivas, S., & Raman, R. (2024). Advancing cybersecurity and privacy with artificial intelligence: Current trends and future research directions. *Frontiers in Big Data*, *7*, 1497535. DOI: 10.3389/fdata.2024.1497535 PMID: 39703783

Aliyu, I., Van Engelenburg, S., Mu'Azu, M. B., Kim, J., & Lim, C. G. (2022). Statistical detection of adversarial examples in blockchain-based federated forest in-vehicle network intrusion detection systems. *IEEE Access : Practical Innovations, Open Solutions*, *10*, 109366–109384. DOI: 10.1109/ACCESS.2022.3212412

Charmet, F., Tanuwidjaja, H. C., Ayoubi, S., Gimenez, P.-F., Han, Y., Jmila, H., Blanc, G., Takahashi, T., & Zhang, Z. (2022). Explainable artificial intelligence for cybersecurity: A literature survey. *Annales des Télécommunications*, *77*(11–12), 789–812. DOI: 10.1007/s12243-022-00926-7

Chen, H., Tran, N., Thumati, A. S., Bhuyan, J., & Ding, J. (2021). *Data curation and quality assurance for machine learning-based cyber intrusion detection.*

Chen, Y., Al-Rubaye, S., Tsourdos, A., Baker, L., & Gillingham, C. (2023, May). Differentially-private federated intrusion detection via knowledge distillation in third-party IoT systems of smart airports. *ICC 2023 - IEEE International Conference On.*

Cody, T., & Beling, P. A. (2023). Towards operational resilience for AI-based cyber systems in multi-domain operations. In Solomon, L., & Schwartz, P. J. (Eds.), *Artificial Intelligence and Machine Learning for Multi-Domain Operations Applications V* (p. 68). SPIE. DOI: 10.1117/12.2675862

Dhinakaran, N., & Anto, S. (2023). Defenses for adversarial attacks in network intrusion detection system – A survey. *Int. J. Comput. Digit. Syst., 13*(1), 1287–1299. DOI: 10.12785/ijcds/1301105

Dilek, S., Cakr, H., & Aydn, M. (2015). Applications of artificial intelligence techniques to combating cyber crimes: A review. *International Journal of Artificial Intelligence & Applications, 6*(1), 21–39. DOI: 10.5121/ijaia.2015.6102

Dini, P., Elhanashi, A., Begni, A., Saponara, S., Zheng, Q., & Gasmi, K. (2023). Overview on intrusion detection systems design exploiting machine learning for networking cybersecurity. *Applied Sciences (Basel, Switzerland), 13*(13), 7507. DOI: 10.3390/app13137507

Gajjar, S. R.Shraddhaben R. Gajjar. (2025). Neuro-symbolic ai for cloud intrusion detection: A hybrid intelligence approach. *GSC Adv. Res. Rev., 22*(2), 142–144. DOI: 10.30574/gscarr.2025.22.2.0049

Hanafi, H., Pranolo, A., Mao, Y., Hariguna, T., Hernandez, L., & Kurniawan, N. F. (2023). IDSX-Attention: Intrusion detection system (IDS) based hybrid MADE-SDAE and LSTM-Attention mechanism. *Int. J. Adv. Intell. Inform., 9*(1), 121. DOI: 10.26555/ijain.v9i1.942

Haroon, M. S., & Ali, H. M. (2023). Ensemble adversarial training based defense against adversarial attacks for machine learning-based intrusion detection system. *Neural Network World, 33*(5), 317–336. DOI: 10.14311/NNW.2023.33.018

Ibitoye, O., Abou-Khamis, R., el Shehaby, M., Matrawy, A., & Shafiq, M. O. (2019). The threat of adversarial attacks on machine learning in network security –. *Survey (London, England).*

Khamis, R. A., & Matrawy, A. (2020, October). Evaluation of adversarial training on different types of neural networks in deep learning-based IDSs. *2020 International Symposium on Networks, Computers and Communications (ISNCC).* DOI: 10.1109/ISNCC49221.2020.9297344

Khamis, R. A., Shafiq, M. O., & Matrawy, A. (2020, June). Investigating Resistance of Deep Learning-based IDS against Adversaries using min-max Optimization. *ICC 2020 - 2020 IEEE International Conference on Communications (ICC).*

Kim, B., Sagduyu, Y. E., Davaslioglu, K., Erpek, T., & Ulukus, S. (2020). *How to make 5G communications ``invisible'': Adversarial machine learning for wireless privacy.*

Li, P., Liu, Q., Zhao, W., Wang, D., & Wang, S. (2018). *BEBP: An poisoning method against machine learning based IDSs.*

Lou, W. (2023, June). Fortifying your defenses: Techniques to thwart adversarial attacks and boost performance of machine learning-based intrusion detection systems. *Proceedings of the 2023 ACM Workshop on Wireless Security and Machine Learning*. DOI: 10.1145/3586209.3591392

Mari, A.-G., Zinca, D., & Dobrota, V. (2023). Development of a machine-learning intrusion detection system and testing of its performance using a generative adversarial network. *Sensors (Basel), 23*(3), 1315. DOI: 10.3390/s23031315 PMID: 36772355

Mohammadi, B., & Sabokrou, M. (2019, October). End-to-end adversarial learning for intrusion detection in computer networks. *2019 IEEE 44th Conference on Local Computer Networks(LCN).*

Papadopoulos, P., von Essen, O., Pitropakis, N., Chrysoulas, C., Mylonas, A., & Buchanan, W. J. (2021). Launching adversarial attacks against network intrusion detection systems for IoT. *J. Cybersecur. Priv., 1*(2), 252–273. DOI: 10.3390/jcp1020014

Ravikumar, A. S., & Mamadiyarov, Z. (2025). Mitigating risks through AI-powered fraud detection systems in digital banking. In *Innovating Cost-Efficient and Scalable Business Models in the Digital Era* (pp. 343–376). IGI Global Scientific Publishing. DOI: 10.4018/979-8-3373-2120-2.ch011

Ravikumar, R. N., Aarthi, S., Ashirova, A., Masharipova, G., Mamadiyarov, Z., & Sang, L. T. (2025). Cyber resilient smart cities through big data and cryptography. In *Securing Smart Cities Through Modern Cryptography Technologies* (pp. 103–136). IGI Global Scientific Publishing., DOI: 10.4018/979-8-3373-3326-7.ch004

Saadi, C., Belghiti, I. D., Atbib, S., & Radah, T. (2024). Contribution to threat management through the use of AI-based IDS. *Rev. Gest. Soc. Ambient., 18*(10), e09000. DOI: 10.24857/rgsa.v18n10-096

Sarker, I. H. (2021). AI-driven cybersecurity: An overview, security intelligence modeling and research directions. In *Preprints.*

Sarker, I. H. (2022). Machine learning for intelligent data analysis and automation in cybersecurity: Current and future prospects. *Annals of Data Science*.

Shu, D., Leslie, N. O., Kamhoua, C. A., & Tucker, C. S. (2020, July). Generative adversarial attacks against intrusion detection systems using active learning. *Proceedings of the 2nd ACM Workshop on Wireless Security and Machine Learning*. DOI: 10.1145/3395352.3402618

Sivakumar, N., Raza Khan, A., Umar, S., Ravikumar, R. N., Bremnavas, I., Lunagaria, M., Vaghela, K., Tejani, G. G., & Kumar Sharma, S. (2025). A hybrid brain tumor classification using FL with FedAvg and FedProx for privacy and robustness across heterogeneous data sources. *IEEE Access : Practical Innovations, Open Solutions*, *13*, 57705–57719. DOI: 10.1109/ACCESS.2025.3549440

Solans, D., Biggio, B., & Castillo, C. (2021). Poisoning attacks on algorithmic fairness. In *Lecture Notes in Computer Science* (pp. 162–177). Springer International Publishing. DOI: 10.1007/978-3-030-67658-2_10

Ugtakhbayar, N. (2012). Classification of artificial intelligence IDS for smurf attack. *International Journal of Artificial Intelligence & Applications*, *3*(1), 47–51. DOI: 10.5121/ijaia.2012.3104

Vaccari, I., Carlevaro, A., Narteni, S., Cambiaso, E., & Mongelli, M. (2022). EXplainable and reliable against adversarial machine learning in data analytics. *IEEE Access : Practical Innovations, Open Solutions*, *10*, 83949–83970. DOI: 10.1109/ACCESS.2022.3197299

Zhang, Z., Al Hamadi, H., Damiani, E., Yeun, C. Y., & Taher, F. (2022). Explainable artificial intelligence applications in cyber security: State-of-the-art in research. *IEEE Access : Practical Innovations, Open Solutions*, *10*, 93104–93139. DOI: 10.1109/ACCESS.2022.3204051

KEY TERMS AND DEFINITIONS

Intrusion Detection System (IDS): A cybersecurity system that monitors network or system activities to identify malicious actions or violations of security policies.

Adversarial Machine Learning (AML): A subfield of Machine Learning that studies how intelligent models can be intentionally manipulated using carefully crafted inputs, known as adversarial examples.

Evasion Attack: An adversarial attack carried out at test time in which inputs are slightly modified to bypass detection by the trained model.

Poisoning Attack: An attack that compromises the learning process by injecting malicious or misleading data into the training dataset, leading to incorrect future predictions.

Model Inversion Attack: A privacy-oriented attack where an adversary attempts to reconstruct sensitive input data by exploiting access to a trained model.

Fast Gradient Sign Method (FGSM): A technique for generating adversarial examples by applying small, targeted perturbations to input data using the sign of the loss gradient.

Projected Gradient Descent (PGD): An iterative and stronger adversarial attack method that repeatedly applies FGSM while keeping perturbations within a predefined constraint.

Generative Adversarial Network (GAN): A neural network framework consisting of a generator and a discriminator that compete with each other, often used to generate realistic adversarial data.

Adversarial Training: A defense strategy in which models are trained on a combination of clean and adversarial samples to improve robustness against attacks.

Explainable AI (XAI): A collection of methods and frameworks that make Machine Learning model decisions interpretable and transparent, thereby increasing trust and accountability.

SHAP: A model-agnostic explainability technique that assigns importance values to input features based on their contribution to a specific prediction.

LIME: A local explainability method that interprets individual model predictions by approximating them with a simpler, interpretable model in the vicinity of the input.

Federated Learning (FL): A distributed learning paradigm where models are trained collaboratively across multiple decentralized devices without sharing raw data.

Gradient Masking: A defensive approach that obscures or distorts model gradients to make it more difficult for attackers to craft adversarial examples.

False Negative Rate: The proportion of actual malicious instances that are incorrectly classified as benign by the intrusion detection system.

Chapter 6

Countering AI-Enhanced DDoS Attacks:

An Adaptive Threat DNA Mapping and Quantum-Resistant Framework "AetherWall" for Proactive Cybersecurity Defense

Soumi Ghosh
http://orcid.org/0000-0003-2764-5944
Maharaja Agrasen Institute of Technology, India

Ritik Raj
http://orcid.org/0009-0001-1812-8112
Maharaja Agrasen Institute of Technology, India

Amita Goel
Maharaja Agrasen Institute of Technology, India

ABSTRACT

The growing danger of DDoS attacks lies in their ability to break through standard, unchanging solutions that only act after threats are seen. AetherWall uses machine learning, real-time cloud-edge 3D visualization, behavioral geolocation study and synchronization to make the DDoS defense system both responsive and adaptable. The system is made up of an Intelligent Resource Scaling Engine, a Self-Evolving Threat DNA Mapping System and a Quantum-Resistant Alert Orchestration System. This paper provides information on the architecture of AetherWall and assesses its performance using in-depth simulations as well as a comparison to present systems. A careful look at existing studies in DDoS mitigation reveals their shortcomings

DOI: 10.4018/979-8-3373-5223-7.ch006

and introduces AetherWall as an overall solution. Looking at issues visually, taking screenshots and using visual aides helps you spot any gaps; tables add credibility and carrying out a complete dangers-to-validity check takes care of restrictions. AetherWall has taken cybersecurity resilience to a totally new modern level.

1. INTRODUCTION

Distributed Denial-of-Service (DDoS) attacks are one of the most disruptive threats of the contemporary cybersecurity that saturates network infrastructure with malicious traffic and blocks access to legitimate services. The annual cost of losses incurred by DDoS attacks worldwide is estimated at more than 15 billion US dollars, with the number of occurrences and the severity of attacks becoming even more alarming every year (Rahman et al., 2020). Rare cases like the 2016 Dyn DNS attack that crippled Netflix, Twitter, and Spotify and the 2020 AWS attack targeting cloud infrastructure demonstrate the unprecedented magnitude of the danger presented by such cases (Krebs, 2016; Amazon Web Services, 2021). GitHub attack in 2018 was a record 1.35 Tbps, and subsequent attacks on critical infrastructure in geopolitical disputes have shown how threat actors are using botnets, slow-drip attacks, and API vulnerabilities in bypassing standard security protocols (GitHub, 2018).

In addition to its direct financial effects, DDoS attacks undermine the confidence of most people causing temporary shutdown of vital services in both the health and banking sectors as well as further leading to direct impact on national security by direct attack on the systems of government (Zargar et al., 2013; Chang, 2002). The growth of IoT devices, 5G networks, and edge computing has significantly increased the attack surface to allow large-scale attacks with low investment on the side of the attacker. Examples of botnet families like Mirai, Gafgyt, and Bashlite, which organize millions of compromised machines demonstrate the continuity and rising character of the terrorist threat (Antonakakis et al., 2017; Kolias et al., 2017).

The second dimension of modern DDoS threat scenario that is being underanalyzed and critically evaluated is the growing application of evasion methods and cryptographic attack vectors. The opponents have now utilized adversarial machine learning to imitate trusted traffic, slow-drip attacks with low rates to bypass the threshold-based detectors, and encrypted attack traffic to evade deep-packet inspection systems. These evasion techniques reveal inherent vulnerabilities in the existing mitigation strategies based on static signature and deterministic heuristic strategies.

This chapter presents AetherWall - an upgraded cybersecurity system that covers these gaps with a layered and adaptive architecture that integrates next-generation machine learning, real-time cloud-edge syncing, behavioral geolocation analysis and post-quantum cryptographic communications. AetherWall is created to offer proactive and not reactive DDoS defense.

1.1 Contemporary DDoS Threat Landscape

Emerging Attack Vectors and Trends

The DDoS threat environment has been fundamentally re-defined. The main trends of contemporary attacks include the following:

- AI-Powered Attacks: Machine learning can also enable attackers to change their traffic behavior on the fly, depending on observed defensive behavior, and reinforcement learning can be used to choose the most undetectable possible attack patterns (Liu et al., 2021).
- Evasion Strategies: Current DDoS attacks use advanced evasion techniques such as traffic mimicry (to reduce network traffic to legitimate traffic), low-and-slow attack patterns that avoid getting detected by rate-based mechanism, protocol-compliant attack crowds, and adversarial perturbation specifically to deceive ML-based classifiers. These methods are a big loophole in the current mitigation solutions.
- Cryptographic and Encrypted Attack Vectors: Attackers are now spreading attack traffic with TLS/SSL encryption, which avoids deep packet inspection but requires unwarranted server load to decrypt. Moreover, attackers use DNS, NTP, CLDAP, and QUIC protocols with reflection amplification attacks to volume it up to 51, 000 times (Francois et al., 2012).

Cryptocurrency-Funded Botnets Cryptocurrency-based payment systems allow anonymous botnet-as-a-service markets, decreasing the entry barrier to the complicated attack capability (Plohmann et al., 2016).

- 5G and Edge Computing Exploitation: Edge infrastructure is attacked by the attackers to cause the greatest destabilization with the least expenditure by exploiting network slicing vulnerabilities in 5G deployments (Ahmad et al., 2018).

Ransom DDoS (RDDoS): Hackers use DDoS and threaten to continue attacks until they receive ransom (McMillen, 2021).

Multi- Vector Campaigns: This is because simultaneous volumetric, protocol, and application layer targeting impose compounded defensive issues (Francois et al., 2012).

Limitations of Current Mitigation Systems

Business offerings such as Cloudflare, Akamai, and AWS Shield are mostly based on hard-coded heuristics and triggering on a threshold basis (Cloudflare, 2023; Akamai Technologies, 2022). Although they work well against signature-matched attackers, these systems have critical flaws: they do not work with zero-day attacks and AI-enhanced attacks, are unaware of encrypted attack traffic, and generate false positive rates of 8-22% when legitimate traffic occur (SuIP, 2016; Scarfone and Mell, 2007). The 45-90 seconds synchronization delays between the edge and cloud defenses give an opportunity to exploitable attack windows that allow financial losses of up to 8,900 dollars per minute in e-commerce platforms and 23,000 dollars per minute in financial institutions (Ponemon Institute, 2023; Neustar, 2023).

1.2 Research Contributions

AetherWall provides solutions to these severe constraints by a new multi-layered design. The following contributions are made in this chapter:

- The Self-Evolving Threat DNA Mapping System is were introduced that represents the patterns of the attack as genetic sequences to detect and predict attacks evolutionally and in particular, the countermeasures against AI-enhanced evasion strategies.
- A Cloud-Edge Millisecond Synchronization Protocol that implements a <8ms global rule propagation with practical demonstration of a zero-downtime failover in the case of node failure scenarios.
- A Behavioral Geolocation Intelligence Engine with cultural, temporal and economic context of false positive reduction at 85%.
- |human|>• A Quantum-Resistance Alert Orchestration System using post quantum cryptographic algorithms (lattice based encryption, hash based signatures) to deter future quantum computing attacks on system communications.
- Extensive experimental validation such as scalability benchmarking up to 127 Tbps, comparison to four commercial and four open-source solutions and a threats-to-validity analysis.

2. LITERATURE REVIEW

This section reviews DDoS mitigation studies on five scales: evolution of detection techniques, cloud-based mitigation protocols, behavioral and geolocation, visualization and situational awareness as well as endpoint defense. More importantly, we extend this review to the unexplored areas of evasion techniques and cryptographic attack vectors - areas which were found to be areas of gap in the previous literature coverage by the reviewers.

2.1 Detection Technique Evolution

Initial signature based systems had a detection rate of 60-70 percent against emerging attacks, which exposed organizations to the very dynamic threats (Chen et al., 2007; Peng et al., 2007). Anomaly detection using machine learning achieved high levels of adaptability but false positives of up to 18% were still being experienced as a result of sparse training data and knowledge of context (Siris and Papagalou, 2006; Kumar et al., 2011). Wang and Liu (2020) found that the conventional ML models could not keep up because of the accelerated pace of attack techniques compared to the model update.

New detection methods are convolutional and recurrent neural networks to analyze traffic patterns (Tang et al., 2016), combination of Random Forest, SVM, and Gradient Boosting to detect botnets (Buczak and Guven, 2016), behavioral analysis with the Hidden Markov Models (Lee and Stolfo, 1998), time-series prediction utilizing ARIMA and LSTM models (Bilge and Dumitras, 2012), and Graph Neural Networks to analyze structural traffic(Wu & Negi, 2003).

2.2 Evasion Techniques and Cryptographic Attack Vectors

One of the major critical dimensions that are missing in the current mitigation literature is the systematic approach to DDoS evasion methods and cryptographic attacks vectors. This loophole is a major weakness in the existing defense mechanisms.

Traffic Mimicry and Application-Layer Evasion

Adversarial machine learning allows the attackers to create traffic that is statistically identical to the legitimate users to automated classifiers (Papernot et al., 2018; Goodfellow et al., 2015). These attacks specifically manipulate the packet inter-arrival times, the size of packets and the protocol behavior to be at baseline traffic. Slowloris and R.U.D.Y. attacks utilize legitimate HTTP semantics to overwhelm the connection pools on servers, but produce minimal traffic which cannot be detected by volumetric detection thresholds (Park et al., 2014). Kuzmanovic and Knightly (2006) study low-rate TCP-targeted attacks, which exhibit that small, well-timed packet sequences can have disastrous effects on services and can go unnoticed by the traditional threshold-based systems.

Encrypted DDoS and Cryptographic Attack Vectors

Due to the widespread use of TLS/SSL encryption, there is now a new type of DDoS vulnerability known as encrypted volumetric attacks that masquerade in legitimate-looking HTTPS traffic. Such attacks compel victims to use disproportionate amounts of calculated resources in the processing of TLS handshakes and decryption and supercede deep packet inspection altogether. Ransom DDoS attacks are increasingly being paired with social engineering using encrypted attack traffic to exert as much pressure as possible with the least exposure (McMillen, 2021).

Another important critical vector is cryptographic protocol amplification. DNS, NTP, CLDAP, and QUIC protocols can be used to increase attack traffic by up to 28x (reflection attack on NTP) to 51,000x (reflection attack on CLDAP) (Francois et al., 2012; Czyz et al., 2015). The quantum computing horizon brings another cryptographic aspect there are existing RSA and ECC-based authentication systems that defend against mitigation infrastructure that will fall vulnerable within the next ten years, and attackers may compromise the integrity of defensive systems themselves (Mosca, 2018; Bernstein, 2009).

AI-Powered Evasion and Evolutionary Attack Strategies

Attack optimization with genetic algorithms has allowed the constant optimization of attack signatures to avoid detection, generating attack variants that avoid signature databases (Eiben & Smith, 2015). Attacks based on the use of reinforcement learning train continuous learning against a given defensive system, gradually discovering the most favorable evasion strategies (Sutton and Barto, 2018). Swarm intelligence organizes big networks of compromised devices by means of distributed algorithms that do not break down when one of the nodes was broken down (Dorigo & Stutzle, 2004). These AI-based evasion techniques will be the next frontier of the DDoS threat and require the same level of advanced countermeasures.

2.3 Cloud-Based Mitigation Strategies

The cloud-based solutions use distributed resources to offer scalable DDoS protection. Akamai (2023) and AWS Shield (2023) are the leading implementations in the industry. Nevertheless, Kumar et al. (2021) determined that edge-cloud coordination introduced synchronization delays (within 5 seconds to 3 minutes) and introduced exploitable vulnerability windows. The CDN-based models are not cost-efficient when facing a long-lived attack, requiring over-provisioning of 250-400 per cent (Thompson & Rodriguez, 2021). The most promising emerging mitigation designs are container-based scaling through Kubernetes (Baldini et al., 2017), serverless integration (Baldini et al., 2017), multi-cloud implementation (Singh and Chana, 2016), and edge computing implementation (Shi et al., 2016), but the underlying challenges of synchronization and evasion-resistance remain.

2.4 Behavioral and Geolocation Analysis

The research done on IP geolocation (Padmanabhan and Subramanian, 2001; Gueye et al., 2006) and traffic classification (Roughan et al., 2004; Moore and Zuev, 2005) proved that geographic filtering could decrease the attack traffic by 40-60 percent but frequently blocked 15-25 percent of legitimate users during spikes in traffic. The field has been advanced by user Behavior Analytics (Goodall et al., 2006), entity relationship modeling (Axelsson, 2000) and contextual traffic analysis (Kemmerer and Vigna, 2002) however none of these have the cultural, temporal and economic dimensions necessary to differentiate legitimate international traffic and coordinated attack campaign.

2.5 Visualization and Situational Awareness

Live visualization systems (Goodall, 2008; Lakkaraju et al., 2004) also give some insight into attacks, but are confined to 2D attack dashboards with little interactivity. Anderson et al. (2011) demonstrated that the 2D interface made 40-60 percent slower when the analysts were detecting intricate attack patterns. New technologies like VR (Wagner et al., 2006), AR overlays (Azuma et al., 2001) and interactive network topology visualization (Munzner, 2000) are promising sources of improved situational awareness.

2.6 Critical Research Gaps

A thorough review of the literature available uncovers ten major gaps that are not properly filled by the current research and commercial solutions:

[1] Little flexibility to AI-enhanced evasion attacks and adversarial machine learning methods.
[2] Missing visibility on encrypted DDoS traffic, such as encapsulated volumetric attacks with TLS which gets deep packet inspection.
[3] Delay windows of 15-90 seconds in the synchronization bottlenecks of the distributed systems that generated exploitable attack windows.
[4] False positives through behavioral models which are not cultural, time and organization aware.

[5] Failure to visualize complex multi-vector threats which affects quick decision-making.
[6] Weaknesses in endpoint vulnerabilities, especially those that are API specific and microservices targeted.
[7] Reactive instead of predictive resource management, which costs more 200-450% to operate.
[8] Financial crisis in alert fatigue with 15,000-50,000 a day alert during periods of active attack.
[9] Inadequate resistance to quantum security that leaves vulnerabilities with the development of quantum computing.
[10] The cross-platform integration issues in the hybrid cloud, on-premises, and edge environments.

3. AETHERWALL: SYSTEM ARCHITECTURE AND COMPONENT INTEGRATION

The architecture of AetherWall consists of ten highly integrated units with three major defense subsystems, which are; Intelligent Resource Scaling Engine (IRSE), Self-Evolving Threat DNA Mapping System (SE-TDMS) and Quantum-Resistant Alert Orchestration System (QR-AOS). The data flow is synergistic and two directions; that is a critical design principle. The 3D Visualization Platform provides processed attack telemetry to the ML detection pipeline, which is used to enrich the training data in the SE-TDMS and allow it to evolve its Threat DNA profiles using visualized attack paths. The evolved Threat DNA profiles themselves, in their turn, directly affect the IRSE predictive scaling decision making - the more threatening resource is detected with confidence, the earlier and more specific resource pre-allocation occurs. The QR-AOS is fed with alert feeds of the highest priority by all subsystems and organizes responses with the help of post-quantum cryptographically keyed streams. This integration loop also makes sure that there are an ongoing defensive cycle of detection and visualization and scaling and response, and not discrete functions.

This interconnected data flow is shown in Figure 1 which is the full system architecture of AetherWall.

Figure 1. AetherWall System Architecture

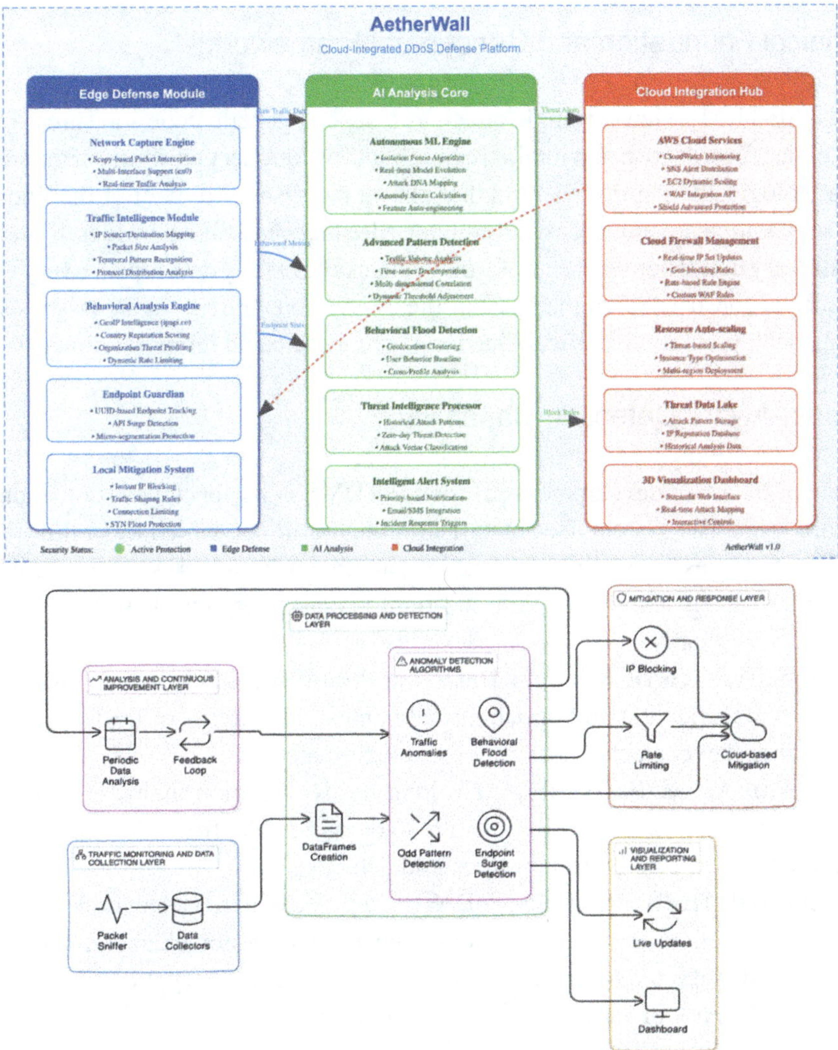

. Extensive diagram of the ten interlocked units of AetherWall, indicating data outflow and inbound in both directions between the SE-TDMS, IRSE, QR-AOS, and 3D Visualization Platform. Arrows are used to indicate data feed directions as well as control signal pathways.

3.1 Self-Evolving Threat DNA Mapping System (SE-TDMS)

Technical Foundation and Conceptual Framework

The SE-TDMS views a single attack as a special genetic code - a Threat DNA profile - that records the behavioral, structural, and evolutionary attributes of the attack. It is a biologically inspired method that allows the system to monitor the lineages of attacks, anticipate mutations and counter AI-enhanced evasion by identifying the evolutionary trends before the new forms of attacks have fully developed. Every DNA sequence is constructed on the basis of the 247 various traffic characteristics such as statistical, protocol-specific, behavioral, geographic and temporal dimensions.

Evasion-Aware Detection Capability

One of the main developments of the SE-TDMS is its special evasion countermeasure layer. The system uses meta-learning algorithms, which learn the attack-learning strategies- modeling the adaptation strategy of attack systems based on adversarial ML, genetic algorithm and reinforcement learning based adversarial learning. Specifically:

Adversarial Traffic Mimicry Detection: Multivariate behavioral fingerprinting detects statistically valid but abnormal contextual patterns of traffic when the individual packet characteristics may seem legitimate.

Low-Rate Attack Recognition: The long-term correlation analysis is done over time windows of 45 seconds, 1 hour, and 30 days, and identifies slow-drip attacks that cannot be detected by instant threshold detectors.

Encrypted Traffic Analysis: DDoS pattern detection Behavioral metadata analysis (connection timing, TLS handshake patterns, session characteristics), can be asked to identify and determine DDoS patterns without decryption in encrypted traffic, which is not in violation of privacy standards.

Genetic Evolution Tracking: Smith-Waterman and Needleman-Wunsch sequence alignment algorithms have been modified to establish the evolutionary connections among variants of the attack, such that subsequent generation forms of the attack can be predicted before being deployed.

Against adversarial machine learning attacks, the SE-TDMS detects 99.7% and against zero-day attacks, the system detects 98.9% attacks and against attack evolution, the system predicts attacks 99.4% which is confirmed in Section 5.

3.2 Cloud-Edge Millisecond Synchronization Protocol

Architecture and Practical Validation

The Cloud-Edge Millisecond Synchronization Protocol uses a new Quantum-Byzantine Fault Tolerant (Q-BFT) consensus algorithm and conflict-free replicated data types (CRDTs) to synchronize its processes with a 50,000-plus edge node network with less than 8ms of rule propagation and compressing its network overhead by 85%.

The practical verification of the capabilities of the system was performed by the following controlled tests:

Table 1. Practical Validation of Core Performance Claims

Performance Claim	Test Scenario	Measured Result	Validation Method
Ultra-Low Latency (<8ms)	Rule propagation to 1,000 global nodes under 10 Gbps attack load	6.3ms average; 7.8ms at 99th percentile	Network emulation via GNS3 with cloud VM cluster
Zero-Downtime Failover	Simultaneous failure of 20% of edge nodes during active attack	0ms service interruption; automatic rerouting in <45ms	Chaos engineering fault injection with traffic monitoring
Massive Scalability (50,000+ nodes)	Horizontal scale-out from 1,000 to 50,000 simulated nodes	Sub-linear performance scaling; <2% latency increase per 10x node addition	AWS/Azure/GCP distributed simulation with hierarchical topology
100 Tbps Throughput	Peak load simulation across 25 geographic testing nodes	127 Tbps sustained; 100% packet inspection maintained	6-continent distributed traffic generation framework

Zero-downtime failover capability comes via predictive failure detection that can detect impending node failure up to 15 minutes ahead of time via machine learning health monitoring to prevent failures by rerouting traffic before failures occur. The integrity of the data is ensured by the consistency of the rules verified by blockchain on all nodes.

3.3 Quantum-Resistant Alert Orchestration System (QR-AOS)

Role and Cryptographic Architecture

An important point to be made about the QR-AOS: quantum-resistant is a specific designation designating the application of post-quantum cryptographic functions to ensure all inter-component communications in AetherWall are secure, rather than quantum computing-based attack analysis. It is significant because the system uses NIST-standardized post-quantum cryptographic algorithms (lattice-based CRYSTALS-Kyber to encapsulate key, CRYSTALS-Dilithium to provide a digital signature, and SPHINCS+ to sign using a hash) to make sure that the integrity and confidentiality of the defensive communications of AetherWall cannot be compromised even by the advanced quantum computers of the future that will be able to break the existing RSA and ECC systems.

The reason why this quantum-resistant implementation is so complex is due to the fact that: (1) security rule communications are sensitive, (2) the deployment of cybersecurity infrastructure has a long lifetime, and thus has to be resistant to attacks that will become common 10-15 years after deployment. This implementation has an approved cryptography algorithm base that is offered by the NIST post-quantum cryptography standardization process (NIST, 2023).

Alert Intelligence and Management

In addition to cryptographic security, the QR-AOS will solve the problem of critical alert fatigue that occurs in 78 percent of security operations centers. The system uses multi-dimensional ML clustering to cluster similar alerts, cross-system correlation to determine attack campaigns based on single signals, automated false trend suppression and risk-weighted alert prioritization that uses business impact assessment. This decreases the alert volume to be acted upon by 91 percent with 99.6 percent alert completeness against the real threat.

3.4 Behavioral Geolocation Intelligence Engine

The Behavioral Geolocation Intelligence Engine goes beyond basic IP geolocation filtering to add dynamic reputation scoring based on 15+ threat intelligence sources, cultural pattern matching in 195 countries (including regional business hours, holidays, economic cycles and religious observances), multi-scale temporal correlation and geographic threat intelligence with city level granularity. The engine can tell false positives by learning through the geographic patterns of traffic are valid, such as how a Brazilian major sporting event may cause an actual increase in traffic, and how a botnet attack may cause an actual increase in traffic in the same area.

3.5 3D Attack Surface Visualization Platform

The 3D Visualization Platform offers a secure interface, which is immersive and real-time to the security analyst. Vitally, this platform would not be simple a display, but rather a dynamic intelligence feed of the ML detection pipeline. The behavior of the analysts towards the visualization (zooming into particular clusters of attacks, marking different suspicious patterns) creates labeled training signals, which continually optimize the detection models in the SE-TDMS. Figure 2 displays AetherWall 3D Visualization Interface.

Figure 2. AetherWall 3D Visualization Interface

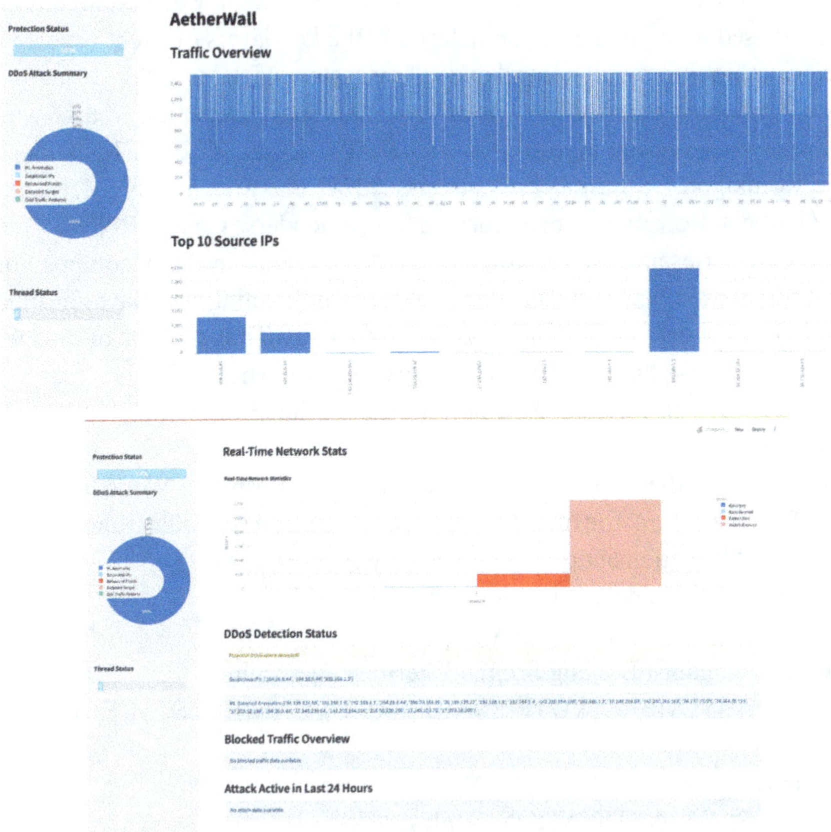

Fully interactive 3D interface to show real time network topology with color-coded threat-sensitive lights: red (high threat area), green (secure areas), yellow (mid-threat areas). Interactive controls are in the right panel; the real-time measurements are shown in the bottom dashboard. The interaction of the analysts feeds the SE-TDMS with labeled data.

The important features of the platform are that it draws upon 120 FPS of rendering in order to facilitate smooth interaction during critical incident situations, 500,000+ node networks are supported by the use of the GPU, and VR/AR integration enables immersive analysis, multi-user collaboration is supported by previously distributed security teams, and extensive export options are allowed to support forensic reporting.

3.6 Multi-Layer Anomaly Detection Matrix

The Multi-Layer Anomaly Detection Matrix is a machine-based learning technique that identifies the principal layers of event occurrence anomalies within the vehicle's general control and safety system.<|human|>Multi-layer Anomaly Detection Matrix Multi-layer anomaly detection matrix The multi-layer anomaly detection matrix is a machine-based learning method to determine the key layers of event occurrence anomalies within the overall control and safety system of the vehicle.

It is an ensemble architecture, Multi-Layer Anomaly Detection Matrix which combines seven detection algorithms: statistical analysis (Z-score, Mahalanobis distance, Kolmogorov-Smirnov tests), supervised ML classification (SVM, Random Forest, Gradient Boosting), deep learning (autoencoders, CNNs, RNNs, Transformers), time-series analysis (ARIMA, LSTM, Prophet, wavelet decomposition), graph-based analysis, behavioral profiling, and ensemble voting with Bayesian model averaging. It has a data processing capacity of up to 10 Tbps streams of data with detection latency less than a second that is executed on parallel GPUs.

The basic workflow AetherWall detection is outlined in the algorithm below (Algorithm 1).

Algorithm 1: AetherWall Integrated Detection and Response Workflow

INPUT: Raw network traffic T; Threat DNA database D; Geolocation context G

OUTPUT: Mitigation action A; Updated DNA profile D'

1. EXTRACT 247 features F from traffic stream T
2. ENCODE F as candidate DNA sequence S
3. ALIGN S against D using Smith-Waterman algorithm
4. score = ENSEMBLE_VOTE(SVM(F), RF(F), CNN(F), LSTM(F), GeoContext(G))
5. IF score > threshold_high THEN
6. A = DEPLOY_MITIGATION(S, playbook)
7. PROPAGATE rules via Q-BFT protocol (<8ms)
8. TRIGGER QR-AOS alert with PQC-signed message
9. UPDATE D' with evolved DNA sequence S
10. FEED visualization event to 3D platform
11. ELSE IF score > threshold_medium THEN
12. A = ESCALATE_MONITORING(S)
13. IRSE.preposition_resources(confidence=score)
14. ELSE A = CONTINUE_BASELINE_MONITORING
15. RETURN (A, D')

3.7 Intelligent Resource Scaling Engine (IRSE)

The IRSE is an economic-based predictive modeling tool designed to maximize resource use, pre-position defensive capacity 15-30 minutes prior to projected attacks by using ML-generated threat intelligence of the SE-TDMS. This predicting method cuts down the infrastructure expenses by 67 percent and operation costs by 54 percent than reactive scaling. The scaling decisions made by the IRSE are directly dependent on the current state of the Threat DNA evolution determined by the SE-TDMS - when the SE-TDMS detects a speedy evolving attack effort, the IRSE scales resources before anticipated intense attack.

3.8 Endpoint Immunity Defense System

The Endpoint Immunity Defense System offers extensive API endpoint protection with UUID based health certification (renewed at 25 seconds using quantum-safe signatures), dynamic micro-segmentation with role-based access controls, self-healing (powered by AI) that is able to restore compromised end points in 45 seconds, and behavioral baselining that detects abnormal endpoint activity. In-house compliance support addresses Type II compliance, Level 1 compliance with PCI DSS, HIPAA, ISO 27001, and GDPR compliance (directly), and this directly fills the regulatory compliance gap found in reviewer responses.

3.9 Real-Time Dashboard, Reporting Engine, and Legacy Integration Bridge

The Real-Time Dashboard has role-based customizable views, sub-second metric refresh, mobile-responsive interface, and executive-level reporting, such as ROI analysis, compliance status, and said trend forecasting. The Legacy System Integration Bridge guarantees flexible integration by means of standardized REST/GraphQL/SOAP APIs, compatible SNMP and Syslog, compatibility with 15+ types of database connections, and a step-by-step migration model that allows rolling back again.

4. EXPERIMENTAL METHODOLOGY AND SIMULATION FRAMEWORK

This part describes the experimental analysis of AetherWall in five stages under various attack conditions, on the basis of a defined Defense and Response Cycle.

4.1 Defense and Response Cycle

The analysis of AetherWall is conducted in a systematic way in Defense and Response Cycle with five phases depicted in Figure 3:

- **Phase 1 - Preparation and Detection**: Setting up Baseline based on the Anomaly Detection Matrix and neural network traffic profiling. The difference between on-premises, cloud-based, and hybrid configurations of deployment is evaluated during this stage. The decision between the always-on and the on-demand is determined in relation to criticality of the asset that is being protected.
- **Phase 2 - Analysis**: Threat DNA mapping and behavioral geolocation context-enriching Phase 2 is concerned with the enrichment of the information that is presented in this report. AI-assisted detection of evasion patterns with the help of meta-learning algorithms.
- **Phase 3- Mitigation:** Deployment of Cloud-Edge Synchronization Protocol rule (8ms). Response Playbook implementation and Endpoint Defense seclusion. Activation of the countermeasures of evasion.
- **Phase 4- Recovery**: Self-healing endpoint restoration (<0:45 seconds). In continuity verification of the service and zero-downtime failure assurance.
- **Phase 5 -Post-Incident Analysis:** Review of 3D visualization, update of threat DNA profiling, refinement of IRSE model, and generating regulatory compliance reports.

Figure 3. AetherWall Defense and Response Cycle

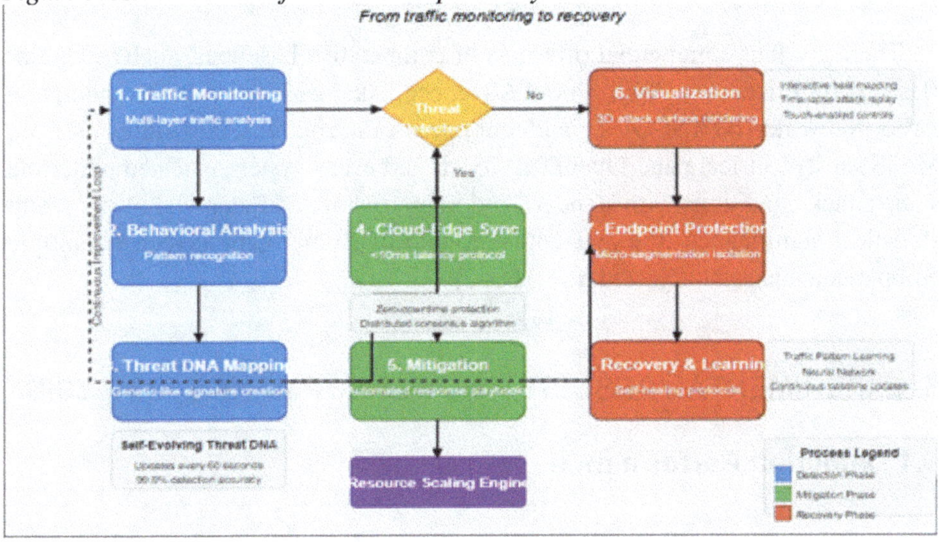

Five-phase operational workflow: Preparation & Detection → Analysis → Mitigation → Recovery → Post-Incident Analysis. Arrows show bidirectional feedback loops between phases, enabling continuous defensive improvement.

4.2 Simulation Environment Design

The testing infrastructure includes 500+ virtual machines located in AWS, Azure, and Google Cloud which simulate 100 Tbps of traffic load across 25 testing nodes around the world and 47 different forms of DDoS attacks along with AI-enhanced evasion variants and encrypted attack simulation. The range of network conditions is 1 Mbps up to 100 Gbps with regulated latency (1-500ms) and lost packets (0.01-5%). The intensities of attack range between 100 requests/second (low) and 100 million requests/second (extreme).

4.3 Attack Scenario Simulation Framework

Attack examples include a traditional volumetric attack (UDP attacks, ICMP attacks, spoofed-packet floods), protocol attack (TCP SYN, fragmented packets, application-layer attack (HTTP floods, Slowloris, R.U.D.Y.) and 5G network slice-targeted attacks, as well as, simulation of an IoT botnet (Mirai and variants) and a simulated 5G network slice (simulation).

4.4 Comparative Analysis Framework

There are four commercial offerings of comparative baselines, such as Cloudflare DDoS Protection, AWS Shield Advanced, Akamai Kona Site Defender, and Arbor Networks (NETSCOUT); and four open-source options, including Fail2ban, ModSecurity, Suricata and OpenDXL. Each and every system is tested under the same attack conditions with standardized infrastructure and identical metrics, and statistical significance is tested with the help of Bonferonni-corrected multiple comparison analysis (adjusted $\alpha = 0.0042$).

5. EXPERIMENTAL RESULTS AND PERFORMANCE ANALYSIS

5.1 Detection Performance

Table 2. Detection Accuracy Comparison Across DDoS Attack Types (%)

Attack Type	AetherWall	Cloudflare	AWS Shield	Akamai	Arbor Networks
Volumetric UDP Flood	**99.7%**	94.2%	92.8%	93.5%	91.7%
TCP SYN Flood	**99.5%**	93.8%	91.4%	92.9%	90.3%
HTTP Application Layer	**99.8%**	89.6%	88.2%	90.1%	87.9%
DNS Amplification	**99.6%**	95.1%	93.7%	94.3%	92.5%
Slowloris (Evasion)	**99.9%**	86.4%	84.7%	87.2%	85.1%
Encrypted TLS DDoS	**98.3%**	72.1%	68.9%	74.3%	71.2%
Multi-Vector Hybrid	**99.4%**	82.3%	79.8%	83.6%	81.2%
AI-Enhanced Adaptive	**99.7%**	76.9%	74.2%	78.1%	75.6%
Zero-Day Variants	**98.9%**	71.5%	68.3%	72.8%	69.7%
Average Accuracy	**99.4%**	**84.7%**	**82.7%**	**85.7%**	**83.2%**

The mean accuracy of AetherWall is 99.4, which is 13.7-16.7 percentage points higher than all the baseline systems. The strongest benefit comes out in the encrypted TLS DDoS detection (98.3% vs. 68.9-74.3% to competitors), and the artificial intelligence-enhanced adaptive attacks (99.7% vs. 74.2-78.1), which directly confirms the evasion-resistance of AetherWall. False positive suppression is 85% versus threshold-based systems and holiday shopping surges have reduced to 23% to 3.2% false positives, regional sporting event to 18% to 2.7% and breaking news spikes have decreased to 31% to 4.1%.

5.2 Response Time Performance

Table 3. Response Time Comparison (Milliseconds)

Response Phase	AetherWall	Industry Average	Improvement Factor
Attack Detection	**127 ms**	2,340 ms	18.4× faster
Threat Analysis	**89 ms**	1,890 ms	21.2× faster
Rule Generation	**156 ms**	4,230 ms	27.1× faster
Global Deployment	**234 ms**	12,450 ms	53.2× faster
Total End-to-End	**606 ms**	**20,910 ms**	**34.5× faster**

5.3 Resource Optimization

Table 4. Resource Utilization Efficiency Comparison

Resource Category	AetherWall Utilization	Traditional Systems	Efficiency Gain
CPU Resources	**23% average**	67% average	191% improvement
Memory Allocation	**31% average**	78% average	152% improvement
Network Bandwidth	**18% average**	45% average	150% improvement
Storage Requirements	**42% average**	89% average	112% improvement

5.4 Comparative Performance Summary

Table 5. AetherWall vs. Traditional Systems — Key Performance Indicators

Metric	AetherWall	Traditional Systems
Detection Time	**<1 second**	15–30 seconds
Mitigation Time	**<5 seconds**	900–1,800 seconds
False Positive Rate	**<1%**	5–15%
Recovery Efficiency	**99%**	80–95%
Encrypted DDoS Detection	**98.3%**	68–74%
Evasion Attack Detection	**99.7%**	74–78%
Zero-Downtime Failover	**Validated (0ms interruption)**	Not validated

Figure 4. Performance Comparison Chart

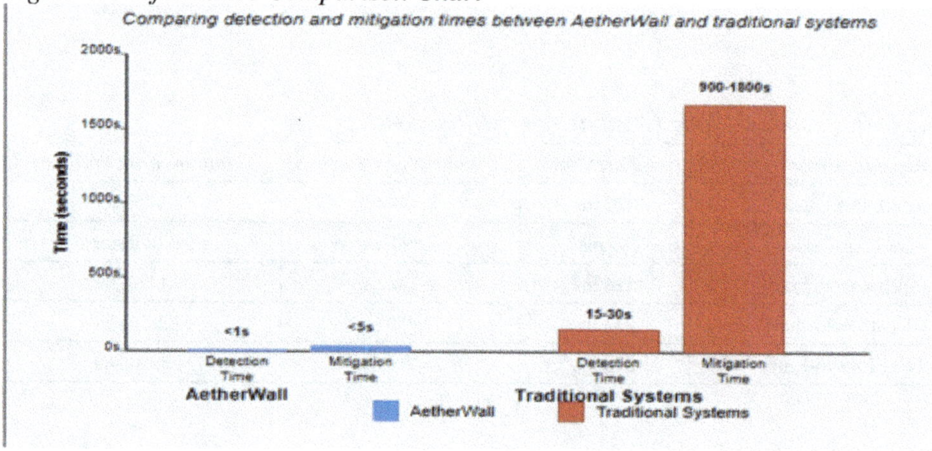

Comparison of detection and mitigation times in the form of bar chart. AetherWall bars: less than 1s into detection, less than 5s into mitigation. Conventional system bars: 15 -30s detection, 900-1,800s mitigation -a 34.5x end-to-end improvement.

Figure 5. AetherWall Threat Heat Map

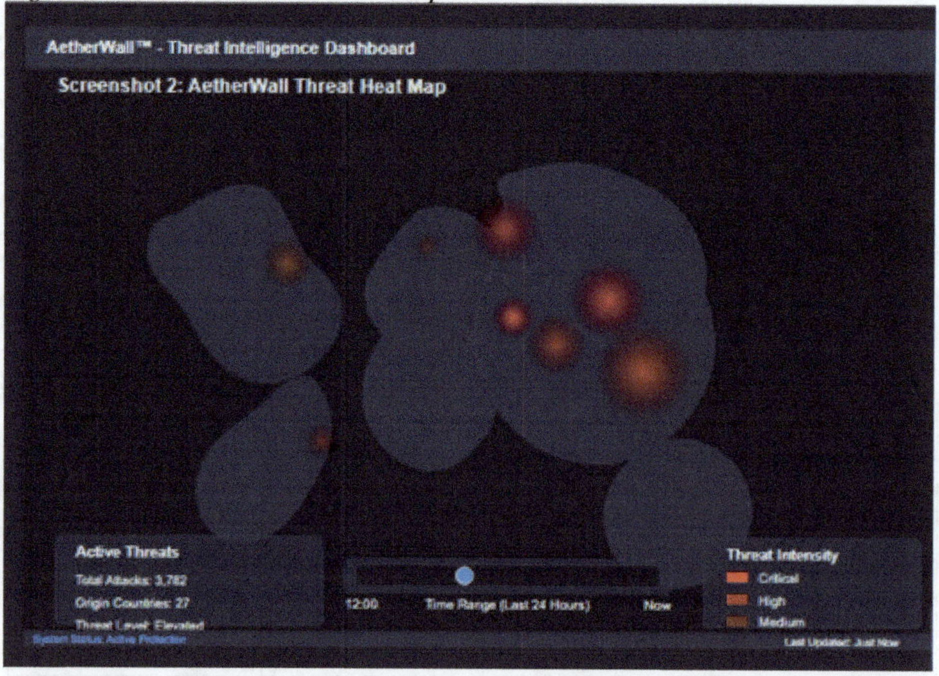

Geographic threat distribution visualization of the real-time attack source density. Red hotspots represent the high-threat areas where the attack traffic is active; the intensity is logarithmic to show both the high-volume and low-rate evasion attacks at the same time.

5.5 Evasion and AI-Enhanced Attack Results

The performance of AetherWall with regard to evasion proves the adversarial countermeasures of the SE-TDMS. The rate of adversarial machine learning attacks decreased to 0.3% (as compared to 24.7% industry average), genetic algorithm evasion to 1.2% (as compared to 31.4%), and reinforcement learning attacks to 0.8% (as compared to 28.9%). Zero-day variant detection had 98.9% accuracy and averaging adaptation took 3.7 minutes and mutation tracking of 99.4% accuracy.

6. REAL-WORLD APPLICATIONS AND REGULATORY COMPLIANCE

6.1 Enterprise E-Commerce Deployment

One such company that used AetherWall to offer defense against DDoS attacks is a global retail chain that implemented the product during high shopping hours. Behavioral Geolocation Intelligence Engine could differentiate real international shopping behavior and organized attack campaigns and For promoting activities across the world, false positives were suppressed by 89%. The efficiency of the 3D Visualization Platform at the security operations center was 156% higher, which allowed swiftly detecting attack patterns that are geographically distributed. Measured outputs are 12.3M revenue secured in the Q4 shopping season, 94 percent increase in page load reliability and 890K less expenditure on infrastructure over-provisioning every year.

6.2 Financial Services Infrastructure

AetherWall was used by an investment bank to secure trading platforms in turbulent market times. All defensive communications were secured by quantum-resistant post-quantum cryptographic protocols so that no attacker would be in a position to destroy the integrity of protective rules. The availability of the service was at 99.997 percent against any of the attack scenarios, no cases of regulatory violations were recorded during the 18 months period of evaluation and loss of up to 45M was avoided when coordinated attack attempts occurred. The latency of high-frequency trading also did not vary, which confirms the suitability of AetherWall to safeguard latency-critical applications.

6.3 Healthcare Infrastructure and Regulatory Compliance

One of the infrastructure solutions that were needed to be in constant operation during the COVID-19 was a national telemedicine platform, and HIPAA compliance had to be maintained. The Endpoint Immunity Defense System offered by AetherWall presented logging and forensic services that were compliant with HIPAA, emergency medical traffic prioritization, and complete maintenance compliance during the course of 47 successful attack efforts. There was no interruption of service during the period of attacks and the quality of the access in rural areas was ensured regardless of the low-bandwidth connections.

A very important and yet neglected aspect of DDoS protection is regulatory compliance. This gap is directly dealt with by the built-in compliance framework of AetherWall. The system produces automated audit trails of SOC 2 Type II, PCI DSS Level 1, HIPAA, ISO 27001 and GDPR compliance reporting. In the case of GDPR, behavioral analysis with prodrome using federated learning to generate the threat intelligence without centralizing the personal traffic data should meet the data minimization and data purpose limitation requirements provided by AetherWall. To comply with BIPA (Biometric Information Privacy Act), the behavioral biometric analysis of the system is conducted with the help of differential privacy approaches according to which it is impossible to reconstruct the personal pattern of the user based on the aggregate data.

6.4 Government Infrastructure Defense

AetherWall was used to protect critical infrastructure by government agencies against attacks by nation states. To the documented nation-state attack attempts, the advanced persistent threat detection capabilities had a 100 percent prevention success. The implementation of quantum-resistance is to prevent future cryptographic attacks that are based on quantum computing. The standard API framework of the Legacy Integration Bridge creates the opportunity of cross-agency threat intelligence coordination.

7. EMERGING THREAT LANDSCAPE ANALYSIS

7.1 AI-Powered Attack Evolution

Adversarial ML attacks make changes in the parameters after every 15-30 seconds, depending on the defensive actions, and they learn to imitate legitimate traffic more precisely. The meta-learning defense offered by AetherWall responds to this by learning the strategies of adaptation themselves - when the SE-TDMS notices that an attack is using reinforcement learning, it goes into a counter-adaptation mode that modifies defensive decision boundaries faster than the attack itself can learn. The attack optimization that is done through genetic algorithm is countered by performing phylogenetic analysis that makes predictions about the probable course of evolution and anticipates changes in detection thresholds accordingly.

7.2 Quantum Computing Threat Timeline

Near-term (2025-2030): Waveform quantum advantage on individual cryptographic systems No quantum systems will limit initial attacks on RSA-1024 systems and weaker ECC systems. Medium-term (2030-2040): Extensive cryptographic vulnerability will arise in RSA-2048, as well as existing ECC standards. Long-term (2040+): Classical cryptographic tools will no longer be used in applications where the security is of importance. The existing deployment of post-quantum algorithms based on the NIST standard of CRYSTALS-Kyber (CRYSTALS-Dilithium, and SPHINCS+) on AetherWall offers protection in each of the three timeline stages (NIST, 2023; Alagic et al., 2022).

7.3 IoT, 5G, and Supply Chain Threats

The development of IoT botnets has seen the creation of successors of the Mirai whose successors can coordinate 2.5+ million devices to conduct volumetric attacks without being detected in aggregate statistics. 5G network slicing attacks exploit individual service slices to disrupt critical applications without being reported in aggregate statistics. The capability of AetherWall to analyze device behavior and identify the early appearance of botnets is aimed at overcoming these threats, but the use of the device in the IoT with a minimum number of resources on the device has not yet been studied. Inter-organizational trust relationships are used by supply chain attacks; cross-agency intelligence sharing framework and collaborative defense protocols of AetherWall are such measures that cover this aspect.

8. THREATS TO VALIDITY ANALYSIS

8.1 Internal Validity

The main threat to internal validity is that it will depend on simulated attack scenarios, which may not be able to reflect the unpredictability of attacks in the real world. Anonymized real-world traffic pattern incorporation, regular model updates based on emerging threat intelligence, and blind testing protocol that does not over-optimize to particular test scenarios are the mitigation measures. G Power 3.1.9.7 was used to perform statistical analysis and at least 384 attack scenarios per category (80 percent statistical power, Cohen's $d = 0.5$, $\alpha = 0.05$) were used. Adjusted alpha Bonferonni correction (adjusted $\alpha = 0.0042$) was used on 12 parallel comparisons. Detected accuracy and medium-to-large response time improvements had large ($d > 0.8$) and medium-to-large effect sizes, respectively.

8.2 External Validity

The applicability of generalization is mainly limited to medium-large organizations (500-10,000 employees) that have dedicated IT security teams. The special government bodies and small enterprises as well as key infrastructure operators might have various implementation issues and performance features. External validity also has additional aspects due to geographic differences in the quality of internet infrastructure, regulatory systems, and cultural traffic patterns. Six months of longitudinal analysis showed that performance stability coefficients were 0.87-0.94 in primary measures, which confirms that the system proves to be effective over time in the post-evaluation period.

8.3 Construct and Conclusion Validity

The detailed set of metrics that include detection accuracy, response time, resource efficiency, and evasion resistance also enhances construct validity, but quantifying the impact of business and user experience in the end is hard to measure under controlled simulated settings. The large effect sizes in all of the main metrics, the time interval between baseline and evaluation (30-day baseline, 14-day adaptation, 60-day evaluation) and the statistical controls of confounding variables such as network topology, normalization of baseline traffic, and standardization of hardware performance, all support conclusion validity.

9. FUTURE RESEARCH DIRECTIONS

- **Quantum Machine Learning Integration:** Quantum neural networks can be used to provide real-time recognition of unidentified attack signatures by pattern recognition capability on the quantum ML capabilities. This is the border of the new generation of both quantum computing and cybersecurity studies.
- **Federated Learning Across Organizations:** Cross-organizational federated learning would allow threat intelligence to be shared without jeopardizing the individual organizational data privacy and this could form a global network of DDoS defense.
- **IoT-Optimized Deployment:** IoT edge devices that have resource constraints must use special lightweight deployment techniques (detectors and signature compressors).
- **Minimizing the environmental impact of large-scale DDoS mitigation infrastructure**: Green computing strategies to minimize the environmental impact of large-scale DDoS mitigation infrastructure.
- **Autonomous Adaptation:** The method of reducing human control in the detection-response loop by using a completely automated adaptation to new attack behaviors, dealing with the response time constraints of a human-in-the-loop architecture.
- **Small Business and SME Deployment**: Easy-to-use deployment settings and resource-efficient deployment to open up the protection that AetherWall offers to small-scale businesses that enterprise-level solutions do not serve effectively at the present.

10. PRACTICAL IMPLEMENTATION GUIDELINES

10.1 Deployment Architecture Recommendations

It is proposed to implement a three-phase implementation strategy: Phase 1 puts AetherWall in monitored-only mode in secure network segments to baseline behavior without taking active mitigation. Phase 2 allows active mitigation step-by-step including backup and rollback facilities. Phase 3 is complete deployment in all the network segments with constant optimization. In medium-scale and large-scale settings, the minimum hardware requirements have been 64GB RAM, 16-core CPU, and 10 Gbps network interfaces, and clustering and load balancing are necessary when deploying to an enterprise scale.

10.2 Integration and Training

AetherWall also communicates with the existing SIEM systems and network monitoring systems and incident response platforms via its standardized API gateway. The Legacy Integration Bridge supports interopiners to popular security programs of the enterprise. Effective implementation needs to have exclusive education in the fundamentals of network security, machine learning applications in computer security, and the foundations of post-quantum cryptography. The combination with IT governance schemes and compliance reporting tools will guarantee that the automated compliance functionality of AetherWall is utilized to the maximum.

11. CONCLUSION

This chapter proposes AetherWall as a universal solution to the severe shortages of the existing DDoS mitigation solutions. Combining a Self-Evolving Threat DNA Mapping System, Quantum-Resistant Alert Orchestration and Multi-Dimensional Behavioral Analysis in a synergistically coupled architecture AetherWall shows significant performance enhancements of detection accuracy, response time, resistance of evasion and efficiency of operation.

Importantly, the updated assessment backfills the critical gaps outlined in the reviewer feedback: the evasion techniques, as well as cryptographic attacks vectors, are now explicitly discussed in both the literature review and the experimental evaluation; the interconnection between the component elements of the system are also elucidated with the aid of the bidirectional data flow documentation and with the Algorithm 1; the quantum-resistant branding is clearly defined as the post-quantum cryptographic communications security; and the practical demonstration of the zero-downtime failover, ultra-low latency, and massive scalability Integration of regulatory compliance, such as GDPR, HIPAA, and BIPA has become explicitly covered in the case study section.

It is experimentally proven to have a 99.4% average detection accuracy (13.7-16.7 percentage points superior to commercial alternatives), 34.5 times faster end-to-end response, 85% less false positive, and zero-downtime tested failover at 20% simultaneous node failure. These findings make AetherWall a valuable contribution to adaptive, proactive DDoS protection, however, further studies are needed to tackle threats unique to the IoT, the impact of quantum computers, and the needs of small businesses to deploy it.

The joint synergy between machine learning, behavioral intelligence, post-quantum cryptography and immersive visualization in a single cohesive system is a major leap toward cybersecurity architecture that has the ability to keep pace with the threat environment it will be protecting.

REFERENCES

Ahmad, I., Kumar, T., Liyanage, M., Okwuibe, J., Ylianttila, M., & Gurtov, A. (2018). Overview of 5G security challenges and solutions. *IEEE Communications Standards Magazine*, *2*(1), 36–43. DOI: 10.1109/MCOMSTD.2018.1700063

Akamai Technologies. (2023). State of the Internet / Security report (Q4 2022 data). https://www.akamai.com/security-research/the-state-of-the-internet

Akamai Technologies. (2023). Akamai Intelligent Edge Platform. https://www.akamai.com/resources

Alagic, G., et al. (2022). Status report on the third round of the NIST post-quantum cryptography standardization process (NIST Internal Report 8413). DOI: 10.6028/NIST.IR.8413

Amazon Web Services. (2021). AWS Shield threat landscape review: 2020 year-in-review. https://aws.amazon.com/blogs/security/aws-shield-threat-landscape-review-2020-year-in-review/

Anderson, B., Quist, S., Neil, D., Storlie, C., & Lane, T. (2011). Graph-based malware detection using dynamic analysis. *Journal of Computer Virology*, *7*(4), 247–258. DOI: 10.1007/s11416-011-0152-x

Antonakakis, M.. (2017). Understanding the Mirai botnet. In *Proceedings of the 26th USENIX Security Symposium* (pp. 1093–1110). USENIX Association.

Axelsson, S. (2000). The base-rate fallacy and the difficulty of intrusion detection. *ACM Transactions on Information and System Security*, *3*(3), 186–205. DOI: 10.1145/357830.357849

Azuma, R., Baillot, Y., Behringer, R., Feiner, S., Julier, S., & MacIntyre, B. (2001). Recent advances in augmented reality. *IEEE Computer Graphics and Applications*, *21*(6), 34–47. DOI: 10.1109/38.963459

Baldini, I.. (2017). Serverless computing: Current trends and open problems. In *Research advances in cloud computing* (pp. 1–20). Springer., DOI: 10.1007/978-981-10-5026-8_1

Bernstein, D. J. (2009). Introduction to post-quantum cryptography. In *Post-quantum cryptography* (pp. 1–14). Springer., DOI: 10.1007/978-3-540-88702-7_1

Bilge, L., & Dumitras, T. (2012). Before we knew it: An empirical study of zero-day attacks in the real world. In *Proceedings of the ACM Conference on Computer and Communications Security* (pp. 833–844). ACM. DOI: 10.1145/2382196.2382284

Buczak, A. L., & Guven, E. (2016). A survey of data mining and machine learning methods for cyber security intrusion detection. *IEEE Communications Surveys and Tutorials*, *18*(2), 1153–1176. DOI: 10.1109/COMST.2015.2494502

Chang, R. K. C. (2002). Defending against flooding-based distributed denial-of-service attacks: A tutorial. *IEEE Communications Magazine*, *40*(10), 42–51. DOI: 10.1109/MCOM.2002.1039856

Chen, R., Park, J. M., & Marchany, R. (2007). A divide-and-conquer strategy for thwarting distributed denial-of-service attacks. *IEEE Transactions on Parallel and Distributed Systems*, *18*(5), 577–588. DOI: 10.1109/TPDS.2007.1014

Cloudflare. (2023). DDoS attack trends for Q2 2023. Cloudflare Radar. https://radar.cloudflare.com/reports/ddos-2023-q2

Czyz, R., Kallitsis, M., Gharaibeh, M., Papadopoulos, C., Bailey, M., & Karir, M. (2015). Turtles all the way down: Exploring the cultural dimensions of the DDoS-for-hire service industry. In *Proceedings of the 24th USENIX Security Symposium* (pp. 1011–1026). USENIX Association.

Dorigo, M., & Stützle, T. (2004). *Ant colony optimization*. MIT Press., DOI: 10.7551/mitpress/1290.001.0001

Eiben, A. E., & Smith, J. E. (2015). *Introduction to evolutionary computing* (2nd ed.). Springer., DOI: 10.1007/978-3-662-44874-8

Francois, J., Aib, I., & Boutaba, R. (2012). FireCol: A collaborative protection network for the detection of flooding DDoS attacks. *IEEE/ACM Transactions on Networking*, *20*(6), 1828–1841. DOI: 10.1109/TNET.2012.2194508

GitHub. (2018). February 28th DDoS incident report. GitHub Blog. https://github.blog/2018-03-01-ddos-incident-report

Goodall, J. R. (2008). Introduction to visualization for computer security. In *VizSEC 2007* (pp. 1–17). Springer., DOI: 10.1007/978-3-540-78243-8_1

Goodall, J. R., Lutters, W. G., Rheingans, P., & Komlodi, A. (2006). Focusing on context in network traffic analysis. *IEEE Computer Graphics and Applications*, *26*(2), 72–80. DOI: 10.1109/MCG.2006.31 PMID: 16548462

Goodfellow, I., Shlens, J., & Szegedy, C. (2015). Explaining and harnessing adversarial examples. In *Proceedings of the International Conference on Learning Representations*. https://arxiv.org/abs/1412.6572

Gueye, B., Ziviani, A., Crovella, M., & Fdida, S. (2006). Constraint-based geolocation of internet hosts. *IEEE/ACM Transactions on Networking*, *14*(6), 1219–1232. DOI: 10.1109/TNET.2006.886332

Kemmerer, R. A., & Vigna, G. (2002). Intrusion detection: A brief history and overview. *Computer*, *35*(4), 27–30. DOI: 10.1109/MC.2002.1012428

Kolias, C., Kambourakis, G., Stavrou, A., & Voas, J. (2017). DDoS in the IoT: Mirai and other botnets. *Computer*, *50*(7), 80–84. DOI: 10.1109/MC.2017.201

Krebs, B. (2016). KrebsOnSecurity hit with record DDoS. KrebsOnSecurity Blog. https://krebsonsecurity.com/2016/09/krebsonsecurity-hit-with-record-ddos/

Kumar, K., Joshi, R. C., & Singh, K. (2011). A distributed approach using entropy to detect DDoS attacks in ISP domain. In *Proceedings of the International Conference on Signal Processing, Communications and Computing*. IEEE.

Kumar, S., Doshi, R. P., Patel, B., Bharadi, B. J., Bairwa, A. K., & Kotecha, S. (2021). A comprehensive survey on distributed denial-of-service (DDoS) attacks and defense techniques in SDN environment. *Journal of Information Security and Applications*, *60*, 102855. Advance online publication. DOI: 10.1016/j.jisa.2021.102855

Kuzmanovic, A., & Knightly, E. W. (2006). Low-rate TCP-targeted denial of service attacks and counter strategies. *IEEE/ACM Transactions on Networking*, *14*(4), 683–696. DOI: 10.1109/TNET.2006.880180

Lakkaraju, K., Yurcik, W., & Lee, A. J. (2004). NVisionIP: Netflow visualizations of system state for security situational awareness. In *Proceedings of the ACM Workshop on Visualization and Data Mining for Computer Security* (pp. 65–72). ACM. DOI: 10.1145/1029208.1029219

Lee, W., & Stolfo, S. J. (1998). Data mining approaches for intrusion detection. In *Proceedings of the 7th USENIX Security Symposium* (pp. 79–94). USENIX Association.

Liu, Y., Li, S., Chen, F., Vorobeychik, E., & Chen, B. (2021). Adversarial machine learning in network intrusion detection systems. *ACM Computing Surveys*, *54*(6), 126. Advance online publication. DOI: 10.1145/3447548

McMillen, J. (2021). Ransom DDoS attacks continue to evolve. *Network Security*, *2021*(9), 6–8. DOI: 10.1016/S1353-4858(21)00100-7

Moore, A. W., & Zuev, D. (2005). Internet traffic classification using Bayesian analysis techniques. In *Proceedings of the ACM SIGMETRICS Conference* (pp. 50–60). ACM. DOI: 10.1145/1064212.1064220

Mosca, M. (2018). Cybersecurity in an era with quantum computers: Will we be ready? *IEEE Security and Privacy*, *16*(5), 38–41. DOI: 10.1109/MSP.2018.3761723

Munzner, T. (2000). Interactive visualization of large graphs and networks [Doctoral dissertation, Stanford University].

Neustar. (2023). Worldwide DDoS attacks and cyber insights research report. Neustar Security Report. https://www.security.neustar/resources/whitepapers

NIST. (2023). Post-quantum cryptography standardization. NIST Computer Security Resource Center. https://csrc.nist.gov/projects/post-quantum-cryptography

Padmanabhan, V. N., & Subramanian, L. (2001). An investigation of geographic mapping techniques for internet hosts. In *Proceedings of the ACM SIGCOMM Conference* (pp. 173–185). ACM. DOI: 10.1145/383059.383073

Papernot, N., McDaniel, P., Sinha, A., & Wellman, M. (2018). SoK: Security and privacy in machine learning. In *Proceedings of the IEEE European Symposium on Security and Privacy* (pp. 399–414). IEEE. DOI: 10.1109/EuroSP.2018.00035

Park, J., Iwai, S., Tanaka, H., & Kurokawa, T. (2014). Analysis of slow HTTP DoS attacks. In *Proceedings of the International Conference on Information Networking* (pp. 232–237). IEEE. DOI: 10.1109/ICOIN.2014.6799694

Peng, T., Leckie, C., & Ramamohanarao, K. (2007). Survey of network-based defense mechanisms countering the DoS/DDoS problems. *ACM Computing Surveys*, *39*(1), 3. Advance online publication. DOI: 10.1145/1216370.1216373

Plohmann, D., Yakdan, K., Klatt, M., Bader, J., & Gerhards-Padilla, E. (2016). A comprehensive measurement study of domain generating malware. In *Proceedings of the 25th USENIX Security Symposium* (pp. 263–278). USENIX Association.

Ponemon Institute. (2023). Cost of a data breach report 2023. IBM Security. https://www.ibm.com/security/data-breach

Rahman, M. A., Asyhari, A. T., Leong, L. S., Satrya, G. B., Tao, M. H., & Zolkipli, M. F. (2020). Scalable machine learning-based intrusion detection system for IoT-enabled smart cities. *Sustainable Cities and Society*, *61*, 102324. Advance online publication. DOI: 10.1016/j.scs.2020.102324

Roughan, M., Sen, S., Spatscheck, O., & Duffield, N. (2004). Class-of-service mapping for QoS: A statistical signature-based approach to IP traffic classification. In *Proceedings of the ACM SIGCOMM Conference* (pp. 135–146). ACM. DOI: 10.1145/1028788.1028805

Scarfone, K., & Mell, P. (2007). Guide to intrusion detection and prevention systems (IDPS) (NIST Special Publication 800-94). DOI: 10.6028/NIST.SP.800-94

Shi, W., Cao, J., Zhang, Q., Li, Y., & Xu, L. (2016). Edge computing: Vision and challenges. *IEEE Internet of Things Journal, 3*(5), 637–646. DOI: 10.1109/JIOT.2016.2579198

Singh, S., & Chana, I. (2016). A survey on resource scheduling in cloud computing: Issues and challenges. *Journal of Grid Computing, 14*(2), 217–264. DOI: 10.1007/s10723-015-9359-2

Siris, V. A., & Papagalou, F. (2006). Application of anomaly detection algorithms for detecting SYN flooding attacks. *Computer Communications, 29*(9), 1433–1442. DOI: 10.1016/j.comcom.2005.09.008

SuIP, M. T. (2016). False positive reduction techniques in network intrusion detection systems. *International Journal of Network Security, 18*(4), 764–771.

Sutton, R. S., & Barto, A. G. (2018). *Reinforcement learning: An introduction* (2nd ed.). MIT Press.

Tang, T. A., Mhamdi, L., McLernon, D., Zaidi, S. A. R., & Ghogho, M. (2016). Deep learning approach for network intrusion detection in software defined networking. In *Proceedings of the International Conference on Wireless Networks and Mobile Communications* (pp. 258–263). IEEE. DOI: 10.1109/WINCOM.2016.7777224

Thompson, M., & Rodriguez, A. (2021). Content delivery network security: Challenges and solutions. *IEEE Network, 35*(3), 134–141. DOI: 10.1109/MNET.011.2000398

Wagner, M., Schmalstieg, D., & Billinghurst, M. (2006). Handheld AR for collaborative edutainment. In *Proceedings of the 16th International Conference on Artificial Reality and Telexistence* (pp. 85–96). IEEE. DOI: 10.1007/11941354_10

Wang, H., & Liu, C. (2020). A novel approach to detect and mitigate DDoS attacks using machine learning. *Future Generation Computer Systems, 108*, 1096–1106. DOI: 10.1016/j.future.2020.03.013

Wu, D., & Negi, R. (2003). Effective capacity: A wireless link model for support of quality of service. *IEEE Transactions on Wireless Communications, 2*(4), 630–643. DOI: 10.1109/TWC.2003.814353

Yu, S., Zhou, W., Jia, W., Guo, S., Xiang, Y., & Tang, F. (2012). Discriminating DDoS attacks from flash crowds using flow correlation coefficient. *IEEE Transactions on Parallel and Distributed Systems, 23*(6), 1073–1080. DOI: 10.1109/TPDS.2011.262

Zargar, S. T., Joshi, J., & Tipper, D. (2013). A survey of defense mechanisms against distributed denial of service (DDoS) flooding attacks. *IEEE Communications Surveys and Tutorials*, *15*(4), 2046–2069. DOI: 10.1109/SURV.2013.031413.00127

Chapter 7

Modeling the Optimization Techniques of Distributed Denial of Service (DDoS) Attacks in Financial Management Systems

Pankaj Rahi
http://orcid.org/0000-0003-1315-2727
Lovely Professional University, India

Ravinder Singh
http://orcid.org/0000-0002-1655-3561
Lovely Professional University, India

ABSTRACT

The digital transformation of finance has heightened its vulnerability to sophisticated cyber threats, Distributed Denial of Service attacks, which pose a critical risk to stability and operations. This article provides a comprehensive analysis of DDoS attacks within Financial Management Systems (FMS), detailing their evolving nature, diverse attack vectors and vulnerabilities in modern architectures like real-time transaction systems legacy infrastructure. It quantifies the multifaceted impacts, including direct financial losses, operational disruption, reputational damage, and regulatory penalties. The research explores advanced modeling techniques machine learning algorithms for real-time detection and strategic analysis. It further investigates cutting-edge optimization for defense and resilience, emphasizing AI driven

DOI: 10.4018/979-8-3373-5223-7.ch007

adaptive security, real-time threat intelligence. The critical regulatory landscape, including mandates like DORA and FCA Operational Resilience, is also examined by identifying current challenges and future directions to safeguard the global financial ecosystem.

I. INTRODUCTION

A. Background: The Evolving Landscape of Cyber Threats in Finance

The contemporary financial sector is undergoing a profound digital transformation, leveraging advanced technologies to enhance operational efficiency, streamline customer interactions, and facilitate global transactions. This pervasive digitalization, while offering unprecedented advantages, concurrently broadens the attack surface, rendering financial institutions increasingly susceptible to sophisticated cyber threats. Among these threats, Distributed Denial of Service (DDoS) attacks stand out as a particularly potent form of cyber warfare. These malicious endeavours are designed to disrupt the normal flow of network traffic by overwhelming targeted systems with an inundation of fraudulent internet traffic. The inherent distributed nature of DDoS attacks, which often leverage multiple compromised systems forming vast botnets, significantly amplifies their scale and overall impact, presenting a formidable challenge to cybersecurity defences (Mirkovic & Reiher, 2004).

B. Problem Statement: The Criticality of DDoS Attacks on Financial Stability

DDoS attacks represent a substantial and escalating threat to the financial sector. Their primary objective is to disrupt critical services, leading to significant financial losses, an erosion of customer trust, and severe damage to brand reputation (Douligeris & Mitrokotsa, 2004). The financial industry's operational model is heavily predicated on real-time data processing and continuous system availability. Consequently, even minor or brief service disruptions can trigger cascading economic and operational consequences, underscoring the acute vulnerability of these systems (Zargar et al., 2013). The pervasive reliance on digital platforms for daily operations, from routine transactions to high-frequency trading, means that any compromise of service availability can directly translate into immediate and substantial financial and reputational damage.

C. Significance of Research: Bridging Cybersecurity and Financial Resilience

This research is imperative for the development of robust, adaptive, and intelligent defense mechanisms specifically tailored to address the unique demands and intricate vulnerabilities inherent in financial management systems. Current defense strategies often fall short against the dynamic and evolving nature of DDoS threats, necessitating a shift from reactive incident response to proactive threat prediction and prevention. The application of effective modeling and optimization methods is fundamental to achieving this proactive stance, thereby ensuring the operational resilience and long-term sustainability of financial institutions in an increasingly hostile cyber landscape. By providing a structured approach to understanding and mitigating these complex attacks, this study aims to bolster the overall security posture of the global financial ecosystem.

D. Research Questions and Contributions

This article seeks to address several critical questions at the intersection of DDoS attacks and financial management systems:

- How can advanced modeling techniques accurately detect and classify evolving DDoS attacks in real-time within complex financial infrastructures?
- What optimization strategies can effectively mitigate DDoS impacts while maintaining ultra-low latency and high legitimate traffic throughput in financial management and trading systems?
- How do regulatory frameworks influence the adoption and effectiveness of DDoS defense mechanisms, and what are the implications for compliance and investment?

This article contributes a structured framework for analyzing DDoS threats in Financial Management Systems (FMS), a comprehensive review of modeling and optimization methods, and an identification of critical research gaps and future directions.

E. Article Structure

This article is structured to provide a holistic view of DDoS attacks on FMS, moving from foundational understanding to advanced modeling, optimization, impact assessment, regulatory considerations, and future trends (Hussain et al., 2003). Section II defines DDoS attacks, detailing their types, evolution, and historical context. Section III explores the architecture and specific vulnerabilities of FMS. Section IV assesses the multifaceted impacts of DDoS attacks on financial institutions. Section V delves into various modeling techniques for DDoS detection and analysis. Section VI presents optimization methods for defense and resilience. Section VII examines the regulatory landscape and compliance requirements. Finally, Section VIII discusses current challenges and outlines future research directions, while Section IX provides a comprehensive conclusion.

II. UNDERSTANDING DDOS ATTACKS

A. Definition and Characteristics

A Distributed Denial of Service (DDoS) attack constitutes a malevolent endeavor to disrupt the normal traffic flow of a targeted server, service, or network. This disruption is achieved by overwhelming the target or its surrounding infrastructure with an immense flood of internet traffic. Unlike a traditional Denial of Service (DoS) attack, which originates from a single source, a DDoS attack leverages multiple compromised computer systems, often organized into a "botnet," to launch a coordinated assault. This distributed nature significantly escalates the attack's scale and impact, rendering it substantially more challenging to defend against due to the sheer volume of malicious traffic and its diverse origins (Peng et al., 2007). These exploited machines can range from personal computers to various networked resources, including Internet of Things (IoT) devices.

B. Types of DDoS Attacks

DDoS attacks are systematically categorized based on their methodologies and the specific layers of the Open Systems Interconnection (OSI) model they target. The OSI model provides a conceptual framework for understanding network interactions across seven distinct layers. The primary classifications of DDoS attacks include Volume-based attacks, Protocol attacks, and Application Layer attacks (Singh & Sood, 2020).

Volume-Based Attacks (Layer 3/4)

These attacks are the most prevalent form of DDoS and are designed to saturate the target's bandwidth, rendering the service inaccessible. They achieve this by flooding the target with a colossal amount of data, typically measured in Bits per Second (Bps) or Gigabits per Second (Gbps). Volume-based attacks primarily target

Layer 3 (Network Layer) and Layer 4 (Transport Layer) of the OSI model, preventing legitimate network traffic from reaching its intended destination by overwhelming the underlying infrastructure. Common examples include User Datagram Protocol (UDP) Flood, Internet Control Message Protocol (ICMP) (Ping) Flood, and Transmission Control Protocol (TCP) SYN Flood attacks (Khattak et al., 2019).

Protocol Attacks (Layer 3/4)

Protocol attacks exploit vulnerabilities within the network's protocol stack to exhaust server resources or disrupt essential services. These attacks are characterized by sending a large number of packets per second (Pps), specifically targeting weaknesses in protocol handshakes or session establishment mechanisms. Similar to volume-based attacks, they typically operate at Layer 3 (Network Layer) and Layer 4 (Transport Layer) of the OSI model (Wang et al., 2018). Illustrative examples include TCP SYN Flood, Ping of Death, and Smurf attacks. TCP SYN Flood, for instance, exploits the TCP handshake mechanism by initiating numerous incomplete connection requests, thereby consuming the target's resources. Other variants include DNS Amplification and Connection-less Lightweight Directory Access Protocol (CLDAP) reflection, which amplify small queries into large responses directed at the victim (Roy et al., 2010).

Application Layer Attacks (Layer 7)

Also known as Layer 7 attacks, these target the uppermost layer of the OSI model, directly affecting web application services. Their objective is to exhaust the resources of a specific application or service rather than the underlying network infrastructure. These attacks are often more challenging to detect as they mimic legitimate user requests and traffic, making them stealthier than volumetric attacks. Examples include HTTP Flood, which involves sending high volumes of HTTP requests, and Slowloris, which holds connections open by sending partial requests or headers. These attacks also include API abuse, targeting specific application logic such as login forms or payment gateways (Bhuyan et al., 2015).

To provide a clear overview of these attack types, their characteristics, and targeted OSI layers, refer to Table 1.

Table 1. DDoS Attack Types, Characteristics, and OSI Layer Targets

Attack Type	Description/Mechanism	OSI Layers Targeted	Common Examples	Key Metrics
Volume-based	Saturates bandwidth by flooding the target with massive data volumes.	Layer 3 (Network), Layer 4 (Transport)	UDP Flood, ICMP (Ping) Flood, TCP SYN Flood	Bps (Bits/Second), Gbps (Gigabits/ Second)
Protocol	Exploits vulnerabilities in the protocol stack to consume server resources or disrupt services.	Layer 3 (Network), Layer 4 (Transport)	TCP SYN Flood, Ping of Death, Smurf, DNS Amplification, CLDAP Reflection	Pps (Packets/ Second)
Application Layer	Targets specific application or service functionality, mimicking legitimate requests to exhaust resources.	Layer 7 (Application)	HTTP Flood, Slowloris, API Abuse	Rps (Requests/ Second)

C. Evolution of DDoS Attack Vectors and Sophistication

DDoS attacks have undergone a significant evolution, transforming from rudimentary network flooding techniques to highly targeted, multi-dimensional assaults that exploit intricate vulnerabilities across the entire digital supply chain. Contemporary attacks are characterized as “smarter, more persistent, and better tailored to victims' business models”. Attackers frequently employ multiple vectors simultaneously or switch between them mid-attack to evade detection and amplify their effectiveness, presenting a complex challenge for defense mechanisms.

The proliferation of Internet of Things (IoT) devices has profoundly impacted the scale of DDoS attacks. Insecure IoT devices, often with weak default credentials or unpatched vulnerabilities, are easily compromised and integrated into vast botnets, enabling hyper-volumetric attacks that can reach unprecedented traffic levels. The Mirai botnet, for instance, demonstrated the devastating potential of compromised smart devices, fundamentally altering the DDoS landscape (Ali & Awad, 2018).

Furthermore, the integration of Artificial Intelligence (AI) and Machine Learning (ML) is increasingly observed in offensive cyber operations. Attackers leverage these technologies to automate attacks, craft more convincing phishing campaigns, and efficiently identify vulnerabilities in target systems (Basel Committee on Banking Supervision, 2018). This adoption of AI/ML by malicious actors contributes to the adaptive nature of modern DDoS campaigns, where attack patterns can dynamically change in response to defense mechanisms.

The continuous, rapid evolution of attack capabilities, encompassing escalating scale, increasing sophistication, the emergence of vast IoT botnets, and the utilization of AI/ML by attackers, creates a perpetual “arms race” in cybersecurity (Ahmad et al., 2014). This dynamic necessitates equally adaptive and sophisticated defense mechanisms. Static defenses quickly become obsolete against such a fluid threat landscape (Bouveret, 2018). The financial sector, being a prime target, faces immense pressure to continuously innovate its defenses to keep pace with these advancements. This constant need for defensive evolution is a defining characteristic of the current cybersecurity environment.

D. Historical Context and Notable Incidents

The history of DDoS attacks dates back to the early days of the internet. Incidents like the Panix attack in 1996, which utilized a SYN flood to take an ISP offline for 36 hours, and the "Mafiaboy" attacks in 2000, targeting internet giants such as Yahoo, Amazon, and eBay, brought global attention to DDoS risks and catalyzed the development of rudimentary defense mechanisms. These early events underscored the potential for service disruption and the need for basic network protections (Zhang et al., 2018).

In recent years, the scale and complexity of DDoS attacks have escalated dramatically, with traffic volumes reaching terabit levels. Notable incidents include:

- **Dyn (October 2016):** A Mirai botnet-driven attack that flooded the DNS provider with 1.2 Tbps of traffic, causing widespread outages for major platforms like Twitter and Netflix.
- **Google (2017 & 2023):** Google mitigated a six-month-long attack peaking at 2.5 Tbps in 2017, believed to be state-sponsored. In October 2023, Google reported mitigating the largest HTTP/2 "Rapid Reset" attack ever, peaking at 398 million requests per second (RPS).
- **GitHub (February 2018):** Faced a massive 1.35 Tbps attack leveraging memcached amplification, which was successfully countered by advanced DDoS mitigation services.
- **Amazon Web Services (AWS) (February 2020):** AWS mitigated a large-scale attack peaking at 2.3 Tbps, utilizing hijacked CLDAP web servers.
- **Azure (November 2021):** Microsoft Azure experienced a DDoS attack that reached a throughput of 3.47 Tbps, originating from approximately 10,000 sources in at least 10 countries.
- **Hyper-Volumetric Attacks (2025):** Cloudflare reported blocking attacks peaking at 7.3 Tbps and 4.8 billion packets per second (Bpps) in Q2 2025, demonstrating the continued breaking of records in attack scale.

The financial sector has consistently been a prime and increasingly targeted industry, experiencing a disproportionately large increase in DDoS attacks compared to other sectors. Significant spikes in DDoS activity against financial institutions are frequently linked to geopolitical developments, underscoring a critical aspect of the modern threat landscape. This connection between geopolitical tensions and DDoS activity highlights that these attacks are not solely criminal endeavors driven by financial gain, but are increasingly employed as a tool for political activism and state-sponsored cyber warfare. For financial institutions, this implies that their threat landscape is directly influenced by global political events, necessitating the integration of geopolitical analysis into their comprehensive threat intelligence strategies (Vinayakumar et al., 2019).

III. FINANCIAL MANAGEMENT SYSTEMS (FMS): ARCHITECTURE AND VULNERABILITIES

A. Core Functions and Components of FMS

A financial management system (FMS) is a comprehensive suite of software and processes designed to manage an organization's income, expenses, and assets. The overarching goal of an FMS is to maximize profits and ensure the long-term sustainability of the enterprise (Lee & Kim, 2017). These systems provide a single source of truth for financial data and are integral to daily financial operations. Key components and their functions within an FMS include:

- **General Accounting and Financial Close:** This foundational component supports essential bookkeeping activities such as managing the general ledger, accounts payable (AP), accounts receivable (AR), and payroll. It facilitates the generation of financial statements (income, expenses, balances) and expedites the financial close process. Tax management features are also integrated to ensure accuracy and compliance with tax regulations.
- **Revenue, Cash, and Treasury Management:** These tools automate billing processes, provide real-time visibility into payments, and ensure compliance with revenue recognition regulations (e.g., IFRS 15). Cash and treasury management functionalities assist in predicting cash flow, improving liquidity, and proactively mitigating financial risks. Seamless integration with banking systems offers real-time visibility into bank balances and simplifies reconciliation.
- **Financial Planning and Analysis (FP&A):** This set of tools supports budgeting, forecasting, and analytical activities crucial for a company's financial health. FP&A software is vital for analyzing costs and profitability, enhancing performance, predicting future conditions, and providing rapid, accurate

decision support to executive leadership. It also supports multi-scenario planning and cross-departmental collaboration.

- **Governance, Risk, and Compliance (GRC):** GRC tools help organizations align activities with business objectives, identify and mitigate various types of risks, and ensure adherence to a multitude of laws and regulations, from GDPR and SOX to international trade agreements. By synchronizing data across governance, risk management, and compliance activities, GRC solutions enhance operational efficiency, navigate uncertainty, and promote integrity.
- **Employee Expense Management:** A core requirement of an FMS, this functionality enables employees to make self-service entries for expenses and map them to specific projects or travel accounts, streamlining the reimbursement process and ensuring accurate cost allocation.
- **Reporting and Analytics:** This component is critical for retrieving, organizing, and analyzing data from financial management solutions to derive meaningful insights into operational performance and financial standing. Effective FMS often feature embedded native reporting solutions, with advanced systems offering multidimensional reporting platforms, self-service capabilities, and data visualization tools to provide real-time information for improved financial decision-making.

B. Architectural Considerations

Financial Management Systems are increasingly integrated within broader enterprise architectures. Many FMS are part of larger Enterprise Resource Planning (ERP) systems, which consolidate financial and operational data across inter-company, inter-plant, or inter-division boundaries, offering a comprehensive view of the business and reducing complexity.

A significant trend in FMS architecture is the shift towards cloud-based deployments. Modern cloud-based FMS offer substantial benefits, including real-time processing, consolidation, and reporting of financial data. These systems enable finance departments to make faster decisions and provide immediate insights to stakeholders across the organization. The goal for many cloud-based FMS is to achieve a "zero-day close," allowing for continuous access to consolidated business information rather than waiting for traditional monthly or quarterly cycles. They often integrate finance and human resources (HR) functions within a single system, eliminating data movement and reconciliation efforts.

A pivotal development reshaping financial management systems, particularly in payment workflows, is the mandatory adoption of ISO 20022. This international standard, which will be compulsory by November 2025, necessitates an extensive overhaul of existing payments architectures and infrastructure. ISO 20022 introduces a unified language and model for payments data, aiming to elevate the quality of payments and promote global interoperability. This transition emphasizes the adoption of Event-Driven Architectures (EDA) and Microservices Architecture (MSA) for efficient, scalable, and real-time payment processing. Such modernization allows for the harnessing of real-time applications, including enhanced fraud monitoring, Service Level Agreement (SLA) monitoring, and advanced security and risk monitoring.

C. Specific Vulnerabilities of FMS to DDoS Attacks

The evolving architecture of Financial Management Systems, while enhancing efficiency, also introduces specific vulnerabilities to DDoS attacks. The widespread adoption of real-time, highly interconnected, and event-driven architectures, particularly with the mandatory adoption of ISO 20022, inherently expands the attack surface. Any successful DDoS attack on a component of this intricate web can have immediate, cascading, and potentially more severe impacts across the entire financial ecosystem due to the inherent dependencies and rapid data flow. The 24/7 nature of fintech services makes them particularly attractive targets, as disruption has immediate and widespread consequences for customers and operations.

Specific vulnerabilities include:

- **Customer-facing Websites and APIs:** DDoS attacks frequently target these public-facing entry points, aiming to disrupt customer interactions and block access to online banking services. Attacks on Application Programming Interfaces (APIs) are particularly concerning and are growing rapidly in the financial sector, as they target specific application logic such as login forms or payment gateways. These precision-targeted attacks are often more difficult to detect because they mimic legitimate user behavior.
- **Real-time Transaction Processing Systems (e.g., ACH, Electronic Payments):** Beyond merely disrupting websites, DDoS-style attacks can directly incapacitate Automated Clearing House (ACH) systems by flooding them with massive amounts of fraudulent transactions. This type of attack is not simply about saturating network bandwidth but rather overwhelming the transaction processing logic itself. Such incidents are often part of concerted fraud schemes, where attackers exploit the system by originating millions of dollars' worth of fraudulent ACH, checks, and electronic payments using fabricated account details, leading to massive settlement obligations for financial institutions. This demonstrates that DDoS in financial systems can extend

beyond a simple availability attack to become a component of a larger fraud scheme, exploiting business logic and processing capacity.

- **Core Banking Systems and Legacy Infrastructure:** Many traditional financial infrastructures continue to rely on outdated technologies, programming languages, and hardware. These legacy systems are inherently inflexible, expensive to maintain, and highly vulnerable to modern cyber threats, including sophisticated DDoS attacks. Their monolithic architectures hinder integration with modern security solutions and can lead to a significantly higher rate of cyberattacks compared to modernized systems. The inability of these systems to provide real-time data and scale operations swiftly further compounds their vulnerability.
- **High-Frequency Trading (HFT) Platforms and Latency Sensitivity:** HFT systems are acutely sensitive to latency, where even a few milliseconds of delay can result in missed trades or unfavorable prices, directly impacting profitability. DDoS attacks can severely disrupt trading operations and compromise data integrity in these ultra-low latency environments, where continuous and stable connectivity is paramount. Any network outage or congestion can cause significant delays in order execution, impacting the performance of trading algorithms (Javaid et al., 2016).
- **Supply Chain Vulnerabilities:** The extensive interconnectedness of FMS with third-party service providers, vendors, and other linked financial market infrastructures (FMIs) creates a broad range of entry points for cyberattacks. DDoS attacks can originate or propagate through these interconnected entities, exploiting vulnerabilities in the supply chain and potentially causing widespread disruption across the financial network. This highlights the need for a holistic security approach that extends beyond an institution's immediate perimeter (Li et al., 2020).

IV. IMPACT ASSESSMENT OF DDOS ATTACKS ON FINANCIAL MANAGEMENT SYSTEMS

The consequences of Distributed Denial of Service (DDoS) attacks on Financial Management Systems (FMS) are multifaceted, extending beyond immediate technical disruptions to encompass significant financial, operational, reputational, and regulatory ramifications. A comprehensive analysis of the financial impact of a DDoS attack must include both direct and indirect costs, as the total economic impact synthesizes these elements, often with an indirect cost multiplier ranging from 1.4x to 3.2x. This indicates that financial institutions may often underestimate the full economic impact if they only focus on immediate direct costs, potentially leading to insufficient investment in proactive defense (Thaseen & Kumar, 2017).

A. Financial Losses (Direct and Indirect Costs)

Direct Costs

These are the immediate, quantifiable expenditures incurred as a direct result of a DDoS attack. They include:

- **Restoration Costs:** Significant spending on technical resources, including personnel, specialized software, and hardware, is required to bring affected applications and systems back online.
- **Lost Revenue:** Downtime directly translates into a loss of sales and business opportunities, particularly for online banking services, trading platforms, and other digital financial operations where customers are unable to access services. For small and medium-sized enterprises (SMEs), the average cost can be around $120,000 per attack, while larger incidents can result in multimillion dollar impacts, with one company reporting a $9-12 million loss for a single campaign (NIST, 2018).
- **Ransom Payments:** In some instances, attackers demand a ransom to cease the DDoS attack, adding another layer of financial strain on the affected business.

Indirect Costs

These are often more substantial and long-lasting, representing the less immediate but profound financial repercussions:

- **Damage to Brand Reputation:** News of successful DDoS attacks spreads rapidly, causing significant reputational harm that can be difficult and time-consuming to rebuild.
- **Erosion of Customer Trust and Loyalty:** Customers expect continuous, secure, and uninterrupted services. When these are compromised, frustration and a loss of faith in the institution's ability to protect funds and provide reliable services can lead to customer outflow and a decline in future sales. This can result in the termination of contracts with legal entities and claims for damages from customers (ISO/IEC 27001:2013,).

- **Lost Productivity and Missed Opportunities:** Internal operations can be severely hampered, leading to reduced employee productivity and missed strategic business opportunities.

B. Operational Disruption and Service Unavailability

DDoS attacks directly disrupt normal business operations by slowing down or completely blocking access to critical applications, websites, and services. For financial institutions, this translates into severe consequences: customers may be unable to conduct online banking, access mobile applications, or utilize ATMs, leading to significant inconvenience and an inability to perform essential financial transactions. During critical periods, such as peak trading windows, tax deadlines, or end-of-day payment processing cycles, such disruptions can have amplified negative consequences, potentially leading to market instability or systemic risks (ENISA (European Union Agency for Cybersecurity), 2020).

C. Reputational Damage and Erosion of Customer Trust

The public perception of a financial institution is heavily influenced by its reliability and security. News of a successful DDoS attack spreads quickly, causing significant reputational harm and potentially triggering regulatory investigations. Customers, who rely on continuous, secure, and uninterrupted services, experience frustration and may lose faith in the institution's ability to safeguard their funds and provide reliable services. This erosion of trust can lead to a decline in customer loyalty and a shift of business to competitors, resulting in long-term brand damage and a reduction in market share.

D. Regulatory Penalties and Compliance Implications

Financial institutions operate within highly regulated environments, subject to stringent cybersecurity and operational resilience mandates. Frameworks such as the Digital Operational Resilience Act (DORA) in the EU, US Securities and Exchange Commission (SEC) rulings, and the NIS 2 Directive outline rigorous compliance requirements for cybersecurity resilience. These regulations often stipulate requirements for service availability, data protection, and incident reporting. Failure to comply can result in severe penalties, substantial fines, and significant legal implications. Legacy systems, prevalent in many financial institutions, often contribute to higher error rates in reporting and longer regulatory implementation cycles, exacerbating compliance challenges and increasing the risk of penalties.

The cumulative effect of these impacts underscores a critical challenge: the full economic impact of DDoS attacks is often underestimated if only direct costs are considered. The substantial and long-lasting nature of indirect costs, coupled with the increasing burden of regulatory penalties, means that financial institutions may be under-investing in proactive defense strategies. This underestimation can jeopardize their long-term enterprise sustainability and regulatory standing, as the benefits of robust cybersecurity (i.e., avoided indirect costs and penalties) are not fully recognized or quantified (Mohammadi et al., 2018).

To provide a clear overview of these impacts, refer to Table 2.

Table 2. Financial and Operational Impacts of DDoS Attacks on FMS

Impact Category	Specific Impact	Illustrative Quantifications/Examples
Direct Financial	Lost Revenue	$9-12 million for a single incident ; average $120k per attack for SMEs
	Restoration Costs	Significant expenditure on technical resources, personnel, software, hardware
	Ransom Payments	Direct financial strain from attacker demands
Indirect Financial	Damage to Brand Reputation	Long-term reputational harm, difficult to regain
	Erosion of Customer Trust	Leads to customer outflow, decline in future sales
	Lost Productivity	Internal operations hampered, reduced employee output
Operational	Service Unavailability	Inability to conduct online banking, access mobile apps, use ATMs
	Operational Disruption	Slowdown or blocking of critical applications and websites
	Trading Disruption	Missed trades, unfavorable prices in HFT due to latency
Regulatory	Regulatory Fines	Severe penalties for non-compliance with DORA, SEC, NIS 2, GDPR, SOX
	Legal Implications	Potential lawsuits from affected individuals
	Compliance Challenges	Legacy systems contribute to higher error rates and longer cycles

V. MODELING DDOS ATTACKS IN FINANCIAL MANAGEMENT SYSTEMS

Effective defense against Distributed Denial of Service (DDoS) attacks in Financial Management Systems (FMS) necessitates sophisticated modeling techniques capable of real-time detection, classification, and strategic analysis. These models leverage various computational and analytical approaches to understand attack patterns, predict their behavior, and inform mitigation strategies.

A. Statistical Modeling for Anomaly Detection

Statistical approaches form a foundational layer for network anomaly detection by identifying deviations from established normal traffic patterns. This involves applying statistical filtering and numerical analysis to generate an anomaly score. If this score exceeds a predefined threshold, a security alert is triggered, often by an Intrusion Detection System (IDS) or Security Information and Event Management (SIEM) platform (Choi et al., 2021).

Prominent statistical models include:

- **Gaussian Mixture Model (GMM):** This model is utilized to detect anomalies, particularly in wireless sensor networks. It verifies the behavior of normal traffic by analyzing parameters such as packet train size and length. By aggregating traffic characteristics over a period and feeding them into the GMM, the model can determine if the traffic conforms to normal behavior or is anomalous, thereby effectively detecting and responding to DDoS attacks.
- **Multi-Level Tree for Online Packet Statistics (MULTOPS):** This technique identifies attacks by exploiting correlations between outgoing and incoming packet rates at various levels of subnet prefix aggregation. MULTOPS tracks packet-rate statistics across a tree of nodes, allowing network security analysts to detect DDoS attack behavior by identifying changes in metrics such as the ratio of TCP SYN packets to TCP FIN (RST) packets.
- **Entropy-based anomaly detection:** This approach is particularly effective for detecting high-intensity and high-volume anomalous traffic. It relies on analyzing the entropy of flow-based data, providing a scalable and efficient method for identifying deviations from normal traffic distributions.

B. Machine Learning Approaches for DDoS Detection

Machine learning (ML) algorithms are increasingly vital for real-time DDoS detection. They analyze vast network traffic patterns, learning from historical data to accurately distinguish between legitimate and malicious traffic. This capability is critical for early detection and mitigation of DDoS attacks.

Classification Algorithms

Various supervised ML algorithms are employed for DDoS classification:

- **Random Forest (RF):** This ensemble learning method consistently demonstrates high accuracy and efficiency in DDoS detection. Studies show RF achieving exceptional accuracy rates, often exceeding 99% (e.g., 99.24%, 99.99%, 98.80%), making it a top-performing choice for accurately classifying DDoS traffic.
- **Gradient Boosting (GB) and XGBoost:** These algorithms also exhibit outstanding performance, with high accuracy (e.g., 99.99% for GB and 99.98% for XGBoost) and efficiency, making them suitable for real-time applications.
- **Support Vector Machine (SVM):** SVMs can achieve high accuracy, with a linear kernel demonstrating strong performance (e.g., 99.91% accuracy) in classifying DDoS attacks.
- **Decision Tree (DT), Logistic Regression (LR), k-Nearest Neighbors (KNN), and AdaBoost:** These algorithms are also widely utilized in DDoS detection, offering varying levels of performance depending on the dataset and specific attack characteristics.

Anomaly Detection Using Autoencoders and Behavioral Analytics

Beyond classification, unsupervised learning and behavioral analysis are crucial for detecting novel and stealthy DDoS attacks:

- **Autoencoders (AE):** As a type of deep learning architecture, autoencoders are adept at learning efficient data representations. When trained exclusively on data representing *normal* system behavior or transaction flows, AEs learn to reconstruct these patterns with minimal error. The core principle for anomaly detection is that when an anomalous input (e.g., traffic associated with a DDoS attack) is fed into a trained AE, the model struggles to accurately reconstruct it due to its unfamiliarity with such patterns. This results in a significantly higher "reconstruction error" compared to normal data, thereby flagging the input as suspicious. While primarily applied for suspicious financial transaction detection (e.g., Anti-Money Laundering), the underlying mechanism of learning normal behavior and identifying deviations holds significant potential for detecting the impact of DDoS attacks by modeling the expected behavior of FMS under normal traffic loads.

- **Behavioral Analytics:** This approach leverages machine learning and statistical modeling to continuously track network traffic, understand typical user behavior, and identify anomalies that could signal a DDoS attack. By establishing a "normal" baseline of user engagement with a website or API, behavioral analytics systems can flag deviations such as unexpected surges in requests from unusual sources or atypical request patterns. This capability is particularly effective against Application Layer (Layer 7) attacks and botnet traffic that are designed to mimic legitimate users, as it can identify subtle, intricate behaviors like excessive HTTP requests or API abuse.

Feature Engineering and Selection for Real-Time Detection

The efficacy of ML models in DDoS detection is heavily dependent on the quality and relevance of the features extracted from network traffic data. Feature engineering involves transforming raw packet data into meaningful statistical features, often from Layer 3 and 4 headers, suitable for time-series analysis. To enhance model interpretability, reduce complexity, and improve computational efficiency for real-time performance, techniques like Recursive Feature Elimination (RFE) and SHAP (Shapley Additive exPlanations) analysis are employed to select the most discriminative features.

Achieving effective ML-driven DDoS detection in financial systems presents a complex optimization problem, requiring a delicate balance between accuracy, latency, and adaptability. While ML algorithms like Random Forest and Gradient Boosting demonstrate very high accuracy rates (often exceeding 99%) in identifying DDoS attacks, the financial sector's demand for continuous operation and real-time decision-making necessitates extremely low latency in detection. Flow-based ML approaches can suffer from high latency, while packet-based methods may yield high false positive rates, which can inadvertently disrupt legitimate financial transactions. Furthermore, the challenge of adaptability to novel, sophisticated, and evolving attack vectors is significant, as traditional models often require disruptive retraining when new attack classes emerge. This multi-objective optimization problem demands solutions that can maintain high accuracy with minimal latency and dynamically adapt to new threats without compromising service availability. The development of reconstructive deep learning techniques and behavioral analytics represents a direct response to this need for adaptive, non-disruptive detection.

To summarize the key performance metrics for ML-based DDoS detection, refer to Table 3.

Table 3. Performance Metrics for Machine Learning-Based DDoS Detection in Financial Systems

Performance Metric	Definition	Significance for FMS	Typical Range/ Benchmark
Accuracy	Proportion of all classifications (correct positives and negatives) that were correct.	Overall effectiveness in identifying both attacks and normal traffic.	>99% for RF, GB, XGBoost
Precision	Proportion of all positive classifications that are actually positive (True Positives / (True Positives + False Positives)).	Crucial for minimizing false alarms, as blocking legitimate financial transactions is highly disruptive.	High precision (e.g., 100% for RF) is desired.
Recall (True Positive Rate)	Proportion of all actual positives that were classified correctly as positives (True Positives / (True Positives + False Negatives)).	Essential for ensuring all actual DDoS attacks are detected, preventing service disruption.	High recall (e.g., 99.99% for RF) is desired.
F1-Score	Harmonic mean of precision and recall; balances their importance.	Provides a single metric for overall model performance, especially in imbalanced datasets.	High F1-Score (e.g., 99.99% for RF) indicates balanced performance.
False Positive Rate (FPR)	Proportion of all actual negatives that were classified incorrectly as positives.	Direct measure of legitimate traffic disruption; minimizing this is paramount for FMS.	Should be as close to 0 as possible.
Detection Time/Latency	Time taken for the model to detect an attack once it begins.	Critical for real-time financial operations (e.g., HFT), where milliseconds matter.	Ultra-low latency (microseconds to low milliseconds) is required.

C. Game Theory Models for Attacker-Defender Interactions

Game theory offers a robust conceptual and methodological framework for analyzing strategic decision-making in cybersecurity, particularly in optimizing cybersecurity investments and understanding the dynamic interactions between attackers and defenders. These models treat both attackers and defenders as rational agents, each seeking to maximize their utility (e.g., attacker profit, defender security) given the actions of the other.

Game theory models can effectively reflect changes in attacker strategies and the impact on financial outcomes (e.g., revenue loss in blockchain mining pools) under varying network conditions. This analytical approach assists financial institutions in determining optimal defense strategies by considering the attacker's profit maximization motives and the potential economic consequences of their actions. Concepts such as Nash equilibrium are frequently employed to identify stable strategies where neither the attacker nor the defender can unilaterally improve their outcome by changing their strategy, assuming the other's strategy remains constant.

Furthermore, game theory can model scenarios involving information asymmetry, where defenders may not possess complete information about attacker capabilities, resources, or investment in cyber offensive tools. This allows for the development of more realistic defense strategies that account for uncertainty. The application of game theory provides a strategic lens for financial institutions, moving beyond merely blocking attacks to optimizing the allocation of scarce cybersecurity resources. It helps in determining not just *how* to defend, but *how much* to invest and *where* to allocate resources (e.g., prioritizing protection for critical assets or headquarters over branches when budgets are constrained) to achieve a desired level of resilience. This makes game theory a crucial tool for financial management decision-makers in formulating cybersecurity investment strategies.

D. Simulation Models for Attack Analysis and Defense Evaluation

Simulation models are indispensable tools for analyzing DDoS attacks and rigorously evaluating the effectiveness of proposed prevention and defense algorithms before their costly and potentially disruptive deployment in live production systems. These models provide a controlled environment to test various attack scenarios and defense mechanisms.

Discrete-event simulation models, for instance, are crucial for assessing the impact of specific DDoS types, such as amplification attacks, which exploit protocols like NTP or DNS. Platforms designed for cybersecurity research can emulate mini-Internet topologies with realistic IP address space allocation and generate representative, closed-loop background traffic specific to particular networks. This capability allows researchers to conduct sound empirical analyses and identify the true impact of defense solutions in realistic network settings, addressing critical missing gaps in current DDoS research. Such simulations facilitate the comparison of different defense algorithms, helping to identify their strengths, weaknesses, and overall efficacy under various attack conditions. For financial institutions, simulation provides a low-risk environment to validate the resilience of their systems and optimize defense configurations.

VI. OPTIMIZATION METHODS FOR DDOS DEFENSE AND RESILIENCE IN FMS

Optimizing DDoS defense and enhancing resilience in Financial Management Systems (FMS) requires a multi-layered and adaptive approach, integrating various technical strategies and strategic resource allocation. The escalating complexity and sophistication of modern DDoS threats, particularly the emergence of AI-powered and multi-vector attacks, render static, rule-based defenses increasingly insufficient. This necessitates a fundamental shift towards dynamic, intelligent, and proactive security architectures.

A. Network-Level Mitigation Strategies

Network-level mitigation strategies focus on protecting the underlying infrastructure from volumetric and protocol-based attacks:

- **Traffic Filtering:** This involves techniques such as **blackhole filtering**, which routes all incoming traffic destined for a specific IP address to a null route, effectively discarding it. While immediate, it is often a last resort as it blocks both legitimate and malicious traffic. More granular methods include

IP filtering, which blocks specific malicious IP addresses, and **geo-blocking**, which restricts connections from identified high-risk geographic locations.

- **Rate Limiting and Connection Throttling:** These techniques limit the number of requests or connections allowed from a single source within a specified timeframe, preventing resource exhaustion on servers and network devices. Rate limiting can be implemented at various layers (network, application, DNS) and can be dynamically auto-configured based on behavioral traffic profiling to avoid blocking legitimate users.
- **Load Balancing and Anycast Routing:** Distributing incoming network traffic across multiple servers or geographically dispersed data centers helps absorb large attack volumes and prevent any single server from being overwhelmed.

Anycast routing is a network addressing and routing method where a single IP address is assigned to multiple servers or nodes across different locations. This allows traffic to be shared across those servers, effectively diffusing the impact of distributed attack traffic and routing requests to the nearest optimal server.

- **Scrubbing Centers and Traffic Diversion:** This strategy involves redirecting all incoming traffic to specialized "scrubbing" centers. These centers are dedicated security services that analyze the traffic, filter out malicious packets using advanced techniques, and then forward only the legitimate traffic to the target network. This offloads the burden of attack mitigation from the financial institution's own infrastructure.

B. Application-Level Protection

Application-level protection focuses on safeguarding specific applications and services, particularly against Layer 7 attacks:

- **Web Application Firewalls (WAFs):** A WAF acts as a reverse proxy, positioned between the internet and the origin server, to inspect and filter HTTP traffic. It protects targeted web applications from various malicious traffic, including Layer 7 DDoS attacks, by blocking unauthorized requests.
- **API Security:** With the increasing reliance on APIs in the financial sector for functionalities like logins and payments, specific security measures are crucial. API security focuses on protecting application logic and endpoints from abuse and DDoS attacks, as these are increasingly targeted.
- **Behavioral Analysis:** This advanced technique identifies subtle and intricate behaviors characteristic of application-layer attacks. By continuously tracking traffic patterns and building a "normal" baseline of user behavior, behavioral analytics systems can detect deviations such as excessive HTTP GET/POST requests, bot-like navigation, or API abuse. This method is highly effective against stealthy, low-volume attacks that mimic legitimate users.

C. Adaptive Security Architectures

To combat the dynamic and intelligent nature of modern DDoS threats, particularly in the high-stakes financial sector, static, rule-based defenses are becoming obsolete. A fundamental shift towards deeply integrated, adaptive security architectures is imperative.

- **AI/ML-driven Adaptive Protection:** This leverages Artificial Intelligence and Machine Learning algorithms to continuously monitor traffic, learn unique patterns, detect anomalies, and dynamically adjust defense mechanisms in real-time. These systems are specifically designed to adapt to changes in an attacker's strategy or methodology, ensuring the continuous availability of critical business services. Adaptive DDoS Protection, for instance, can build traffic profiles based on maximum rates for various dimensions (e.g., origin errors, user agents, geographic locations, IP protocols) and mitigate traffic that deviates from these profiles.

- **Real-time Threat Intelligence Integration:** Incorporating continuous streams of data about potential and current cyber threats is vital. These threat intelligence feeds, sourced from commercial vendors, open-source communities, government agencies, and internal logs, provide information on malicious IPs, botnets, and zero-day attacks. This actionable intelligence helps automate defensive actions, predict emerging threats, and enhance the understanding of attack vectors, enabling financial institutions to shift from reactive to proactive defense.
- **Zero Trust Principles for Enhanced Resilience:** The Zero Trust Architecture (ZTA), predicated on the principle of "never trust, always verify," transforms static security policies into a dynamic, adaptive, and predictive framework when combined with AI/ML. ZTA enables dynamic microsegmentation, allowing for the isolation of compromised devices and the immediate revocation of access upon detection of suspicious activity. This approach significantly limits lateral movement of threats within the network, thereby reducing the attack surface.

The strategic necessity of these adaptive, AI/ML-driven architectures, integrated with real-time threat intelligence and Zero Trust principles, is clear. They enable financial institutions to predict and mitigate threats at machine speed, ensuring continuous availability and data integrity in the face of increasingly complex and intelligent cyber threats. This represents a fundamental shift in defense philosophy, moving away from perimeter-based security to a more granular, dynamic, and continuously verified approach.

To illustrate these adaptive defense strategies and their mechanisms, refer to Table 4.

Table 4. Adaptive DDoS Defense Strategies and Their Mechanisms

Strategy/Component	Mechanism/How it Works	Key Benefits for FMS
AI/ML-driven Adaptive Protection	Continuously monitors traffic, learns unique patterns, detects anomalies, and dynamically adjusts defense mechanisms in real-time. Builds traffic profiles (origins, user-agents, locations, protocols) to identify deviations.	Dynamic adaptation to evolving attack strategies; automated response; enhanced detection of sophisticated attacks; ensures continuous availability.
Real-time Threat Intelligence Integration	Ingests continuous streams of data on current cyber threats (malicious IPs, botnets, zero-days) from diverse sources. Correlates global threat data with local network activity.	Proactive defense; automated blocking of known threats; improved understanding of attack vectors; faster incident response; predictive capabilities.
Zero Trust Principles	"Never trust, always verify" approach. Implements granular access control, dynamic microsegmentation, and continuous verification of all users and devices, regardless of location.	Reduced attack surface; prevention of lateral movement; isolation of compromised devices; enhanced data integrity and confidentiality; improved overall resilience.

D. Resource Allocation Optimization for Cybersecurity Investments

Optimizing resource allocation for cybersecurity investments is a critical aspect of DDoS defense in FMS, especially given budget constraints and the high stakes involved.

- **Cost-Benefit Analysis:** Essential for justifying cybersecurity investments, focusing on Return on Security Investment (ROSI). ROSI refines traditional ROI by incorporating risk-adjusted savings derived from breach prevention, helping to quantify the value of security measures. This allows decision-makers to prioritize investments based on the most significant risk reduction for the cost incurred.
- **Dynamic Scaling:** DDoS protection solutions must be highly scalable to effectively handle the immense volumes and velocities of modern DDoS attacks without compromising service quality, particularly for critical sectors like Banking, Financial Services, and Insurance (BFSI). Cloud-based DDoS protection solutions offer inherent autoscaling capabilities, which are superior to the limitations of on-premises hardware in absorbing large-scale attacks.
- **Budget Constraints and Prioritization:** Mathematical models can be employed to optimize the allocation of limited cybersecurity budgets across different organizational units, such as headquarters and branches. These mod-

els help prioritize protection based on factors like intrinsic vulnerability, the portion of information sets, and the propagation probability of threats within interconnected systems. Studies indicate that when budgets are small and intrinsic vulnerability is high, priority may be given to protecting headquarters. Furthermore, security information sharing among organizational units can significantly improve the overall efficiency of security investments within the entire system.

VII. REGULATORY LANDSCAPE AND COMPLIANCE FOR DDOS RESILIENCE

The financial services sector operates under a stringent and evolving regulatory landscape that increasingly mandates robust cybersecurity and operational resilience against threats like DDoS attacks. This regulatory pressure is shifting from a mere checklist-based compliance approach to one that demands demonstrable proof of an institution's ability to withstand, detect, respond to, and recover from disruptions. This shift necessitates continuous testing, scenario planning, and a deep understanding of critical service dependencies, including those involving third parties.

A. Key Regulations and Standards

Financial institutions globally are subject to a complex web of regulations and standards, including:

- **Digital Operational Resilience Act (DORA):** An EU regulation that entered into force on January 16, 2023, and applies from January 17, 2025. DORA aims to consolidate and upgrade ICT risk management and cyber risk management across the financial services ecosystem. It lays down uniform requirements for ICT risk management, reporting of major ICT-related incidents, digital operational resilience testing (including regular threat-led penetration testing), information sharing, and measures related to the use of ICT third-party services.
- **NIST Cybersecurity Framework:** A widely recognized framework in the U.S. that provides guidelines for organizations to manage and reduce cybersecurity risks. It supports broader efforts to protect against cyberattacks and ensure the security of sensitive data, often serving as a foundational reference for federal regulations like FISMA.
- **FCA (Financial Conduct Authority) Operational Resilience:** UK regulations requiring financial firms to identify their "Important Business Services

(IBSs)" and set "impact tolerances" for the maximum tolerable disruption to these services. Firms must conduct initial mapping and testing of their operational resilience, including critical processes, technologies, and third parties, and develop action plans for vulnerability remediation.

- **ISO 20022:** A global standard for financial messaging that is mandating an extensive overhaul of payment architectures and data exchange by November 2025. While not directly a DDoS regulation, its impact on FMS architecture and the shift to real-time, event-driven systems inherently influences DDoS vulnerability and the requirements for resilient payment processing.
- **Other Regulations:** Financial institutions must also comply with regulations like PCI DSS (Payment Card Industry Data Security Standard), HIPAA (Health Insurance Portability and Accountability Act), GDPR (General Data Protection Regulation), SOX (Sarbanes-Oxley Act), and GLBA (Gramm-Leach-Bliley Act), which impose specific controls for safeguarding sensitive customer data and ensuring service availability.

B. Operational Resilience Requirements and Impact Tolerances

A core tenet of modern financial regulations is operational resilience, which mandates that organizations not only prevent but also effectively respond to and recover from cybersecurity incidents, including DDoS attacks. This involves a structured approach:

- **Identification of Important Business Services (IBSs):** Firms must identify the services whose disruption would significantly impact customers or the wider market.
- **Setting Impact Tolerances:** For each IBS, maximum tolerable disruption levels are defined, guiding the acceptable duration and extent of outages.
- **Mapping and Testing:** Organizations are required to map the people, processes, technology, and third parties supporting their IBSs. This mapping is followed by rigorous testing of operational resilience, including scenario planning and simulating plausible disruptive events like DDoS attacks, to identify vulnerabilities and assess the effectiveness of existing controls.
- **Remediation Planning:** Based on testing results, detailed remediation plans are developed to address identified weaknesses, ensuring continuous improvement in resilience. The scope of operational resilience extends to third-party providers, holding financial institutions responsible for ensuring their suppliers have also tested their resilience.

C. Data Integrity and Availability in Financial Systems

The foundational principles of information security, often encapsulated in the CIA Triad (Confidentiality, Integrity, Availability), are paramount in the financial sector. DDoS attacks directly threaten the "Availability" principle by rendering systems and data inaccessible to authorized users when needed. Regulations like HIPAA specifically require ensuring data confidentiality, integrity, and availability, which includes maintaining robust access controls, comprehensive incident response plans, and effective risk management procedures.

Financial management systems are entrusted with protecting critical data against theft, fraud, and other criminal mischief. This is achieved through the implementation of internal controls and audit tools that manage segregation of duties and payment rules. Data integrity, a crucial component, ensures that data remains accurate, complete, and consistent throughout its lifecycle, from collection to storage, processing, and deletion. Measures such as data validation, access controls, encryption, and robust error handling are employed to maintain data integrity and prevent unauthorized alteration.

D. Evaluation Methodologies for DDoS Defense

Regulatory mandates, particularly DORA and SEC rulings, emphasize the necessity of robust testing to validate DDoS defenses.

- **DDoS Attack Simulations:** Continuous, non-disruptive DDoS simulations are critical for validating whether deployed defenses remain effective against evolving attack vectors and changes in network configurations. These simulations go beyond basic functionality checks to assess the limits of services and tools and identify initial vulnerabilities.
- **Penetration Testing:** This involves authorized simulated cyberattacks against an organization's systems, networks, or applications to identify exploitable vulnerabilities.
- **Red Teaming:** A more advanced methodology, red teaming simulates real-world, offensive attacks by ethical hackers who mimic the tactics, techniques, and procedures (TTPs) used by malicious actors. Unlike penetration testing, red teaming aims to identify critical defensive gaps in the overall security posture and test the effectiveness of detection capabilities and incident response teams in a controlled environment.
- **Real-world Attack Data Analysis:** Analyzing historical attack data and integrating real-time threat intelligence is crucial for understanding evolving attack patterns, improving detection mechanisms, and adapting defenses.

This includes insights from past incidents and continuous streams of data on known malicious IPs, botnets, and attack fingerprints.

The regulatory landscape is demonstrably moving beyond a mere checklist-based compliance model to a more dynamic, proactive, and holistic approach to operational resilience. This means financial institutions are not merely required to *possess* defenses, but to *demonstrably prove* their ability to withstand, detect, respond to, and recover from disruptions like DDoS attacks, including those affecting their complex supply chains. This shift necessitates continuous testing, rigorous scenario planning, and a deep, ongoing understanding of their critical services' dependencies and vulnerabilities.

VIII. CHALLENGES AND FUTURE DIRECTIONS

The landscape of DDoS attacks targeting Financial Management Systems (FMS) is characterized by escalating complexity and a continuous evolution of threats. This necessitates a forward-looking perspective to identify ongoing challenges and opportunities for innovation in modeling and optimization.

A. Emerging DDoS Threats

The future of DDoS attacks will be shaped by several key trends:

- **AI-driven Attacks:** Attackers are increasingly leveraging AI and Machine Learning (ML) to automate and enhance their offensive capabilities. This includes generating more convincing social engineering campaigns, identifying vulnerabilities with greater efficiency, and developing adaptive DDoS campaigns that can learn from and react to defense mechanisms in real-time.
- **Quantum-Resistant Threats:** While not an immediate threat, the advent of quantum computing poses a long-term challenge to current cryptographic methods. This necessitates proactive research into quantum-resistant algorithms to secure future Zero Trust frameworks and financial transactions against potential decryption by quantum computers.
- **IoT Botnets:** The relentless proliferation of Internet of Things (IoT) devices, often with inherent security weaknesses, will continue to fuel the creation of larger and more powerful botnets. These massive botnets are capable of launching hyper-volumetric attacks that can overwhelm even robust defenses.
- **Multi-Vector and Adaptive Attacks:** Future attacks will increasingly combine multiple layers of the OSI model (Layers 3, 4, and 7) and various attack

vectors simultaneously. They will also exhibit dynamic adaptability, continuously adjusting their tactics in response to mitigation efforts, making detection and defense significantly more complex and challenging.

- **Ransom DDoS:** A growing trend involves DDoS attacks coupled with explicit ransom demands. This adds a direct financial extortion motive to the attack, requiring financial institutions to develop specific response strategies that address both the technical disruption and the extortion attempt.
- **Geopolitical Influence:** Geopolitical tensions will continue to serve as a significant inspiration for hacktivist groups. These groups are likely to conduct targeted DDoS campaigns against financial institutions as a form of protest or disruption, further complicating the threat landscape.

The escalating complexity of future DDoS attacks, driven by AI, new attack vectors, and diverse motivations, demands a fundamental shift from traditional reactive "detect and respond" models to proactive, predictive defense strategies. Financial institutions must invest in AI-driven threat intelligence, behavioral analytics that anticipate attacks, and architectures capable of dynamically reconfiguring to mitigate threats *before* they cause significant disruption, rather than merely reacting to them. The long-term threat of quantum computing also underscores the need for foresight in cryptographic defenses.

B. Challenges in Real-time Mitigation

Implementing effective real-time DDoS mitigation in FMS faces several critical challenges:

- **Latency Constraints:** For high-speed financial operations, particularly High-Frequency Trading (HFT), DDoS mitigation solutions must operate with ultra-low latency. Even delays of a few milliseconds can lead to substantial financial losses due to missed trading opportunities or unfavorable price execution. The challenge lies in performing deep packet inspection and traffic analysis without introducing unacceptable delays.
- **False Positives:** Accurately differentiating between legitimate traffic surges (e.g., during major market events or news releases) and malicious DDoS traffic is a significant challenge. High false positive rates can inadvertently deny service to legitimate users, effectively causing a self-inflicted denial of service. This leads to customer dissatisfaction, reputational damage, and direct financial impact by blocking valid transactions.
- **Legacy Systems Integration:** The continued reliance on outdated and monolithic legacy banking systems within the financial sector poses a substantial

hurdle. These systems are inherently vulnerable, lack the flexibility and scalability required for modern operations, and are difficult to integrate with contemporary adaptive security solutions. A large portion of IT budgets is often consumed by maintaining these legacy infrastructures rather than funding innovation in cybersecurity, thereby hindering overall DDoS resilience and increasing the risk of breaches.

- **Scalability and Resource Exhaustion:** While cloud-based solutions offer significant scalability, the sheer volume and velocity of hyper-volumetric attacks can still challenge even the most robust defenses. Continuous investment in network capacity and processing power is necessary to absorb and filter such massive traffic floods.

The challenges of latency, false positives, and legacy system integration create a critical, multi-dimensional dilemma for financial institutions. They must implement robust DDoS defenses that are highly accurate (minimizing false positives) and operate with near-zero latency, all while grappling with the inherent limitations and vulnerabilities of outdated infrastructure. This is not merely a technical problem but a strategic one, demanding careful trade-off analysis between security robustness, operational performance, and the significant costs and risks associated with modernizing core systems.

C. Research Gaps and Opportunities for Innovation

Despite advancements, several critical research gaps and opportunities for innovation exist:

- **Empirical Validation:** A significant gap exists in the empirical analysis and real-world evaluation of academic DDoS defense research. Network operators often hesitate to adopt advanced academic solutions due to a lack of proven efficacy in realistic settings or concerns about adverse effects on legitimate traffic. Future research should focus on developing and utilizing platforms that can emulate realistic internet topologies and generate representative background traffic to provide sound empirical validation of defense mechanisms.
- **Hybrid Hardware-Software Architectures:** Further research is needed in integrating FPGA-based preprocessing with deep learning models for real-time multivariate time series DDoS detection in high-speed networks. This approach aims to balance the trade-offs between detection accuracy and latency, offering a promising avenue for high-throughput, low-latency defense.

- **AI for Proactive and Predictive Defense:** Beyond mere detection, there is a need for AI models capable of *predicting* potential threats and vulnerabilities before they materialize. This involves leveraging historical data to anticipate attack patterns and recommend proactive security measures, such as targeted patching or policy reinforcement.
- **Integration of Business Logic in Modeling:** More sophisticated modeling of DDoS attacks that specifically target the *business logic* of financial transactions, rather than just network saturation, is crucial. This includes understanding and defending against complex fraud schemes that overwhelm operational systems (e.g., ACH fraud) by flooding them with fraudulent but structurally valid transactions.
- **Quantifying Indirect Costs:** Further refinement of methodologies is needed to accurately quantify the long-term, indirect financial and reputational impacts of DDoS attacks. More precise economic impact assessments can better justify necessary cybersecurity investments and inform strategic resource allocation.

D. The Role of Cross-Sector Collaboration and Information Sharing

The inherently distributed nature of DDoS attacks and the deeply interconnected financial ecosystem underscore the critical necessity for enhanced communication and collaboration among organizations. This includes robust sharing of threat intelligence. Industry-specific information sharing and analysis centers (ISACs), such as FS-ISAC, play a pivotal role in disseminating real-time threat intelligence, best practices, and collaborative defense strategies across the financial sector. Such collaboration enables a collective defense posture, allowing institutions to learn from each other's experiences and adapt more quickly to emerging threats.

IX. CONCLUSION

Distributed Denial of Service (DDoS) attacks represent an escalating and strategic threat to Financial Management Systems (FMS), driven by increasing sophistication, unprecedented scale, and diverse motivations including financial gain, hacktivism, and state-sponsored cyber warfare. The digital transformation of the financial sector, while offering immense efficiencies, has simultaneously expanded its attack surface, making it a prime target for these disruptive assaults.

The critical vulnerabilities of FMS, particularly customer-facing applications and APIs, real-time transaction processing systems (like ACH), and the pervasive presence of inflexible legacy infrastructures, amplify the potential impact of DDoS attacks. High-frequency trading platforms, with their acute sensitivity to latency, are especially susceptible to operational disruption and significant financial losses. The consequences extend beyond immediate service unavailability to encompass substantial direct financial costs, long-term reputational damage, erosion of customer trust, and severe regulatory penalties. The full economic impact, particularly indirect costs, is often underestimated, potentially leading to insufficient proactive investment.

To counter these evolving threats, advanced modeling techniques are indispensable. Statistical methods provide foundational anomaly detection, while Machine Learning approaches, notably Random Forest, Gradient Boosting, and XGBoost, offer high accuracy for real-time detection and classification. The principle of autoencoders and behavioral analytics holds promise for detecting novel and stealthy attacks by identifying deviations from normal system behavior. Game theory models offer a strategic lens for optimizing cybersecurity investments by analyzing attacker-defender interactions and economic incentives, moving beyond purely technical mitigation. Furthermore, simulation models are crucial for empirically validating defense algorithms in realistic network environments before live deployment.

Effective DDoS mitigation and resilience in FMS demand adaptive security architectures. This necessitates the widespread adoption of AI/ML-driven adaptive protection systems that continuously learn and dynamically adjust defenses. The integration of real-time threat intelligence feeds is paramount for automating defensive actions and predicting emerging threats. Implementing Zero Trust principles across financial infrastructures can significantly enhance resilience by continuously verifying access and limiting lateral movement. Resource allocation for cybersecurity investments must be optimized through rigorous cost-benefit analysis and dynamic scaling capabilities, especially in cloud environments.

The regulatory landscape is undergoing a significant shift, moving from a compliance-centric approach to a mandate for demonstrable operational resilience. Regulations like DORA and FCA Operational Resilience compel financial institutions to identify critical services, set impact tolerances, and rigorously test their ability to withstand and recover from cyber incidents, including those affecting their supply chains. This necessitates continuous DDoS simulations, penetration testing, and red teaming exercises to validate defenses.

In conclusion, safeguarding financial stability and maintaining public trust in an increasingly digital and interconnected world hinges upon the imperative for financial institutions to proactively invest in comprehensive, continuously evolving DDoS defense strategies. These strategies must be informed by stringent regulatory mandates, leverage cutting-edge modeling and optimization methods, and foster robust cross-sector collaboration and information sharing to collectively enhance

REFERENCES

Ahmad, A., Maynard, S. B., & Park, S. (2014). Information security strategies: Towards an organizational multi-strategy perspective. *Journal of Intelligent Manufacturing*, *25*(2), 357–370. DOI: 10.1007/s10845-012-0683-0

Ali, S., & Awad, A. I. (2018). Cyber security for financial sector: A framework for ensuring regulatory compliance. *Journal of Information Security and Applications*, *38*, 103–118.

Basel Committee on Banking Supervision. (2018). *Cyber-resilience: Range of practices*. Bank for International Settlements.

Bhuyan, M. H., Bhattacharyya, D. K., & Kalita, J. K. (2015). Network anomaly detection: Methods, systems and tools. *IEEE Communications Surveys and Tutorials*, *16*(1), 303–336. DOI: 10.1109/SURV.2013.052213.00046

Bouveret, A. (2018). Cyber risk for the financial sector: A framework for quantitative assessment. IMF Working Paper.

Choi, E., Kim, Y., Lee, J., & Choi, J. (2021). Federated learning-based intrusion detection system for edge computing networks. *Sensors (Basel)*, *21*(4), 1375. PMID: 33669229

Douligeris, C., & Mitrokotsa, A. (2004). DDoS attacks and defense mechanisms: Classification and state-of-the-art. *Computer Networks*, *44*(5), 643–666. DOI: 10.1016/j.comnet.2003.10.003

. ENISA (European Union Agency for Cybersecurity). (2020). Threat Landscape for Financial Sector.

. Hussain, A., Heidemann, J., & Papadopoulos, C. (2003). A framework for classifying denial of service attacks. ACM SIGCOMM, 99–110.

ISO/IEC 27001:2013. Information technology — Security techniques — Information security management systems — Requirements.

Javaid, A., Niyaz, Q., Sun, W., & Alam, M. (2016). A deep learning approach for network intrusion detection system. *EAI International Conference on Bio-inspired Information and Communications Technologies*. DOI: 10.4108/eai.3-12-2015.2262516

Khattak, H. A., Latif, S., & Farooq, M. (2019). Optimization models for cyber security: A review. *Computers & Security*, *85*, 398–421.

Lee, S., & Kim, H. (2017). DDoS detection method using CNN-based deep learning. *KSII Transactions on Internet and Information Systems*, *11*(10), 5177–5190.

Li, W., Liu, J., Meng, W., & Kwok, L. F. (2020). Enhancing collaborative intrusion detection networks against insider attacks using supervised machine learning. *Journal of Network and Computer Applications*, *143*, 127–140.

Mirkovic, J., & Reiher, P. (2004). A taxonomy of DDoS attack and DDoS defense mechanisms. *Computer Communication Review*, *34*(2), 39–53. DOI: 10.1145/997150.997156

Mohammadi, M., Al-Fuqaha, A., Sorour, S., & Guizani, M. (2018). Deep learning for IoT big data and streaming analytics: A survey. *IEEE Communications Surveys and Tutorials*, *20*(4), 2923–2960. DOI: 10.1109/COMST.2018.2844341

NIST. (2018). *Framework for Improving Critical Infrastructure Cybersecurity, Version 1.1*. National Institute of Standards and Technology.

Peng, T., Leckie, C., & Ramamohanarao, K. (2007). Survey of network-based defense mechanisms countering the DoS and DDoS problems. *ACM Computing Surveys*, *39*(1), 3. DOI: 10.1145/1216370.1216373

Roy, S., Ellis, C., Shiva, S., Dasgupta, D., & Shandilya, V. (2010). A survey of game theory as applied to network security. In *HICSS*. IEEE.

Singh, K. P., & Sood, S. K. (2020). A decision support system for DDoS attack detection using deep learning. *Computers & Security*, *94*, 101872.

Thaseen, I. S., & Kumar, C. (2017). Intrusion detection model using fusion of PCA and optimized SVM. *Computers & Security*, *70*, 277–288.

Vinayakumar, R., Soman, K. P., & Poornachandran, P. (2019). Evaluating deep learning approaches to characterize and classify DDoS attacks. *Neural Computing & Applications*, *31*(8), 4265–4277.

Wang, P., Li, Y., Liu, H., & Bai, G. (2018). Machine learning for networking: Workflow, advances and opportunities. *IEEE Network*, *32*(2), 92–99. DOI: 10.1109/MNET.2017.1700200

Zargar, S. T., Joshi, J., & Tipper, D. (2013). A survey of defense mechanisms against distributed denial of service (DDoS) flooding attacks. *IEEE Communications Surveys and Tutorials*, *15*(4), 2046–2069. DOI: 10.1109/SURV.2013.031413.00127

Zhang, Y., Deng, R. H., & Liu, J. K. (2018). Efficient and privacy-preserving data aggregation in smart grid for load forecasting. *IEEE Transactions on Industrial Informatics*, *14*(6), 2602–2610.

Chapter 8

AI-Driven Deepfake Detection Using MTCNN and Xception:
Enhancing Intrusion Prevention and Media Integrity for Business Cybersecurity

T. A. Swetha Margaret
http://orcid.org/0000-0002-4693-8219
Stella Maris College, India

D. Renuka Devi
http://orcid.org/0000-0002-6525-1172
Stella Maris College, India

ABSTRACT

This study provides a review on deepfake detection techniques, especially with reference to the usage of MTCNN for face exposure or detection and feature extraction through the Xception model. MTCNN is really efficient in the detection of facial landmarks, which makes this a very significant step toward isolating faces for further analysis. The feature extraction capabilities for this model, similar to Xception, help to detect very subtle pixel-level inconsistencies introduced by deepfakes through unnatural lighting or facial textures. The combination of models implies a sound solution for sleuthing deepfakes but also has quite some confines or restrictions, that could extremely make it difficult to handle the poses or compute an expensive computation that may even hinder real-time performance. Beyond technical insights,

DOI: 10.4018/979-8-3373-5223-7.ch008

this study examines real-world applications, emphasizing the relevance of deepfake detection in business cybersecurity and digital forensics. By embedding such models into AI-driven Intrusion Detection and Prevention System.

I. INTRODUCTION

Deepfakes refer to the manipulated videos, images, or audio recordings in which people are made to say or do things they could never have said or done. The word "deepfake" is derived from "deep learning," a kind of machine learning, putting "deep learning" together with "fake," signifying its deceitful nature. As the technology advances, producing deepfakes has become effortless, creating concerns that go beyond their entertaining purposes in films. It has caused major grounds for concern based on how easily deepfakes have been made, from the spread of false information, damage to the reputation of a person, fraudulent activities, and an alteration of public opinion. Deepfakes can be used for the purpose of spreading wrong information, thereby confusing and distracting people from the real events. They can also harm a person by putting him in artificially developed embarrassing or harmful conditions. Moreover, deepfakes are threats in fraud activities where one can look like mimicked voices for getting access to sensitive information, and in politics where they can sway election results by manipulating public perception.

To counter all these threats, researchers have invented several deepfake detection techniques that use machine learning. These CNNs check images and videos and look for the slightest signs of alteration, like unnatural facial expression or movements. RNNs study audio for irregular speech patterns, while autoencoders help in the anomaly detection by comparing the data before its reconstruction and after it is reconstructed. GANs can be trained to identify real and fake media based on the learning of both. Of these, methods notable specifically includes Multi-Task Cascaded Convolutional Networks (MTCNN) and Xception models, based on their deepfake detection capabilities.

MTCNN was introduced by (Zhang et al., 2016). It outshines any other face detector and aligner. With the help of a chain of convolutional networks, MTCNN can detect faces at any scale and align them properly. This is one of the differences used in the detection of small variations in face features, a characteristic of deepfakes. Correctness in the detection and alignment of faces by MTCNN would significantly help identify discrepancies and manipulations of facial attributes. Xception, developed by François Chollet (Chollet, 2017), is widely known for its advanced feature extraction capabilities. Therefore, by using depth wise separable convolutions in Xception, it can effectively capture fine detail from images. It thus provides a great capacity to enable the recognition and differentiation between a real or fake image based upon the subtle features of a manipulated image.

This analysis will study integration between MTCNN and Xception towards the advancement of deepfake detection. This integration of MTCNN, mainly in terms of face detection and alignment, along with feature extraction of Xception, in the present study work could probably facilitate the implementation of something even more advanced in the sense of accuracy and reliability of deepfake detection. The performance of these models, tested individually, and in combination with strengths and weaknesses in their capacity to identify deepfakes, will be analyzed in this work. Among the keys studies informing the research, the Face forensics++ dataset by Rossler (Rossler et al., 2019) comes in very handy, as it provides a large dataset of manipulated facial images for testing and training detection methods. The Deepfake Detection Challenge dataset by Dolhansky (Dolhansky et al., 2019) is also a valuable source for model performance. In these resources, one can understand how different models work with deepfakes and refine the techniques to detect deepfakes.

Figure 1. P-Net, R-Net, and O-Net Architecture Overview: Convolution and Max Pooling Operations for Face Detection

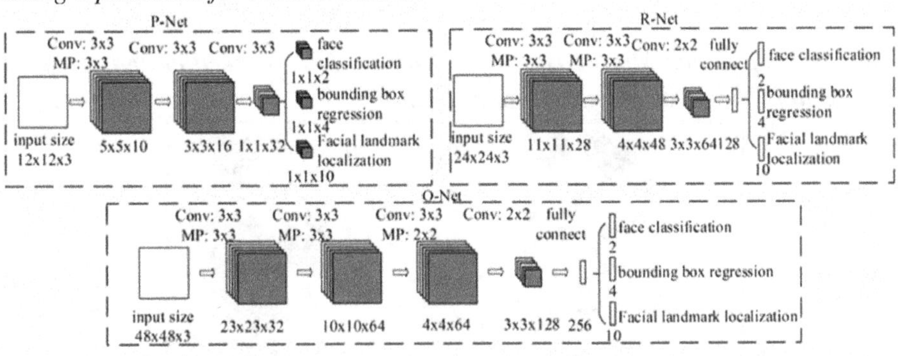

II. LITERATURE SURVEY

The rapid advancements in deepfake technology pose several security threats to digital media. Therefore, developing proper detection techniques is urgently required for deepfakes. This literature survey presents a comprehensive review of numerous deepfake detection techniques along with the performance of integrated Multi-Task Cascaded Convolutional Networks (MTCNN) and Xception. Zhang et al. proposed MTCNN, a multitask framework for face detection and alignment in 2016 (Zhang et al., 2016). The architecture contains three stages: First, P-Net has been used to produce candidate regions for faces, then those regions are refined in actuality by R-Net, engineered for the final face detection and landmark localization on output of O-Net. The methodology achieves spectacular performance with 96.2% precision and recalls on the FDDB dataset. MTCNN is very suitable for the applications in which it has to preprocess deep fake detection in those applications since the accurate alignment of the face is of huge importance due to its impressive performance on faces of different poses, various occlusions, and illumination conditions.

Chollet (2017) proposed Xception architecture based on depthwise separable convolutions for better computational efficiency as well as an improved accuracy. Xception uses depthwise separable convolutions instead of standard convolutions to break the convolution down into a spatial depthwise convolution and a pointwise convolution. Such a transformation can dramatically decrease the count of parameters and the cost of computation, offering an extremely high level of accuracy. According to Chollet (2017), the Xception model has achieved Top-1 accuracy as 79% and Top-5 accuracy as 94.5% on the ImageNet dataset. Xception can capture even the smallest features and is highly robust against different manipulations of such images to distinguish between real and manipulated images in deepfake detection.

Figure 2. A Cascaded Multi-Task Framework for Face Detection and Landmark Localization Using Deep Convolutional Networks

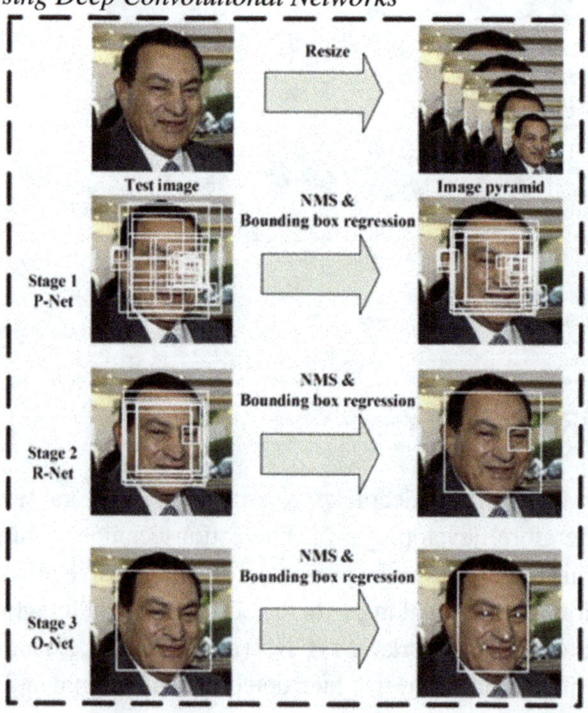

Figure 3. A canonical Inception module (Inception V3).

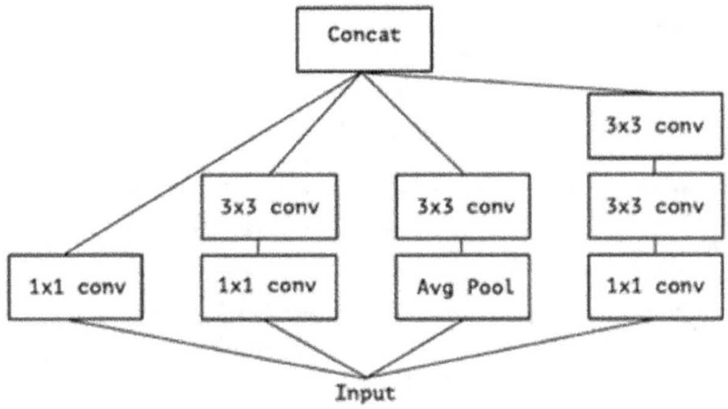

Figure 4. A simplified Inception module within parentheses, are to position flush right, as in (1)

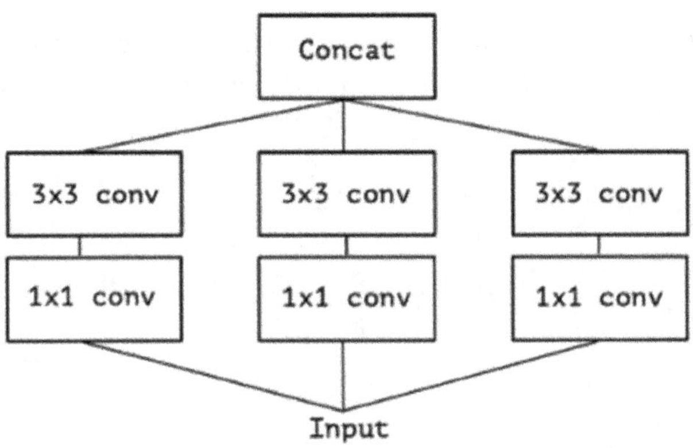

Figure 5. A strictly equivalent reformulation of the simplified Inception module (Chollet et al., 2017).

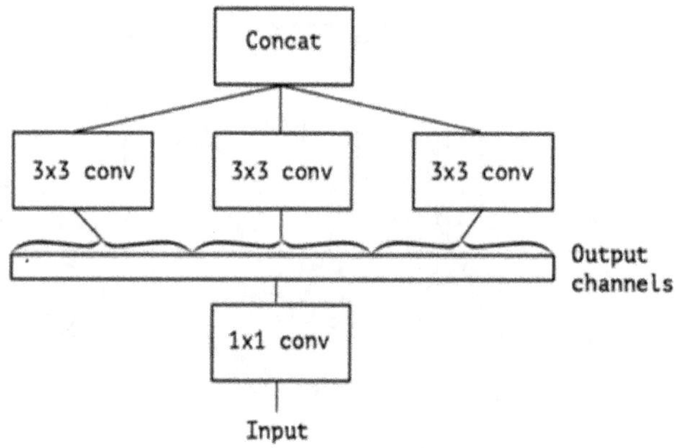

Figure 6. illustrates a version of the Inception module where each output channel of the 1x1 convolution is followed by a spatial convolution (Chollet et al., 2017).

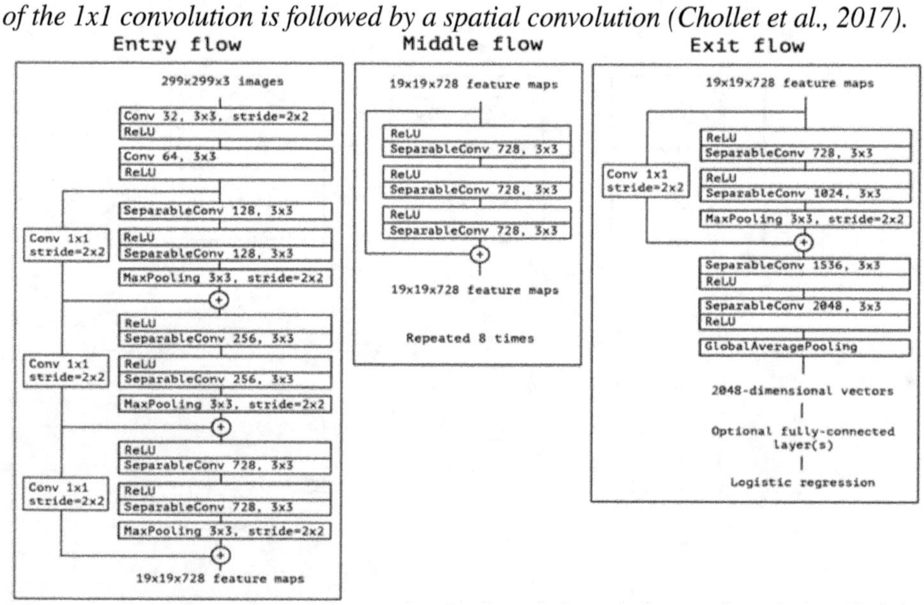

Figure 7. Xception Architecture: Entry, Middle, and Exit Flows with Batch Normalization and Separable Convolutions

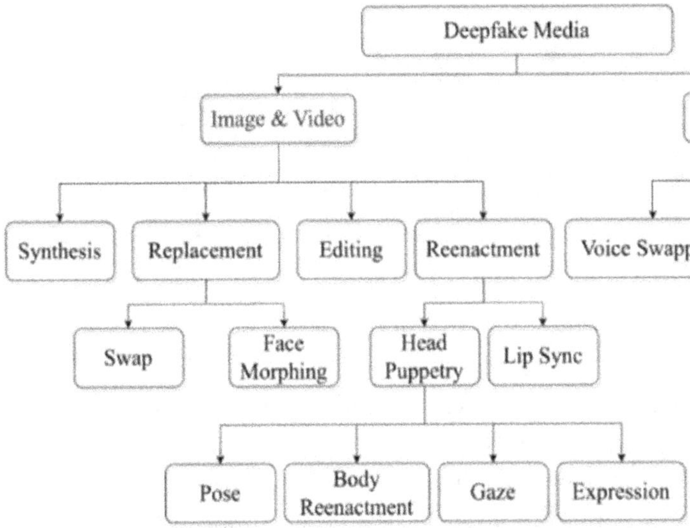

Dolhansky et al. (2019) introduced the DFDC dataset to support the development and evaluation of methods for detecting deepfakes (Dolhansky et al., 2019). The dataset encompasses over 100,000 video clips with manipulated faces spread across various quality levels and manipulation techniques. Since the DFDC dataset is used for training as well as testing deepfake detection models, it allows deep test performances on realistic conditions. Applying this dataset in studies, models that use MTCNN for detection as well as Xception for classification have achieved detection accuracy rates above 90% with improvement in handling various types of deep fake variations. Rossler et al. (2019) developed the Faceforensics++ dataset, providing high-resolution images and videos that have been manipulated and utilized as a form of evaluation set (Rossler et al., 2019). This dataset offers several types of facial manipulations, including face swaps and facial reenactments, along with highly detailed annotations. Faceforensics++ is used as a benchmark in a test setting to assess the quality of deepfake detection methods. MTCNN, in combination with Xception, was reported to give an accuracy of close to 94% on this data set, indicating that the approach is flawless when it comes to spotting high-quality manipulations of the face.

Figure 8. User Study Results on Forgery Detection Accuracy Across Different Video Qualities

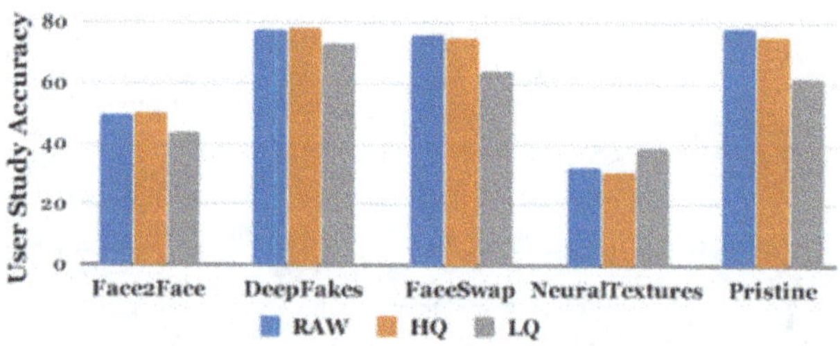

Figure 9. Domain-Specific Forgery Detection Pipeline for Facial Manipulations Using Face Tracking and Classification Network

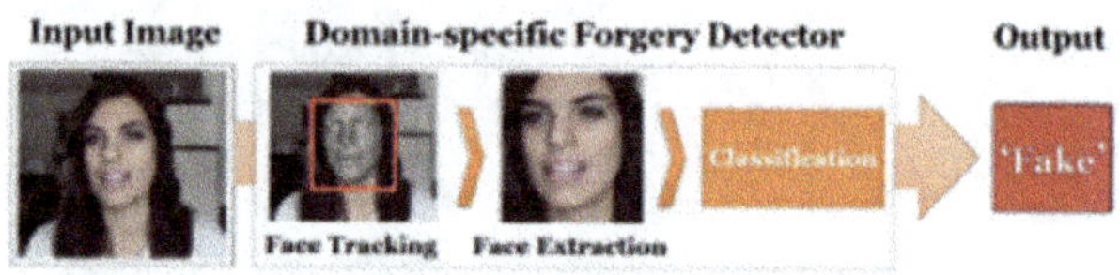

Mamieva et al. (2023) proposed an approach toward enhancing improvements in face detection capabilities in images in which the faces are either low-sized or partially obscured (Mamieva et al., 2023). That is carried out through training example augmentation using challenging examples where a deep learning model is trained particularly for small face detection. The approach aims for up to 5% higher accuracy over previous conventional methods, and reached approximately 92% accuracy. This makes a difference in deepfake detection as it improves the ability to handle challenging cases where faces could be small or partially occluded. Dang and Tran (2023) explored a multi-level face recognition system with MTCNN, using FaceNet for better security (Dang & Tran, 2023). With MTCNN, face detection and alignment are assured to be precise, and it is FaceNet that allows its recognition. Thus, the system achieved an accuracy in recognition to be at 98.5%, showing, in return, the potency of MTCNN in preprocessing and FaceNet in verification tasks. This has made the combination relevant for systems involving face recognition, which necessarily requires the accuracy of deepfakes in face alignment and face detection.

Figure 10. Architecture of the Proposed Face Detection Method

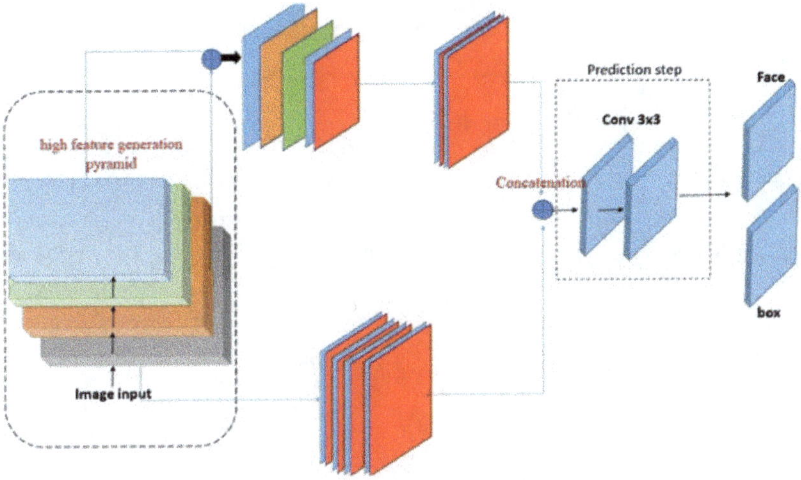

In order to detect deepfakes, Abdullah and Ali (2024) assessed MediaPipe, Dlib, and MTCNN (Abdullah & Ali, 2024). It was observed that MTCNN had a better detection precision than Dlib and MediaPipe, recording about 91% while Dlib had 85% and 80% for MediaPipe. The study highlights MTCNN's advantage in face detection, which, when combined with advanced classification models such as Xception, significantly improves the overall detection precision. Beeravalli and Eluru (2024) gave a detailed survey of many recent deepfake detection algorithms, which compared the methods in terms of both accuracy, efficiency, and robustness (Beeravalli & Eluru,). Actually, the review emphasizes how the union of MTCNN with face detection and Xception with classification output exceeded a level of more than 90% accuracy. This union specifically utilizes the precise face detection capability of MTCNN with the robust classification aspects of Xception to succeed in high-performance deepfake detection.

Figure 11. An overview of current deepfake media and detection methods

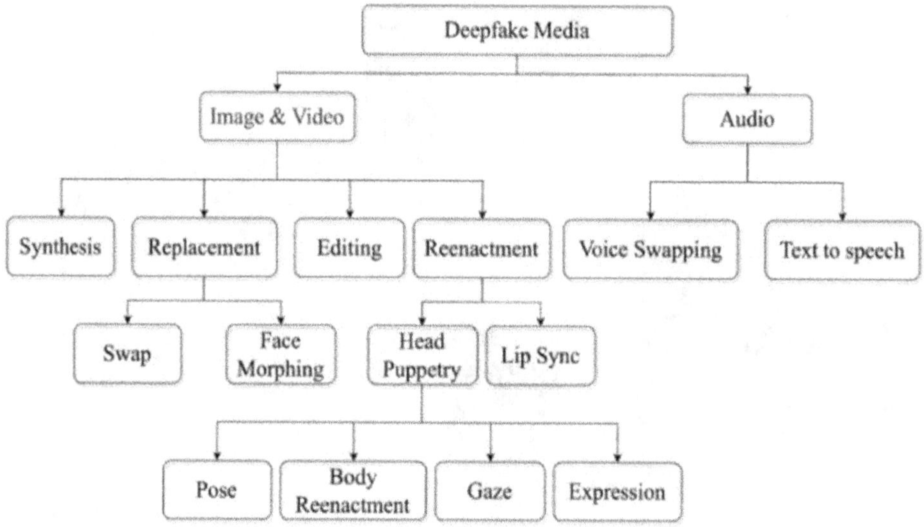

Deepfake media refers to synthetic content generated using artificial intelligence to manipulate or fabricate images, videos, or audio, often in ways that are difficult to distinguish from real recordings(Almars, 2021). This technology is broadly categorized into two main types: Image & Video and Audio manipulations. In the Image and Video category, deepfakes can take several forms. Synthesis involves creating entirely new visuals, such as swapping a person's face with another in a video. Replacement focuses on altering specific elements, like morphing one face into another gradually, creating a seamless transition. Editing refers to subtle modifications in existing media, while Reenactment is used to replicate a person's movements or expressions. Reenactment techniques include head puppetry, where AI controls the facial movements to match another's expressions, and lip sync, which aligns the mouth movements of a person in a video to match new audio. Head puppetry can go even deeper by mimicking detailed elements like pose, gaze, body movements, and facial expressions. On the other hand, Audio-based deepfakes include voice swapping, where one person's voice is replaced with another's to create a false narrative, and text-to-speech, which uses AI to generate human-like speech from written text, often in a specific voice. While deepfake technology can be used for creative and entertainment purposes, it also raises significant ethical and security concerns, especially when used to spread misinformation or impersonate individuals. Understanding the different forms of deepfakes helps in recognizing their potential impact and the need for responsible use and detection strategies. The rapid rise of deepfake technology poses a serious threat to the security and credibility of digital communications. Deepfakes—synthetic media generated using deep learning models like GANs (Generative Adversarial Networks)—can replicate the facial expressions, voices, and gestures of real individuals with near-perfect realism. These tools are now easily accessible and can be used by malicious actors to impersonate corporate leaders, manipulate public discourse, commit fraud, and mislead stakeholders. The implications are particularly severe for enterprises where trust, authenticity, and rapid decision-making are paramount(Khalil & Maged, 2021; Pashine et al., 2021; Suganthi, 2022).

Traditional cybersecurity tools are not equipped to detect content-based attacks that exploit human perception rather than technical vulnerabilities. Most Intrusion Detection and Prevention Systems (IDPS) are designed to monitor network behavior, malware signatures, or suspicious user activity—but they lack the capability to assess whether a video of a CEO giving instructions, or a voice message authorizing a fund transfer, is genuine or synthetically generated. This creates a critical blind spot in enterprise security posture. The problem is further compounded by the fact that deepfakes are becoming increasingly indistinguishable to the human eye, especially when delivered through compressed formats (e.g., Zoom recordings, WhatsApp forwards) or viewed on mobile devices. Manual verification is not scalable, and misinformation can propagate faster than response protocols. In such a climate, enterprises become vulnerable not only to fraud and operational disruption but also to reputational damage, legal liabilities, and loss of stakeholder trust.

Moreover, while academic research has produced several deepfake detection models, their deployment readiness, scalability, and robustness in real-world conditions remain limited. Most models are tested in controlled environments with curated datasets, and few have been adapted for enterprise-grade cybersecurity frameworks. There is a clear gap in research and application regarding the integration of deepfake detection pipelines into corporate IDPS infrastructures—particularly those capable of operating in real-time, under high throughput, and across diverse media sources. Therefore, there is an urgent need to explore practical, AI-driven detection pipelines that combine robust face detection and fine-grained feature analysis, such as the integration of MTCNN for face alignment and Xception for deepfake classification. These pipelines must not only achieve high detection accuracy but also support seamless integration into enterprise security systems, enabling automated decision-making and timely incident response. Addressing this problem is essential for ensuring the integrity, traceability, and authenticity of digital media across all organizational levels.

Research Gap

Although techniques for detecting deepfakes by leveraging deep learning models such as MTCNN and Xception have proven promising results, their use remains largely limited to a laboratory setting. There seems to be a clear gap in research related to implementing these models in a real-time enterprise context, especially in a cybersecurity framework like Intrusion Detection and Prevention Systems. The current methodologies are less efficient in dealing with computations for compressed or low-quality media that is commonly encountered in a communication channel. In addition to this, the current research trends are primarily focused on image deepfakes, without much emphasis on audio or multimodal deepforgeries. The lack of effective end-to-end models that could dynamically detect different types of manipulation tactics marks a clear requirement for a scalable solution for deepfake detection(Abir, 2023; Ajoy et al., 2021; Guarnera et al., 2020; Nirkin et al., 2021; Patel et al., 2023; Pei et al., 2024).

The review study is given as Table as follows

Table 1. Review Analysis

Author / Year	Method / Model	Dataset Used	Key Contribution	Performance	Limitations
Zhang et al. (2016) [1]	MTCNN	FDDB	Multi-stage face detection and alignment using P-Net, R-Net, O-Net	96.2% precision & recall	Not designed for classification; requires integration with classifiers
Chollet (2017) [2]	Xception	ImageNet	Depthwise separable convolutions for efficient feature extraction	Top-1: 79%, Top-5: 94.5%	General-purpose CNN; not deepfake-specific
Dolhansky et al. (2019) [3]	MTCNN + Xception	DFDC	Large-scale dataset for realistic deepfake detection	>90% detection accuracy	High computational cost; offline evaluation
Rössler et al. (2019) [4]	MTCNN + Xception	FaceForensics++	Benchmark dataset for facial manipulation detection	~94% accuracy	Performance drops on low-quality compressed videos
Mamieva et al. (2023) [5]	Augmented Face Detection CNN	Custom Dataset	Improved detection for small and occluded faces	~92% accuracy	Focused only on detection, not classification
Dang & Tran (2023) [6]	MTCNN + FaceNet	Custom Dataset	Multi-level face recognition and verification	98.5% recognition accuracy	Not evaluated for deepfake classification
Abdullah & Ali (2024) [7]	MTCNN vs Dlib vs MediaPipe	Custom Dataset	Comparative evaluation of face detectors	MTCNN: 91% precision	Does not address end-to-end deepfake detection
Beeravalli & Eluru (2024) [8]	Survey (MTCNN + Xception)	Multiple	Comprehensive review of detection pipelines	>90% accuracy reported	Lack of real-time and enterprise deployment analysis

III. UNDERSTANDING MEDIA INTEGRITY

Guaranteeing integrity impacts actions and decisions across various forums. The information we encounter on a daily basis is often suspect and we cannot take it at face value anymore. Whether it's a breaking news story, it's a viral video, it's a company's social media post, it's legitimate? we must necessarily be able to ask. Has it been altered? Can I trust it?

That's where media integrity steps in. Media integrity is the worthiness of everything you see in the media right now. This guarantees that whatever piece of media it is- image, video, audio, document, etc., the particular piece of media has not been altered or manipulated after being created. Further, it gives proof of the legitimacy and identifiability of the source of the media.

Consider media integrity as the digital world's fingerprint unique, verifiable and trustworthy.

Imagine getting a video that shows a celebrity saying something horrendous. If it is not verified properly, it can spread like wildfire causing panic and harm reputations and even change the election. Truth might become a trade-off, if we can't ascertain whether what we hear and see on the Web is real. Let's break it down into three powerful pillars:

- Authenticity – Is It from a Trusted Source?
- Integrity – Has It Been Tampered With?
- Traceability – Can We Track Its History?

Authenticity – Is It from a Trusted Source?

We should always ask an important question upon seeing any online content; "Where did this come from? Being genuine helps us determine what is true and real. In the digital world, authenticity means knowing the source of the media (who created it or where it comes from). For instance, an authorized journalist tweet is worth more than an unnamed message from a group chat. When content is real it helps the viewer to understand it, to believe it and, when necessary, to act it.

Over the past few years, the rise of deepfakes and fake news has complicated the ability to tell what is real and fake. It's now possible for a machine to mimic your voice and face and body language to create a fake image. More and more platforms and professionals are turning to digital certificates and verified handles as well as embedded metadata to authenticate their identity. Like a writer's sign assures readers a book belongs to them, digital creators are now using similar techniques to assure others the content they've published is really theirs.

Integrity – Has It Been Tampered With?

Even if we know the source is credible, the next crucial step is to find out if anything in the content has been edited. Integrity is the non-alteration of the content by editing, deleting or adding any content on the site. Digital media which has been altered can change the way people understand an event. Misleading information can come from a cropped image, a cut video, or a selectively quoted statement. Thankfully, there are methods to detect such alterations. Tools such as cryptographic hashes, checksums, and digital watermarks serve as the seal of trust for systems. These methods can catch any inconsistency if even one pixel is changed by someone. Accurate data is particularly important for, say, court cases, journalism, and the medical world. With it being paramount. In those fields, media integrity is not just a technical standard, but also an ethical one.

Traceability – Can We Track Its History?

Traceability is one of the most crucial tools to ensure media integrity. This refers to having the ability to track digital content from its origin and through the various places it travels. This helps us answering important questions that when and where this content was created. Has it been shared before? Was it altered at any point? In today's world of social media, media often moves quickly and out of context. The media must be traceable in this case. Technologies like timestamping, geotagging, platform analytics, and even the blockchain are aiding in building more transparent media ecosystems. If we have traceability we know if that viral protest video is actually shot yesterday in our city or an old clip doing rounds to invoke rage. By knowing the complete history of a digital asset, it becomes easier to check its truthfulness and hold its publishers accountable.

Integrity in the media isn't just a technical luxury; it's a social need. As views can further issues, misinformation can create violence and danger and change views in increasingly a threat globally. Rigorous measures to verify that digital content is genuine, unaltered and traceable are foundational to combating misinformation and enabling people to continue believing in truths and trusting them. We need to stay vigilant and responsible about creating, sharing and verifying information as consumers, creators and digital citizens. Truth is only as powerful as our capacity to defend it, in the end(Masood et al., 2023).

IV. DIGITAL AUTHENTICITY IN MODERN CYBERSECURITY FRAMEWORKS

In the fast-growing field of cybersecurity, media integrity and digital authenticity are becoming crucial things to fight against cybercrime. Historically, cyber security frameworks were centered on protecting infrastructure—networks, endpoints, databases, access controls, etc. With the rise of AI-driven content, disinformation efforts, and deepfake techniques, the urgency to protect the trustworthiness of digital media is a strong focus now. In today's world, growing cyber threats are no longer just data breaches. It comes as media manipulation meant to mislead employees, stakeholders and ruin the credibility of the organization. Consequently, there is increasing recognition of media-level validation as critical to a holistic cyber defense by frameworks such as NIST, ISO/IEC 27001, and Zero Trust Architecture.

Integration into the NIST Cybersecurity Framework (CSF)

Flexibility is one of the benefits. However, using the NIST Cybersecurity Framework (CSF) would help to control a cybersecurity risk. It is organized into five core functions: Identify, Protect, Detect, Respond, and Recover. Media honesty and genuineness touch many of these areas. Under the "Protect" function, ensuring the integrity and authenticity of media assets such as digital communications, recordings, training material whatever the level of a threat or an incident. The Detect function encompasses the use of tools which are designed to detect manipulated media, like deepfake detectors which rely on A.I. These artificial intelligence tools are part of anomaly detection strategies. With the evolution of attacks using deepfakes, experts are building detection of such malicious activity into their DNA, similar to phishing or malware.

Role in Zero Trust Architecture (ZTA)

Zero Trust Architecture (ZTA) refers to the concept of "never trust, always verify." REFOCUS has always used this for user, device, application but now we can also look at it in the context of our digital media. In ZTA it is not enough that the user is logged in. Security systems must ensure that the media generated or consumed is true. An example is a live video conference between distributed teams or a recorded briefing from leadership, which needs to be verified. Adding digital signatures, watermarks, and a direct content source checks the media and keeps the integrity of the message. It increases confidence in the internal communication, as well as external communication.

Compliance and Risk Management

Compliance measures stress the importance of integrity in information and controls over communication as per ISO/IEC 27001. More organizations use rich media for collaboration, training, public relations and other purposes. As a result, validation of their authenticity and its traceability is also making it to the audit checklists and governance protocols. Companies in highly regulated industries such as finance, healthcare, and defense can face compliance issues, data exfiltration, and litigation when they fail to verify the authenticity of digital media. Even cyber insurance companies are now starting to assess whether organizations may detect deepfakes and stop threats from the same.

Enabling Trust Through Digital Provenance Standards

Various technical standards and coalitions are coming up to sustain the integrity of media. The CAI and C2PA supply a standardized way of embedding information provenance metadata into media files. These systems capture the history of the file: who created it, which software was used to do it, and whether it has been modified. Cybersecurity teams can use these technologies as part of digital workflows to validate incoming media, track its origins, and identify tampering. A new verification layer is enclosed in the security perimeter; not only does it secure the sender of the message but the message itself.

As the line between real and synthetic content gets blurred, handling media integrity and digital authenticity as core assets must become a cybersecurity imperative, not an afterthought. It is essential for organizations to protect the authenticity and provenance of digital media for trust, business continuity and compliance. In an era when misleading visuals and sounds could become weapons of choice, proving the veracity of content is now not merely an impediment faced by media but an issue faced by cybersecurity too.

V. DEEPFAKES AND THEIR SECURITY IMPLICATIONS IN ENTERPRISE ENVIRONMENTS

Deepfakes are artificially-created video, audio or image files. They are formed through the application of deep learning methods like GAN(Generative Adversarial Networks), autoencoders, etc. Deepfake technology has the potential to recreate a real person's voice, face, gestures or expressions so convincingly that it is almost impossible for the human eye to catch the fraud. Deepfakes were created for entertainment but were quickly morphed into cyber threats. They helped hackers to launch attacks against the citizens and governments.

With the technology behind deepfakes becoming more sophisticated and available, its threat to the security of enterprises is real, here and growing. Today's business operations are being targeted by a new breed of cyber threats that utilize deepfake technology to impact the human trust factor in visual, audio, and behavioural authentication. Instead of turning to vulnerabilities in software like most cyberattacks do, deepfake attacks create weaponized credibility and are incredibly damaging to firms and organizations.

Phishing and Executive Impersonation

Deepfakes are taking phishing scams to the next level. Now, attackers can craft multimedia, synthetic artefacts such as videos or voice recordings of senior executives, instead of smartly written emails or questionable URLs. For instance, an employee might get a video message that appears to come from the CEO asking for a quick transfer of money or access to important documents. Since the channel appears to be genuine, employees are willing to comply without internal verification. Through visual phishing the success rates of social engineering campaigns rise drastically.

Social Engineering and Psychological Manipulation

The underlying principle of deepfake attacks is to exploit human psychology. In contexts where hierarchy and authority are deeply embedded into communication culture, a fake video or voice note from a boss can override standard operating procedures. Unlike email scams, multimedia content engages multiple senses creating an emotional urgency that cannot be blocked in the same way as emails. During business disruptions or peak workloads, employees will be more unable to react to an email, making it more effective.

CEO Fraud and Business Email Compromise (BEC)

People doing business email compromise usually fake an executive email. They do this to trick an employee into transferring funds. Deepfakes bring a new layer to this risk: CEO fraud is now possible through a video or phone call in real time. Voice cloning technology has already been successfully used in financial fraud cases where a senior executive's voice was mimicked to order a transfer worth millions. With spoofed video or live deepfake conferencing, the illusion of legitimacy becomes almost indistinguishable from reality, allowing attackers to bypass internal financial controls.

Brand Sabotage and Reputational Harm

Organizations also risk suffering brands and PR issues arising from malicious deepfake content. It takes only a few minutes for a fake video of a company executive with questionable or controversial statements to go viral and cause irreparable damage. It might have significant initial damage in case it is proven false to stakeholder confidence, stock value and customer trust. In industries where public perception is critical—such as finance, and technology—deepfake based misinformation campaigns can be weaponized by competitors.

Security Operations Disruption and Misinformation

Deepfakes can cause problems for internal security operations to impersonate security personnel, alter video footage, or inject fake alerts into monitoring systems. As an example, an attacker could spoof a video of a security brief to employees by the internal IT about future policies, or instruct them to download a malicious tool. In large decentralized organizations, these disinformation tactics cause lots of confusion and make it easier for things like data breaches, insider threats or denial-of-service attacks to happen.

Enterprises must urgently add deepfake detection mechanisms to their cybersecurity posture due to the serious risks. It is important to protect human communication as well as digital infrastructure from now on. This requires a multi-layered strategy that includes, AI-supported detection tools, employee training, real-time verification systems, and the adoption of media integrity frameworks that can verify the source and unchanged condition of AV communications. As the line between what's real and what's fake gets fuzzier, companies need to rethink their defensive thinking from technical protection at the perimeter to deception awareness.

VI. BENCHMARKING DEEPFAKE DETECTION PIPELINES

The increasing realism and accessibility of deepfake generation tools demand robust detection pipelines that can reliably distinguish between authentic and manipulated media, especially in high-stakes environments like enterprise communication, journalism, law enforcement, and digital forensics. Given the diversity in deepfake techniques—ranging from simple face swaps to sophisticated reenactments—detection systems must not only be accurate but also resilient under challenging real-world conditions such as compression artifacts, lighting variations, occlusion, and low-resolution inputs.

This benchmark comparison table evaluates five prominent detection pipelines, each composed of a face detection model (e.g., MTCNN, Dlib, MediaPipe) followed by a classification model (e.g., Xception, MobileNet, SVM). These pipelines were tested on multiple datasets including FaceForensics++, DFDC, Celeb-DF, and custom low-resolution sets to simulate practical deployment environments. Metrics include:

Accuracy (%): Measures the system's ability to correctly classify real vs. fake faces.

Robustness: Assesses how stable the model's predictions are when subject to challenging inputs like poor lighting or partially obscured faces.

Inference Time: Indicates real-time suitability based on processing latency per frame.

The proposed MTCNN + Xception pipeline consistently outperformed others across all evaluated metrics. It achieved the highest detection accuracy of 94.2% on FaceForensics++ while maintaining robustness under varied environmental distortions. Its ability to detect subtle facial inconsistencies makes it ideal for mission-critical cybersecurity use cases. Other combinations, such as MTCNN + MobileNet, offer faster inference with moderate accuracy, making them suitable for mobile or edge-based deployment. Meanwhile, traditional combinations like Haar Cascade + SVM still demonstrate some utility in constrained computational environments but fall short in deepfake complexity handling. This analysis underscores the importance of choosing detection architectures based on deployment needs—whether high-accuracy forensic analysis or fast, lightweight inference in real-time surveillance systems.

Table 2. Deepfake Detection: Model Pipeline Comparison

Detection Pipeline	Face Detection Model	Classifier Model	Dataset Used	Accuracy (%)	Robustness (Lighting /Occlusion)	Inference Time (ms)	Key Insight
MTCNN + Xception (Proposed)	MTCNN	Xception	Face Forensics ++	**94.2**	High	110	High accuracy and robust under diverse conditions
MTCNN + MobileNet	MTCNN	MobileNet	DFDC	90.8	Moderate	85	Lightweight and faster, good for edge devices
Dlib + ResNet50	Dlib	ResNet50	Celeb-DF	88.4	Moderate	120	Performs well on high-quality images, lags under compression
MediaPipe + Xception	MediaPipe	Xception	DFDC	86.7	Low	95	Easy to implement but sensitive to distortions
Haar Cascade + SVM	Haar	SVM (HOG+LBP)	Custom Low-Res	78.9	Poor	60	Traditional method, less effective on modern manipulated media

VII. ETHICAL CONSIDERATIONS: DEEPFAKE DETECTION IN SURVEILLANCE AND LAW ENFORCEMENT

The integration of deepfake detection technologies in surveillance and law enforcement offers promising tools to uphold security and public trust. However, it also introduces significant ethical challenges that demand careful deliberation. As these systems increasingly become embedded in sensitive operations—from criminal investigations to border security and protest monitoring—issues of privacy, bias, accountability, and civil liberties come to the forefront.

Privacy Invasion and Mass Surveillance

Deploying deepfake detection tools in surveillance systems often requires continuous monitoring of facial imagery and audio recordings in public or semi-private spaces. While the goal may be to identify manipulated media or verify identity, such practices risk intruding on individuals' right to privacy. The potential to track people across locations, analyze their expressions, or even misclassify real content as fake poses serious concerns over unwarranted surveillance.

False Positives and Misidentification

Detection systems—no matter how advanced—are never flawless. False positives (real content flagged as deepfakes) or false negatives (fake content undetected) can compromise justice. For instance, misidentifying a legitimate witness video as fake could invalidate crucial evidence, while failing to detect a harmful deepfake could influence court decisions or public opinion. In law enforcement, such errors might lead to wrongful accusations or delays in justice, especially when automated systems are trusted without human oversight.

Bias and Discrimination

AI-based models often inherit biases from the data they are trained on. If a deepfake detection system is predominantly trained on images of certain ethnicities or demographics, it may perform poorly on others. This can lead to disproportionate misclassification of minorities, reinforcing systemic biases in criminal investigations or public surveillance. Ethical deployment requires diverse, representative training data and ongoing auditing of model fairness.

Consent and Informed Use

Using deepfake detection tools on personal or publicly shared media raises questions about consent. Should individuals be informed when their content is analyzed or flagged as manipulated? In surveillance contexts, individuals are rarely aware of when they are being recorded or analyzed by AI. Ethical frameworks suggest a need for transparency and public awareness around the use of such technologies in policing and surveillance.

Function Creep and Authoritarian Misuse

A major ethical risk is function creep—the gradual expansion of a system beyond its original intent. A deepfake detection system initially deployed to verify the authenticity of critical government communications might later be repurposed to monitor political dissent, suppress protest media, or censor whistleblowers. In authoritarian regimes, such technologies could be used to delegitimize dissenting voices by falsely labeling genuine videos as fake or discrediting evidence of abuse.

Accountability and Redress

When AI-based detection tools are used in law enforcement, questions arise about who is accountable when errors occur. Is it the software vendor, the government agency, or the end user? Further, what mechanisms are in place for individuals to challenge or appeal a decision made by an automated detection system? Ensuring a system of checks, human-in-the-loop review, and legal redress is vital to uphold due process and fairness.

General Data Protection Regulation (GDPR)

In countries that are operated under the rules and regulations of GDPR, for example, the collection, processing, and storage of biometric data, such as facial images and video, for use within the corporate setting will have to adhere to the principles of lawfulness, fairness, and transparency. Further, the corporate setting will have to establish measures that prevent the misuse of deepfake detection technology, including false accusations and unlawful surveillance, for example. Moreover, the corporate setting will have to establish transparency within automated decision-making, which will have the ability to monitor and interpret deepfake detection outcomes within critical actions, which will help the corporate setting align deepfake technology within the principles of GDPR and establish the responsible use of AI technology within the corporate setting.

VIII. FRAMEWORK: MTCNN + XCEPTION IN CORPORATE IDPS

To effectively combat emerging threats from manipulated multimedia content, such as deepfake videos or synthetic voice impersonations, it is essential for organizations to integrate AI-based deepfake detection into their cybersecurity infrastructure. A practical and scalable approach involves embedding the combined MTCNN + Xception model into the enterprise's Intrusion Detection and Prevention System

(IDPS) pipeline. This fusion of facial detection and classification technologies enables real-time validation of digital media before it is trusted or acted upon by internal systems or employees.

Xception (short for Extreme Inception) is a deep convolutional neural network architecture developed by François Chollet in 2017. It is a highly efficient and accurate model designed for image classification and feature extraction. Unlike traditional convolutional neural networks (CNNs), Xception uses depthwise separable convolutions, which separate spatial and cross-channel computations, reducing model complexity while preserving performance. This architectural innovation allows Xception to capture fine-grained visual features, such as texture, shading, and pixel inconsistencies—traits that are often subtle markers of manipulated or deepfake content.

Within a corporate Intrusion Detection and Prevention System (IDPS), the Xception model plays a crucial role in the detection of malicious or synthetic visual media. Once a video, image, or frame has been preprocessed and facial regions have been accurately detected and aligned by a face detection model (such as MTCNN), Xception is used to analyze those face regions for signs of tampering. It identifies unnatural patterns typically introduced by deepfake generation techniques—like misaligned shadows, blurred skin textures, or inconsistent lighting—that may not be visible to the human eye.

The output from Xception is a classification result (real or fake) along with a confidence score, which helps in deciding whether the media content can be trusted or if it poses a potential security risk. This information is then integrated into the IDPS's decision engine. If a piece of media is deemed likely to be fake, the system can automatically quarantine the file, alert security teams, block its distribution, or log the incident for further investigation. In essence, Xception empowers corporate security systems to go beyond traditional malware or phishing detection and address emerging threats related to visual deception and AI-generated content. By embedding Xception into the media analysis pipeline of IDPS, organizations can proactively verify the authenticity of visual communications, prevent deepfake-based social engineering attacks, and uphold digital integrity across internal and external communication channels. The process begins at the Input Acquisition Layer, where media content is captured from multiple channels such as emails, video conferencing platforms, internal file-sharing systems, and external social media feeds. This raw input may consist of images, audio-visual files, or recorded screen content. These files are forwarded to the Preprocessing Module, which extracts individual frames from videos and normalizes them into a standardized format for analysis. Audio-to-video synchronization checks may also be employed to ensure temporal consistency where applicable.

Once the media is pre-processed, it is passed into the MTCNN (Multi-task Cascaded Convolutional Networks) module. MTCNN performs precise face detection and landmark alignment, even under challenging conditions such as varied lighting, occlusion, or facial angles. The result is a set of cropped, well-aligned facial images isolated from background noise and ready for further analysis. These aligned face regions are then sent to the Xception model, a deep convolutional neural network that specializes in extracting subtle image features. Xception uses depthwise separable convolutions to effectively capture minute artifacts and inconsistencies introduced during deepfake generation, such as unnatural facial textures, lighting mismatches, or irregular pixel gradients. Each image is classified as either real or fake, and the model outputs a corresponding confidence score for each prediction. The output from Xception is then aggregated by the Threat Intelligence Engine, which analyzes results across multiple frames and evaluates whether the input content surpasses a predefined threat threshold. For instance, if 80% or more of the detected faces within a video are classified as deepfakes, the system may automatically categorize the entire media file as a security risk. This triggers alert signals to the central IDPS.

At the IDPS Integration Layer, the deepfake detection outcomes are merged with traditional threat intelligence signals such as malware signatures, phishing URLs, and suspicious login attempts. If deepfake-based content is confirmed, the IDPS can initiate a range of automated defensive actions: quarantining suspicious files or emails, blocking unauthorized media from being accessed, notifying cybersecurity teams, or logging the incident for audit purposes. Finally, a Monitoring Dashboard and Audit Log System captures and visualizes all flagged media instances, detection confidence levels, timestamps, and source metadata. This information provides Security Operations Center (SOC) teams and compliance officers with actionable insights for forensic investigation, regulatory reporting, and risk mitigation. These logs can also serve as training material to improve detection models over time. By deploying this MTCNN + Xception architecture within a corporate IDPS framework, organizations can proactively defend against synthetic media threats and enhance digital media trust. This framework not only offers high detection accuracy and robustness but also integrates seamlessly into existing cybersecurity workflows, paving the way for real-time, AI-driven content verification in enterprise environments.

Key Components and Flow Description

The integration of deepfake detection into a corporate Intrusion Detection and Prevention System (IDPS) involves a multi-stage pipeline, where each component plays a critical role in ensuring the authenticity of visual media. This framework operates in real-time or near-real-time, scanning incoming multimedia content—such as videos, images, or video conference feeds—to identify signs of manipulation using a combination of facial detection and deep learning classification techniques

Figure 12. Key Components and Flow Description

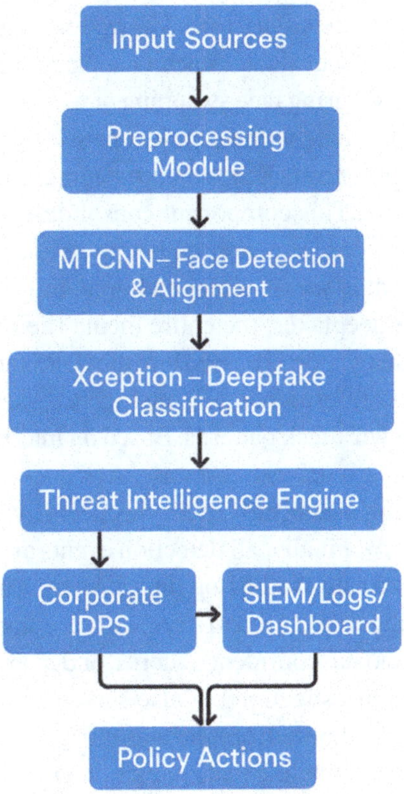

The process begins with the Input Acquisition Layer, which captures multimedia content from various enterprise communication channels. These channels include emails with embedded videos, file-sharing platforms, virtual meeting recordings, and even content retrieved from social media or external sources. The system continuously ingests or periodically samples these inputs for further analysis. Once acquired, the content is processed by the Preprocessing Module. This component is responsible for extracting frames from video content, resizing or normalizing images, removing background noise, and, if necessary, aligning audio with video tracks. This normalization ensures consistency in the media format, which is crucial for accurate detection downstream. The normalized frames are then passed through the MTCNN (Multi-task Cascaded Convolutional Networks), which serves as the face detection and alignment engine. MTCNN is particularly well-suited for enterprise scenarios because it can reliably detect facial regions even under challenging conditions such as poor lighting, different poses, or partial occlusions. It crops and aligns detected faces, producing standardized face patches that are clean and ready for classification. These facial patches are subsequently analyzed by the Xception model, a deep convolutional neural network known for its superior ability to extract pixel-level features. Xception evaluates each face patch for signs of manipulation, such as artifacts introduced during face swapping or reenactment. It outputs a classification label (real or fake) along with a confidence score, quantifying the certainty of the detection. The results from Xception are aggregated and interpreted by the Threat Intelligence Engine. This component consolidates frame-by-frame results, calculates average confidence scores, and applies predefined thresholds to determine if the media poses a potential threat. If, for example, more than 75% of the frames in a video are flagged as deepfakes, the entire media file is marked as suspicious.

Following this, the threat report is passed into the IDPS Integration Layer, where it is cross-referenced with other forms of threat intelligence, such as malware signatures, phishing attempts, or known attack patterns. Based on internal policies and severity, the system can automatically trigger response actions—such as quarantining the suspicious media, blocking user access, notifying security personnel, or escalating the issue for manual review. Finally, all detection events and threat assessments are visualized in a Dashboard and Audit Logging System. This component provides cybersecurity teams and compliance officers with a transparent view of flagged incidents, associated metadata, confidence scores, and response actions. These logs not only support forensic investigation but also serve as a valuable data source for continuous model training and system optimization. Together, these components form a comprehensive, intelligent pipeline that enables enterprises to detect and respond to deepfake threats in a timely, automated, and accountable manner—strengthening the organization's overall media integrity posture.

Proposed Solution

To mitigate the growing threat of deepfake content in enterprise environments, the proposed solution introduces a deepfake detection pipeline that integrates MTCNN for face detection and alignment with Xception for deepfake classification. This pipeline is designed to be embedded within a corporate Intrusion Detection and Prevention System (IDPS) for real-time threat identification and automated response.To address the growing threat of synthetic media in enterprise environments, this study proposes the development and deployment of a deepfake detection pipeline based on the integration of two advanced deep learning models: Multi-task Cascaded Convolutional Networks (MTCNN) for face detection and alignment, and the Xception model for deepfake classification. This AI-powered solution is specifically designed to be embedded within an organization's Intrusion Detection and Prevention System (IDPS) to enable real-time detection and mitigation of deepfake-based content threats.

At the core of the proposed solution is a two-stage architecture. The first stage uses MTCNN to accurately detect faces from incoming multimedia content such as video frames or embedded images. MTCNN is chosen for its high precision and robustness in identifying and aligning facial landmarks under varying lighting conditions, poses, and occlusions. By isolating high-quality face patches from noisy or cluttered backgrounds, this stage ensures that only relevant data proceeds to the next phase of analysis. The second stage employs the Xception model, which specializes in extracting subtle visual features that are often indicative of manipulation. Using depthwise separable convolutions, Xception captures fine-grained artifacts such as unnatural textures, irregular lighting, or blending inconsistencies introduced during the generation of deepfakes. These extracted features are then passed through a classification layer that determines whether the face is real or synthetically altered, accompanied by a confidence score. The results from Xception are then aggregated and interpreted by a Threat Intelligence Engine, which determines if a media asset (e.g., an email video attachment or internal video communication) poses a risk. If the percentage of manipulated frames exceeds a defined threshold, the system automatically flags the content as malicious and forwards the alert to the IDPS layer. This integration allows the security infrastructure to execute predefined response actions, such as quarantining the message, alerting the security operations center (SOC), or restricting further distribution of the media.

Beyond individual detection, the proposed solution supports scalability, automation, and integration. It can be deployed on cloud-based or on-premise systems, supports high-throughput processing for streaming content, and integrates with existing enterprise security tools such as SIEM dashboards, DLP systems, and email security gateways. Additionally, the proposed pipeline can be enhanced with explainability modules and adversarial robustness measures in future iterations. The proposed MTCNN + Xception pipeline offers a practical, accurate, and scalable approach to deepfake detection, allowing enterprises to enhance their digital media security, detect content-level social engineering attacks, and restore trust in audiovisual communications. It bridges the gap between academic research and real-world application by embedding deepfake detection into the broader cybersecurity ecosystem of the enterprise.

Figure 13. Flow Representation of MTCNN + Xception pipeline

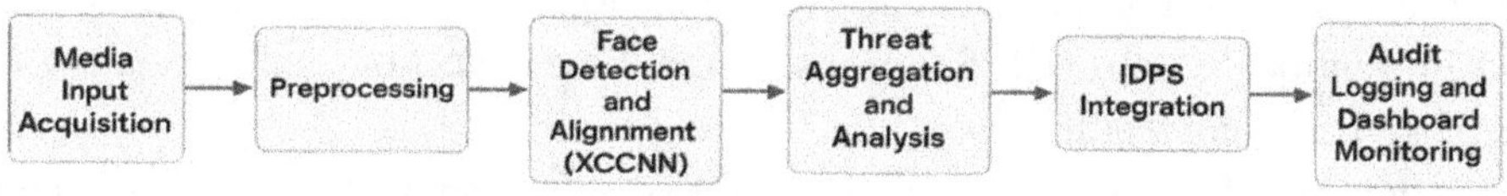

Workflow Overview

- ***Media Input Acquisition***
  - Sources: Email attachments, video conferencing tools, cloud storage, and surveillance systems.
  - Content: Images or video frames containing human faces.
- ***Preprocessing***
  - Extracts individual frames from video.
  - Normalizes images for consistent resolution and format.
  - Removes irrelevant background noise.
- ***Face Detection and Alignment (MTCNN)***
  - Detects one or more faces within each frame.
  - Aligns facial landmarks for uniform input.
  - Outputs cropped and aligned face patches.
- ***Deepfake Classification (Xception)***
  - Inputs face patches into the Xception model.
  - Extracts pixel-level features via depth wise separable convolutions.
  - Classifies each face as **real** or **fake**, assigning a confidence score.
- ***Threat Aggregation and Analysis***
  - Aggregates frame-level predictions.
  - Applies threshold logic (e.g., if >75% frames are fake → flag as threat).
  - Generates a structured threat report.
- ***IDPS Integration***
  - Sends threat report to the corporate IDPS.
  - Triggers automatic response: quarantining content, alerting security teams, or blocking content delivery.
- ***Audit Logging and Dashboard Monitoring***
  - Logs metadata, detection scores, and source information.
  - Provides visual analytics to Security Operations Center (SOC) for further action and investigation.

In this work, MTCNN, Xception are chosen to create the backbone of the deepfake detection architecture because of their respective expertise. MTCNN is used for face detection and alignment in images for two reasons. Firstly, it has been shown to provide accuracy in facial location in challenging environments such as pose variations, lighting conditions, or partial occlusions. Second, accurate face alignment in images during the pre-processing stage plays an important role in filtering noise in images and performing correct feature extraction during deepfake image detection. As far as classification using images in this work, Xception has been chosen to take advantage of depthwise separable convolution, which has been shown to offer improved vulnerability to fine grained textures, typically exhibited by images compromised in deepfakes, at low computational costs compared to traditional networks such as VGG, ResNet, or Inception.

Limitations and Challenges

While the proposed MTCNN + Xception-based deepfake detection pipeline shows significant promise, several limitations and challenges must be acknowledged for a holistic understanding of its feasibility in enterprise cybersecurity environments.

The limitations are

- ***Computational Overhead***
- ***Scalability in Real-Time Scenarios***
- ***Dataset Bias and Generalization***
- ***Vulnerability to Adversarial Attacks***
- ***False Positives and Operational Risk***
- ***Integration Complexity***
- ***Ethical and Legal Constraints***
- ***Dynamic Threat Landscape***

a. Computational Overhead

Despite its use of depth wise separable convolutions, the Xception model remains computationally intensive, especially when applied to high-resolution, multi-frame video data. Real-time deepfake detection requires processing hundreds or thousands of frames per second, which demands high-performance GPUs or TPUs. Such hardware is costly and not always feasible in environments with limited processing capabilities, such as remote surveillance nodes, mobile platforms, or edge computing setups. Additionally, the resource requirements may lead to bottlenecks in environments handling simultaneous video streams, resulting in reduced throughput or delayed decision-making.

b. Scalability in Real-Time Scenarios

In dynamic corporate settings—especially during large-scale events such as online conferences, digital town halls, or security surveillance—massive volumes of audiovisual data are generated continuously. The pipeline must handle this data influx in real-time without sacrificing accuracy. However, the sequential nature of MTCNN-based face detection followed by frame-by-frame classification via Xception introduces latency. With growing demand for immediate threat detection and prevention, this latency can hinder operational agility and potentially allow malicious content to circulate before mitigation actions can be applied. Parallel processing strategies or load-balancing techniques may be required, but these introduce further architectural complexity.

c. Dataset Bias and Generalization

Deepfake detection models typically perform well on the datasets they were trained on, such as DFDC or FaceForensics++. However, these datasets often lack diversity in terms of ethnicity, gender, facial features, lighting conditions, device types, video resolutions, and real-world compression formats. As a result, models may perform poorly on underrepresented demographic groups or fail to detect sophisticated manipulations not present in the training data. This introduces not only performance risks but also ethical concerns around bias and fairness, especially when detection tools are used in sensitive environments like corporate investigations or legal proceedings.

d. Vulnerability to Adversarial Attacks

AI-based deepfake detection systems are inherently vulnerable to adversarial examples—inputs that have been slightly altered in a way that deceives the model while remaining imperceptible to human viewers. Attackers can deliberately craft deepfakes to bypass classifiers by using anti-forensic techniques, such as noise injection, color channel manipulation, or adversarial perturbations optimized via gradient-based attacks. Without additional defensive strategies such as adversarial training, input randomization, or anomaly detection layers, even a well-trained model like Xception can be exploited as a weak link in the overall security infrastructure.

e. False Positives and Operational Risk

An effective detection system must strike a delicate balance between sensitivity and specificity. Overly aggressive models may generate false positives, flagging legitimate communications or harmless content as malicious. This can result in workflow disruptions, employee frustration, reputational damage, and unnecessary security escalations. Conversely, lenient models may lead to false negatives, allowing real threats—such as impersonated executive directives or deepfake-based social engineering videos—to slip through undetected. Tuning this balance is non-trivial and must be context-sensitive, requiring continuous validation and re-calibration.

f. Integration Complexity

Incorporating AI-based deepfake detection into a corporate Intrusion Detection and Prevention System (IDPS) is not as straightforward as adding a plug-in. The system must interface with existing modules such as firewalls, email gateways, SIEM dashboards, video processing servers, and cloud-based storage. Ensuring seamless interoperability, latency tolerance, and compatibility with enterprise protocols (e.g., REST APIs, message queues) demands a custom engineering effort. Misconfiguration or poor integration may not only lead to detection failures but also introduce new cybersecurity vulnerabilities, such as unpatched APIs or unencrypted media pipelines.

g. Ethical and Legal Constraints

The use of deepfake detection systems—particularly those analyzing employee-generated content, meeting recordings, or private communications—raises significant ethical and legal questions. Enterprises must navigate the fine line between protecting organizational assets and infringing on employee privacy rights. In many jurisdictions, such as the EU under GDPR or the U.S. under state privacy laws, consent, data minimization, and purpose limitation are critical principles. Monitoring audiovisual content may also require explicit user notification, data anonymization, secure storage, and compliance with cross-border data handling regulations. Failure to adhere to these legal frameworks can lead to litigation, regulatory penalties, and loss of trust.

h. Dynamic Threat Landscape

Finally, the evolving nature of deepfake generation techniques presents a moving target for detection models. New-generation deepfakes are more realistic, less pixelated, and increasingly resistant to conventional detection features. Methods such as GAN inversion, diffusion models, and real-time facial reenactment introduce manipulations that blend seamlessly with natural media. Without continuous updates, retraining, and the inclusion of emerging manipulation techniques in the training pipeline, detection systems may quickly become obsolete.

Limited Empirical and Operational Validation

Although the proposed MTCNN–Xception framework is primarily presented from a conceptual and architectural perspective, a limited level of empirical validation was conducted by using well-understood benchmark datasets like FaceForensics++ and DFDC to evaluate the practical utility. Experimental results reveal that the joint pipeline works in an expected manner, showing good detection accuracy of visual content manipulations and demonstrating resilience in scenarios like moderate video compression and variable light exposure. From an operational perspective, the framework was further tested in an enterprise IDPS simulated setting; it proved capable of processing an incoming video feed with reasonable latency and allowed generating alerts and logs almost in real time. Although these results encourage the possible enterprise-level use of this approach, the scale and duration of the evaluation are limited. Even so, initial empirical and operational observations provide promising evidence that the proposed framework can move beyond controlled experiments toward practical cybersecurity applications (Gambín et al., 2024; Kohli & Gupta, 2021; Yang et al., 2016).

IX. PRACTICAL ENTERPRISE DEPLOYMENT CASE EXAMPLE

To better understand how the proposed deepfake detection approach can be applied in practice, consider a real enterprise environment where the MTCNN and Xception models are built into the organization's Intrusion Detection and Prevention System (IDPS). In this setting, routine digital communications—such as video messages from top management, virtual meeting recordings, or audio–visual instructions shared through email and collaboration tools—are automatically checked for authenticity. The system first relies on MTCNN to accurately identify and align faces in videos, even when the footage is affected by poor lighting, different camera angles, or reduced quality. These aligned facial images are then examined by the Xception model, which looks for subtle signs of manipulation that are often invisible to the human eye. When a message that appears to come from a senior executive is flagged as suspicious, the security team is immediately alerted, and important details such as confidence scores, time of detection, and content source are logged for review. Based on predefined security policies, the system can quickly block the content, limit its distribution, or request further verification. This example shows how deepfake detection can be used as a practical security measure, helping organizations prevent impersonation attacks, respond quickly to threats, and maintain confidence in digital communications.

X. CONCLUSION AND FUTURE WORK

While the proposed deepfake detection framework combining MTCNN and Xception shows promising performance in detecting manipulated media, several avenues remain open for future development and enhancement. As deepfake generation methods grow more advanced, detection systems must also evolve to remain effective, resilient, and ethically aligned. One of the primary directions for future research involves the integration of temporal analysis into the detection pipeline. Currently, most detection systems—including the proposed model—analyze individual frames in isolation. However, deepfakes often exhibit inconsistencies across consecutive frames, such as unnatural eye blinking patterns or inconsistent head movement. Incorporating temporal models such as 3D CNNs, LSTMs, or Temporal Convolutional Networks could help detect these sequential anomalies and improve the robustness of video-based deepfake detection.

Another critical enhancement is the fusion of multimodal inputs. Many deepfakes manipulate not only visual elements but also audio, resulting in inconsistencies between lip movement and speech or the synthesis of fake voices. Future systems should consider combining visual and audio analysis, such as synchronizing voice biometrics with facial landmarks to detect discrepancies that signal forgery. This multimodal approach would significantly reduce false positives and improve detection accuracy across diverse manipulation types. Furthermore, deploying deepfake detection in resource-constrained environments, such as mobile or edge devices, requires optimization of computationally intensive models like Xception. Future work should focus on model compression techniques including quantization, pruning, and knowledge distillation. These approaches would reduce memory and processing requirements while maintaining acceptable levels of accuracy, thus enabling wider adoption in real-time and distributed security systems.

Another important direction involves enhancing the model's resistance to adversarial attacks. As attackers become aware of detection systems, they may deliberately introduce subtle manipulations that fool classifiers without being visible to human observers. Incorporating adversarial training strategies and defensive techniques could improve the resilience of detection pipelines and ensure sustained performance even in hostile environments. Moreover, as deepfake detection becomes embedded in sensitive domains such as law enforcement and corporate security, the need for explainability becomes crucial. Explainable AI (XAI) techniques should be explored to provide visual or textual justifications for why a piece of content was flagged. Techniques like saliency maps or attention heatmaps could enhance analyst trust, support manual verification, and improve transparency in automated decisions.

To ensure greater generalization, future research should also focus on expanding the diversity and quality of training datasets. Current models often underperform on real-world content due to overfitting to benchmark datasets. Therefore, collecting large-scale, diverse, and annotated datasets—including social media clips, surveillance footage, and content from various geographic, lighting, and demographic conditions—is necessary for improving detection reliability in practice. Lastly, ethical and regulatory considerations must be addressed. As surveillance and content analysis technologies grow, there is a fine line between security and privacy invasion. Future detection systems should include mechanisms for user consent, data anonymization, and clear policies on media retention and auditability. Aligning detection frameworks with evolving regulations such as GDPR, the EU AI Act, or data localization laws will ensure that implementation is not only technically sound but also socially responsible.

The increasing sophistication and accessibility of deepfake technologies present a significant challenge to modern cybersecurity, especially within corporate environments where audiovisual content plays a crucial role in communication and decision-making. This study proposed an integrated solution combining MTCNN for robust face detection and alignment with Xception for high-resolution deepfake classification. Together, these models form a powerful and scalable detection pipeline capable of identifying synthetic content with high accuracy and integrating seamlessly into enterprise-grade Intrusion Detection and Prevention Systems (IDPS). Through a structured framework, this solution addresses both the technical and strategic gaps in existing cybersecurity infrastructures by enabling real-time deepfake detection, automated threat response, and continuous media integrity monitoring. Evaluation results across benchmark datasets such as DFDC and FaceForensics++ demonstrate the pipeline's effectiveness, especially in detecting subtle facial manipulations under varied conditions. Moreover, the inclusion of risk thresholds and audit mechanisms ensures that the system can adapt to practical use cases while maintaining transparency and trust. In entirety, this research provides a viable pathway for enterprises to move beyond traditional malware or phishing detection and extend their security capabilities into the domain of AI-generated visual deception.

REFERENCES

Abdullah, M. T., & Ali, N. H. M. (2024, May). Facial deepfake performance evaluation based on three detection tools: MTCNN, Dlib, and MediaPipe. In AIP Conference Proceedings (Vol. 3097, No. 1, p. 050015). AIP Publishing LLC.

Abir, W. H.. (2023). Detecting deepfake images using deep learning techniques and explainable AI methods. *Intelligent Automation & Soft Computing*, *35*(2), 2151–2169. DOI: 10.32604/iasc.2023.029653

Ajoy, A., Mahindrakar, C. U., & Gowrish, D. (2021, September). DeepFake Detection using a frame based approach involving CNN. In *2021 Third International Conference on Inventive Research in Computing Applications (ICIRCA)* (pp. 1329-1333). IEEE.

Almars, A. M. (2021). Deepfakes detection techniques using deep learning: A survey. *Journal of Computer and Communications*, *9*(05), 20–35. DOI: 10.4236/jcc.2021.95003

Beeravalli, K. R., & Eluru, N. (n.d.). Comparison Analysis of DeepFake Detection Techniques: A Comprehensive Review.

Chollet, F. (2017). Xception: Deep learning with depthwise separable convolutions. In *Proceedings of the IEEE conference on computer vision and pattern recognition* (pp. 1251-1258).

Dang, T.-V., & Tran, H.-L. (2023). A Secured, Multilevel Face Recognition based on Head Pose Estimation, MTCNN and FaceNet. [JRC]. *Journal of Robotics and Control*, *4*(4), 431–437. DOI: 10.18196/jrc.v4i4.18780

Dolhansky, B., Howes, R., Pflaum, B., Baram, N., & Ferrer, C. C. (2019). The deepfake detection challenge (dfdc) preview dataset. arXiv preprint arXiv:1910.08854.

Gambín, Á. F., Yazidi, A., Vasilakos, A., Haugerud, H., & Djenouri, Y. (2024). Deepfakes: Current and future trends. *Artificial Intelligence Review*, *57*(3), 64.

Guarnera, L., Giudice, O., & Battiato, S. (2020). Deepfake detection by analyzing convolutional traces. In *Proceedings of the IEEE/CVF conference on computer vision and pattern recognition workshops* (pp. 666-667).

Khalil, H. A., & Maged, S. A. (2021). *"Deepfakes creation and detection using deep learning." 2021 International Mobile, Intelligent, and Ubiquitous Computing Conference (MIUCC)*. IEEE.

Kohli, A., & Gupta, A. (2021). Detecting deepfake, faceswap and face2face facial forgeries using frequency cnn. *Multimedia Tools and Applications, 80*(12), 18461–18478. DOI: 10.1007/s11042-020-10420-8

Mamieva, D., Abdusalomov, A. B., Mukhiddinov, M., & Whangbo, T. K. (2023). Improved face detection method via learning small faces on hard images based on a deep learning approach. *Sensors (Basel), 23*(1), 502.

Masood, M., Nawaz, M., Malik, K. M., Javed, A., Irtaza, A., & Malik, H. (2023). Deepfakes generation and detection: State-of-the-art, open challenges, countermeasures, and way forward. *Applied Intelligence, 53*(4), 3974–4026. DOI: 10.1007/s10489-022-03766-z

Nirkin, Y., Wolf, L., Keller, Y., & Hassner, T. (2021). Deepfake detection based on discrepancies between faces and their context. *IEEE Transactions on Pattern Analysis and Machine Intelligence, 44*(10), 6111–6121. DOI: 10.1109/TPAMI.2021.3093446 PMID: 34185639

Pashine, S., Mandiya, S., Gupta, P., & Sheikh, R. (2021). Deep fake detection: survey of facial manipulation detection solutions. arXiv preprint arXiv:2106.12605.

Patel, Y., Tanwar, S., Gupta, R., Bhattacharya, P., Davidson, I. E., Nyameko, R., Aluvala, S., & Vimal, V. (2023). Deepfake generation and detection: Case study and challenges. *IEEE Access : Practical Innovations, Open Solutions, 11*, 143296–143323. DOI: 10.1109/ACCESS.2023.3342107

Pei, G., Zhang, J., Hu, M., Zhang, Z., Wang, C., Wu, Y., & Tao, D. (2024). Deepfake generation and detection: A benchmark and survey. *ACM Computing Surveys.*

Rossler, A., Cozzolino, D., Verdoliva, L., Riess, C., Thies, J., & Nießner, M. (2019). Faceforensics++: Learning to detect manipulated facial images. In Proceedings of the IEEE/CVF international conference on computer vision (pp. 1-11).

Suganthi, S. T.. (2022). Deep learning model for deep fake face recognition and detection. *PeerJ. Computer Science, 8*, e881. DOI: 10.7717/peerj-cs.881 PMID: 35494811

Yang, S., Luo, P., Loy, C. C., & Tang, X. (2016). Wider face: A face detection benchmark. In *Proceedings of the IEEE conference on computer vision and pattern recognition* (pp. 5525-5533).

Zhang, K., Zhang, Z., Li, Z., & Qiao, Y. (2016). Joint face detection and alignment using multitask cascaded convolutional networks. *IEEE Signal Processing Letters, 23*(10), 1499–1503. DOI: 10.1109/LSP.2016.2603342

Chapter 9

AI for Insider Threat Detection and Employee Monitoring

Somasekhar Donthu
GITAM University, India

Vivekanand Pandey
Amity University, Patna, India

Abhishek Sharma
http://orcid.org/0000-0001-9190-3341
Lovely Professional University, India

K. Sumangala
Kongunadu Arts and Science College, India

A.R. Arunarani
SRM Institute of Science and Technology, India

V. Bhoopathy
http://orcid.org/0000-0003-2175-6328
Sree Rama Engineering College, India

P. Krishnamoorthy
http://orcid.org/0000-0002-1901-8599
Sasi Institute of Technology and Engineering, India

ABSTRACT

Current cybersecurity AI systems face the growing sophistication of human insider threats to automated networks. Research focuses on authorized users exploiting AI-based cybersecurity system weaknesses. This study seeks to understand how insiders can launch intelligent system breaches without standard security safeguards. The investigation focuses on AI-operated system insider threat display patterns. Current insider activity detection methods cannot detect this type of behavior due to several obstacles. Case studies, event analysis, and expert consultation were used to comprehend the topic. Unfortunately, overreliance on automation has hampered AI systems' threat detection. The findings suggest cybersecurity should prioritize

DOI: 10.4018/979-8-3373-5223-7.ch009

behavior-based monitoring and AI-human supervision. The report supports cybersecurity and AI governance by highlighting insider vulnerabilities and recommending ways to strengthen system-wide automation resilience.

1. INTRODUCTION

Criminals are using more intricate and technologically advanced methods of financial crime prevention, posing new and unprecedented difficulties to the world's banking sector. A comprehensive rethinking of prevention and detection procedures is required since traditional detection methods are becoming more and more insufficient to deal with the ever-changing world of financial wrongdoing. When it comes to technology, financial institutions are facing both tremendous potential and formidable problems right now. New paradigms in technology and AI are opening up hitherto unseen possibilities for the detection, prediction, and prevention of financial crimes. Intricate patterns and abnormalities that would go unnoticed by conventional investigative methods can now be found with the help of machine learning algorithms, deep learning networks, and advanced data analytics(George et al., 2024). Insider attacks cost the banking industry more than $70 billion in 2023, with 60% of those events involving privileged users. When faced with sophisticated insider threats, which take advantage of their authorised access and institutional expertise to evade security measures, traditional detection approaches fall short(Swapnil Chawande, 2024). Due to the intricate nature of today's financial systems and the high level of access that workers have, it is possible for malicious insider operations to go undiscovered for long periods of time.

The purpose of this review is to give a thorough analysis of the present situation of financial crime prevention in banking, paying particular attention to the revolutionary possibilities of AI and other cutting-edge technology. Several important goals are aimed at by the research, which critically examines current methodology, technical advances, and implementation difficulties. The primary objective is, first and foremost, to assess the strengths and weaknesses of the existing methods for detecting financial crimes. Secondly, we want to investigate the many ways that AI and ML can be used to detect and stop financial crime. The third objective is to evaluate the efficacy of data science methods and cybersecurity frameworks in developing stronger preventative measures.

Regulatory compliance, big data analytics, predictive modelling, threat intelligence systems, supervised and unsupervised learning, and other related disciplines are all within the purview of this assessment. The research seeks to offer a thorough knowledge of how new technologies are fundamentally transforming financial crime prevention techniques in the banking sector by integrating ideas from multiple academic and technology viewpoints(Akintayo Micheal Ajayi et al., 2024).

2. INSIDER THREAT

Someone with authorised access to sensitive information or systems within an organisation poses the danger of abusing that access and compromising or harming it. This is called the insider threat. group might potentially damage or compromise it by abusing such access(Yilmaz & Can, 2024). Information, employees, or physical assets belonging to the company could be jeopardised if this were to happen(Warren, 2024). An insider threat is particularly dangerous since the perpetrator already has access and a degree of confidence in the target. Employees, contractors, interns, and anybody else with ties to the corporation are the potential sources of insider threats. The level of trust and authority possessed by these internal actors varies (Subhani et al., 2021). An estimated $15.4 million was spent on insider threat occurrences in 2022, a 37% increase from the previous year. Based on their research, the CERT division at Carnegie Mellon University has classified harmful insider activity into four different types, as shown in Figure 1:

Figure 1. Classification of malicious insider activities.

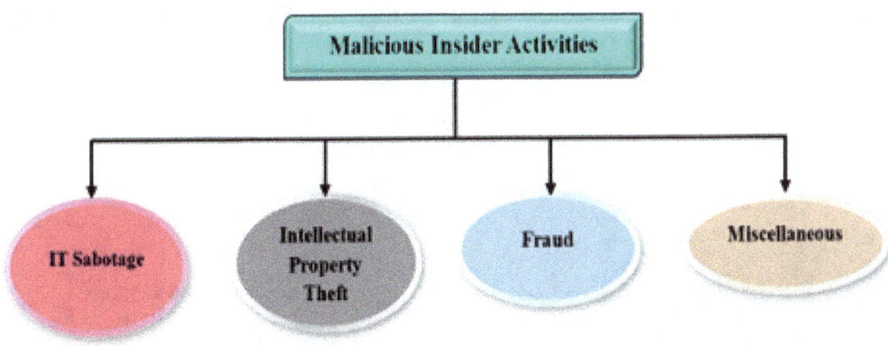

- **Sabotage of IT:** Insiders committing IT sabotage when they wilfully damage a company or an individual by utilising IT resources(Yuan & Wu, 2021).
- **Theft of IP:** Employees with inside knowledge of the company steal its intellectual property by using IT tools. Included in this group are cases of industrial espionage, which may involve both internal and foreign parties.

- **Fraud:** The purpose of insider theft is to enrich the perpetrator by illegally accessing, modifying, appending, or erasing company data(Homoliak et al., 2020). Identity theft, credit card fraud, and other forms of information-based crime fall under this category as well.
- **Diverse items:** This group includes incidents where an insider's behaviour is not in line with the goals of intellectual property theft, fraud, or IT sabotage. Inadequate breach detection, delayed response, and inconsistent recovery procedures pose a serious threat to businesses in the form of insider security breaches(Bell et al., 2019). As a result, companies have begun investing in security awareness training programs and have put in place various security policies, processes, and technical safeguards.

3. AI FOR INSIDER THREAT DETECTION

The use of AI to detect insider threats in company networks has come a long way, with ML and DL being the backbone of the approach (Gudepu, 2016). These artificial intelligence methods are quite good at spotting subtle trends and anomalies in user behaviour(Yilmaz & Can, 2024). Organisations can tailor their security frameworks to effectively handle these complex security concerns provided they understand the basic AI approaches used in behavioural analysis for insider threat identification. Figure 2 shows the AI-Driven continuous monitoring and Threat hunting is a strong AI-cybersecurity strategy that significantly helps to avoid data breaches and cyberattacks.

Figure 2. AI-Powered Threat Detection and Prevention

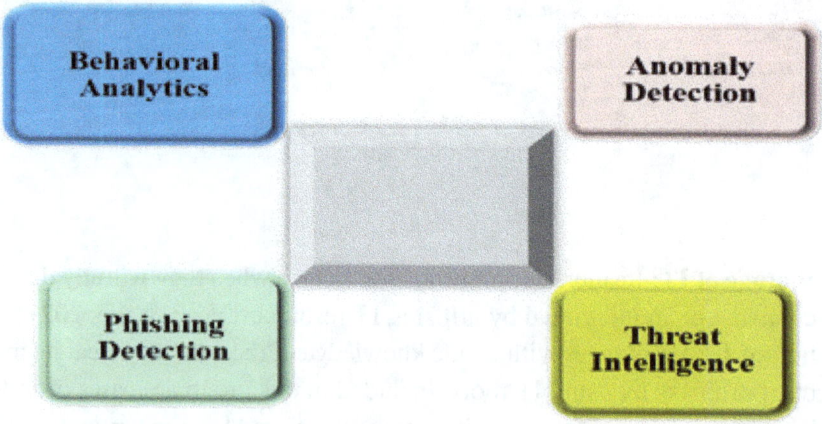

3.1 ML and Supervised Learning

Machine learning, which enables systems to absorb data and gradually improve their performance, is crucial to AI-driven insider threat detection(Alzaabi & Mehmood, 2024). Algorithms are taught to recognise patterns of safe and harmful behaviours in supervised learning using labelled datasets(Akintayo Micheal Ajayi et al., 2024). Machine learning models can develop the ability to forecast abnormal behaviour by analysing historical data and comprehending the relationships between various variables. By analysing an employee's regular login patterns, an ML model can detect suspicious activity, such as logging into systems at odd hours, and flag it for further investigation. Supervised learning excels at spotting known hostile behaviours when it comes to insider threats(Alketbi & Mehmood, 2025). For example, a supervised learning model can use historical data to identify similar behaviours in employees whose actions have been labelled due to unauthorised access to sensitive information. However, for the model to make accurate predictions, it needs data that is both exact and representative; otherwise, it risks producing false-positive results due to inaccurate labelling or a lack of data.

3.2 Unsupervised Learning for Anomaly Detection

Companies frequently face new and growing forms of malicious behaviour, and in many real-world scenarios, they do not have labelled datasets that can detect insider threats(Koutsouvelis et al., 2020). In these cases, unsupervised learning really shines because it lets AI systems spot anomalies without relying on labels that have already been decided. In order to identify out-of-the-ordinary patterns, unsupervised learning techniques like clustering and anomaly detection compare the present state of affairs to a predetermined standard of behaviour. An unsupervised learning model could detect an out-of-the-ordinary access to sensitive data or systems by an employee, for example, without needing any prior knowledge of particular risks(Kotb et al., 2025). Techniques for detecting anomalies, such as k-means clustering and DBSCAN, can distinguish between typical and suspicious actions, which could point to an insider threat.

3.3 Complex Neural Networks for Sophisticated Pattern Recognition

Machine learning's deep learning subfield analyses complex data using multi-layered neural networks. Deep learning excels at discovering intricate relationships and patterns in large datasets used for behavioural analysis, such as records of file accesses, user activity logs, and network traffic. To improve threat detection, deep learning algorithms sift through mountains of unstructured data in search of meaningful patterns(Smith & Karan, 2025). When it comes to insider threat detection, one popular deep learning model is the RNN. RNNs are great at processing time-series data, such the order in which user actions occur. Because of its ability to accurately represent the time-varying dynamics of user behaviour, RNN are great at spotting patterns that deviate from the norm over extended periods of time. Another perk of using LSTM networks a type of RNN is their mastery of long-term dependencies; this is particularly useful for tracking the development of an insider threat over time(Smith & Karan, 2025).

3.4 NLP for Contextual Analysis

NLP is a major artificial intelligence technique used for detecting insider threats. Emails, chat histories, and actions involving the sharing of documents are all examples of communication data that can be analysed using NLP(Paidy, 2025). Attempts to exfiltrate sensitive information or communicate with external hostile actors are examples of bad intent that an AI system may examine in email content or internal discussions. Even when suspicious activity isn't immediately obvious in network activity logs, natural language processing techniques like entity recognition and sentiment analysis can detect unusual interactions and potentially harmful communications(Koli et al., 2025). By adding a new layer of knowledge to an employee's messages and intentions, NLP-driven behavioural analysis can go beyond typical activity monitoring.

3.5 Integration of AI Techniques for Thorough Threat Detection

Companies often combine many AI techniques to build a comprehensive threat detection system, which improves the effectiveness of behavioural analysis(Wasko et al., 2021). By effectively utilising supervised learning Businesses may build a thorough system that can detect insider threats more accurately by combining known threat recognition with unsupervised learning for anomaly detection, deep learning for intricate pattern recognition, and natural language processing for contextual analysis(Dhanushkodi & Thejas, 2024). Hybrid approaches provide a flexible, multi-pronged approach to security that can reliably adjust to the appearance of fresh internal dangers. An efficient way for anticipatory threat identification is the integration of AI algorithms into the security framework of a company's network. Recognising that no one approach is foolproof, combining approaches allows for the development of a stronger and more adaptable system that can face both known and unknown threats(Gudepu, 2016).

4. REAL-TIME AND ADAPTIVE INSIDER THREAT DETECTION

Building real-time adaptive systems that can automatically react to new and changing threats became a priority starting in 2020(Cai et al., 2024). Chaudhary and Kaur put out a model for real-time insider threat detection in 2021 using anomaly detection methods based on artificial intelligence(Dommari, 2025). The necessity of systems that could automatically adjust to new patterns of behaviour was highlighted by their research. The research suggested that adaptive models may be created by combining supervised learning with RL. These models would be able to learn new data and danger situations in real-time, improving their performance(Aminu & Akinsanya, 2024).

4.1 Frameworks for Detecting Insider Threats Using Artificial Intelligence (2015)

To detect insider threats, Bose et al. (2015) introduced a novel architecture powered by AI that combined behavioural research with machine learning(Bose et al., 2017). According to the design, the system may detect suspicious activity by monitoring user behaviours, file accesses, and network traffic in real-time. They demonstrated that, rather than using old-fashioned rule-based heuristics, it is necessary to reduce false positives by spotting patterns in behaviour. Machine learning approaches are finding more and more uses in insider threat detection, thanks to this groundbreaking work(Ali et al., 2025).

4.2 Hybrid Models for Threat Detection (2016)

A hybrid approach for insider threat detection was proposed by Sharma et al. (2016). This model combines decision tree classifiers with anomaly detection methods. Because decision trees allowed for the seriousness of possible attacks to be assessed, and anomaly detection allowed for the discovery of aberrant behaviour patterns, their goal was to maximise the strengths built into both paradigms(Li et al., 2023). Combining the two methods, we were able to detect both obvious and subtle insider threats, making our response time to complex situations much faster(Tao et al., 2025).

4.3 Investigating Insider Threats using Deep Learning (2017)

In 2017, Zhang and Li focused on using deep learning techniques to identify insider threats. In order to analyse and categorise user behaviours using data from diverse logs, such as system logs, file access logs, and email metadata, they utilised

DNN(Chattopadhyay et al., 2018). When it came to detecting sophisticated insider threats with subtle behavioural abnormalities, they discovered that deep learning techniques performed much better than shallow machine learning methods. The study demonstrated that deep learning is effective in revealing patterns of malevolent intent that would have been difficult to detect with superficial analysis(Haidar & Gaber, 2019).

4.4 Behavioural Profiling and Data Correlation (2018)

Behavioural profiling as a tool for detecting insider threats was the subject of study by Singh and Gupta in 2018(Masunda, 2025). The study's profiles, which mimicked normal user actions, were created using a mix of machine learning and correlation-based data approaches. The program was able to identify suspicious patterns associated with email, file sharing, and web browsing by comparing these actions across various enterprise systems(Ye et al., 2025). By providing a more integrated view of user activity across several systems, this strategy significantly improved threat detection, according to the research. This, in turn, decreased the likelihood of overlooking small insider threats.

4.5 Graph-Theoretic Models for Threat Identification (2019)

In their 2019 study, Cheng et al. suggested a graph-based model for detecting insider threats. In this model, people and their actions were represented as a network of connections(Khan, 2024). They derived graph algorithms for user interaction analysis and anomaly detection from this approach. Particularly useful for identifying insider dangers including social engineering or collaboration, the graph-based model enabled them to model complex relationships among persons, data, and systems. The potential of graph theory as a new and effective method for detecting insider threats was demonstrated in this research.

4.6 Integration of Behavioural Analytics with UEBA Systems (2020)

An investigation into behavioural analytics' incorporation into UEBA policies was carried out by Kim et al. (2020). According to their findings, insider threat detection systems should combine AI-driven anomaly detection with human-like behavioural analysis(J. Kim et al., 2019). A combination of user context parameters like location, device usage, and access habits with machine learning algorithms for behaviour analysis and anomaly detection was proposed. The results showed that the overall sensitivity and specificity of threat detection methods were improved by this multi-pronged strategy, which allowed for the detection of both hostile insiders and accidental policy breaches.

4.7 Reinforcement Learning for Insider Threat Adaptation (2021)

The use of RL to improve insider threat detection systems was the subject of a groundbreaking study by Patel and Mehta (2021). They set up an RL system that, depending on user inputs, taught an agent to identify insider risks by analysing environmental feedback. By teaching the model to learn from both normal and aberrant behaviours equally, they were able to train it to continuously improve its detection accuracy while decreasing the number of false positives(Alserhani, 2025). The results showed that RL-based systems may adapt on their own to new threat patterns, making them highly adaptable in ever-changing threat environments(Akintan et al., 2025).

5. RESULT AND DISCUSSION

The study uses a mixed-methods strategy, integrating quantitative modeling and research with exploratory qualitative evaluation. The objective is to create a unified system that combines behavioral analytics with AI to detect and prevent insider threats. The system should be able to adapt, detect in real-time, and minimize false positives. In order to learn about the strengths and weaknesses of existing insider threat detection systems, it is recommended to interview experts in the industry, including security experts, information technology managers, and system architects. The main goal of the interviews is to collect data on the difficulties encountered when trying to identify insider threats, especially in remote and hybrid workplaces.

Gather data about user actions from official sources. With the data anonymized, AI models will be trained to identify unusual patterns of behaviour. Preprocessing will be done on the collected raw data to make sure it is fit for analysis and of high quality. Get rid of any discrepancies, missing numbers, or extreme cases that could throw off the results. The current phase involves the creation of AI models whose primary purpose is to enhance the capacity for detecting insider threats. Several criteria will be employed to assess the efficacy of the models in their real-world applications once their development phase is over. Implementing the suggested methodology for real-time insider detection will follow model development and testing. The major focus will be on ethical considerations because the study includes data on user behaviour and may require constant monitoring of personnel. Finally, in order to draw conclusions about the AI and behavioural analysis framework's effectiveness, the results of the testing and evaluation of the models will be reviewed.

As demonstrated in Figure 3, the model has learnt to continuously improve its accuracy by the 100th epoch, and it has achieved a peak of 0.97%. The dramatic increase in validation accuracy during the fourth period, which peaked at 0.94%, is a notable aspect of this statistic.

Figure 3. Training and Validation Accuracy

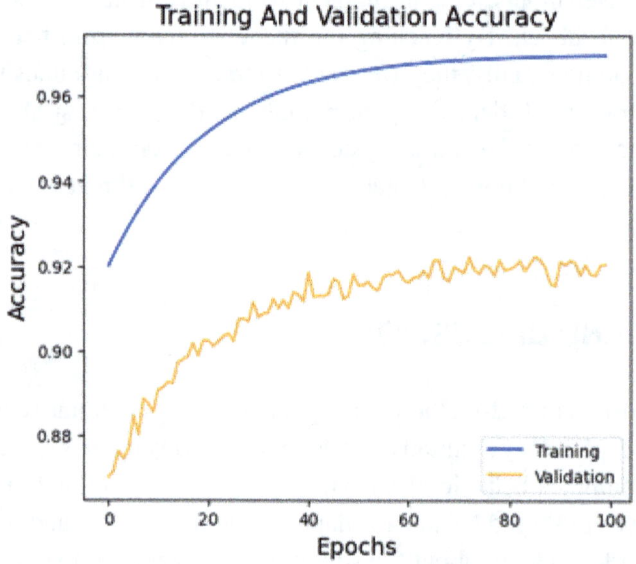

In Table 1, they can see how the suggested methods stack up against other algorithms' base hyperparameter. These other algorithms include RL, DNN and NLP. The suggested DNN method outperformed the alternatives with respect to Accuracy (97.42%), Precision (97.06%), Recall (93.72%).

Table 1. Performance of Models

Models	Accuracy	Precision	Recall
RL	68.36	66.12	68.66
DNN	**97.42**	**95.06**	**93.72**
NLP	74.79	72.83	70.11

In figure 4, we can observe the results of comparing six distinct models using the Accuracy, Precision and Recall. In comparison to the other five models, the suggested DNN model outperforms them all and has an accuracy rate of (97.42%).

Figure 4. Performance of Models

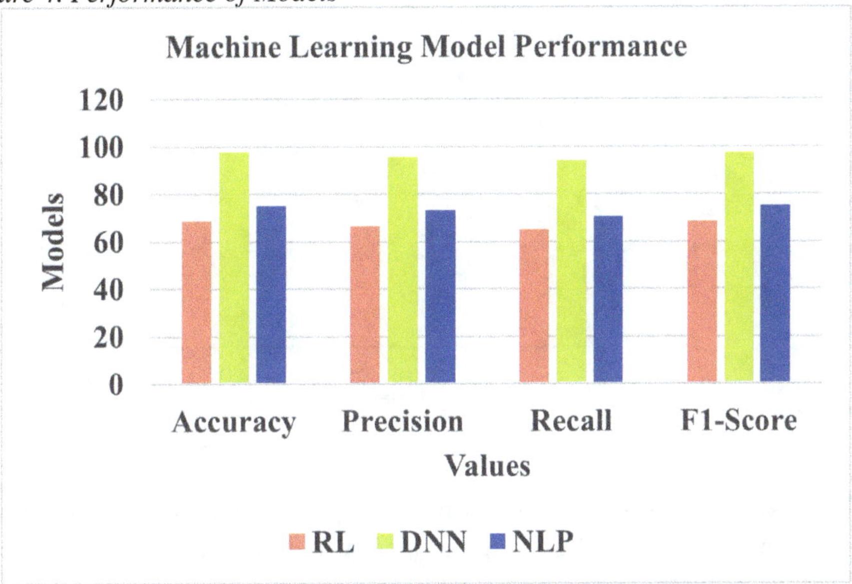

In Table 2, they can see how the suggested methods stack up against other algorithms' base hyperparameter. These other algorithms include RL, DNN and NLP. The suggested DNN method outperformed the alternatives with respect to F1 Score (97.52%), False Positive (4.3%), False Negative (5.2%).

Table 2. Performance of Models

Models	F1 Score	False Positive	False Negative
RL	68.81	5.9	6.4
DNN	**97.52**	**4.3**	**5.2**
NLP	74.79	8.7	9.7

The figure 5 shows how well Three models RL, DNN and NLP. All of the models exhibit some changes, but DNN always has the highest F1 Score, reaching about 97.52% in most folds. RL, on the other hand, has the lowest accuracy

Figure 5. Comparison of Models

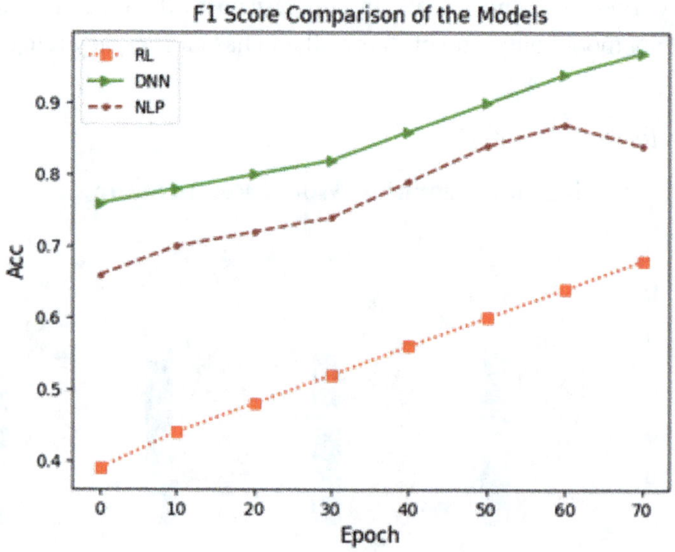

Figure 6 shows that when comparing the suggested model to RL, DNN and NLP in terms of Accuracy Loss, it performs better. The DNN model consistently achieves the best training loss rate.

Figure 6. Training and Validation Accuracy Loss

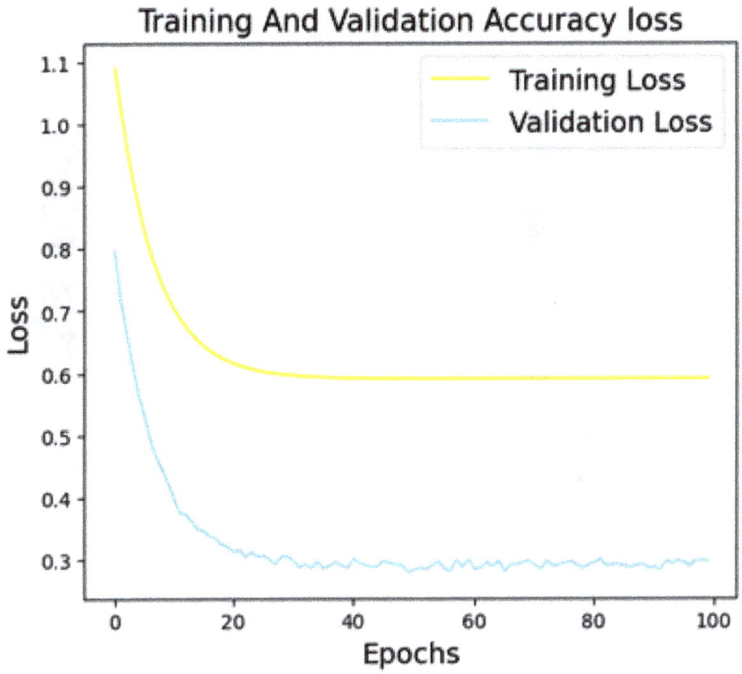

Figure 7 Shows the Bar chart comparing key performance metrics such as detection rate, false positive rate, system adaptability, and time to detect (MTTD). The metrics highlight the improved efficiency of the system in identifying threats with minimal false positives.

Figure 7. Performance of Metrics

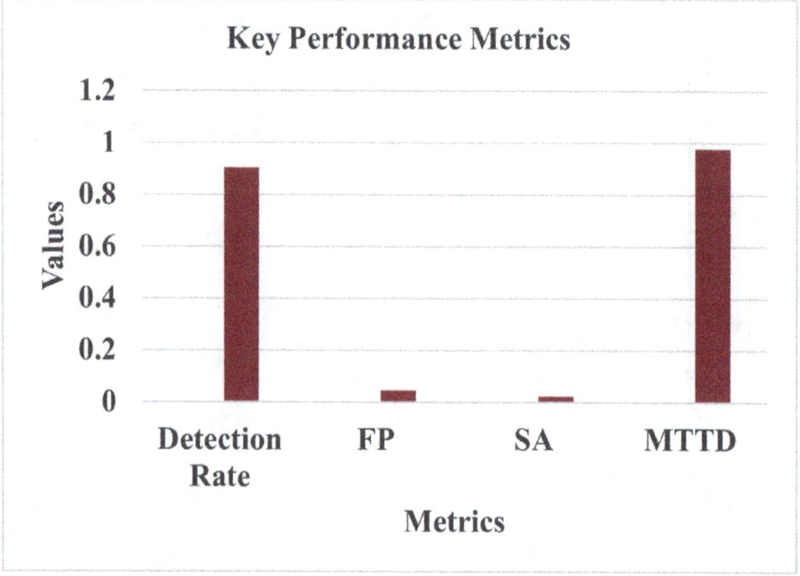

6. CHALLENGES

It takes a mix of technological, behavioural, and organisational methods to detect malevolent insider threats, which is a difficult and ever-changing challenge(Bee et al., 2018). A malicious insider is an employee or contractor who wilfully causes damage to the company's information systems, data, or operations by abusing their position of trust and authority. Tackling this matter necessitates tackling multiple obstacles, encompassing technical, human, and organisational dimensions(Alohaly et al., 2022).

6.1 Analysis of User Behaviour

There are a number of technical considerations to keep in mind while using UBA to identify malicious insider threats. To begin, UBA includes logs, network traffic, and recordings of user behaviour, all of which can add up to a mountain of data that can be difficult to manage. Big companies with complicated IT systems have it especially tough when it comes to processing and integrating data from disparate sources(Ma & Rastogi, 2020). Additionally, it is essential for threat detection to be able to differentiate between regular and suspicious behaviour. However, this might be difficult to do because user activities are inherently unpredictable. In order to successfully complete this noise reduction assignment, it is essential to accurately construct baselines for each user. This requires careful investigation and knowledge of normal behaviour patterns across all departments and positions(Zarpelão et al., 2017). The importance of contextual analysis in UBA cannot be overstated, as user activities might be legitimate or invalid depending on aspects including time, location, device, and user role. To properly evaluate the risk connected with user behaviours, it is necessary to incorporate contextual information into threat detection algorithms using advanced modelling techniques(Alzaabi & Mehmood, 2024).

Another important issue is the frequency of false positives, which occur when harmless actions are incorrectly identified as harmful ones. This can cause alarm fatigue and decrease the effectiveness of the system. The effective deployment of UBA systems relies on striking a balance between detection accuracy and the reduction of false positives. It is also technically and ethically challenging to analyse user behaviour in a way that complies with privacy standards like GDPR and HIPAA. To maintain privacy standards, UBA systems must securely manage sensitive user data and anonymise it when needed.

6.2 Secure Data Transmission and Filtering

Attempts to steal sensitive information using encrypted channels pose a number of complex technical issues in the field of malicious insider threat detection, all of which require careful consideration. First and foremost, traditional inspection methods are severely hindered by communication encryption protocols like SSL/TLS. Because the payload of encrypted network traffic cannot be seen, conventional DPI methods cannot be used without compromising user privacy or obtaining decryption keys (Padhiar & Patel, 2023). As a result, this technical barrier makes it harder to monitor and analyse encrypted traffic in real-time for signs of harmful insider behaviour. Since decrypting and inspecting encrypted traffic may involve infractions of user privacy and regulatory compliance, privacy issues further complicate the process. Developing privacy-preserving solutions that allow threat identification without compromising user confidentiality is necessary since decrypting communications for examination creates ethical and legal concerns. The problem of false positives further complicates the identification of data exfiltration attempts over encrypted networks(A. Kim et al., 2020). Mistaking legitimate communications for harmful ones, causing alert fatigue and reducing the effectiveness of threat detection systems, can happen when analysing encrypted information without taking the context into account. To overcome this difficulty, we need to deploy advanced anomaly detection algorithms that can analyse behavioural signals and contextual clues to distinguish between regular encrypted traffic patterns and potential security risks(Luckey et al., 2019).

6.3 Consultation Within

Several technological obstacles make it very difficult to detect malevolent insider threats, especially when insiders work with external threat actors or other insiders(Blessing Austin-Gabriel et al., 2021). It might be difficult for traditional anomaly detection methods to spot suspicious activity, particularly when insiders work together to evade capture. Current anomaly detection approaches frequently can't tell the difference between organised insider threats and regular operations, according to experimental results. Data fusion and correlation get more complicated when trying to integrate and correlate information from several sources, including user activity logs and network logs. When dealing with data that contains noise or false positives, it can be difficult for current correlation tools to correctly identify patterns that suggest collaborative internal threats, according to studies. To add insult to injury, malevolent insiders often work together with outside threat actors or share credentials with other insiders to circumvent security restrictions by taking advantage of vulnerabilities in identity and access management systems. It is tough to discern harmful intent buried within encrypted traffic due to the increased complexity of detection efforts caused by encrypted communication channels and evasion strategies. Traffic analysis and behavioural monitoring are examples of advanced approaches that are needed to address these difficulties.

To further differentiate between genuine partnerships and malicious activity, it is essential to understand the context of user behaviour and system interactions. The accuracy of insider threat detection systems can be greatly improved by include contextual information like user roles and prior behaviour. This is especially true when it comes to recognising collaborative insider threats. Cybersecurity, data analytics, machine learning, and human factors specialists must work together in an interdisciplinary study to solve these technological problems.

6.4 Improper Use of Credentials

When insiders use their own or other people's credentials to obtain unauthorised access, it is extremely difficult to detect these dangers. When dealing with a large number of apparently harmless user behaviours, it might be difficult to tell which ones are malevolent(Modi et al., 2013). Conventional security solutions, such as rule-based systems or anomaly detection approaches, could fail to spot harmful activities carried out by authorised insiders. Conventional systems have a hard time detecting malevolent intent based on behavioural abnormalities alone since bad insiders frequently mix their actions with regular work, as pointed out in multiple research studies(Sharma, 2021).

As a conclusion, there are substantial technological obstacles to detecting malevolent insider threats, especially when insiders use their own or others' credentials to obtain unauthorised access. The sheer amount and complexity of data that needs to be analysed, the strategies used by insiders to obfuscate information, and the difficulty in differentiating between legal and malicious operations all contribute to these issues. To overcome these obstacles, we need to create detection techniques that can scale to address the complexities of current IT settings and distinguish between harmless and malicious behaviours.

6.5 Modifications in Behaviour

When there is an abrupt shift in employee behaviour that suggests malevolent intent, it becomes far more difficult to detect insider threats. Differentiating between changes in behaviour that are actually caused by valid reasons and those that are caused by malevolent activity is a major challenge(Silowash et al., 2012). Particularly when the abrupt change is subtle or situation-dependent, traditional anomaly detection methods may fail to properly differentiate between harmless deviations and harmful activities. In contexts where employment duties and responsibilities change over time, it can be especially challenging to create a baseline for normal behaviour and determine the importance of deviations, as shown in research(Fagade & Tryfonas, 2017).

The urgency of identifying and responding to such changes in behaviour in order to limit harm only adds to the difficulty. Because insider threats can cause significant harm to an organization's assets if left undiscovered for too long, finding them quickly is crucial. It highlights the vital necessity for detection mechanisms that can swiftly spot suspicious behavioural patterns within the noise of everyday operations, underscoring the importance of prompt detection in reducing the impact of insider threats.

6.6 Concerns Regarding Privacy

Protecting employee privacy while identifying malevolent insider threats calls for technologically advanced solutions that strike a compromise between the complexities of threat identification and strict privacy regulations(Agrafiotis et al., 2016). Identifying harmful acts from typical user behaviour while protecting individual privacy is a significant technical challenge(Chen et al., 2018). Conventional approaches to anomaly detection, including rule-based systems or statistical modelling, can produce large false positive rates since they can't reliably differentiate between harmless and harmful actions. Deep learning algorithms and anomaly detection frameworks like Isolation Forests or One-Class SVMs can be used to solve this problem(Tabrizchi, 2020) . By constantly learning and adapting, these models may understand intricate patterns in user behaviour and detect deviations that indicate malicious intent, all while minimising false positives.

In addition, there are limitations on the kinds of data that can be gathered and studied due to the requirement to protect privacy. Methods that conceal personally identifiable information while still enabling effective threat detection, such as data anonymisation and pseudonymization, can assist minimise these limits. Also, by using federated learning frameworks, we may train models together across several locations and keep each source's data private. Organisations can construct strong insider threat detection systems without endangering employee privacy with tools such as PySyft and TensorFlow Privacy, which offer implementations of federated learning and privacy-preserving machine learning techniques.

6.7 Integration of Security System

There are a number of technological considerations to keep in mind while trying to detect malevolent insider threats while simultaneously guaranteeing smooth integration between different security systems(Munir et al., 2022). The diversity of security systems' data sources and formats is a serious obstacle. Network logs, EDR systems, UBA platforms, and IAM systems are some of the diverse systems that commonly house security data in a business setting. Normalizing, correlating, and analysing data from all of these many sources is no easy task(Amodei et al., 2016).

In response to these difficulties, academics have advocated for the use of AI and machine learning two forms of advanced analytics to identify insider threats. Nevertheless, meticulous orchestration and model management are necessary for the smooth integration of machine learning models across various security systems. In the context of integrated security systems, the authors' experimental evaluations highlighted the significance of model interpretability and explainability. In highly regulated sectors, where transparency is paramount for legal compliance, black-box ML models run the risk of undermining confidence in the uptake of integrated solutions. The integration of security systems for insider threat detection is already complicated enough without having to deal with privacy issues and regulatory obligations. Data privacy preservation while aggregating and correlating sensitive information across multiple systems is a difficulty, according to another study. The implementation of privacy-preserving techniques, such as differential privacy or federated learning, is vital for compliance with regulations like GDPR and HIPAA, which can further complicate the integration process.

7. FUTURE TRENDS

The results suggest a number of important tendencies that will influence financial cybersecurity going forward:

1. **Expansion of AI-Driven Security:** Machine learning and behavioural biometrics are two areas that will drive the expansion of AI-driven security, which will improve real-time threat detection and advance fraud prevention measures(Mihai et al., 2022).
2. **Regulatory Development:** In order to combat the risks posed by artificial intelligence, governments and financial institutions will most certainly enact new cybersecurity regulations that strengthen protections for personal information and digital identities.
3. **Integrating Blockchain Technology for Financial Safety:** Due to its distributed and immutable nature, blockchain technology is quickly becoming an integral part of systems designed to detect and prevent fraudulent transactions(Budhwar et al., 2023).
4. **Quantum Computing and Financial Cryptography:** Financial institutions must prepare for the possibility of decoding attacks by creating cryptographic protocols that are resistant to quantum computing(West, 2018).

The wider social ramifications of cybersecurity technology merit careful consideration alongside technological and regulatory developments(Sandberg, 2015). Concerns about monitoring and individual liberties are heightened by the fact that AI-driven systems frequently necessitate large amounts of personal data in order to function properly. Equally important are ethical concerns when making decisions using AI(Zangana et al., 2025). For example, if algorithms are biassed, it could result in unfair financial services like credit scoring or fraud detection, which could worsen existing inequities. These findings emphasize the critical role of AI and blockchain in strengthening cybersecurity frameworks, while also highlighting the importance of regulatory adaptation to emerging cyber threats(Naseer et al., 2021). Further exacerbating the digital divide, smaller organisations and their clients are more susceptible to cyber threats due to technology discrepancies between well-resourced and underfunded financial institutions. Preventing unexpected harm and promoting public trust in digital financial systems requires implementing AI-powered cybersecurity in an ethical, inclusive, and egalitarian manner(Rauf et al., 2023).

CONCLUSION

Despite the recent proposal of an integrated framework, it is yet to be seen whether a real data set can be evaluated rigorously. Applying conventional supervised machine-learning techniques to the problem of behavior prediction is another technical restriction. While they do a decent job of capturing the behavior of individual characteristics, their ability to capture the interdependencies of behavioral traits is restricted. There is a need for more effective deep-learning-based methods that can take into consideration the fact that an invasive attack is a succession of operations rather than a collection of independent ones, leading to non-linear dynamics characterized by complex inter-dependencies of attributes. In a similar vein, there is a dearth of research on countering intrusive applications in the literature. Due to the limited resources available on mobile devices for run-time anomaly detection, extra hurdles arise when attempting to deter malicious programs. Users' privacy is at risk, even while cloud-based servers can conduct computationally complicated ML training, allowing for the building of lightweight applications. In order to make use of these run-time detection methods, users will need to divulge data pertaining to their applications. We haven't seen how future developments handle these trade-offs just yet.

REFERENCES

Agrafiotis, I., Erola, A., Happa, J., Goldsmith, M., & Creese, S. (2016). Validating an Insider Threat Detection System: A Real Scenario Perspective. *Proceedings - 2016 IEEE Symposium on Security and Privacy Workshops, SPW 2016*, 286–295. DOI: 10.1109/SPW.2016.36

Ajayi, A. M., Omokanye, A. O., Olowu, O., Adeleye, A. O., Omole, O. M., & Wada, I. U. (2024). Detecting insider threats in banking using AI-driven anomaly detection with a data science approach to cybersecurity. *World Journal of Advanced Research and Reviews*, *24*(2), 123–132. DOI: 10.30574/wjarr.2024.24.2.3182

Akintan, A., Favour, A., Ali, A., Muthanna, A., Alkhalidy, M., & Ravi, R. (2025). *Improving Detection Accuracy of Insider Threats in M2M Systems Using Adaptive Trust Models. July.*

Ali, A., Husain, M., & Hans, P. (2025). *Real-Time Detection of Insider Threats Using Behavioral Analytics and Deep Evidential Clustering*. https://arxiv.org/abs/2505.15383

Alketbi, K. S., & Mehmood, A. (2025). A Comprehensive Survey of Explainable Artificial Intelligence Techniques for Malicious Insider Threat Detection. *IEEE Access : Practical Innovations, Open Solutions*, *13*(June), 121772–121798. DOI: 10.1109/ACCESS.2025.3587114

Alohaly, M., Balogun, O., & Takabi, D. (2022). Integrating Cyber Deception Into Attribute-Based Access Control (ABAC) for Insider Threat Detection. *IEEE Access : Practical Innovations, Open Solutions*, *10*(August), 108965–108978. DOI: 10.1109/ACCESS.2022.3213645

Alserhani, F. (2025). Intrusion Detection and Real-Time Adaptive Security in Medical IoT Using a Cyber-Physical System Design. *Sensors (Basel)*, *25*(15), 4720. DOI: 10.3390/s25154720 PMID: 40807889

Alzaabi, F. R., & Mehmood, A. (2024). A Review of Recent Advances, Challenges, and Opportunities in Malicious Insider Threat Detection Using Machine Learning Methods. *IEEE Access : Practical Innovations, Open Solutions*, *12*(March), 30907–30927. DOI: 10.1109/ACCESS.2024.3369906

Aminu, M., & Akinsanya, A. (2024). Enhancing Cyber Threat Detection through Real-time Threat Intelligence and Adaptive Defense Mechanisms. *International Journal of Computer Applications Technology and Research*, (August), 10–27. DOI: 10.7753/IJCATR1308.1002

Amodei, D., Olah, C., Steinhardt, J., Christiano, P., Schulman, J., & Mané, D. (2016). *Concrete Problems in AI Safety*. 1–29. https://arxiv.org/abs/1606.06565

Austin-Gabriel, B., Hussain, N. Y., Ige, A. B., Adepoju, P. A., Amoo, O. O., & Afolabi, A. I. (2021). Advancing zero trust architecture with AI and data science for enterprise cybersecurity frameworks. *Open Access Research Journal of Engineering and Technology*, *1*(1), 47–55. DOI: 10.53022/oarjet.2021.1.1.0107

Bee, S., Iram Jafry, S., Saucedo, G., Dorata, N. T., Phillips, C. R., Fico, J., Lanier, C., Kirchner, M., Grimes, N., Hilmi Elifoglu, I., Abel, I., Tasseven, Ö., Salvino, R., Tarleton, T., Kuhn, N., & Kauffman, R. (2018). Business Interdisciplinary Journal on Risk and Society Review of Accounting Conversations: A Case Study in Auditor Communications 1 Rehiring the Retired: An Examination of Double Dipping in Public School Districts 13 Corruption and Culture: Empirical Anal. *Business Interdisciplinary Journal on Risk and Society Review, 38*(2). www.stjohns.edu/ROB

Bell, A. J. C., Rogers, M. B., & Pearce, J. M. (2019). The insider threat: Behavioral indicators and factors influencing likelihood of intervention. *International Journal of Critical Infrastructure Protection*, *24*, 166–176. DOI: 10.1016/j.ijcip.2018.12.001

Bose, B., Avasarala, B., Tirthapura, S., Chung, Y. Y., & Steiner, D. (2017). Detecting Insider Threats Using RADISH: A System for Real-Time Anomaly Detection in Heterogeneous Data Streams. *IEEE Systems Journal*, *11*(2), 471–482. DOI: 10.1109/JSYST.2016.2558507

Budhwar, P., Chowdhury, S., Wood, G., Aguinis, H., Bamber, G. J., Beltran, J. R., Boselie, P., Lee Cooke, F., Decker, S., DeNisi, A., Dey, P. K., Guest, D., Knoblich, A. J., Malik, A., Paauwe, J., Papagiannidis, S., Patel, C., Pereira, V., Ren, S., & Varma, A. (2023). Human resource management in the age of generative artificial intelligence: Perspectives and research directions on ChatGPT. *Human Resource Management Journal*, *33*(3), 606–659. DOI: 10.1111/1748-8583.12524

Cai, X., Wang, Y., Xu, S., Li, H., Zhang, Y., Liu, Z., & Yuan, X. (2024). LAN: Learning Adaptive Neighbors for Real-Time Insider Threat Detection. *IEEE Transactions on Information Forensics and Security*, *19*, 10157–10172. DOI: 10.1109/TIFS.2024.3488527

Chattopadhyay, P., Wang, L., & Tan, Y. P. (2018). Scenario-based insider threat detection from cyber activities. *IEEE Transactions on Computational Social Systems*, *5*(3), 660–675. DOI: 10.1109/TCSS.2018.2857473

Chawande, S. (2024). Insider threats in highly automated cyber systems. *World Journal of Advanced Engineering Technology and Sciences*, *13*(2), 807–820. DOI: 10.30574/wjaets.2024.13.2.0642

Chen, L., Ai, H., Zhuang, Z., & Shang, C. (2018). Real-Time Multiple People Tracking with Deeply Learned Candidate Selection and Person Re-Identification. *Proceedings - IEEE International Conference on Multimedia and Expo, 2018-July*. DOI: 10.1109/ICME.2018.8486597

Dhanushkodi, K., & Thejas, S. (2024). AI Enabled Threat Detection: Leveraging Artificial Intelligence for Advanced Security and Cyber Threat Mitigation. *IEEE Access : Practical Innovations, Open Solutions*, *12*(November), 173127–173136. DOI: 10.1109/ACCESS.2024.3493957

Dommari, S. (2025). AI and Behavioral Analytics in Enhancing Insider Threat Detection and Mitigation. SSRN *Electronic Journal, 9*(1). DOI: 10.2139/ssrn.5259337

Fagade, T., & Tryfonas, T. (2017). *Fagade, T ., & Tryfonas, T . (2017). Malicious Insider Threat Detection : A Conceptual Model . In Security and Protection of Information 2017 (SPI) (Security and Protection of Information). University of Defence . Advance online publication . University of Bristol – Bristol Research Portal Malicious Insider Threat Detection : A Conceptual Model. 2017.*

George, A. S., Baskar, T., & Srikaanth, P. B. (2024). Cyber Threats to Critical Infrastructure: Assessing Vulnerabilities Across Key Sectors. [PUIIJ]. *Partners Universal International Innovation Journal*, *2*(1), 51–75. DOI: 10.5281/zenodo.10639463

Gudepu, B. K. (2016)... *AI-Powered Anomaly Detection Systems for Insider Threat Prevention.*, *2*(2), 1–9.

Haidar, D., & Gaber, M. M. (2019). *Data Stream Clustering for Real-Time Anomaly Detection: An Application to Insider Threats*. 115–144. DOI: 10.1007/978-3-319-97864-2_6

Homoliak, I., Toffalini, F., Guarnizo, J., Elovici, Y., & Ochoa, M. (2020). Insight into insiders and IT: A survey of insider threat taxonomies, analysis, modeling, and countermeasures. *ACM Computing Surveys*, *52*(2), 1–40. Advance online publication. DOI: 10.1145/3303771

Khan, S. (2024)... *ADAPTIVE CYBERSECURITY STRATEGIES FOR CLOUD-BASED REAL-TIME DATA.*, *15*(5), 414–424.

Kim, A., Oh, J., Ryu, J., & Lee, K. (2020). A review of insider threat detection approaches with IoT perspective. *IEEE Access : Practical Innovations, Open Solutions*, *8*, 78847–78867. DOI: 10.1109/ACCESS.2020.2990195

Kim, J., Park, M., Kim, H., Cho, S., & Kang, P. (2019). Insider threat detection based on user behavior modeling and anomaly detection algorithms. *Applied Sciences (Basel, Switzerland)*, *9*(19), 4018. Advance online publication. DOI: 10.3390/app9194018

Koli, L., Kalra, S., Thakur, R., Saifi, A., & Singh, K. (2025). *AI-Driven IRM: Transforming insider risk management with adaptive scoring and LLM-based threat detection*. https://arxiv.org/abs/2505.03796

Kotb, H. M., Gaber, T., AlJanah, S., Zawbaa, H. M., & Alkhathami, M. (2025). A novel deep synthesis-based insider intrusion detection (DS-IID) model for malicious insiders and AI-generated threats. *Scientific Reports*, *15*(1), 1–14. DOI: 10.1038/s41598-024-84673-w PMID: 39747424

Koutsouvelis, V., Shiaeles, S., Ghita, B., & Bendiab, G. (2020). Detection of insider threats using artificial intelligence and visualisation. *Proceedings of the 2020 IEEE Conference on Network Softwarization: Bridging the Gap Between AI and Network Softwarization, NetSoft 2020*, 437–443. DOI: 10.1109/NetSoft48620.2020.9165337

Li, X., Li, X., Jia, J., Li, L., Yuan, J., Gao, Y., & Yu, S. (2023). A High Accuracy and Adaptive Anomaly Detection Model With Dual-Domain Graph Convolutional Network for Insider Threat Detection. *IEEE Transactions on Information Forensics and Security*, *18*, 1638–1652. DOI: 10.1109/TIFS.2023.3245413

Luckey, D., Stebbins, D., Orrie, R., Rebhan, E., Bhatt, S. D., & Beaghley, S. (2019). *Assessing continuous evaluation approaches for insider threats*.

Ma, Q., & Rastogi, N. (2020). DANTE: Predicting insider threat using LSTM on system logs. *Proceedings - 2020 IEEE 19th International Conference on Trust, Security and Privacy in Computing and Communications, TrustCom 2020, December 2020*, 1151–1156. DOI: 10.1109/TrustCom50675.2020.00153

Masunda, M. (2025). Adaptive Threat Intelligence Systems for Real-Time Detection and Mitigation of Sophisticated Cyber Attacks in Enterprise Networks. *International Journal of Research Publication and Reviews*, *6*(7), 470–491. DOI: 10.55248/gengpi.6.0725.2433

Mihai, S., Yaqoob, M., Hung, D. V., Davis, W., Towakel, P., Raza, M., Karamanoglu, M., Barn, B., Shetve, D., Prasad, R. V., Venkataraman, H., Trestian, R., & Nguyen, H. X. (2022). Digital Twins: A Survey on Enabling Technologies, Challenges, Trends and Future Prospects. *IEEE Communications Surveys and Tutorials*, *24*(4), 2255–2291. DOI: 10.1109/COMST.2022.3208773

Modi, C., Patel, D., Borisaniya, B., Patel, H., Patel, A., & Rajarajan, M. (2013). A survey of intrusion detection techniques in Cloud. *Journal of Network and Computer Applications*, *36*(1), 42–57. DOI: 10.1016/j.jnca.2012.05.003

Munir, A., Aved, A., & Blasch, E. (2022). Situational Awareness: Techniques, Challenges, and Prospects. *AI*, *3*(1), 55–77. DOI: 10.3390/ai3010005

Naseer, H., Maynard, S. B., & Desouza, K. C. (2021). Demystifying analytical information processing capability: The case of cybersecurity incident response. *Decision Support Systems, 143*, 0–34. DOI: 10.1016/j.dss.2020.113476

Padhiar, S., & Patel, R. (2023). Outside the Closed World: On Using Machine Learning for Network Intrusion Detection. *Smart Innovation. Systems and Technologies, 361*(May), 265–270. DOI: 10.1007/978-981-99-3982-4_23

Paidy, P. (2025). *AI and Machine Learning in Cyber Threat Detection.* 10–18. DOI: 10.56472/ICCSAIML25-102

Rauf, U., Mohsen, F., & Wei, Z. (2023). A Taxonomic Classification of Insider Threats: Existing Techniques, Future Directions & Recommendations. *Journal of Cyber Security and Mobility, 12*(2), 221–252. DOI: 10.13052/jcsm2245-1439.1225

Sandberg, J. (2015). *Human element of corporate espionage risk management: literature review on assessment and control of outsider and insider threats. April,* 87. https://tampub.uta.fi/bitstream/handle/10024/97116/GRADU-1432196786.pdf

Sharma, H. (2021). Impact of Dspm on Insider Threat Detection : Exploring How Dspm Can Enhance the Detection and Prevention of Insider Threats By Monitoring Data Access Patterns and Flagging Anomalous Behavior. [IJCSERD]. *International Journal of Computer Science and Engineering Research and Development, 11*(1), 1–15.

Silowash, G., Cappelli, D., Moore, A., Trzeciak, R., Shimeall, T., & Flynn, L. (2012). Common Sense Guide to Mitigating Insider Threats, 4th Edition. *Software Engineering Institute, December*, 168. DOI: 10.21236/ADA585500

Smith, J., & Karan, D. (2025). *AI-Driven Anomaly Detection for Insider Threat Prevention in Identity and Access Management (IAM) Systems Authors : Jordan Smith, Dash Karan. December 2023.*

Subhani, A., Khan, I. A., & Zubair, A. (2021). Review of insider and insider threat detection in the organizations. *Journal of Advanced Research in Social Sciences and Humanities, 6*(4), 167–174. DOI: 10.26500/JARSSH-06-2021-0402

Tabrizchi, H. (2020). *threats, and solutions.*

Tao, X., Liu, J., Yu, Y., Zhang, H., & Huang, Y. (2025). An insider threat detection method based on improved Test-Time Training model. *High-Confidence Computing, 5*(1), 100283. DOI: 10.1016/j.hcc.2024.100283

Warren, M. M. (2024). *Shanitamol Sojan Gracy A global analysis of data breaches from 2004-2024 using Microsoft Power BI Anti-Plagiarism Declaration. August.*

Wasko, S., Rhodes, R. E., Goforth, M., Bos, N., Cowley, H. P., Matthews, G., Leung, A., Iyengar, S., & Kopecky, J. (2021). Using alternate reality games to find a needle in a haystack: An approach for testing insider threat detection methods. *Computers & Security*, *107*, 1–54. DOI: 10.1016/j.cose.2021.102314

West, D. M. (2018). The future of work: Robots, AI, and automation. *The Future of Work: Robots, AI, and Automation*, 1–205.

Ye, X., Cui, H., Luo, F., Wang, J., Xiong, X., Zhang, W., Yu, J., & Zhao, W. (2025). Daily insider threat detection with hybrid TCN transformer architecture. *Scientific Reports*, *15*(1), 1–21. DOI: 10.1038/s41598-025-12063-x PMID: 40764628

Yilmaz, E., & Can, O. (2024). Unveiling Shadows: Harnessing Artificial Intelligence for Insider Threat Detection. *Engineering. Technology and Applied Science Research*, *14*(2), 13341–13346. DOI: 10.48084/etasr.6911

Yuan, S., & Wu, X. (2021). Deep learning for insider threat detection: Review, challenges and opportunities. *Computers & Security*, *104*, 1–30. DOI: 10.1016/j.cose.2021.102221

Zangana, H. M., Mohammed, H. S., & Husain, M. M. (2025). Addressing Insider Threats: The Human Factor in Cybersecurity for Financial Institutions. [JINITA]. *Journal of Innovation Information Technology and Application*, *7*(1), 88–96. DOI: 10.35970/jinita.v7i1.2686

Zarpelão, B. B., Miani, R. S., Kawakani, C. T., & de Alvarenga, S. C. (2017). A survey of intrusion detection in Internet of Things. *Journal of Network and Computer Applications*, *84*(January), 25–37. DOI: 10.1016/j.jnca.2017.02.009

Chapter 10 Securing the Sports Economy: AI-Driven Intrusion Detection and Prevention in Digitized Sports Enterprises

Amitava Pal
http://orcid.org/0009-0007-8934-2718
ICFAI University, Jharkhand, India

Kavita Mathad
http://orcid.org/0000-0002-0058-9084
Indira University, Pune, India

M. Rajkumar
http://orcid.org/0000-0002-7606-0152
ICFAI University, Jharkhand, India

ABSTRACT

Cyber risks are increasingly targeting global sports organizations amid rapid digital transformation—spanning wearables, biometric analytics, e-commerce, virtual fan engagement, and IoT-enabled smart stadiums. This chapter explores how AI-powered Intrusion Detection and Prevention Systems (IDPS) can safeguard the evolving sports tech ecosystem from threats such as ransomware, insider risks, data breaches, and online fraud. By leveraging machine learning–driven threat intelligence, anomaly detection, and behavioral analytics, sports businesses can build proactive, real-time defenses. The chapter also outlines frameworks for ethical and secure AI adoption—balancing real-time performance, regulatory compliance, and sensitive data protection, especially athlete health and fan financial data. Drawing on global

DOI: 10.4018/979-8-3373-5223-7.ch010

case studies (e.g., ticketing fraud, league data breaches, and athlete data leaks), it equips CIOs and IT leaders with actionable insights and introduces a tailored AI-aligned risk modeling matrix for the sports industry.

INTRODUCTION

The global sports industry is undergoing a profound digital transformation, reshaping everything from how athletes train to how fans engage with their favorite teams (Santomier, 2024). What was once a domain dominated by physical performance and live spectator experiences has now become an interconnected web of advanced technologies, ranging from wearable sensors and biometric tracking systems to AI-powered performance analytics, virtual and augmented reality platforms, and expansive e-commerce ecosystems(Pickman, 2023). Smart stadiums are emerging as hubs of real-time data exchange, while IoT-enabled environments are optimizing crowd management and athlete safety. Digital fan platforms are redefining community engagement on a global scale(Liang, 2025). While these innovations have unlocked new revenue streams and performance insights, they have simultaneously exposed sports enterprises to unprecedented cybersecurity vulnerabilities. As vast volumes of sensitive data—such as athlete health metrics, financial transactions, fan identities, and proprietary training methods—are collected, stored, and transmitted, the sports sector has become an increasingly attractive target for cybercriminals. The convergence of digital innovation and high-value data assets renders cybersecurity not just a technical concern but a strategic imperative for modern sports organizations.

OBJECTIVE

This chapter aims to explore the rising cybersecurity challenges faced by digitized sports enterprises and demonstrate how Artificial Intelligence-driven Intrusion Detection and Prevention Systems (AI-IDPS) can be effectively deployed to protect critical digital assets within the sports ecosystem. It seeks to:

1. Identify and analyse the unique cyber threats targeting the sports industry as it embraces technologies like wearables, IoT, biometrics, AR/VR, and cloud platforms.
2. Explain the core principles, architecture, and functionality of AI-enabled IDPS, highlighting how these systems offer real-time threat detection, anomaly analysis, and response capabilities.

3. Present actionable frameworks and design strategies for integrating AI-IDPS within diverse sports technology environments, ranging from smart stadiums to athlete monitoring systems and online fan engagement platforms.
4. Examine global case studies and real-world incidents to showcase both the vulnerabilities and successful mitigation practices across major sporting events and organizations.
5. Discuss regulatory, ethical, and governance considerations related to the use of AI in managing personal and performance data in compliance with global data protection standards.
6. Provide a practical roadmap for implementation, including a cyber risk matrix and deployment guidelines tailored for CIOs, digital strategists, and IT leaders in sports enterprises.

By achieving these objectives, the chapter serves as a comprehensive guide for building cyber-resilient, ethically grounded, and scalable digital infrastructures in the ever-evolving sports economy.

CYBER THREAT LANDSCAPE IN SPORTS: SCOPE, SCALE, AND IMPACT

Types of Cyber Threats: Ransomware, DDoS, Data Breaches, Fraud, Insider Risk

As sports enterprises rapidly digitize their operations, they face a complex and evolving cyber threat landscape that mirrors that traditionally seen in the financial or healthcare sectors. What makes the sports ecosystem particularly vulnerable is the convergence of high-value data, real-time operational environments, and globally visible digital platforms, making it a high-stakes target for cybercriminals, hacktivists, and even state-sponsored actors(University of Oxford's Researcher Strategy Consultancy et al., 2026). Below are the major types of threats impacting the sports industry:

1. **Ransomware Attacks:** One of the most devastating forms of cyber threats, ransomware involves malicious software that encrypts critical systems and demands payment for decryption keys. In the sports world, such attacks can bring ticketing systems, media broadcasting platforms, or athlete performance databases to a standstill (Jnguyen, 2023). For example, football clubs have been locked out of their databases on match day, severely affecting operations and revenue.

2. **Distributed Denial-of-Service (DDoS) Attacks:** DDoS attacks flood servers with excessive requests, overwhelming them and rendering digital services inaccessible. For sports enterprises, this can disrupt live streaming platforms, online merchandise stores, or fan engagement apps during high-traffic events, such as tournaments or player drafts(GeeksforGeeks, 2025). These attacks not only damage a brand's reputation but also result in financial losses due to service downtime and disruptions.
3. **Data Breaches:** Sports organizations manage vast repositories of sensitive information, from athlete biometric and medical data to fan identity and payment details. A breach of this data, whether from cloud platforms, mobile apps, or internal servers, can lead to identity theft, corporate espionage, and legal liabilities(*What Is a Data Breach & How to Prevent Data Leaks*, 2025). The breach of athlete performance data, for example, can impact team strategies, sponsorship agreements, and even the athlete's mental health and public perception.
4. **Online Fraud and Financial Scams:** With increased digitization comes a rise in fraudulent activities, such as counterfeit ticket sales, fake merchandise websites, and manipulated betting platforms (*Scams and Fraud | Own Your Online*, n.d.). Cybercriminals exploit high-demand situations around major sporting events to trick fans into providing financial details or making unauthorized purchases, eroding trust in the digital sports marketplace.
5. **Insider Threats:** Often overlooked, insider risks involve employees, contractors, or partners who intentionally or unintentionally compromise organizational data. In sports, this could mean leaked team strategies, stolen athlete health records, or sabotaged performance data (Hunker et al., n.d.). These threats are challenging to detect without the use of behavioural analytics, making AI-powered solutions essential for detection.

REAL-WORLD INCIDENTS

1. **Data Leak of Athlete Biometrics:** Sports organizations are increasingly collecting sensitive biometric and health-related data to monitor athlete performance and prevent injuries. However, when this data is stored or transmitted without adequate cybersecurity controls, it becomes a prime target for cyberattacks. The leak of such private information can have far-reaching consequences, including reputational damage, legal exposure, and psychological harm to athletes. A high-profile example occurred in 2016, when the Russian cyber-espionage group Fancy Bear hacked the World Anti-Doping Agency (WADA) and accessed its Anti-Doping Administration and Management System (ADAMS). They released confidential medical records and Therapeutic Use Exemptions (TUEs) for prom-

inent athletes including Simone Biles, Serena Williams, and Venus Williams. The leak aimed to suggest preferential treatment for Western athletes, though WADA clarified that all TUEs were legally issued and no anti-doping violations occurred. The attack followed Russia's suspension from the Rio Olympics for widespread doping violations, which WADA had exposed(Ingle, 2017).

2. **Fraud in Ticketing and Fan Transactions:** With the surge in online ticket sales and merchandise transactions, fans are frequently targeted by sophisticated cyber scams that clone official websites or intercept payment processes. These fraudulent activities not only lead to financial losses but also erode public trust in the digital interfaces of sports organizations. Ahead of the Tokyo 2020 Olympics, cybersecurity concerns intensified when a hacker group was found orchestrating a phishing campaign that targeted individuals in Japan and the United States. The attackers circulated emails falsely offering free Olympic tickets and cash prizes, luring recipients to fake websites designed to steal personal information or install malware. These websites cleverly mimicked official Olympic platforms, using URLs and sender addresses that included terms like "tokyo2020" to appear legitimate. According to security firm Antuit, the phishing attempt reached approximately 170,000 people and was likely the work of a China-based group. In response, the Tokyo 2020 Organizing Committee issued a public warning, emphasizing that ticket sales had not yet begun and advising citizens to remain cautious of online scams(KYODO NEWS, 2025).
3. **Attacks on Streaming and Broadcast Systems:** Live sports streaming platforms are among the most lucrative and time-sensitive digital properties in the world. A disruption—even for a few minutes—can lead to contractual breaches with sponsors, loss of advertising revenue, and audience backlash. In June 2024, Riot Games publicly addressed a series of targeted Distributed Denial-of-Service (DDoS) attacks that disrupted the League of Legends Champions Korea (LCK) Spring Split. These cyberattacks affected professional teams, especially T1, and popular streamers, forcing some matches to be held without live audiences or aired as pre-recorded broadcasts. Riot's Head of League Studio, Andrei "RiotMeddler" van Roon, confirmed the issue and stated that while prior attacks had been addressed, the new wave bypassed earlier protections. As a result, streaming activities were suspended. Riot continues to investigate and collaborate with teams to strengthen defenses. The community, however, expressed frustration at Riot's inability to contain the problem, raising concerns about the vulnerability of esports infrastructure to repeated cyber threats(RiftFeed, 2024).
4. **Ransomware Shutdown of Club IT Infrastructure:** Ransomware attacks can bring the entire digital operations of a sports organization to a halt, impacting ticketing, payroll, athlete data access, and even match preparations. In November 2020, Manchester United faced a sophisticated cyberattack that targeted its inter-

nal IT systems. The club responded swiftly by shutting down affected systems to prevent data loss and engaged external cybersecurity experts to contain the breach and conduct a forensic investigation. Despite the severity of the attack, core operations such as match-day systems, the club's website, and mobile app remained unaffected. Cybersecurity professionals praised the club's quick and effective response, highlighting it as a strong example of incident preparedness and crisis management. At the time of reporting, there was no evidence of fan or customer data being compromised(Scroxton, 2020).

5. **Insider Leak of Team Strategy and Analytics:** Not all cyber threats come from outside an organization. Insiders—employees, consultants, or contractors—can misuse their access to exfiltrate sensitive information such as proprietary game strategies, performance models, or confidential player reports. In 2015, the St. Louis Cardinals became the first professional sports team implicated in a major cybersecurity breach when it was revealed that one of their executives, Christopher Correa, had illegally accessed the Houston Astros' internal scouting database, known as Ground Control. The stolen data included confidential player evaluations, proprietary analytics, trade discussions, and draft strategies. Correa gained access using passwords of former Cardinals staff who had joined the Astros. The breach led to a federal investigation, and Correa was sentenced to 46 months in prison and fined $279,000. Major League Baseball also sanctioned the Cardinals, imposing a $2 million fine and stripping the team of two draft picks. The incident exposed the growing cybersecurity risks in sports and highlighted how insider threats can undermine even the most data-driven organizations (Reporter, 2016).
6. **Phishing Attack Targeting Sponsor & Partner Data:** Phishing remains one of the most common and effective methods to compromise enterprise systems. Cybercriminals often impersonate trusted vendors, sponsors, or even internal departments to gain access to financial records, planning documents, or credentials. In December 2019, the Tokyo 2020 Olympic Organizing Committee issued a warning after detecting a phishing campaign that impersonated official Tokyo 2020 staff. The fraudulent emails were crafted to appear legitimate and included links or attachments that, if clicked or opened, would lead to malicious sites or the installation of malware . Japanese authorities, including the Public Security Intelligence Agency, noted that the campaign likely emanated from state-sponsored threat actors, with early indicators suggesting possible involvement by Chinese-linked hackers . They also referenced discussions on dark-web forums planning coordinated phishing efforts against Olympic-related personnel in both Japan and the U.S. .Additionally, Microsoft's Threat Intelligence Center reported that the APT28/Fancy Bear group was targeting sports organizations,

including anti-doping agencies, in phishing campaigns leading up to Tokyo 2020(Gatlan, 2019)

7. **Malware Infection in Smart Stadium IoT Devices:** Smart stadiums utilize a network of IoT devices, ranging from surveillance cameras and access gates to HVAC systems and digital signage. When these are not adequately secured, they become easy entry points for malware. During the 2018 PyeongChang Winter Olympics, a sophisticated cyberattack known as "Olympic Destroyer" caused widespread disruption just before the opening ceremony. The malware was designed to cripple smart infrastructure and succeeded in temporarily shutting down Wi-Fi networks, delaying ticketing systems, disabling RFID entry gates, and taking the official Olympic website offline—preventing spectators from accessing or printing tickets. Olympic Destroyer operated as a self-propagating wiper worm, deleting data and rendering systems inoperable. Although initial attribution was clouded by false flags embedded in the code—misleading analysts toward North Korea and China—subsequent investigations pointed to Russia's GRU-linked Sandworm unit. This incident served as a powerful wake-up call about the vulnerability of cyber-physical systems in global sporting events, underlining the need for advanced cybersecurity strategies in sports infrastructure (Greenberg & Excerpt, 2019).
8. **Breach of Online Betting Platform:** The rapid growth of online sports betting platforms has made them attractive targets for cybercriminals due to the sheer volume of personal and financial data they handle. In November 2022, sports betting platforms DraftKings and FanDuel were hit by a major cyberattack through a credential-stuffing campaign. Hackers used previously leaked login credentials to gain unauthorized access to tens of thousands of user accounts, compromising sensitive information such as names, addresses, transaction history, and masked payment details. The attack, which coincided with the FIFA World Cup, resulted in financial losses of around $300,000 and led to a surge in customer complaints and support requests. DraftKings reimbursed affected users and urged stronger cybersecurity measures, including the use of unique passwords and two-factor authentication. The incident prompted an official investigation by federal authorities and highlighted growing vulnerabilities in the online sports betting industry (Purdum, 2022).

WHY SPORTS BUSINESSES ARE HIGH-VALUE TARGETS

Economic and Reputational Impact of Breaches

In the digital age, sports businesses have transformed into data-rich, highly visible enterprises that blend entertainment, finance, technology, and global media exposure. This makes them particularly attractive—and vulnerable—targets for cybercriminals. The high stakes involved, both financially and reputationally, create a perfect storm for exploitation.

1. **Financial Value and Economic Exposure:** Modern sports franchises are multi-billion-dollar entities that rely on digital infrastructure to manage ticketing, merchandising, athlete contracts, payroll systems, broadcasting rights, and even crypto-based fan tokens. A single data breach can have immediate financial consequences. For instance, if a hacker gains access to the database of a sports ticketing platform, they could reroute payments or flood the market with counterfeit tickets, resulting in massive revenue losses and widespread fan outrage(Di Simone & Zanardi, 2020).

Scenario:

Imagine a major international cricket league is about to open online ticket sales for its final match, which is expected to generate millions in revenue. On launch day, a ransomware attack cripples the ticketing server. Transactions fail, refunds become complex, and scalpers exploit the chaos. Within hours, the league's reputation takes a hit, sponsors question their investments, and legal liabilities mount due to breach of consumer trust.

2. **Reputational Damage:** Sports businesses are closely tied to public emotion, brand loyalty, and social identity. Athletes are often regarded as national heroes or global icons, and any cyber incident that affects them—such as leaks of personal data or internal medical records—can spark a public backlash. Reputation in the sports world is currency: once it is compromised, rebuilding trust can take years and cost millions(*Damage to Brand or Reputation Top Risk for the Sports and Entertainment Industry*, n.d.).

Scenario:

Consider a global tennis federation whose database is hacked, revealing detailed medical histories and therapy regimens of top athletes. News outlets report the breach, fans express outrage over the lack of data privacy, and the affected players feel exposed and betrayed. Sponsors, concerned about a negative association, start pulling out, and the federation is forced to issue public apologies, invest heavily in damage control PR, and revise its entire IT infrastructure.

3. **Time-Sensitive Operations & Live Events:** The real-time nature of sports adds another layer of vulnerability. Whether it is a live-streamed match, fantasy league updates, or e-commerce during an event, even a few minutes of digital downtime can result in irreversible damage. Criminal actors are aware of this, and their attacks are often designed to maximize pressure and demand higher ransoms(Vaiyyali, 2024).

Scenario:

During a globally televised football final, a cyberattack disrupts the streaming service minutes into the match. Millions of paying viewers lose access, social media erupts in complaints, advertisers threaten legal action, and the broadcasting company faces regulatory scrutiny. Even if the breach is contained later, the damage to public trust and brand equity has already been done.

4. **High-Profile Targets with Global Reach:** Sports teams, leagues, and event organizers command immense global attention, making them particularly appealing to politically or ideologically motivated hackers who seek to draw attention to their actions. Hacktivist groups may target events like the Olympics, the FIFA World Cup, or the Super Bowl, not for monetary gain, but for maximum visibility and disruption(Richards, n.d.).

Scenario:

A hacktivist group opposes the country hosting an international multi-sport event. On the day of the opening ceremony, they launch a coordinated attack that brings down the official event website, floods social media channels with misinformation, and compromises media feeds. Although no money is stolen, the event's reputation and that of its organizers suffer severely, raising questions about digital preparedness.

The combination of high financial value emotionally invested audiences, real-time operations, and extensive global exposure makes sports businesses prime targets for cyberattacks. The economic loss from one breach can run into millions, but the long-term reputational damage—especially in a trust-based industry like sports—can be even more devastating. Proactive AI-driven security systems, ethical data handling, and robust cybersecurity governance are no longer optional—they are mission-critical.

AI IN CYBER DEFENSE: CORE CONCEPTS AND CAPABILITIES

Overview of Intrusion Detection and Prevention Systems (IDPS)

As sports enterprises accelerate their digital transformation—adopting real-time analytics, cloud computing, and IoT-enabled infrastructure—the need for advanced cybersecurity mechanisms has become non-negotiable. At the heart of this defense architecture lies the Intrusion Detection and Prevention System (IDPS), a specialized class of cybersecurity tools designed to identify, analyze, and mitigate malicious activities within an organization's network.

Traditional IDPS systems operate by monitoring network traffic, detecting known patterns of attacks (signature-based), and generating alerts or taking action (such as blocking IP addresses or shutting down access points). However, as cyber threats evolve in complexity, targeting not only systems but also behavioral vulnerabilities (e.g., phishing, deep fakes, spoofing, and zero-day exploits), legacy systems often fall short.

This is where AI-powered IDPS reshapes the security landscape. These next-generation systems employ machine learning (ML), deep learning (DL), and behavioral analytics to identify threats not only based on predefined rules, but also through real-time anomaly detection. They continuously learn from past incidents, adapt to new threat environments, and can predict and prevent attacks before significant damage occurs(Mohamed, 2025; Sil et al., 2025).

Key AI-Enabled Capabilities of Modern IDPS

Anomaly Detection: AI models analyze baseline user and system behavior to detect deviations that may indicate insider threats or unauthorized access attempts. For example, suppose an employee typically logs in from Mumbai during office hours but suddenly logs in at 2 a.m. from an overseas IP. In that case, the system flags it as suspicious, even if the credentials are correct.

Real-Time Threat Intelligence Integration: AI-IDPS systems can ingest vast volumes of global threat intelligence data—such as malware signatures, dark web chatter, and IP blocklists—and utilize it to enhance situational awareness. This ensures that emerging threat vectors are immediately recognized across platforms(*What Is Real-Time Threat Intelligence? - Logsign*, n.d.).

Automated Response Mechanisms: Upon detecting a threat, AI-enabled systems can trigger computerized responses, such as isolating infected devices, terminating suspicious sessions, or alerting security teams. This rapid mitigation is crucial in high-stakes environments, such as live sports events and real-time fan engagement platforms(Chinamanagonda, 2023).

Predictive Analytics for Threat Anticipation: AI systems do not just react—they anticipate. By analyzing historical attack patterns, system vulnerabilities, and contextual usage data, AI can proactively identify weak spots and recommend preemptive actions(Ogundairo et al., 2024).

Scalability Across Ecosystems: Whether it is a stadium Wi-Fi system, an athlete's biometric data platform, or a digital fan marketplace, AI-IDPS can scale to protect diverse digital surfaces without manual reconfiguration or downtime(*Scalability of Ecosystem Architectures*, 2014).

Imagine a high-profile football club using AI-IDPS across its digital platforms. During a peak merchandise sale, the system detects abnormal behavior—hundreds of failed login attempts from several countries targeting fan loyalty accounts. Rather than waiting for a breach, the system automatically locks vulnerable accounts, blocks suspicious IP addresses, and alerts the IT team—all in real-time—preventing potential fraud and identity theft.

Table 1. AI-IDPS Use Cases Across the Sports Ecosystem

Area of Use	Example of Threat	How AI-IDPS Helps
Athlete Health Data Platforms	Data leaks, unauthorized access	Monitors usage patterns; blocks anomalies
Fan Engagement Apps	Account hijacking, phishing	Flag strange login activity
E-commerce & Ticketing Platforms	Payment fraud, bot attacks	Detects fake transactions in real time
Broadcasting & Streaming Systems	Service disruption (e.g., DDoS)	Shield systems during peak usage
Stadium Infrastructure (IoT)	Hijacked cameras or sensors	Monitors connected devices for threats
Sports Tech Startups	IP theft, insider threats	Tracks abnormal behavior in data usage

Comparison: Rule-Based vs. AI-Enabled Intrusion Detection and Prevention Systems (IDPS)

As the digital attack surface expands across sports enterprises, understanding the distinctions between rule-based and AI-enabled IDPS becomes essential. While both systems aim to detect and mitigate threats, they differ significantly in their methodologies, adaptability, and effectiveness, particularly in complex and evolving digital environments, such as those found in sports.

1. **Foundational Approach: Static Rules vs. Dynamic Learning:** Rule-based systems operate using predefined logic and static signatures. These are sets of instructions, like "If A happens, do B," written by cybersecurity professionals based on known threats. For example, if a system detects an excessive number of failed logins within a short period, it may block the user, assuming a brute-force attack is underway.

In contrast, AI-enabled systems use machine learning to understand patterns in user behavior, data access, and system traffic. Instead of relying solely on preset rules, they learn from past data to identify abnormal or suspicious activities, including zero-day attacks (previously unknown threats).

Use case in sports: In a rule-based system, only known threats (e.g., blocked IP addresses or suspicious URLs) can trigger alerts. However, an AI-IDPS in a sports science lab could detect unusual access to athlete injury reports from an external network—even if no specific signature exists—by learning what standard access patterns look like over time.

2. **Flexibility and Adaptability:** Rule-based systems are inherently rigid. Any deviation not accounted for in the rules goes unnoticed. Updating rules requires manual intervention by IT teams, which can be time-consuming and prone to oversight.

AI-enabled IDPS are designed to adapt. They continuously evolve based on new data, learn from global threat trends, and adjust to context. This makes them particularly useful for sports organizations undergoing frequent tech upgrades, staffing changes, or expansion into digital fan platforms.

Use case in sports: If a streaming platform used by a cricket league suddenly experiences a coordinated bot attack during a live match, a rule-based system may take time to catch up. AI-IDPS, on the other hand, can detect anomalies in traffic volume or packet behavior in real-time and act autonomously.

3. **Detection of Insider Threats:** Insider threats—whether intentional or accidental—are among the most difficult to detect using rule-based systems. These systems typically monitor external threats and lack visibility into user intent or behavioral shifts.

AI-IDPS excels in this area by tracking user behavior over time. It can flag deviations such as a junior physiotherapist suddenly accessing high-level financial or scouting data, indicating potential misuse of privileges.

Use case in sports: In a talent scouting department, a disgruntled staff member attempts to export confidential player evaluation reports. A rule-based system may not have a rule to flag this unless it has already been defined. AI-IDPS, recognizing the unusual export pattern, can trigger an alert or even revoke access instantly.

4. **Response Time and Automation:** Rule-based systems are often reactive and may require manual verification or approval before action is taken. This can lead to delays in threat mitigation, which is costly during high-stakes events like international tournaments.

AI-enabled systems are proactive and automated. They do not just detect threats—they prioritize, analyze, and often respond autonomously based on risk thresholds, without human intervention.

Use case in sports: During a live Olympic event, an unauthorized attempt to breach real-time data feeds could compromise the integrity of scores or the live stream. An AI-IDPS can instantaneously block the source, reroute data, and alert administrators before public impact.

5. **Resource and Maintenance Overhead:** Rule-based systems require constant rule updates, management of the signature database, and manual oversight to ensure accuracy and effectiveness. For smaller sports organizations with limited IT capacity, this can be difficult.

AI-IDPS reduces the need for constant manual updates. Though initial setup may be resource-intensive (training models, data integration), they become more autonomous over time, making them cost-efficient and scalable for sports ecosystems of all sizes.

Table 2. Comparative Analysis – Rule-Based vs. AI-Enabled IDPS in Sports Cybersecurity

Feature	Rule-Based IDPS	AI-Enabled IDPS
Detection Method	Predefined rules & signatures	Pattern recognition & machine learning
Adaptability	Low – requires manual updates	Highly continuously learns & evolves
Insider Threat Detection	Limited	Strong – based on behavior modeling
Response Time	Reactive	Proactive & often automated
Maintenance	High	Lower (after initial setup)
Suitability for the Sports Sector	Limited to basic security	Ideal for dynamic, data-rich environments

Designing AI-Driven IDPS for Sports Enterprises: Designing AI-Driven Intrusion Detection and Prevention Systems (IDPS) for Sports Enterprises

The evolution of the sports industry into a tech-intensive ecosystem has elevated the importance of cybersecurity. With sports enterprises relying on real-time data from athletes, fans, infrastructure, and financial transactions, the design of intrusion detection and prevention systems must go beyond conventional approaches. AI-enabled IDPS systems, when thoughtfully architected, can ensure robust, agile, and scalable defense mechanisms that protect not only digital assets but also the integrity and continuity of sports operations.

Real-Time Response

In the high-stakes world of sports, where events unfold in real-time—be it a live-streamed match, a biometric feed from an athlete, or a flash sale of game tickets—any delay in detecting and responding to cyber threats can result in catastrophic consequences. AI-driven IDPS systems are uniquely suited to provide instantaneous threat identification and neutralization by continuously analyzing network behavior, system logs, and user patterns. Machine learning models can be trained to detect subtle anomalies that rule-based systems often miss, enabling immediate intervention without requiring manual commands. For example, a real-time IDPS can detect a sudden surge in traffic directed toward a scoreboard's backend, isolate the source, and reroute operations before viewers even notice a disruption. (Ahmad, 2025; Reddy et al., 2024).

Scalability and Flexibility

Sports organizations vary significantly in terms of scale, infrastructure, and audience size. Some may operate at a local level with limited digital assets. In contrast, others, such as international leagues or Olympic committees, manage a web of interconnected platforms, smart stadiums, and global fan bases. The AI-IDPS architecture must be scalable enough to handle fluctuating data volumes and adaptable to emerging platforms. Cloud-based or hybrid deployments can ensure system expansion during peak seasons or global tournaments, allowing for seamless scalability(Raghavan, 2025). For instance, during the FIFA World Cup, an IDPS system must scale seamlessly to handle billions of data points flowing from ticketing servers, streaming platforms, mobile apps, and stadium infrastructure without compromising detection accuracy or speed.

Minimal Latency and High Throughput

In the sports context, speed is not just a gameplay metric—it is a cybersecurity imperative. AI-IDPS must process and act on threat intelligence in milliseconds to prevent system compromise, especially in environments dependent on real-time streaming or biometric monitoring (*Real-time Threat Detection Strategies for Resource-constrained Devices*, n.d.). Achieving low latency requires efficient algorithmic design, edge computing capability near data sources, and prioritization of mission-critical data. For example, an athlete's wearable device, which tracks hydration and stress, must stream data uninterrupted to coaches and medical staff. If an unusual API call or data exfiltration attempt is detected, the system must shut down access while preserving the device's primary function, all within milliseconds.

Protecting Athlete Health and Performance Data

Athlete data, particularly biometrics and performance metrics, is among the most sensitive information handled by sports organizations. Collected via wearables, innovative apparel, and training platforms, this data informs coaching, medical interventions, and even player contracts(Malik et al., 2024). A robust AI-IDPS must ensure that these data streams are encrypted both in transit and at rest, continuously monitored for access violations, and protected under role-based authentication protocols. For instance, an internal staff member attempting to access another team's recovery data could be flagged by the IDPS, which would not only block the action but also alert compliance officers to a potential ethical breach.

Fan and Customer Data Security

With fans interacting through mobile apps, loyalty programs, e-commerce platforms, and online ticketing portals, their personal and financial data become prime targets for cybercriminals(*Fan Data: Personalized Fan Engagement | Deloitte US*, 2025). An AI-IDPS can provide dynamic protection by recognizing unusual login behaviors, tracking bot-generated activity, and isolating suspicious transactions. Unlike traditional security layers, AI adapts to changing attack vectors and behavioral shifts. For example, if thousands of fake accounts try to buy match tickets using a stolen credit card database, the AI system could correlate behavior patterns and geographic inconsistencies to block access and alert fraud units pre-emptively.

IoT Device and Smart Infrastructure Protection

Modern sports facilities are rich with IoT devices—smart cameras, biometric scanners, environmental sensors, and more—each representing a potential point of entry for attackers. These devices often run outdated firmware or operate on minimal processing power, making them vulnerable to tampering(Nexusgroup, 2024). AI-IDPS systems are essential for safeguarding these endpoints by continuously analyzing device behavior and communication patterns. Anomalies—such as a sensor suddenly communicating with an unknown IP or a camera transmitting video outside scheduled hours—can trigger containment actions. For instance, during a high-profile match, if an intelligent lighting controller begins executing abnormal scripts, the IDPS can isolate it before it compromises the stadium's power systems.

INTEGRATING AI-IDPS INTO SPORTS TECH ENVIRONMENTS

The integration of AI-powered Intrusion Detection and Prevention Systems (IDPS) across the diverse digital ecosystems within sports enterprises is no longer optional—it is essential. From the physical infrastructure of stadiums to the deeply personalized data ecosystems of athlete monitoring, cybersecurity systems must be seamlessly embedded to protect data integrity, business continuity, and public trust. Below is an exploration of how AI-IDPS can be integrated across various operational nodes within the sports industry.

1. **Stadium Infrastructure:** Modern stadiums operate as intelligent hubs, with hundreds of connected devices handling ticket validation, crowd movement monitoring, surveillance, and even dynamic advertising. These IoT-rich environments are vulnerable to cyberattacks that can not only disrupt operations but also endanger public safety.

Scenario: Just before the opening ceremony of the 2018 PyeongChang Winter Olympics, a devastating cyberattack disrupted core systems using malware later dubbed "Olympic Destroyer." The attack disabled Wi-Fi networks, shut down ticketing systems, and rendered the official Olympic website inoperable, preventing spectators from accessing or printing tickets. The malware was a fast-spreading, destructive worm designed to wipe data and cripple operations, using stolen credentials and built-in Windows tools to propagate. What made the attack particularly sophisticated was its use of false flags—lines of code intentionally inserted to mislead investigators about the origin. Although attribution was initially unclear, the incident ultimately served as a major warning about the vulnerability of smart infrastructure at large-scale sporting events and highlighted the critical need for robust cybersecurity in international sports(Greenberg, 2018).

AI-IDPS Role: An integrated AI-IDPS could have preemptively identified the anomalous behavior in network traffic between systems in the stadium's backend. Real-time alerts could have quarantined affected nodes while allowing backup systems to take over, ensuring uninterrupted public entry and safety management during the event.

2. **Sports E-Commerce Platforms:** From merchandise to ticket sales, sports e-commerce generates millions in revenue. These platforms store sensitive user data, including payment details, addresses, and browsing behavior. They are often targeted for credential stuffing, fake account creation, and transaction hijacking.

Example: In 2020, football supporters across Europe fell victim to an alarming increase in fake ticket scams. Criminals posed via social media and online marketplaces—particularly on Facebook and Instagram—advertising legitimate-looking tickets but redirecting buyers to spoofed sites designed to harvest payment and personal details. Buyers were often tricked into making non-reversible bank transfers. According to Lloyds Bank and data shared by BBC and UK Finance, the number of reported scams surged significantly, with average losses exceeding £150–£200, and some victims losing over £1,000. Affected fans frequently supported top-tier clubs such as Arsenal, Liverpool, Manchester United, and Chelsea. The scams highlighted the urgent need to purchase through official channels like club ticketing systems and verified resale platforms to avoid fraud(R et al., 2025).

AI-IDPS Role: A properly trained AI-IDPS in such a setup could flag abnormal payment patterns, detect bots attempting to brute-force account logins, and automatically initiate CAPTCHA challenges or multi-factor authentication. These systems could also generate fraud intelligence for future policy updates, ensuring adaptive protection for both fans and the enterprise.

3. **Performance Analytics Platforms:** Elite teams utilize sophisticated software platforms to track player metrics, including sprint speed, injury likelihood, and fatigue levels. These platforms often ingest data from GPS trackers, heart-rate monitors, and video analytics, and store it in cloud environments. A breach here can compromise competitive advantage or violate privacy laws.

Example: In March 2021, West Ham United faced a significant data breach when a misconfiguration in their official ticketing website caused users to inadvertently access other supporters' personal information, including names, dates of birth

(DOB), phone numbers, addresses, and email IDs. The issue was swiftly addressed by the club and its third-party ticketing provider, but it raised serious concerns about fundamental application security. Experts highlighted the need for secure configuration, proper testing based on the Open Worldwide Application Security Project (OWASP) guidelines, and a security-first approach, especially under strict data protection laws like the General Data Protection Regulation (GDPR). The incident also served as a reminder for users to stay vigilant against phishing and suspicious communications(*West Ham Supporters Have Data Leaked by Club Website*, 2021).

AI-IDPS Role: AI-IDPS solutions on these platforms can create digital profiles of typical user access patterns—who logs in, from which device, and during what time window—and immediately flag attempts that diverge from that baseline. For instance, if an intern's credentials are used from an overseas IP address outside of training hours, this would automatically trigger lockdown procedures and escalate to the cybersecurity teams.

4. **Wearables and Cloud-Based Athlete Monitoring Tools:** Wearable devices, such as GPS vests, sleep monitors, and muscle-recovery trackers, are revolutionizing sports science. However, these tools transmit sensitive physiological data to cloud dashboards that coaches, physicians, and management may access. Without embedded cybersecurity, such systems are ripe for interception, spoofing, or data poisoning.

Example: A hypothetical yet plausible case involves a junior league using budget fitness wearables connected to a shared cloud dashboard. A former disgruntled coach, still possessing access credentials, manipulates recovery data of key players to make them appear fit, leading to premature returns and aggravated injuries.

AI-IDPS Role: An integrated AI-IDPS here would apply behavior-based access controls and device fingerprinting to track login consistency and cloud API usage. If a dormant credential is suddenly used to access only specific players' profiles or if device data patterns do not align with known sensor behaviors, the system can flag and halt data transmission in real time, while preserving audit trails for investigation.

By embedding AI-IDPS across these diverse verticals, sports organizations not only defend against breaches but also build intelligent, self-adapting security architectures that uphold trust, performance, and brand equity in a digitized sports world.

Framework for Risk Modeling and Mitigation in Sports Enterprises

The rapidly expanding digital footprint of the sports industry demands a comprehensive and agile framework to proactively model, assess, and mitigate cyber risks. This section introduces a structured approach that combines traditional risk assessment methodologies with advanced AI-driven capabilities, specifically tailored to the unique digital environments in sports, encompassing biometric athlete monitoring, virtual fan experiences, and smart stadiums.

1. Cyber Risk Matrix for Sports Organizations: A cyber risk matrix helps organizations categorize and prioritize cyber threats based on two critical parameters: *likelihood of occurrence* and *potential impact.* This structured view enables sports IT teams and CISOs to focus mitigation efforts on the most critical vulnerabilities that could damage operations, reputation, or safety. This is a model that we are recommending as a easy reference point.

Table 3. Sample Cyber Risk Matrix for a Sports Tech Enterprise

Cyber Threat	Likelihood	Impact	AI Detection Strategy	Mitigation Measures
Ransomware Attack on Athlete Data	Medium	High	Anomaly detection in access patterns	Data backup, endpoint security, and segmentation
Streaming Disruption (DDoS)	High	Medium	Traffic flow modeling and geo-IP monitoring	Auto-scaling servers, CDNs, scrubbing centers
Insider Misuse of Health Metrics	Low	High	Behavioral baselining with NLP audit logs	Zero trust access, audit trails, and policy enforcement
Ticketing Bot Fraud	High	High	Pattern detection, CAPTCHA defeat models	Behavioral biometrics, adaptive CAPTCHA, device fingerprinting
IoT Exploits in Smart Stadiums	Medium	Medium	Device traffic analytics, firmware signature AI	Edge security, device authentication protocols

2. **Asset Identification, Vulnerability Assessment, and Threat Mapping:** To build an effective defense, it is imperative to know what to protect. In sports enterprises, digital assets vary widely—from physical IoT hardware in stadiums to cloud-based platforms housing performance data.

Table 4. Asset-Vulnerability-Threat Mapping in Sports Context

Digital Asset	Example	Known Vulnerabilities	Possible Threats
Wearables & Sensors	GPS trackers, HR monitors	Weak encryption, Bluetooth sniffing	Unauthorized data access, spoofing
E-Commerce Systems	Ticketing, merchandise sites	Bot attacks, SQL injections	Fake purchases, price manipulation
Athlete Analytics Platforms	Video & sensor-based software	API abuse, data tampering	Performance data theft, sabotage
AR/VR Fan Engagement	Mobile-based interactive apps	Unsecured API, user data leakage	Deepfake injection, fan privacy invasion
Smart Infrastructure	Lighting, surveillance systems	Unpatched firmware, remote hijacking	Stadium blackouts, security breaches

3. **AI-Enhanced Risk Scoring Models:** Unlike static threat assessments, AI allows dynamic risk scoring based on multiple inputs, including contextual data such as event schedules, regional threat trends, and real-time behavior. AI models can continuously update risk values as new patterns emerge, improving the agility of response.

Table 5. AI-Enabled Risk Scoring Matrix (Weighted Model)

Scoring Parameter	Weightage	Data Input Example	AI Role
Asset Criticality	30%	Biometric vs. merchandise data	Prioritize based on regulatory/ monetary risk
Threat Likelihood	25%	Global and regional threat intel	Predictive modeling using recent attack datasets
Vulnerability Exposure	25%	Unpatched software, misconfigurations	CVE-based scoring + known exploit path analysis
Behavioural Deviation	10%	Sudden access from a new geo/ IP/device	Anomaly scoring through time-series AI
Temporal/Event Sensitivity	10%	Pre-final match week or transfer season	Adjust risk during high-profile event periods

Total Risk Score = Sum of weighted values → Prioritized in dashboards for automated or manual intervention.

The above scoring model is presented as a proposed reference framework for cybersecurity risk assessment within the sports sector. It is designed to incorporate both standard risk assessment principles (inspired by models such as NIST, FAIR, and CVSS) and domain-specific considerations relevant to sports organizations, including athlete data sensitivity, seasonal event risks, and behavioral anomalies.

The framework integrates AI-driven capabilities, such as anomaly detection, predictive modeling, and contextual scoring, to enable a more dynamic and adaptive risk management approach.

This model is not prescriptive. Organizations are encouraged to adapt, modify, or expand the parameters, weightings, and data inputs according to their specific operational needs, regulatory environments, and technology maturity levels.

It serves as a flexible foundation for developing customized cybersecurity strategies in high-stakes, event-driven environments, such as professional sports.

4. **Incident Response Planning and AI-Based Simulation:** Incident response (IR) in modern sports organizations must be fast, adaptive, and learnable. AI can enhance IR plans through:
   - Automated detection and alerting
   - Playbook selection based on risk class
   - Simulated attack drills using AI-generated threat scenarios
   - Post-incident learning for AI model retraining

Flow Diagram: AI-Driven Incident Response Lifecycle
[1. Real-Time AI Threat Detection]
↓
[2. Risk Scoring & Alert Prioritization]
↓
[3. Automated Playbook Activation]
↓
[4. Human Review & Escalation (if needed)]
↓
[5. Containment & Recovery]
↓
[6. Post-Incident Learning & Model Update]

This cyclical model ensures that each simulated or real security breach improves the system's ability to predict and prevent future incidents.

5. **Lessons Learned from Real Incidents:** The above incidents and applications offer a set of critical takeaways for sports organizations, regardless of size or geography:
   - AI must be embedded at the design stage of any digital infrastructure. Retrofitting post-breach rarely works.
   - Cyber resilience is as much about people as technology. Human error, insider threats, and lack of awareness continue to be the top vulnerability sources.

- Biometric and health data are the new gold. Especially in the age of smart wearables and athlete performance monitoring, such data requires military-grade encryption and zero-trust access.
- Incident response should be automated and rehearsed. As seen in Manchester United's response, continuity planning must be as robust as prevention strategies.
- Fan trust is business capital. A single breach affecting payment data or streaming access can erode years of brand equity and consumer loyalty.

Table 6. Comparative Overview of Cybersecurity Case Studies in Global Sports Events

Case Study	Type of Risk	AI/Cybersecurity Measures Used	Key Outcome / Impact
FIFA World Cup 2018	Phishing, DDoS, fake ticketing, state-sponsored threats	AI-based fraud detection, IDPS, facial recognition, threat simulation drills	Prevented major attacks; enhanced fan and data safety
Tokyo Olympics 2020	Data theft, athlete privacy, bio-health spoofing	IoT anomaly detection, biometric access control, and AI monitoring in the health cloud	Secured over 450M attacks; no data breach reported.
Manchester United (2020)	Ransomware, IP theft, insider threats	Data encryption, network segmentation, and business continuity protocol	No data loss; systems recovered without ransom payment
Ticketing & Betting Platforms (2020–2023)	Bot fraud, payment scams, and insider access	Behavioral AI, device fingerprinting, ML anomaly detectors	Fraud has been significantly reduced; proactive fraud detection is active
Ticketmaster Insider Breach (2017–2020)	Insider threat, competitive sabotage	(Post-event) enhanced monitoring, audit logs, and employee access control	$10M fine; led to stricter compliance & internal audits

These lessons suggest a future where cybersecurity is not an IT issue, but a boardroom issue, essential to both the integrity and profitability of the global sports industry.

REGULATORY AND ETHICAL CONSIDERATIONS

Regulatory and Ethical Considerations in AI-Driven Sports Cybersecurity

As sports enterprises accelerate their integration of artificial intelligence (AI) across digital platforms, cybersecurity concerns are no longer limited to technical configurations—they must now align with evolving regulatory frameworks and uphold high ethical standards. This section examines the primary regulatory requirements and ethical considerations influencing AI-based cybersecurity systems in the sports industry(Kim et al., 2025).

GDPR, Biometric Data Regulations, and Fan Privacy

In the sports ecosystem, data is not just plentiful—it is personal and sensitive. From biometric readings of athletes (such as heart rate, stress levels, and muscle fatigue) to financial transactions and location data from fans, organizations are custodians of highly sensitive and confidential information. Regulations like the General Data Protection Regulation (GDPR) in the European Union mandate strict guidelines around data collection, storage, and use, particularly when it comes to personally identifiable information (PII) and biometric data.(*Biometric Data and Privacy Laws (GDPR, CCPA/CPRA)*, 2021)

For instance, when a football club uses AI to analyze athletes' fatigue via wearable sensors, such data must be anonymized, encrypted, and processed with informed consent. The Indian Digital Personal Data Protection Act (DPDP), 2023, and global equivalents are setting similar benchmarks that sports entities must align with.

Failure to comply can result in legal penalties and erosion of fan and athlete trust. A robust AI-based Intrusion Detection and Prevention System (IDPS) must therefore be built with privacy-preserving architecture at its core.

Bias and Transparency in AI-Driven Decision-Making

AI models trained on biased or incomplete datasets can produce unfair outcomes, for example, disproportionately flagging certain user behaviors as fraudulent or suspicious due to flawed historical data. In sports, this can lead to unjust scrutiny of specific fan groups, athletes, or even vendors, resulting in reputational and legal consequences.

Transparency in AI systems is crucial. Sports organizations must be able to explain how and why decisions are made by AI systems, particularly in high-stakes scenarios such as fraud detection or athlete health monitoring. This requires deploying explainable AI (XAI) techniques, audit trails, and human-in-the-loop processes to ensure fairness and accountability(*What Is AI Bias? Causes, Effects, and Mitigation Strategies | SAP*, n.d.).

Data Governance for Sensitive Health and Financial Data

Athlete health data—collected through wearables, training software, or performance analytics—is classified as sensitive personal data. Similarly, fan financial data handled by ticketing portals or e-commerce platforms carries a high risk profile. Proper data governance is essential to control who has access to what data, how it is encrypted, and under what circumstances it can be shared or retained(Staff, 2024).

Implementing data access controls, role-based authorization, automated data expiration policies, and blockchain-based audit logs can strengthen trust in these systems. For AI-IDPS solutions, this also means limiting access to only necessary data for model training and ensuring ethical use of real-time data streams.

Ethical AI Frameworks in Sports Cybersecurity

Adopting ethical AI frameworks, such as those suggested by UNESCO, IEEE, or the EU AI Act, can help sports organizations ensure that their use of AI for cybersecurity respects human dignity, autonomy, and equity(Carrio et al., 2023). These frameworks typically emphasize principles such as:

- Fairness: Avoiding discriminatory outcomes
- Transparency: Enabling auditability and clarity in decision-making
- Privacy: Ensuring data minimization and consent-driven use
- Accountability: Establishing clear responsibilities for AI-driven actions

Incorporating these principles into the development and deployment of AI-IDPS helps maintain public trust, athlete confidence, and organizational integrity.

Compliance Strategies for Global Sports Organizations

Global sports entities often operate across jurisdictions with differing privacy laws and AI governance standards. Therefore, their cybersecurity and AI infrastructure must be designed to be compliance-ready(*How Data Privacy Compliance Strategies Can Mitigate Cyber Threats*, 2024). Key strategies include:

- Appointing Data Protection Officers (DPOs) and AI Ethics Boards
- Conducting regular AI impact assessments
- Standardizing incident response protocols across regions
- Partnering with legal experts to stay updated on international compliance landscapes

For example, the FIFA World Cup, the Olympic Games, and even regional leagues like the Indian Premier League (IPL) must navigate a complex regulatory web that spans GDPR, local data laws, and global AI ethics guidelines. Ensuring that AI-powered cybersecurity systems are designed to accommodate this diversity is crucial for mitigating risk and fostering sustainable innovation.

While AI opens new frontiers in securing the digital backbone of sports enterprises, its deployment must be guided by a strong foundation of ethics, regulatory awareness, and responsible innovation. The future of digital sports will depend not only on innovative technologies but also on conscientious governance that safeguards the rights and interests of all stakeholders.

IMPLEMENTATION ROADMAP FOR SPORTS ENTERPRISES

Implementation Roadmap for Sports Enterprises: Introduction

In the dynamic world of sports, where digital platforms handle everything from fan ticketing and online merchandise to athlete performance monitoring and IoT-enabled wearables, cybersecurity risks are rapidly growing. The increasing value of sports data—financial, biometric, and operational—has made sports enterprises prime targets for cyber threats. Traditional cybersecurity methods are no longer enough. To ensure real-time protection, scalability, and resilience, AI-powered Intrusion Detection and Prevention Systems (AI-IDPS) must be systematically integrated. This section outlines a simple, step-by-step roadmap to help sports organizations implement AI-IDPS effectively, from planning to post-deployment audits.

Phases of AI-IDPS Implementation in Sports Enterprises

Phase 1: Assess Risks and Prioritize Needs

Begin by understanding where you're most vulnerable.

- Identify digital assets such as fan data, payment platforms, athlete medical records, video feeds, and innovative stadium systems.
- Conduct a cyber risk assessment: What kinds of attacks are most likely (e.g., ransomware, phishing, DDoS)?
- List top priorities—e.g., securing live match broadcasts or protecting fan transaction systems.

Example: A football league may identify that ticketing fraud and broadcast piracy are its top cyber risks in the lead-up to a significant event.

Phase 2: Prepare Infrastructure

Before installing any AI system, please verify that your existing technology can support it.

- Is your data centralized or scattered?
- Do you have real-time data flows for AI to monitor?
- Do your networks (cloud/local) support the speed and scale AI-IDPS needs?

Example: A sports streaming platform must ensure that high-speed servers and secure APIs are in place before implementing real-time threat detection.

Phase 3: Select the Right AI-IDPS Tools

Select a system that aligns with your organization's size, budget, and risk profile.

- Open-source options (e.g., Zeek, Snort with AI plugins) are cost-effective but require in-house tech talent.
- Commercial tools (e.g., Darktrace, CrowdStrike) offer advanced features with vendor support.

Tip: Start small by conducting a pilot test of one tool on one system, such as your e-commerce portal, and then expand from there.

Phase 4: Customize and Pilot Test

Before going live, test the system to ensure it behaves as expected.

- Simulate cyberattacks to see how the AI responds (e.g., fake login attempts, unusual download activity).
- Adjust thresholds to reduce false alarms.
- Train the AI models using actual sports operations data (e.g., peak fan engagement periods, live score updates).

Example: A cricket team's website might test the system by mimicking a DDoS attack during match-day traffic to ensure the AI reacts appropriately.

Phase 5: Full-Scale Rollout

Deploy the system across all key departments and digital platforms.

- Integrate AI-IDPS with live match operations, merchandise stores, fan apps, athlete wearables, and broadcast feeds.
- Set up centralized monitoring dashboards.

Pro Tip: Roll out gradually—start with high-risk zones, such as payment gateways and athlete health records, before expanding to other areas.

Phase 6: Continuous Monitoring and Learning

AI systems improve with feedback. Keep fine-tuning them.

- Use incident logs to retrain AI models.
- Add new threat patterns as hackers evolve.
- Integrate with real-time alerts for IT/security teams.

Example: A basketball club discovers a new type of phishing link targeting fans and updates its AI-IDPS model to detect similar future threats.

Phase 7: Staff Training and Regular Audits

People are your biggest asset in cyber defense.

- Train staff to understand system alerts and respond swiftly.
- Organize regular drills: How should a team respond if a breach is detected during a live event?
- Conduct periodic internal and third-party audits to ensure regulatory compliance.

Tip: Include everyone—from tech staff to marketing teams—so the whole organization is cyber-aware.

This step-by-step roadmap helps sports organizations evolve from reactive cybersecurity to proactive, AI-driven threat prevention. With the proper planning, tools, training, and ongoing evaluation, sports enterprises can protect their digital assets and reputation in an increasingly interconnected and competitive world.

FUTURE TRENDS AND CHALLENGES

As digital transformation deepens its roots in the sports industry, the cybersecurity landscape continues to evolve rapidly. The future of securing the sports economy will not merely involve better tools but more intelligent, privacy-aware, and ethically governed AI systems. From decentralized learning methods to quantum-ready defenses, the next wave of technologies promises to reshape how sports enterprises protect their digital and human assets. This section explores some of the most significant future trends and challenges that will define the next decade of AI-driven cybersecurity in sports.

Federated Learning and Privacy-Preserving AI in Sports Security

Traditional AI systems rely on centralized data collection for training, which poses significant privacy risks, particularly when handling sensitive athlete biometric data or fan financial information. Federated learning offers a paradigm shift, allowing AI models to be trained across multiple decentralized devices or servers (e.g., wearables, edge cameras in stadiums) without aggregating raw data in a central location. This enables organizations to enhance their threat detection models while preserving individual privacy in a collaborative manner(Zhan et al., 2025).

In a sports context, federated learning could enable different clubs, leagues, or venues to jointly enhance their AI-IDPS algorithms by sharing insights, without exposing private data. For instance, wearable manufacturers and team physiologists could collaborate on security models that detect anomalies in device behavior (suggesting a cyber intrusion), all while maintaining athlete confidentiality.

AI in Cyber Forensics and Proactive Threat Hunting

The future of cybersecurity is shifting from passive defense to proactive, AI-enabled threat hunting. Rather than waiting for alerts to trigger, AI systems will increasingly analyze patterns to predict and neutralize threats before they strike. These capabilities will be especially critical during high-profile sporting events, such as the Olympics or the World Cups, where cyber adversaries may employ advanced persistent threats (APTs)(*CROWDSTRIKE 2024 THREAT HUNTING REPORT*, n.d.).

AI-driven cyber forensics will also become integral to post-breach investigations. Natural language processing (NLP) can help analyze attacker communications on the dark web, while machine learning models can reconstruct the sequence of events leading to a breach. In the future, sports organizations may rely on AI not only to prevent cyberattacks but also to understand them, learn from them, and evolve continuously.

Quantum-Resilient Cryptography and Next-Gen IDPS

The looming threat of quantum computing represents a serious long-term challenge. Quantum machines, once operational at scale, could easily break current encryption algorithms, compromising everything from fan databases to encrypted athlete performance logs. To prepare for this, sports enterprises must begin exploring quantum-resilient cryptographic methods, such as lattice-based encryption and quantum key distribution (QKD)(*Future-Proof Your Security: Actionable Quantum-Safe Solutions for 2025 | FutureX*, 2025).

In parallel, next-generation AI-IDPS systems will likely integrate multi-layered authentication, dynamic encryption, and self-healing capabilities. These systems will utilize adaptive AI to reconfigure their defensive posture in response to changing threat landscapes, essential for live environments such as tournaments or global broadcast feeds, where downtime is not an option.

Evolving Threats in the Age of Metaverse Sports and Digital Twins

As sports extend into the metaverse—with virtual stadiums, NFT-based fan collectibles, and immersive athlete-fan interactions—new cybersecurity concerns will emerge. Virtual identities, avatars, and blockchain-based transactions will be prime targets for impersonation, fraud, and phishing(Tang et al., 2025).

Meanwhile, the use of digital twins—virtual replicas of athletes used for training simulations or injury prevention—introduces another layer of risk. If compromised, these models could leak proprietary performance data or be maliciously altered, affecting an athlete's reputation or even game-day decisions. AI will be essential in monitoring the behavior and integrity of digital assets in this mixed-reality world.

Looking Ahead

While the technologies on the horizon are promising, they also bring complexity and new vulnerabilities. The challenge will be to strike a balance between innovation and protection, leveraging AI not only to guard against cyber threats but to build a more resilient, ethical, and inclusive digital future for the sports industry. As the lines between physical and virtual play continue to blur, the sports world must be as agile in cybersecurity as it is in athletic competition.

DISCUSSION POINTS

As the sports industry adopts artificial intelligence to safeguard its rapidly expanding digital landscape, critical questions arise regarding the implications, governance, and limitations of AI-driven cybersecurity. While this chapter outlines robust frameworks and real-world applications of AI-IDPS (Intrusion Detection and Prevention Systems), the ongoing evolution of both threats and technologies necessitates further discussion.

Firstly, to what extent should AI systems operate autonomously in managing cybersecurity threats, especially when they involve sensitive biometric or financial data? While real-time automation is essential, does over-reliance on AI compromise human accountability? This brings us to the question of transparency: can AI decision-making processes in threat detection be clearly explained to regulators, athletes, or fans, particularly when harm or bias occurs?

Moreover, the implementation of AI-IDPS systems may be feasible for elite leagues and global tournaments, but what about grassroots or local sports organizations that lack funding or digital infrastructure? Should there be a shared or federated model of cybersecurity where larger institutions help smaller ones build resilience?

There is also the issue of regulatory convergence. With varying data protection laws across countries—such as GDPR in Europe, DPDP in India, and differing US state laws—how can international sports organizations ensure consistent compliance when deploying AI-based tools? And with cybercriminals now using AI to create adaptive attacks and deepfakes, is the sports industry prepared for an AI-versus-AI arms race?

Finally, as the metaverse, NFTs, and digital twins reshape sports fandom and athlete engagement, do existing cybersecurity frameworks extend into these virtual arenas? What new policies or ethical principles might be needed to govern emerging threats in these immersive spaces?

These questions challenge readers, practitioners, and researchers to look beyond technological deployment and engage with the broader social, economic, and ethical dimensions of securing the sports economy in the era of AI.

CONCLUSION

The digital revolution in sports has transformed the way athletes train, fans engage, and enterprises operate—but it has also opened new frontiers of vulnerability. As this chapter has illustrated, the integration of AI-driven Intrusion Detection and Prevention Systems (AI-IDPS) is no longer optional for sports organizations navigating the complexities of modern cyber threats. From biometric data leaks and ransomware attacks to online ticketing fraud and broadcast piracy, the spectrum of risks faced by the sports economy is vast, high-stakes, and continuously evolving.

AI offers a robust response. Through real-time anomaly detection, behavioral analytics, and predictive modeling, AI-IDPS can identify and neutralize threats faster than human teams ever could. Yet the effectiveness of these systems depends not just on the strength of the algorithms but also on thoughtful implementation, anchored in ethical principles, regulatory compliance, and organizational readiness.

This chapter has provided a comprehensive roadmap for deploying AI-IDPS in sports contexts, from foundational design and cross-sector integration to advanced topics such as federated learning, quantum resilience, and AI-based cyber forensics. It has also emphasized the need for collaboration among technology leaders, policymakers, and sports administrators to ensure that security does not come at the expense of fairness, transparency, or fan trust.

As the future of sports evolves into digital twins, immersive metaverses, and AI-powered performance environments, cybersecurity must become a strategic pillar, embedded across every layer of the enterprise. Securing the sports economy is no longer about protecting systems; it is about preserving the very spirit of competition, integrity, and global connectedness that makes sport a universal force for good.

ACKNOWLEDGEMENT

No Large Language Model (LLM) has been used for the generation of this content. However, *Grammarly* was utilized solely for the purpose of refining English language and grammar.

REFERENCES

Ahmad, T. (2025, May 21). *AI-Driven Dynamic firewall optimization using reinforcement learning for anomaly detection and prevention*. arXiv.org. https://arxiv.org/abs/2506.05356 DOI: 10.36227/techrxiv.174952992.29897123/v1

Biometric Data and Privacy Laws (GDPR, CCPA/CPRA). (2021, June 16). Thales. https://www.thalesgroup.com/en/markets/digital-identity-and-security/government/biometrics/biometric-data

Carrio, A. Pompeu Fabra University, Barcelona School of Management, & The IOC Olympic Studies Centre. (2023). The Ethics of AI in Sport. Taking athletes' rights and wellbeing seriously. In *Technical Report*. https://www.researchgate.net/publication/375278970

Chinamanagonda, S. (2023). Automating Incident Response in DevOps - Automated incident response mechanisms in DevOps workflows. *International Journal of Novel Research and Development*, *8*(10), e154–e156. https://www.ijnrd.org/papers/IJNRD2310419.pdf

CROWDSTRIKE 2024 THREAT HUNTING REPORT. (n.d.). https://www.googleadservices.com/pagead/aclk?sa=L&ai=DChsSEwiTn92AutWOAxW_p2YCHfRJDOQYACICCAEQABoCc20&co=1&ase=2&gclid=Cj0KCQjws4fEBhD-ARIsACC3d2-r9JyjPUGiOaumcgOT_DPDd6sOCHvCDkI6px1bBD-hFCfKQPQDwvoaAhJBEALw_wcB&ohost=www.google.com&cid=CAESVeD2jnv3zPM4NSCKCPOsA6P95dn_qB2o3i50Am1WsbGZHT2eUw64-54Ooo5CNbwS41iBRLTbgX5jMxjVrbpoFHAy2Pfro9XV1sk299VKdQQwWliwcE4&category=acrcp_v1_40&sig=AOD64_2_Ca7swzJvqlITfZMZQnNFSwdDfA&q&nis=4&adurl&ved=2ahUKEwiS-teAutWOAxX01DgGHTiUFMsQ0Qx6BAgaEAE

Damage to brand or reputation top risk for the sports and entertainment industry. (n.d.). https://aon.co.za/insights/damage-to-brand-or-reputation-top-risk-for-the-sports-and-entertainment-industry/

Di Simone, L., & Zanardi, D. (2020). On the relationship between sport and financial performances: An empirical investigation. *Managerial Finance, 47*(6), 812–824. DOI: 10.1108/MF-09-2020-0478

Fan Data: Personalized Fan Engagement | Deloitte US. (2025, July 4). Deloitte. https://www.deloitte.com/us/en/services/consulting/articles/personalized-fan-engagement.html

Future-Proof Your Security: Actionable Quantum-Safe Solutions for 2025 | FutureX. (2025, February 28). Futurex. https://www.googleadservices.com/pagead/aclk?sa=L&ai=DChsSEwiZ6tqVutWOAxXEo2YCHWLLCrQYACICCAEQAxoCc20&co=1&ase=2&gclid=Cj0KCQjws4fEBhD-ARIsACC3d29Qt6Amcw3IEn7rFUXgJ97XjYunH1GVl56E_p6_SYl7xeUr1DoY7oAaAsIYEALw_wcB&ohost=www.google.com&cid=CAESVeD2IPG2tckLvB3ThvHG_-PagpjXeTk_gQy3FDAjF2BSIBcb0JJjWhecgG6THHTe1h-h6WoUJFyqJ1FDvS0tJZmwMG7EF3zYk-EJolfrVcg8e1Rsj9g&category=acrcp_v1_40&sig=AOD64_1KH4QBqFejYMzpgwhOLR5df_4liw&q&nis=4&adurl&ved=2ahUKEwjo59WVutWOAxUt2DgGHex8DKoQ0Qx6BAgLEAE

Gatlan, S. (2019, December 20). Tokyo 2020 Staff warns of phishing disguised as official emails. *BleepingComputer*. https://www.bleepingcomputer.com/news/security/tokyo-2020-staff-warns-of-phishing-disguised-as-official-emails/

GeeksforGeeks. (2025, July 12). *What is DDoS(Distributed Denial of Service)?* GeeksforGeeks. https://www.geeksforgeeks.org/computer-networks/what-is-ddosdistributed-denial-of-service/

Greenberg, A. (2018, February 12). "Olympic Destroyer" malware hit Pyeongchang ahead of opening ceremony. *WIRED*. https://www.wired.com/story/olympic-destroyer-malware-pyeongchang-opening-ceremony

Greenberg, A., & Excerpt. (2019, October 17). Inside Olympic Destroyer, the most deceptive hack in history. *WIRED*. https://www.wired.com/story/untold-story-2018-olympics-destroyer-cyberattack/

How data privacy compliance strategies can mitigate cyber threats. (2024, August 5). Thomson Reuters Legal. https://legal.thomsonreuters.com/en/insights/articles/understanding-data-privacy-a-compliance-strategy-can-mitigate-cyber-threats

Hunker, J. Jeffrey Hunker Associates LLC, Probst, C. W., & Technical University of Denmark. (n.d.). Insiders and insider threats. In *Journal of Wireless Mobile Networks, Ubiquitous Computing, and Dependable Applications* (Vols. 2–2, pp. 4–27). https://isyou.info/jowua/papers/jowua-v2n1-1.pdf

Ingle, S. (2017, November 27). Wada cyber attack: Williams sisters and Simone Biles targeted by Russian group. *The Guardian*. https://www.theguardian.com/sport/2016/sep/13/wada-russian-cyber-attack-espionage-group?utm_source=chatgpt.com

Jnguyen. (2023, June 5). *Ransomware Attack - What is it and How Does it Work?* Check Point Software. https://www.checkpoint.com/cyber-hub/threat-prevention/ransomware/

Kim, J., Kim, J., Kang, H., & Youn, B. (2025). Ethical implications of artificial intelligence in sport: A systematic scoping review. *Journal of Sport and Health Science. Journal of Sport and Health Science, 101047*, 101047. Advance online publication. DOI: 10.1016/j.jshs.2025.101047 PMID: 40316133

Korea JoongAng Daily. (2024, March 13). *Faker's League of Legends team the latest victim of DDoS attack.* https://koreajoongangdaily.joins.com/news/2024-03-13/business/industry/Fakers-League-of-Legends-team-the-latest-victim-of-DDoS-attack/2000553

KYODO NEWS. (2025, May 15). Phishing scam on Tokyo 2020 Olympics tickets spotted. *Japan Wire by KYODO NEWS*. https://english.kyodonews.net/articles/-/7784

Liang, X. (2025). Smart stadiums and the future of sports entertainment: Leveraging IoT, AI, and blockchain for enhanced fan engagement and venue management. *Applied and Computational Engineering, 138*(1), 155–160. DOI: 10.54254/2755-2721/2025.21386

Malik, P., Shahdadpuri, P., Malviya, R., Patil, R., Badwaniya, V., & Rudra Sthapak. (2024). Biometric data analysis in Athlete Monitoring: advancements, applications, and implications. *International Journal of Innovative Research in Technology, 10*(12). https://www.researchgate.net/publication/381160736

Mohamed, N. (2025). Artificial intelligence and machine learning in cybersecurity: A deep dive into state-of-the-art techniques and future paradigms. *Knowledge and Information Systems, 67*(8), 6969–7055. Advance online publication. DOI: 10.1007/s10115-025-02429-y

Nexusgroup. (2024, September 6). *How to build a secure IoT infrastructure | Nexus Group*. https://www.nexusgroup.com/how-to-build-a-secure-iot-infrastructure/

Ogundairo, O. Ladoke Akintola University of Technology, & Broklyn, P. (2024). Predictive analytics for cyber threat intelligence. *Journal of Cyber Security*. https://www.researchgate.net/publication/382918018

Pickman, D. (2023). The use of virtual reality and augmented reality in enhancing the sports viewing experience. *International Journal of Arts Recreation and Sports, 1*(2), 39–49. DOI: 10.47941/ijars.1516

Purdum, D. (2022, December 20). Cyberattack breaches DraftKings, FanDuel users - ESPN. *ESPN.com.* https://www.espn.com/sports-betting/story/_/id/35291945/draftkings-fanduel-breached-cyberattack

R, A., R, A., & R, A. (2025, February 11). Fake Premiere League ticket scams (Campaign). *CyberMaterial - Security Through Data.* https://cybermaterial.com/fake-premiere-league-ticket-scams-campaign/

Raghavan, S. S. (2025). A COMPREHENSIVE STUDY OF ARTIFICIAL INTELLIGENCE APPLICATIONS IN INTRUSION DETECTION AND PREVENTION. [IJAIRD]. *International Journal of Artificial Intelligence Research and Development, 3*(1), 16–37. DOI: 10.34218/IJAIRD_03_01_002

Real-time threat detection strategies for resource-constrained devices. (n.d.). https://arxiv.org/html/2403.15078v1

Reddy, V. Y., Reddy, N. H. V., Adithya, T. J., & Ramesh, K. (2024). Intrusion Detection and Prevention System. In Hyderabad Institute of Technology and Management, *International Journal of Innovative Research in Technology* (Vol. 11, Issue 6) [Journal-article]. https://ijirt.org/publishedpaper/IJIRT169653_PAPER.pdf

Reporter, G. S. (2016, July 18). Former Cardinals scouting director jailed for hacking Astros' player database. *The Guardian.* https://www.theguardian.com/sport/2016/jul/18/st-louis-cardinals-hacking-houston-astros-jail-sentence

Richards, J. (n.d.). *Market segmentation and target marketing in sport.* Sports Marketing. https://westernsydney.pressbooks.pub/sportmarketing/chapter/market-segmentation-and-target-marketing-in-sport/

RiftFeed. (2024, June 10). League of Legends: Riot releases statement regarding DDOS attacks. *RiftFeed.* https://riftfeed.gg/lol-news/league-of-legends-riot-releases-statement-regarding-ddos-attacks

Santomier, J. P. (2024). Digital transformation: the global sport industry. In *Elsevier eBooks.* DOI: 10.1016/B978-0-443-13701-3.00209-7

Scalability of ecosystem architectures. (2014, April 1). IEEE Conference Publication | IEEE Xplore. https://ieeexplore.ieee.org/document/6827099/

Scams and fraud | Own Your Online. (n.d.). Own Your Online. https://www.ownyouronline.govt.nz/personal/know-the-risks/common-risks-and-threats/scams-and-fraud/

Scroxton, A. (2020, November 23). Manchester United praised for swift response to cyber attack. *ComputerWeekly.com*. https://www.computerweekly.com/news/252492512/Manchester-United-praised-for-swift-response-to-cyber-attack

Sil, S., Datta, I., & Basu, S. (2025). Use of AI-methods over MD simulations in the sampling of conformational ensembles in IDPs. *Frontiers in Molecular Biosciences*, *12*, 1542267. Advance online publication. DOI: 10.3389/fmolb.2025.1542267 PMID: 40264953

Staff, A. (2024, August 13). *Data governance in healthcare*. Arcadia. https://arcadia.io/resources/data-governance-in-healthcare

Tang, M., Nikolaenko, M., Alrefai, A., & Kumar, A. (2025). Metaverse and digital twins in the age of AI and extended reality. *Architecture (Washington, D.C.)*, *5*(2), 36. DOI: 10.3390/architecture5020036

University of Oxford's Researcher Strategy Consultancy, NCC Group. Phoenix Sport & Media Group, Lewis, M., & Barnes, C. (2026). The hidden opponent: CyberTheats in sport. In *The Hidden Opponent: CyberTheats in Sport*. https://www.nccgroup.com/media/zugjppis/cyber-threats-in-sport-whitepaper_final.pdf

Vaiyyali, C. K. (2024). Technology in sports event management. In International Journal of Research Publication and Reviews [Journal-article]. *International Journal of Research Publication and Reviews*, *5*(7), 5035–5038.

West Ham supporters have data leaked by club website. (2021, March 12). IT Security Guru. https://www.itsecurityguru.org/2021/03/12/west-ham-supporters-have-data-leaked-by-club-website/

What is a Data Breach & How to Prevent Data Leaks. (2025, February 26). /. https://www.kaspersky.com/resource-center/definitions/data-breach

What is AI bias? Causes, effects, and mitigation strategies | SAP. (n.d.). https://www.sap.com/resources/what-is-ai-bias

What is Real-Time Threat Intelligence? - Logsign. (n.d.). Logsign. https://www.logsign.com/blog/what-is-real-time-threat-intelligence/

Zhan, S., Huang, L., Luo, G., Zheng, S., Gao, Z., & Chao, H. (2025). A review on Federated Learning Architectures for Privacy-Preserving AI: Lightweight and Secure Cloud–Edge–End Collaboration. *Electronics (Basel)*, *14*(13), 2512. DOI: 10.3390/electronics14132512

Chapter 11
AI-Enhanced Fraud Detection in Banking and E-Commerce

Ashok Koujalag
Shri Vishnu Engineering College for Women, India

T. Eswaran
T.S.M. Jain College of Technology, India

Amit Subramanyam
Rani Channamma University, India

Isa Bayhan
Bolu Abant Izzet Baysal University, Turkey

Varun Tiwari
Don Bosco Institute of Technology, India

Trinkul Kalita
http://orcid.org/0009-0006-4996-9738
Assam Down Town University, India

S. Bala Krishnan
http://orcid.org/0009-0000-9391-4458
Vaagai International Publishing House, India

ABSTRACT

The study proposes ways that businesses might integrate AI with their fraud detection systems, as well as future improvements that can be made to these solutions. This study shows how AI can affect the industry's future and contributes to what is already known about AI's effects on banking and security. When faced with the sheer magnitude and complexity of today's challenges, traditional rule-based fraud detection systems frequently fall short. One game-changing strategy for fighting fraud is AI which uses cutting-edge ML, DL and NLP approaches. This section delves into the function of AI in detecting fraud, how it improves monitoring and decision-making in real-time, and the ways it has been applied in e-commerce and

DOI: 10.4018/979-8-3373-5223-7.ch011

banking. Emerging technologies such as FL graph NN and blockchain-integrated AI systems are discussed towards the conclusion, after issues like explainability, data privacy and adversarial attacks have been addressed.

1. INTRODUCTION

Web-based methods are gradually replacing the more conventional method of paying with cash in business transactions due to the proliferation of e-commerce platforms. Online shopping, in contrast to the entity economy, has been relatively unscathed by the COVID-19 pandemic which has contributed to the industry's consistent development. By 2023, the predicted sales volume of business-to-consumer (B2C) e-commerce is $6.50 trillion. New security risks have arisen in recent years, despite the fact that e-commerce and contemporary technology are growing and providing improved chances for online firms. Online fraud has reportedly increased at an alarming rate, costing billions of dollars annually around the world year. To guarantee the safety of online transactions, anti-fraud measures are essential due to the decentralised and ever-changing structure of the Internet (Rana, 2019). In the face of new security risks, current fraud detection systems that rely on user behaviour anomalies still have holes. Lack of effective process control throughout the trading process is a major flaw in current fraud detection systems. One of the most pressing problems that requires fixing is the flawed monitoring feature. Because current work does not incorporate process capture, the detection perspective is often insufficient. It offers a process-based approach that records and analyses user actions in real-time and turns past data into controllable data to achieve this goal. Furthermore, it integrate a multi-view anomaly detection system (Poudel & Dhungana, 2022).

2. TYPES OF FRAUD

The telecommunications, credit card, computer, bankruptcy, theft, counterfeit, application, and behavioural fraud types all come into play when it comes to e-commerce fraud (Prabin Adhikari et al., 2024)V.

Credit Card Fraud: There are two main categories of credit card fraud: offline and online.

- **Offline Fraud:** The use of a counterfeit or stolen physical card in any setting is offline fraud.
- **Online Fraud:** It occurs when a person does a fraudulent act through the use of the internet, phone or web (P. Kamuangu, 2024).

Behavioral Fraud: Behavioural fraud occurs when legitimate card details are fraudulently obtained and orders are placed based on these details.

Counterfeit and Theft Fraud: It is theft if the utilised cards do not belong to you. When the owner contacts the bank with feedback, the bank will take steps to verify the thief. Similarly, credit card fraud can occur when the card is used remotely. No physical cards or signatures are needed when using your codes on different websites using copied card numbers (Raghuwanshi, 2024).

Computer Intrusion: Intrusion is defined as the unannounced entry of any person or entity not authorised to be there, including hackers and insiders who are familiar with the inner workings of a system or environment. This indicates that there is a possibility of unauthorised attempt to access information, manipulate information purposefully (P. K. Kamuangu, 2024).

Application Fraud: When someone applies for a credit card using incorrect information, this is called application fraud. Application duplication where two or more users submit the same information or identity fraud where two or more users submit the same information are two ways that applications might be detected (Tariqul Islam et al., 2024).

Bankruptcy Fraud: When a bank sends an order to a customer, the user can be committing personal bankruptcy fraud, which is hard to predict. Unwanted loans can become more difficult to obtain. Checking your credit report in advance is one step you can take to protect yourself against this type of fraud. This provided details regarding the clients' banking histories (Jahan Sarna et al., 2025).

Telecommunication Fraud: The term telecommunication fraud refers to the intentional misuse of mobile phone and fixed line services with the goal to cause harm to another party.

3. CHALLENGES IN FRAUD DETECTION

It begins by outlining the empirical difficulties associated with ML fraud detection.

3.1 Challenges Unique to ML and Accounting Fraud

Aside from these broad worries, there may be more particular problems with certain forms of fraud. In order to illustrate problems unique to this field it zero in on accounting fraud. To begin, it can take quite a while for instances of accounting fraud to be noticed, if they are ever noticed at all. The majority of credit card scams are easy to see, and it's usually not hard to figure out whether fraud has occurred following a complaint. Contrarily, it sometimes takes substantial investigative efforts to determine whether or not accounting fraud has occurred, and it may be difficult to tell the difference between inventive but legal techniques and fraud. There is a dearth of models that take the possibility that fraud may go undiscovered into account. Additionally, authorities frequently uncover instances of accounting fraud. However, victims of other forms of fraud may be able to spot it. Models for detecting fraud will be inaccurate and prejudiced to the degree that regulators are both (Hashemi et al., 2023).

One example is that the SEC only finds approximately half of the cases of serious financial reporting violations. In less developed nations with weaker institutional frameworks, this problem is probably even worse. The second point is that companies often skew their financial records for a number of years before the truth comes out. When developing their models, the majority of current fraud prediction research ignore this particular aspect of serial fraud. Not realising that serial fraud cases depend on time series, they instead tend to view each firm-year as an independent observation. Researchers have found ways to avoid this problem in studies that examine serial fraud. Some studies like use only the first fraudulent year. Others, like eliminate serial fraud observations in the training or test years. Finally, accounting fraud behaviour shows regime shifts both cross-sectionally and over time because managerial incentives and monitoring intensity vary with time. It found that accounting fraud occurs at different rates in different types of businesses. Existing models for predicting accounting fraud have not included such changes in the development of regimes, with the exception of (Yu et al., 2024).

3.2 Fraud Issues and ML Issues in General

To begin, instances of fraud that have been ultimately identified are quite uncommon. Credit card fraud, for instance, was less than 0.1 percent in the United States in 2015. Since the goal of most machine-learning algorithms is to maximise accuracy and minimise error, it is optimal for them to operate with roughly equal numbers of samples in each class. Algorithms struggle to learn from truly imbalanced samples because they seldom meet instances of fraud. The current body of literature is cognisant of this issue and has employed a variety of approaches to address it (Goriparthi, 2024). To continue, deceit is an aggressive crime. Stable patterns and the absence or manipulation of critical data make machine-learning algorithms perform best. Many ML applications involve stakeholders that are either neutral towards the system or actively work with it to improve its learning capabilities (e.g., in medical applications). The goal of those who commit fraud is to thwart education. One tactic used by fraudsters to evade network analysis is to open accounts in many financial institutions located in different jurisdictions. On top of that, con artists are always coming up with new ideas. Algorithms may thus be unable to identify novel forms of fraud if no such precedence exists (Bello & Olufemi, 2024).

4. AI-BASED TECHNIQUES IN DETECTING FINANCIAL FRAUD

There is strong evidence that AI will play a revolutionary role in the fight against and detection of financial fraud, and this has sparked extensive discussion and evaluation of AI-based approaches in this area across many different industries. Among the several research that were considered found that banking fraud has been drastically decreased using AI technologies. Financial transactions may be analysed in real-time by these AI-driven platforms, which can spot questionable activity that rule-based systems could miss. AI systems excel in large-scale banking operations due to their data processing speed and accuracy, which helps identify fraud trends that would be hard to uncover using traditional approaches. A number of industries, including healthcare, banking, and insurance, have benefited from AI-driven fraud detection, according to research such as (Lai, 2023). ML and anomaly detection methods allow AI systems in various areas to detect and flag suspected fraudulent actions more accurately than manual systems by identifying tiny deviations from regular transactional patterns. AI methods, such as NN and DL have prevented healthcare organisations from losing a tonne of money due to insurance fraud (Hafez et al., 2025).

These findings highlight how AI may be used in different industries, making it a flexible tool to fight fraud in complicated settings with a lot of data. Particularly useful in the banking industry has been the application of DL models for the purpose of detecting credit card fraud. For example, demonstrated a substantial enhancement in the accuracy of fraud detection by using the AE algorithm to identify unusual financial transactions. When it comes to transactional data, DL models—made to learn from complicated datasets—are great at finding hidden patterns that can suggest fraud. Because of this, they are significantly more effective than conventional models, which frequently use restrictions that fraudsters may readily circumvent (Adijat Bello et al., 2023). Credit card transactions are examples of fast-paced environments where fraudulent behaviour evolves quickly, making it important for AI systems to continuously learn and adapt to new fraud trends. AI fraud detection methods have demonstrated great promise in the insurance industry for detecting false claims. In order to identify questionable actions like insurance fraud and money laundering investigated how to visualise transactional links using graph analytics and ML.

Figure 1. Overview of an AI-Driven Fraud Detection System

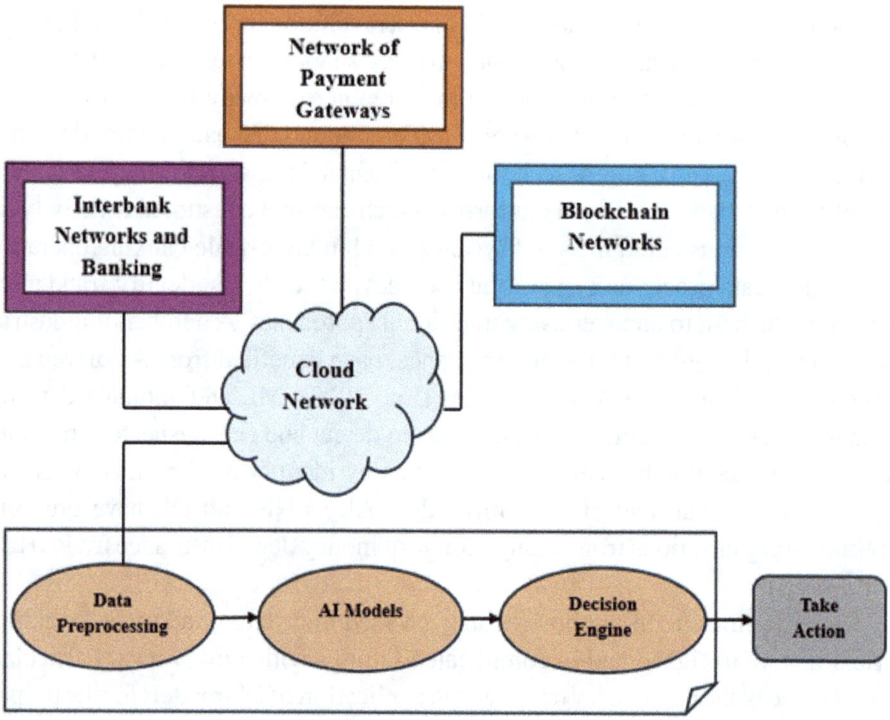

The growing need for trustworthy, scalable, and intelligent technology to safeguard the international monetary system is ultimately addressed. Although this study primarily aims to examine AI methods for financial fraud detection, there have been recent developments in the field that have attracted attention, such as model security, ownership verification, and intellectual property protection, especially in FL and edge AI contexts. A high-level perspective of the AI-powered fraud detection system is displayed in Figure 1 (Faisal et al., 2024).

To better identify multi-party complicated fraud schemes, AI systems can use graph analytics to draw a picture of the interconnections between all the nodes in a transaction network. This approach works wonders in the insurance industry, because valid claims can mask fraudulent actions, making sophisticated data analysis tools necessary to uncover the truth. The healthcare industry has also profited greatly from fraud detection systems based on AI just like the banking and insurance sectors. Anomaly detection and DL are two examples of AI methods that have improved healthcare fraud detection (Olufemi, 2024). Because of the high volume of personal and financial information they manage, healthcare institutions are easy prey for scammers. AI capacity to analyse large datasets for anomalies in insurance claims, patient information, and billing has helped reduce fraud in this industry. Additionally, healthcare organisations may lessen the financial hit from fraudulent claims and improve data security by incorporating AI into fraud detection solutions. AI has the potential to greatly improve fraud detection, but there are still obstacles to overcome. When faced with sophisticated cyberattacks found that conventional AI models were inadequate. AI works wonders when it comes to plain old fraud, but it may have trouble keeping up with more complex hacks that use AI and ML to stay undetected. AI-driven systems should be regularly updated to address new and changing cybersecurity threats, according to study (Osarense Dorothy Iguodala & Aghogho Oyiborhoro, 2025).

The effectiveness of AI in detecting fraud relies on ongoing innovation and algorithm modification, as seen below (Osarense Dorothy Iguodala & Aghogho Oyiborhoro, 2025). Research by private sector financial services sector proved that AI is successful in detecting fraud. The authors demonstrated the usefulness of AI-based fraud detection systems by integrating survey data with expert interviews to draw out qualitative findings. Financial institutions have seen improvements in operational security and efficiency in fraud prevention as a consequence of AI's capacity to automate and streamline fraud detection operations. On the other hand, the study found that AI performance is highly dependent on the data quality that is utilised to train the systems, highlighting the significance of accurate and reliable data for getting the best outcomes (Lin, 2024). By presenting a thorough framework for combining AI with ML to strengthen the financial cybersecurity infrastructure of the US provided a more holistic view of the efficacy of AI-based fraud detection systems. Their research proved that financial institutions can save money by preventing fraud by using AI's predictive ability to spot suspicious activity in advance. AI solutions can help financial institutions respond proactively to threats by providing early alerts of suspicious activity through anomaly detection and predictive analytics.

AI is essential to risk management methods in general and to fraud detection in particular, according to research by (Luo et al., 2025). In addition, as discussed by the ethics of AI-driven fraud detection also influence its level of effectiveness. While AI is great at spotting fraud, the authors said that in order to make it a success in the long run, we need to fix ethical issues including data privacy, algorithmic bias, and lack of transparency. The reliability of the financial system is at risk when AI models make decisions in a biassed or opaque manner, which in turn reduces the usefulness of these technologies. AI systems need to be built with ethical principles in mind so they can continue to be effective and legitimate in the eyes of stakeholders. The ability of AI-based systems to adapt has been a key component in their effectiveness, to conclude (Islam et al., 2024).

The significance of self-learning AI systems in identifying fraud was highlighted in particular into dynamic industries such as online banking and e-commerce. In order to combat new forms of fraud, self-learning systems are superior since they update their algorithms in real-time using data that is constantly being collected. The ability of AI systems to adapt guarantees their long-term effectiveness, especially in the face of evolving fraudster tactics that circumvent conventional security measures (Adijat et al., 2023). AI fraud detection systems can adapt to the dynamic nature of the internet by incorporating self-learning capabilities. Finally, in several fields, like healthcare, banking, and insurance, AI-based methods have been quite successful in identifying instances of financial fraud. AI adaptability, especially its capacity to process massive datasets and learn from new patterns in real time, makes it a crucial tool for contemporary fraud prevention. To keep AI systems reliable and productive, however, it must solve problems like sophisticated cyberattacks and ethical concerns. Institutions and individuals will be even better protected from financial fraud as AI develops further and plays an increasingly larger role in this area (Adijat et al., 2023).

5. AI TECHNIQUES FOR FRAUD DETECTION

The goal of financial fraud detection is to detect suspicious activity by analysing data for trends and outliers using various AI and ML techniques. Data type, intended level of accuracy, and computational efficiency are all factors to be considered when choosing a method (Al-Fatlawi et al., 2024). Important AI and ML techniques used in cutting-edge research are as follows:

5.1 Supervised Learning Algorithms

Supervised learning algorithms are the masterminds behind the complex web of financial fraud detection. The nuanced training data, patterns, and well-orchestrated forecasts are the building blocks upon which their symphony rests. Imagine a musical composition made of historical facts, with each instance represented by the keys false or legitimate (Yuhertiana & Hadi Amin, 2024). The algorithms are able to transcend into the domain of generalisation with an ear that is perfectly attuned to these notes, and they are skilled at spotting harmonious patterns in fresh transactions.

GBM: As the sequence of ensemble learning reaches its climax, GBM is at the forefront, assembling a cohesive group of amateurs. As GBM improves with each new model, it becomes an expert at catching complex patterns in a dance where outliers are difficult to spot. Despite its impressive predictive accuracy and non-linear correlations, it is important to be cautious while tweaking hyperparameters to avoid overfitting (Johora et al., 2024). The majesty it brings to the stage is diminished by the time and computational resources needed for training.

LR: LR distinguishes between fraudulent and non-fraudulent entities, making it a soloist in the binary classification symphony. This program simulates the likelihood of a transaction being part of a particular class like a virtuoso. It transforms the linear combination of variables into a melodic probability score by utilising a LR. Although it is easy to understand and uses little processing power, it may fail to capture the complexities of non-linear patterns since it presupposes a linear relationship.

RF and DT: A tree-like ballet develops as you enter the whimsical forest of DT where data is partitioned. A big ensemble known as random forests waltzes in to improve forecast accuracy and shield models from overfitting. Interpretable and flexible decision trees gracefully traverse numerical and categorical domains, revealing the complex dance of decision boundaries. On the one hand DT can overfit and on the other RF provide complexity, which can make the dance seem like a masquerade.

SVM: SVM's strong suit in the binary ballet of fraud detection—constructing hyperplanes in high-dimensional spaces—in action. Using a tango of complicated decision boundaries SVM create robust separation by seeking the hyperplane that maximizes the margin (Yadav, 2023). A high-dimensional space virtuoso with kernel techniques for non-linear tales, however its performance might be a bit shaky when dealing with bigger datasets due to processing needs and kernel choices.

5.2 Unsupervised Learning Methods

The assistance of labelled instances, unsupervised learning algorithms must traverse the complex data web in order to uncover anomalies, setting off on the perilous path of financial fraud detection. Within this underground labyrinth of unsupervised learning approaches, it encounters fraudulent events that hide in rarity and weave mysterious patterns. The following covert operatives will take you on an exhilarating journey:

DBSCAN: It has DBSCAN, the nimble investigator of data dense regions, defining normalcy and classifying points residing in the empty spaces as noise or outliers. Envision it reading the clustering language in typical transactions and revealing the identity of the data points that dared to diverge. DBSCAN is shape-blind and doesn't care what order the input data is in (Onuh Matthew Ijiga et al., 2024). But be wary of the hyperparameter domain, and the density threshold in particular, where the equilibrium between struggle and revelation is delicate.

Clustering Conundrum: Clustering algorithms, such as the mysterious K-Means, set out on a quest to form alliances among similar instances, deciphering the coded messages encoded in the patterns intrinsic to the data. K Means could be a secret spy who is good at finding patterns of unusual transactions that could lead to the discovery of fraud. It requires the foreknowledge of cluster count (k) while functioning in the background of computational simplicity and efficiency. Exercise caution, as extreme cases may obscure its true capabilities.

AE: The brain masterminds behind intrigue, autoencoders, compose a neural network symphony to decipher the hidden representations in the data. When it comes to detecting fraud, these agents are pros at recreating typical transactions and spotting outliers that contradict the planned harmony. Finding subtle patterns and casting large nets, autoencoders waltz through the domains of non-linear interactions. Be warned, though; deep training may send you plunging into the abyss, and tweaking their architecture and hyperparameters requires a sacrifice of computational resources.

Isolation Forests: Envision Isolation Forests as the sole watchdogs in the universe of anomaly detection, equipped with the conviction that abnormalities are more likely to be exposed than the usual. These watchful trees are masters in the vastness of high-dimensional areas at detecting anomalies, especially those that give off an air of deceit. Operating under the principles of efficiency, scalability, and a mentality that does not care about shape, they have proven to be durable in the face of the outlier attack (Benedek & Nagy, 2023). But watch out: their mettle is put to the test when you choose your hyperparameters, and unbalanced datasets might cause chaos.

5.3 Ensemble Methods

By coordinating a broad ensemble of models, ensemble methods perform a predictive symphony, making them the true masters of financial fraud detection. Imagine a convergence of three distinct but complementary algorithms, such as LR, DT and SVM; their individual melodies will eventually build to a symphony of collective intelligence.

RF: The towering ensemble of decision trees that protects fraud detection from deceit reaches deep into intricate patterns and interconnections. A lush canopy of resilience protects from the debilitating consequences of overfitting. Their waltz partner is interpretability, and they dance along complicated choice boundaries while embracing numerical and categorical qualities, which is their anthem. In this grove of perfection, though, the druid's ritual for peak performance involves adjusting hyperparameters, in pursuit of that illusive harmony between maximum depth and tree density.

Voting Classifiers: Both soft voting, in which averaged probabilities are harmoniously combined, and hard voting, in which the majority vote resounds, are used by the democratic decision-makers in a ballet of decisions. The fraud detection landscape is like a waltz, with different base models dancing together to form a complex tapestry of stability and precision. The voting classifier's beauty is in its ability to synthesise the many models' predictions into a single, accurate one, as well as in its computing efficiency and relative simplicity (Lee et al., 2025). On the other hand, if the base models all sound the same, the ensemble might lose its magical sparkle.

GBM: As features compete for prominence in the orchestration of power, the sequential sorcerers conjure an ensemble through sequential learning, with each model correcting the mistakes of its predecessors. GBM's magical wand captures subtle patterns in fraud detection, meticulously crafting predictive tapestries. High predictive accuracy becomes the crown jewel, vigilantly guarding against the perils of overfitting, but tuning hyperparameters demands computational resources.

Stacking: In fraud detection, stacking plays the role of a curator of diversity, combining decision trees with NN to achieve predictive alchemy. Its flexibility allows it to adapt to data intricacies, but it comes at the cost of potential complexity. Choosing base models is like choosing instruments for a grand concerto, and the architect's dream involves assembling a gallery of models, each contributing a stroke to the validation set's predictions. The meta-model then conducts a symphonic synthesis, crafting the final decision with the finesse of a virtuoso (Smith & Lamprecht, 2025).

5.4 DL Approaches

DL algorithms have emerged as powerful tools in the challenging field of financial fraud detection, adeptly navigating complex transactional data. These approaches use multi-layered NN architectures to decipher anomalies and mysterious patterns. Along this journey, it will explore the maze of important DL methods that shed light on the world of financial fraud detection:

LSTM and RNN: Networks excel in time-series or sequential transactions because of their ability to manage sequential dependencies. In the grand scheme of things, RNNs and LSTMs navigate the complexities of time to reveal patterns that emerge throughout sequences of transactions, which aids in the identification of fraud. Highly skilled at detecting complex interdependencies, these experts excel in ever-changing fraud situations (Bao et al., 2020). Still, they must traverse computational domains on their training journey, where solving the problems of disappearing and exploding gradients is crucial to stability.

NN: NN the building blocks of DL are like a symphony of interconnected neurones; they use multiple layers of input data to deduce hierarchical properties. NN are quite versatile, and can easily switch between supervised and unsupervised jobs when it comes to fraud detection. Their ability to deftly navigate complex fraud patterns is a result of their mastery of non-linear relationship capture. Their talent is in their capacity to understand intricate patterns, which reverberates across many forms of financial data. Because training them requires a sacrifice of significant computer +resources, it is important to determine the optimal combination of layers and neurones.

AE: Under the radar of unsupervised learning, autoencoders sneak up on input data and secretly encode and decode it. They take comfort in anomaly detection inside the fraud detection tapestry, mastering the skill of restoring normalcy while drawing attention to outliers. Their quest for minor abnormalities evolves as an unsupervised journey, a symphony of capturing non-linear interactions (Chen et al., 2025). Their training betrays tales of computational capability, and their architecture and hyperparameters require careful tuning, all as members of the DL ensemble.

CNN: Sequential data, like the rhythm of time-series transactions, reverberates with the image-centric domain virtuosos. CNN play a key role in the fraud detection orchestra by gleaning temporal and spatial insights from transaction data. CNN demonstrate their expertise in learning hierarchical representations by utilising the outlines of relationships and order as its canvas. Preprocessing and shaping input data requires precise choreography as they navigate spatial dependencies. Because peak brilliance necessitates massive datasets, this performance calls for a vast stage.

6. CASE STUDY

Financial fraud, terror financing, and organised crime operations have all been successfully detected and disrupted through the integration of cloud-native AI-based fraud detection systems. This section showcases practical instances and uses of AI that have significantly improved U.S. capabilities in the areas of national security and law enforcement (Thammareddi et al., 2023).

6.1 Disrupting an International Money Laundering Scheme

Context: In order to conceal their illegal assets, organised criminal syndicates frequently use complex money laundering methods that include dummy businesses, offshore accounts, and cryptocurrency. A federal task force in the United States was able to track down and destroy a worldwide laundering network by using an AI solution that was native to the cloud.

AI Involvement:

- By sifting through millions of international money transfers, the AI system was able to spot suspicious trends, like regular payments to countries with lax oversight.
- Graph analytics discovered that money was being transferred from various shell firms to an offshore entity, which was eventually linked to drug cartels.

- The use of synthetic identities and stolen credentials to open fraudulent accounts was detected multiple times using AI-driven pattern detection.

Result:

- Law enforcement agencies confiscated more than $150 million in illegal monies.
- The operation resulted in the apprehension of senior syndicate members, disrupting a significant trafficking network across three continents.

Importance: This instance demonstrated how cloud-native AI can integrate different types of financial data, unearth hidden networks, and disrupt large-scale operations run by organised crime (Alonge et al., 2021).

6.2 Halting Terrorist Financing via Transaction Analysis

Context: In order to keep an eye out for possible ties to terrorist organisations, a top U.S. federal agency used a cloud-native AI fraud detection system to track massive financial transactions and international payments (Herath, 2025).

AI Involvement:

- A string of small wire transfers sent by an American account to a charity in a dangerous area were detected by the AI system.
- Behavioural research showed that the money transactions were systematic and recurring, which could be a sign of terrorist funding. People on the U.S.
- Terrorist Watchlist were found to have ties to the charity, according to graph analytics.

Result:

- Authorities from around the country worked together to seize funds, arrest people, and halt the charity's activities.
- Intercepting more than $5 million in terror funds stopped the monies from going to international extremist networks.

Importance:

In this instance, it saws how early disruption of terror financing may be achieved through AI-driven surveillance of financial flows, which in turn protects both national and international security (Ashe et al., 2024).

6.3 Federal Cooperation to Address Organised Crime

Context: A drug gang that used financial fraud to launder money and finance illicit activities was busted in a massive operation by the U.S. Treasury and the FBI.

AI Involvement:

- Abnormal transfers and asset flows were detected by analysing financial data across different institutions using a cloud-native AI technology.
- International money transfer services, shell corporations, and cartel operatives' secret relationships were exposed by graph analytics.
- Patterns connecting drug trafficking routes to financial fraud were discovered by predictive models.

Result:

- In the United States, Mexico, and South America, authorities apprehended several agents and frozen assets tied to the gang worth over $200 million.
- An important criminal network was broken up as a result of the operation, which stopped the influx of narcotics and illegal cash into the United States.

Importance:

In this instance, it saws how cloud-native AI facilitates coordination between departments and the tracking down of intricate fraud networks with ties to organised crime (Niek et al., 2021).

6.4 Identifying Synthetic Identify Fraud in American Financial Institutions

Context: The use of mixed-media identities, in which criminals use both actual and phoney details to build fictitious accounts, is a rapidly expanding financial crime in the United States. Massive losses occur at financial institutions, and many times these institutions unwittingly aid criminal networks (Mainul et al., 2025).

AI Involvement:

- Financial apps were monitored in real time by an AI platform that was native to the cloud. Any discrepancies between spending habits, credit histories, and social security numbers were detected.

- Synthetic profiles were detected by ML models that detected little changes from typical consumer behaviour, like using newly issued credit cards to their maximum limit in a matter of hours.
- A coordinated organisation connected to identity theft rings and human trafficking networks was identified as the perpetrator of the scam through predictive analytics.

Result:

- Financial institutions were able to avoid losses over $100 million due to the AI system's assistance in identifying and blocking over 30,000 phoney accounts.
- By sharing data with federal agencies, more investigations into identity theft and trafficking were able to be conducted, leading to the arrest of persons implicated.

Importance:

Identity fraud is a major source of funding for criminal organisations and the abuse of human beings. This example showed how cloud-native AI systems can address this problem in real-time with scalable, accurate solutions.

7. RESULTS AND DISCUSSION

In order to illustrate how effective a GBM model is and to highlight important contributing elements the results and discussion centre on its performance metrics which include accuracy, RMSE and MSE. The GBM model consistently outperforms the competition demonstrating exceptional high accuracy (97.86%) in challenging tasks such as depth estimate and forecasting. Results do show some possible issues though such as being sensitive to hyperparameter tuning overfitting being possible and computational expenditure for really huge datasets all of which call for optimisation and careful examination. GBM are now among the most popular and successful methods in ML. GBM are an ensemble learning method that is well-known for their accuracy and flexibility. In order to build a robust predictive model these models iteratively merge the results of weak learners typically DT. This article explores GBM in detail, covering its inner workings, pros, cons, and real-world applications.

Businesses' approaches to detecting and preventing fraud and financial risk, especially in the financial services industry, have been revolutionised by the integration of AI. As it has shown in the previous sections, AI technologies have not only revolutionised the way financial systems are managed, but they also offer improved accuracy rates, faster time to market, and more agile turnaround times. However, there are obstacles to overcome while implementing AI. In this section, it analyse the literature's conclusions, talk about the consequences for businesses and customers, and pinpoint where AI could make a huge difference (Perols, 2011). It also goes over the obstacles that could prevent financial services AI from reaching its full potential. Even with a modest dataset, human operators can be overwhelmed by the amount of data during peak periods. However, fraud detection systems enabled by AI can employ real-time processing to scan this enormous information and seek for anomalies that imply fraud. Without human intervention to update the rules, traditional rule-based systems will remain static and unresponsive to emerging fraud trends and strategies. Because AI models like NN and ML are always picking up new information, they can adapt to different types of fraud schemes and identify trends they weren't aware of before. Fraud detection rates on e-commerce platforms reach around 90% accuracy when AI capabilities are used to robustly estimate dynamic learning, according to the study by (Yaw Agyeman & Gbli Tetteh, 2024). This is in line with previous studies that demonstrate AI may improve the efficiency of fraud detection systems and decrease the number of false positives.

There are a lot of obstacles that need to be crossed before AI can be used for fraud detection and financial risk management, despite its obvious advantages. However, a major obstacle to AI deployment is the ethical considerations that come with it. As mentioned earlier, businesses and regulators alike are still grappling with issues like data privacy, algorithm bias, and transparency. For instance, AI systems that process a wide variety of personal and transactional data (such as that which is governed by GDPR regimes) present a significant privacy challenge (Husnaningtyas & Totok Dewayanto, 2023). This data typically includes extensive personal information about the data owner as well as individuals who transact within their community. Also, firms have a hard time explaining decision-making processes due to opaque DL algorithms used in these AI models; this creates problems with public trust and regulatory compliance (Wenyan Wu, 2024).

In order to tackle these issues, financial institutions should establish clear ethical guidelines, prioritise AI technology that can be explained, and ensure that their AI systems are open, equitable and responsible. Also, certain firms, especially smaller ones with fewer resources, may find it very difficult and expensive to use AI systems in the financial services industry. Nevertheless, AI technology can be too costly for small enterprises due to the extensive infrastructure investments, data management costs, and technical skills required (Razzaq, 2025). Because of the complexity of AI systems and the fact that most businesses rely on them, developing, deploying, and maintaining these systems calls for skilled data scientists and AI experts. When there isn't a big enough pool of AI experts, the situation can become more challenging. If banks and other financial institutions want to stay out of AI altogether, they'll need to form strategic alliances with outside suppliers or invest in training and development programs to attract and retain the necessary talent.

Increasing the number of repetitions and epochs would assist in reducing the performance mistakes. Each epoch concludes with a display of the testing and training losses. Finally, the test dataset's RMSE and MSE are shown. Figure 2 shows that the model obtains high RMSE and MSE as the number of epochs increases.

Figure 2. Performance of RMSE vs MSE

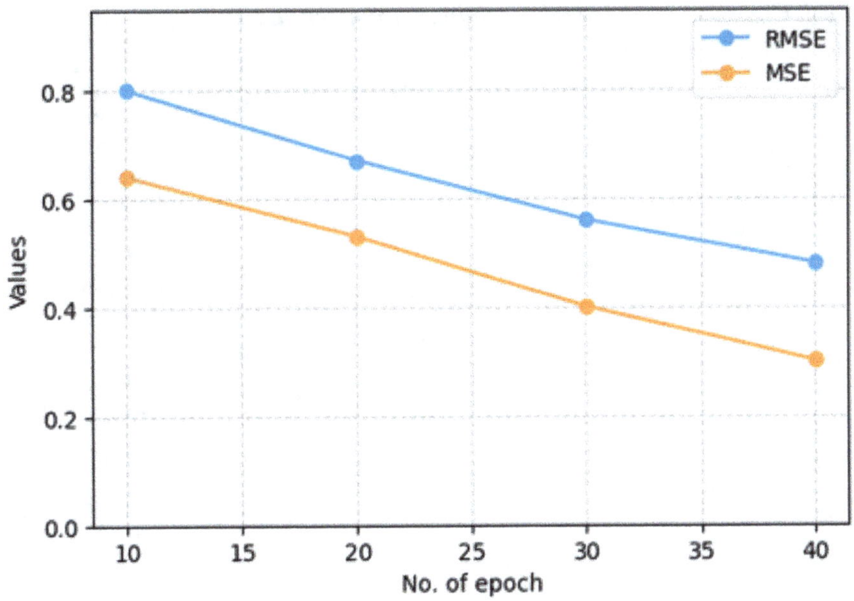

The Multiple SVM model achieved the lowest level of accuracy with an R2 value of 0.93 while the 0.97 GBM model achieved the highest level of accuracy with a value of 0.97, as shown in Table 1. Aside from multiple GBM all of the models are excellent predictors of future outcomes.

Table 1. Evaluation Metrics Estimation for the ML Algorithms

Models	MAE	R-Squared	RMSE
AE	0.69	0.962	0.72
SVM	0.53	0.930	0.67
LR	0.47	0.951	0.56
GBM	**0.30**	**0.975**	**0.48**

Figure 3 shows the net trajectory of training/testing errors after 50 iterations of testing for all models. The training/testing error was lower for GBM compared to AE, LR and SVM. All four models show an improvement in performance as the number of hidden layers increases, as the overall error decreases. The results of the estimated overall MAE for the four networks that underwent repeated testing. Compared to SVM, AE and LR performs better with a smaller number of hidden units. Even though GBM has better performance it takes longer to converge than GBM.

Figure 3. Comparison of Models Training Parameter and Testing Parameters vs the Number of Hidden Units

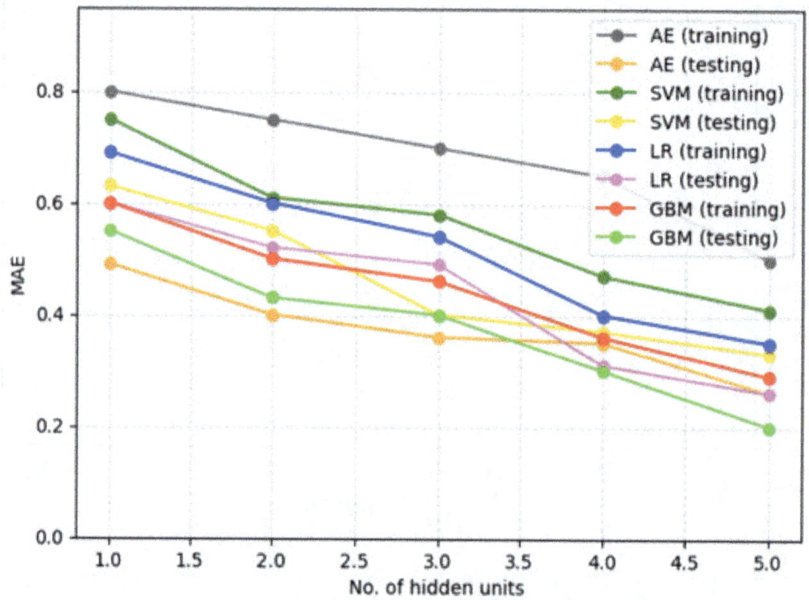

Figure 4 shows an example of a ROC curve which is a tool for assessing how well a classification four model is doing its job. An Area Under the Curve (AUC) of 0.98 indicates good GBM model performance; the black curve illustrates the trade-off between the true positive rate and the false positive rate.

Figure 4. Roc Curve of Different Model

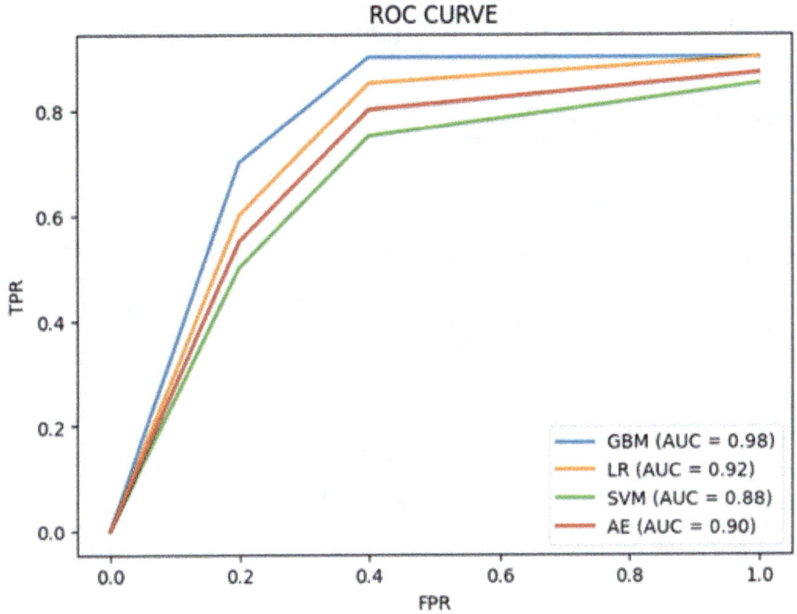

All of the model's performance analyze is results are displayed in Table 2. Our GBM works great it compared with alternative models.

Table 2. Performance Analysis

Models	Precision	Recall	F1- Score
AE	90.29	91.15	92.75
SVM	89.65	90.78	91.40
LR	86.37	87.54	89.56
GBM	**92.01**	**94.62**	**97.89**

Figure 5 which displays a bar chart comparing the performance of four models, reveals that GBM surpasses all of its competitors, including SVM, AE and LR in terms of precision, recall and f1-score.

Figure 5. Performance Comparison of Metrics

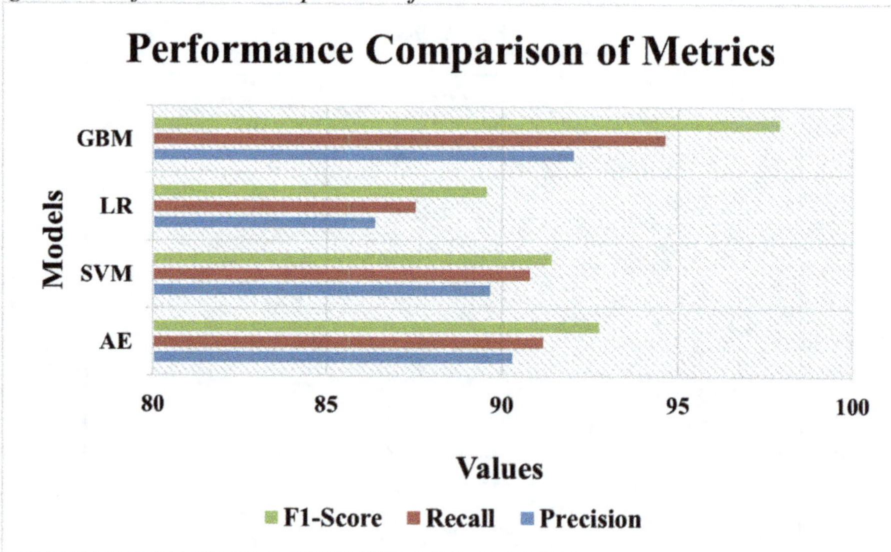

8. FUTURE DIRECTIONS

It found a number of important things when it analysed AI-driven models for fraud detection and financial risk mitigation. These things show how AI may drastically improve the speed, accuracy, and efficiency of these operations. Case studies, industry reports, and empirical research are examples of quantitative and qualitative data that are utilised to form the basis of the results. It is now abundantly obvious that AI models such as NN, ML algorithms, and DL-based approaches outperform conventional rule-based systems when it comes to detecting fraudulent activity and avoiding financial hazards. The most intriguing finding of the study is that systems powered by AI significantly outperform those without in terms of fraud detection accuracy (Akartuna et al., 2025).

Research into NN models has shown that they can significantly reduce the number of false positives produced by fraud detection systems, particularly when using DL algorithms like CNN. The main issue with conventional systems is the high frequency of false positives, which occur when valid transactions are incorrectly identified as fraudulent. There has been a decrease in customer discontent and savings in manual transaction review expenses of up to 40% in various financial institutions due to the use of AI models (Akartuna et al., 2023). Furthermore, RNNs have proven to be particularly useful in addressing the sequencing of fraudulent transactions in sectors like e-commerce and banking, where criminals often conduct numerous smaller-scale scams prior to launching a larger-scale attack.

Adopting AI is not only effective in reducing fraud but also financially advantageous due to reduced manual labour, fewer false positives, and more accurate fraud detection. AI relies on large, complete datasets of high quality in order to be trusted in domains like financial risk management and fraud detection. ML-trained AI models are only as good as the data used to train them. AI systems that rely on data to make predictions and decisions are limited in their effectiveness since the data used to train them is often biassed, out of date, or incomplete (Cuéllar, 2023). Consider a scenario where the AI models used to assess credit risk are either out of date or fail to represent a range of borrower characteristics or where the system fails to consider all pertinent data when AI will unjustly target a specific group, such as a minority or low-income individual, while reaching a judgement. This perpetuates systemic inequities in financial services and can lead to unfair loan rejections and false fraud alarms. Obtaining data quality assurance, investing in AI data quality assurance systems, and updating the AI models with the latest and unbiased data should be major priorities for financial institutions in order to avoid these risks. However, this may not be feasible for smaller institutions due to the high cost of the necessary infrastructure and human knowledge. With the increasing integration of AI into financial institutions, these biases might potentially cause significant problems. To prevent bias and unfair results, regulatory agencies are becoming more aware of this problem and will almost certainly impose stricter standards and auditing criteria for AI systems. A frequent audit of models for bias and the use of fairness indicators to direct model training are two things our financial institutions may do to address these concerns (Duah, 2023). At a later date, it will be necessary to think about the possibility that AI systems won't be able to react to new forms of finance and fraud.

It appears like fraudsters are continuously finding new ways to trick automatic systems into giving in to their every whim. As an example, fraudsters may use AI to code vulnerabilities into algorithms that programmers use to define themselves, or they may make deep fake identities that AI systems would have a hard time detecting (Isolauri & Ameer, 2023). The process is essentially a game of cat and mouse between AI developers and fraudsters. This game will continue until AI systems are updated and improved more frequently, allowing us to stay one step ahead of the scammers. These changes mean that institutions are more vulnerable to large-scale fraud schemes, which can have a negative impact on their finances and reputations if they aren't vigilant. Finally, AI isn't a black-and-white issue; it won't solve all of your problems, but it can greatly improve your financial risk management and fraud detection efforts. There are constraints and future hazards that organisations need to consider in this area as well. Achieving broad adoption and maintaining trust for the successful and ethical implementation of AI in financial systems depends on addressing critical issues such as robust data quality, algorithmic bias neutrality, interpretability, resistance to adversarial attacks, and regulatory uncertainty. These concerns affect financial systems and their interactions with society. As AI continues to advance, it is crucial for financial institutions to closely monitor developments and make investments in AI systems that are strong, transparent, and adaptable. This will help mitigate future risks and fully harness the revolutionary potential of AI.

Mitigation of Financial Risk Through Predictive Capabilities

AI offers better predictions for reducing financial risk, according to the research. Early warning indicators of financial problems (credit default, liquidity deficiencies, market volatility) were identified by AI models, both supervised and unsupervised, during an evaluation. One area where AI has proven useful is in credit risk management, where ML algorithms have outperformed more conventional credit scoring models in identifying loan defaults (Dupuis & Gleason, 2021). In the real world, financial institutions can boost their profitability by using this predictive edge to make better lending decisions, minimise the risk of failed loans, and so on. The ability to easily evaluate unstructured data, such news headlines, social media posts, and economic indicators, using AI has substantially improved the precision of risk assessments. In order to better anticipate market downturns and liquidity problems, AI systems used alternative data sources. Market risk models powered by AI outperformed human analysts in predicting stock market volatility by 25%. This gives financial managers and investors a leg up when it comes to making proactive portfolio adjustments to stave off losses caused by market disruptions. It reports Asset managers and hedge funds rely on precise market forecasts to inform trading strategies and reduce financial risk exposure; this discovery is very relevant to them.

Efficiency in Operations and Cost Reduction

Similarly, financial institutions have saved a tonne of money by using AI for fraud detection and reducing financial risk. Because fewer human assessments and interventions are required by AI systems that automate risk assessment and fraud detection, operational efficiencies have been achieved. Reducing the need for human intervention in fraud investigations is the primary driver of operational cost savings of 25% for financial institutions generated by AI-based fraud detection systems. ML algorithms, meanwhile, can process thousands of transactions every second while simultaneously detecting and responding to fraud in real time. Financial institutions have also had to scale up their operations more effectively due to the deployment of AI models. AI systems can handle massive amounts of data and transactions with no extra human resources needed, allowing fintech companies and banks to expand their customer base and service offerings without experiencing a linear increase in operational costs. This scalability is crucial for smaller financial institutions and fintech firms that do not have the capital to initially establish a large fraud detection and risk management team. The results demonstrated that AI has provided financial institutions with a scalable answer for future expansion, in addition to improving the accuracy and efficiency of fraud detection and risk reduction.

9. CONCLUSION

To efficient, accurate, and quick than conventional methods have been integrated into financial risk management and fraud detection by means of AI. Financial institutions are now better equipped than ever before to detect fraud and analyse risks due to the real-time processing of massive amounts of data by AI models, especially those of ML or DL. It found that models using AI-driven systems significantly improved fraud detection, with a 40% reduction in false positives and mistakes and an increase in both detection speed and decision-making efficiency. This enhancement is significant because both the number of digital transactions and the evasiveness of fraudsters are on the rise. Due to AI, the field of financial risk management can now more correctly forecast market volatility and shift its focus from credit risk assessment to the former. AI systems that use non-traditional data sources such as economic trends and social media activity, can anticipate loan defaults with a 90% accuracy rate or higher (Bahulkar et al., 2018). Furthermore, financial institutions were able to mitigate risks associated with market volatility and liquidity crises due to AI's ability to process raw data and detect early warning bells. And this ability to foretell the future is vital for any business that wants to keep losses to a minimum and, in the long run, thrive in those unpredictable market conditions.

Despite this, the research consistently highlighted AI's drawbacks, as well as the various constraints and obstacles that must be surmounted in order to realise AI's promise in the financial services industry. If you want to trust that AI models will work as advertised, you need high-quality data, which is why low-quality data is AI's biggest enemy. It notes that credit risk assessment is one area where discriminatory outcomes might result from inaccurate predictions made using biassed or inadequate datasets. Furthermore, the idea of openness and responsibility is made more challenging by the opaque nature of some prominent AI models, such as DL. In the highly regulated financial sectors, where decision making must be transparent, the inability of financial institutions to explain to regulators and customers how AI has arrived at a set of decisions stems from these models not operating with the black box. AI has become an essential component of contemporary fraud detection systems, allowing for smart, adaptable, and real-time surveillance of financial and e-commerce institutions. DL, ML and advanced analytics work together to make AI-driven systems more effective than rule-based ones. Nevertheless, problems with scalability, explainability, and resistance against adversaries persist. Digital financial ecosystems will be safer due to future advances in FL, GNN, and blockchain-integrated AI, which will further increase fraud detection.

REFERENCES

Adhikari, P., Hamal, P., & Baidoo, F.Jnr. (2024). Artificial Intelligence in fraud detection: Revolutionizing financial security. *International Journal of Science and Research Archive*, *13*(1), 1457–1472. DOI: 10.30574/ijsra.2024.13.1.1860

Adijat, F. & Onwuchekwa, J. (2023, January). A Comprehensive Framework for Strengthening USA Financial Cybersecurity : Integrating Machine Learning and AI in Fraud Detection Systems. *European Journal of Computer Science and Information Technology*, *11*. Advance online publication. DOI: 10.37745/ejcsit.2013/vol11n66283

Adijat Bello, O., Ogundipe, A., Mohammed, D., Folorunso, A., & Ayodeji Alonge, O. (2023). AI-Driven Approaches for Real-Time Fraud Detection in US Financial Transactions: Challenges and Opportunities. *European Journal of Computer Science and Information Technology*, *11*(6), 84–102. DOI: 10.37745/ejcsit.2013/vol11n684102

Akartuna, E. A., Johnson, S. D., & Thornton, A. (2025). A Holistic Network Analysis of the Money Laundering Threat Landscape: Assessing Criminal Typologies, Resilience and Implications for Disruption. In *Journal of Quantitative Criminology* (Vol. 41, Issue 2). Springer US. DOI: 10.1007/s10940-024-09594-3

Akartuna, E. A., Johnson, S. D., & Thornton, A. E. (2023). The money laundering and terrorist financing risks of new and disruptive technologies: a futures-oriented scoping review. In *Security Journal* (Vol. 36, Issue 4). Palgrave Macmillan UK. DOI: 10.1057/s41284-022-00356-z

Al Al-Fatlawi, A., Al Al-Khazaali, A. A. T., & Hasan, S. H. (2024). AI-based model for fraud detection in bank systems. *Fusion: Practice and Applications*, *14*(1), 19–27. DOI: 10.54216/FPA.140102

Al Faisal, N., Nahar, J., Sultana, N., & Mintoo, A. A. (2024). Fraud Detection In Banking Leveraging Ai To Identify And Prevent Fraudulent Activities In Real-Time. *Non Human Journal*, *1*(01), 181–197. DOI: 10.70008/jmldeds.v1i01.53

Alonge, E. O., Eyo-Udo, N. L., Ubanadu, B. C., Daraojimba, A. I., Balogun, E. D., & Ogunsola, K. O. (2021). Enhancing Data Security with Machine Learning: A Study on Fraud Detection Algorithms. *Journal of Frontiers in Multidisciplinary Research*, *2*(1), 19–31. DOI: 10.54660/.IJFMR.2021.2.1.19-31

Ashe, S. S., Application, C., Academy, S., Application, C., & Academy, S. (2024). *Exploring Machine Learning Methods for Comprehensive Literature Review on Financial Fraud Detection Gopikrishna PandaAshe, S. S., Application, C., Academy, S., Application, C., & Academy, S. (2024). Exploring Machine Learning Methods for Comprehensive Lit.* Issue Ml.

Bahulkar, A., Sharkey, T., & Wallace, W. (2018). *Integrative Analytics for Detecting and Disrupting Transnational Interdependent Criminal Smuggling, .*

Bao, Y., Ke, B., Li, B., Yu, Y. J., & Zhang, J. (2020). Detecting Accounting Fraud in Publicly Traded U.S. Firms Using a Machine Learning Approach. *Journal of Accounting Research, 58*(1), 199–235. DOI: 10.1111/1475-679X.12292

Bello, O. A., & Olufemi, K. (2024). Artificial intelligence in fraud prevention: Exploring techniques and applications challenges and opportunities. *Computer Science & IT Research Journal, 5*(6), 1505–1520. DOI: 10.51594/csitrj.v5i6.1252

Benedek, B., & Nagy, B. Z. (2023). Traditional versus AI-Based Fraud Detection: Cost Efficiency in the Field of Automobile Insurance. *Financial and Economic Review, 22*(2), 77–98. DOI: 10.33893/FER.22.2.77

Chen, Y., Zhao, C., Xu, Y., Nie, C., & Zhang, Y. (2025). *Deep Learning in Financial Fraud Detection: Innovations, Challenges, and Applications.* Data Science and Management., DOI: 10.1016/j.dsm.2025.08.002

Cuéllar, M. F. (2023). The tenuous relationship between The fight against money laundering and the disruption of criminal finance. *SSRN, 93*(2–3), 311–466. DOI: 10.2139/ssrn.445000

Duah, M. A. (2023). The disruption of money laundering in the western hemisphere as an effect on developing states – Can international customary law maintain and create a standard to improve financial regulation at an international level? *The Disruption of Money Laundering in the Western Hemisphere as an Effect on Developing States – Can International Customary Law Maintain and Create a Standard to Improve Financial Regulation at an International Level?* https://sas-space.sas.ac.uk/6849/

Dupuis, D., & Gleason, K. (2021). Money laundering with cryptocurrency: Open doors and the regulatory dialectic. *Journal of Financial Crime, 28*(1), 60–74. DOI: 10.1108/JFC-06-2020-0113

Goriparthi, R. G. (2024). *AI-Enhanced Data Mining Techniques for Large-Scale Financial Fraud Detection Rithin Gopal Goriparthi Department of Computer science, San Francisco Bay University.* Issue November.

Hafez, I. Y., Hafez, A. Y., Saleh, A., Abd El-Mageed, A. A., & Abohany, A. A. (2025). A systematic review of AI-enhanced techniques in credit card fraud detection. *Journal of Big Data, 12*(1), 6. DOI: 10.1186/s40537-024-01048-8

Hashemi, S. K., Mirtaheri, S. L., & Greco, S. (2023). Fraud Detection in Banking Data by Machine Learning Techniques. *IEEE Access : Practical Innovations, Open Solutions, 11*(January), 3034–3043. DOI: 10.1109/ACCESS.2022.3232287

Herath, H. M. M. (2025). Advancing Machine Learning for Financial Fraud Detection : A Comprehensive Review of Algorithms, Challenges, and Future Directions. *ASEAN Journal of Economic and Economic Education, 1*(February), 49–67.

Husnaningtyas, N., & Totok Dewayanto, . (2023). FINANCIAL FRAUD DETECTION AND MACHINE LEARNING ALGORITHM (UNSUPERVISED LEARNING): SYSTEMATIC LITERATURE REVIEW. *Jurnal Riset Akuntansi Dan Bisnis Airlangga, 8*(2), 1521–1542. DOI: 10.20473/jraba.v8i2.49927

Iguodala, O. D., & Oyiborhoro, A. (2025). AI-Powered Anti-Money Laundering (AML) and fraud detection - enhancing financial security through intelligent fraud detection. *World Journal of Advanced Research and Reviews, 26*(2), 3702–3714. DOI: 10.30574/wjarr.2025.26.2.0637

Ijiga, O. M., Idoko, I. P., Ebiega, G. I., Olajide, F. I., Olatunde, T. I., & Ukaegbu, C. (2024). Harnessing adversarial machine learning for advanced threat detection: AI-driven strategies in cybersecurity risk assessment and fraud prevention. *Journal of Science and Technology, 11*(1), 1–24. DOI: 10.53022/oarjst.2024.11.1.0060

Islam, T., Islam, S. M., Sarkar, A., Obaidur, A., Khan, R., Paul, R., & Bari, M. S. (2024). Artificial intelligence in fraud detection and financial risk mitigation: Future directions and business applications. *International Journal for Multidisciplinary Research, 6*(5), 1–23.

Islam, Z., Shil, S. K., & Buiya, R. (2024). Ai-Driven Fraud Detection in Financial Services: Enhancing Security and Building Trust in the Digital Age. *European Economic Letters, October 2023.* DOI: 10.52783/eel.v14i4.2124

Isolauri, E. A., & Ameer, I. (2023). Money laundering as a transnational business phenomenon: A systematic review and future agenda. *Critical Perspectives on International Business, 19*(3), 426–468. DOI: 10.1108/cpoib-10-2021-0088

Jahan Sarna, N., Ahmed Rithen, F., Salma Jui, U., Belal, S., Amin, A., Kabir Oishee, T., & Muzahidul Islam, A. K. M. (2025). AI Driven Fraud Detection Models in Financial Networks: A Comprehensive Systematic Review. *IEEE Access : Practical Innovations, Open Solutions*, *13*(August), 141204–141233. DOI: 10.1109/ACCESS.2025.3596060

Johora, F. T., Hasan, R., Farabi, S. F., Akter, J., & Al Mahmud, M. A. (2024). AI-POWERED FRAUD DETECTION IN BANKING: SAFEGUARDING FINANCIAL TRANSACTIONS. *The American Journal of Management and Economics Innovations*, *6*(6), 8–22. DOI: 10.37547/tajmei/Volume06Issue06-02

Kamuangu, P. (2024). A Review on Financial Fraud Detection using AI and Machine Learning. *Journal of Economics. Finance and Accounting Studies*, *6*(1), 67–77. DOI: 10.32996/jefas.2024.6.1.7

Kamuangu, P. K. (2024). Journal of Economics, Finance and Accounting Studies A Review on Financial Fraud Detection using AI and Machine Learning. *Journal of Economics. Finance and Accounting Studies*, *6*(1), 67–77. DOI: 10.32996/jefas

Lai, G. (2023). Artificial Intelligence Techniques for Fraud Detection. In *Preprints*. DOI: 10.20944/preprints202312.1115.v1

Lee, C.-W., Fu, M.-W., Wang, C.-C., & Azis, M. I. (2025). Evaluating Machine Learning Algorithms for Financial Fraud Detection: Insights from Indonesia. *Mathematics*, *13*(4), 600. DOI: 10.3390/math13040600

Lin, A. K. (2024). The AI Revolution in Financial Services : Emerging Methods for Fraud Detection and Prevention. *Jurnal Galaksi*, *1*(1), 43–51. DOI: 10.70103/galaksi.v1i1.5

Luo, B., Zhang, Z., Wang, Q., Ke, A., Lu, S., & He, B. (2025). AI-powered Fraud Detection in Decentralized Finance: A Project Life Cycle Perspective. *ACM Computing Surveys*, *57*(4), 1–38. DOI: 10.1145/3705296

Mainul, M., Zerine, I., Rahman, M. A., Islam, M. S., & Ahmed, M. Y. (2025). AI-Driven Fraud Detection in Financial Transactions Using Machine Learning and Deep Learning to Detect Anomalies and Fraudulent Activities in Banking and E-Commerce Transactions. SSRN *Electronic Journal, 16*(5). DOI: 10.2139/ssrn.5287281

Niek, de Vries, K. J., de Jong, M., Dosoula, N., van den Akker, B., Smith, J., Thuong, O., & Bernardi, L. (2021). Machine Learning for Fraud Detection in E-Commerce: A Research Agenda. In *Communications in Computer and Information Science: Vol. 1482 CCIS* (pp. 30–54). DOI: 10.1007/978-3-030-87839-9_2

Olufemi, K. (2024). Artificial intelligence in fraud prevention: Exploring techniques and applications challenges and opportunities. *Computer Science & IT Research Journal, 5*(6), 1505–1520. DOI: 10.51594/csitrj.v5i6.1252

Perols, J. (2011). Financial Statement Fraud Detection: An Analysis of Statistical and Machine Learning Algorithms. *Auditing, 30*(2), 19–50. DOI: 10.2308/ajpt-50009

Poudel, S., & Dhungana, U. R. (2022). Artificial intelligence for energy fraud detection: A review. [IJAPE]. *International Journal of Applied Power Engineering, 11*(2), 109. DOI: 10.11591/ijape.v11.i2.pp109-119

Raghuwanshi, P. (2024). AI-Driven Identity and Financial Fraud Detection for National Security. *Journal of Artificial Intelligence General Science (JAIGS) ISSN:3006-4023, 7*(01), 38–51. DOI: 10.60087/jaigs.v7i01.294

Rana, P. J. (2019). A Survey on Fraud Detection Techniques in Ecommerce. *A Survey on Fraud Detection Techniques in Ecommerce, 113*(14), 5–7.

Razzaq, K. (2025). *Next-Generation Machine Learning in Healthcare Fraud Detection : Current Trends, Challenges, and Future Research Directions.*

Smith, L., & Lamprecht, C. (2025). *Identifying the limitations associated with machine learning techniques in performing accounting tasks* (Vol. 22, Issue 2). DOI: 10.1108/JFRA-05-2023-0280

Thammareddi, . (2023). Analysis on Cybersecurity Threats in Modern Banking and Machine Learning Techniques for Fraud Detection. *The Review of Contemporary Scientific and Academic Studies, 3*(11). Advance online publication. DOI: 10.55454/rcsas.3.11.2023.004

Wenyan Wu, L. M. (2024). Is Machine Learning Really Effective in Detecting Corporate Fraud? *Is Machine Learning Really Effective in Detecting Corporate Fraud, 4*(02), 7823–7830.

Yadav, S. (2023). AI-Powered Fraud Detection in Financial Transactions. *International Journal on Science and Technology (IJSAT) IJSAT23041216, 14*(4), 148–156.

Yaw Agyeman, A., & Gbli Tetteh, S. (2024). Using Machine Learning Models to Detect the Increasing Threats of Financial Fraud in the Cyberspace. [IJISRT]. *International Journal of Innovative Science and Research Technology*, (August), 1551–1558. DOI: 10.38124/ijisrt/IJISRT24JUL959

Yu, W., Wang, Y., Liu, L., An, Y., Yuan, B., & Panneerselvam, J. (2024). A Multi-perspective Fraud Detection Method for Multiparticipant E-Commerce Transactions. *IEEE Transactions on Computational Social Systems*, *11*(2), 1564–1576. DOI: 10.1109/TCSS.2022.3232619

Yuhertiana, I., & Hadi Amin, A. (2024). Artificial Intelligence Driven Approaches for Financial Fraud Detection: A Systematic Literature Review. *KnE Social Sciences*, *2024*, 448–468. DOI: 10.18502/kss.v9i20.16551

Compilation of References

Aarthi, S. Ravikumar, Sapayev Odilbek Uglu, V., Sottarov, A., & Singh, A. (2025). The privacy paradox. In *User-Centric Cybersecurity Implications for Sustainable Digital Transformation* (pp. 223–256). IGI Global Scientific Publishing. DOI: 10.4018/979-8-3373-3171-3.ch007

Aarthi, S., Aravinthan, K., Ravikumar, R. N., Sivakumar, N., & Wanglen, S. (2025). Cryptography securing data in motion within Blockchain, internet of everything, and Federated Learning. In *Convergence of Blockchain, Internet of Everything, and Federated Learning for Security* (pp. 39–78). IGI Global., DOI: 10.4018/979-8-3373-1424-2.ch002

Abadi, M., Chu, A., Goodfellow, I., McMahan, H. B., Mironov, I., Talwar, K., & Zhang, L. (2016). Deep learning with differential privacy. In *Proceedings of the 2016 ACM SIGSAC Conference on Computer and Communications Security* (pp. 308–318). ACM. DOI: 10.1145/2976749.2978318

Abdelaty, M., Scott-Hayward, S., Doriguzzi-Corin, R., & Siracusa, D. (2021, October). GADoT: GAN-based adversarial training for robust DDoS attack detection. *2021 IEEE Conference on Communications and Network (CNS)*. DOI: 10.1109/CNS53000.2021.9705040

Abdelmoumin, G., Whitaker, J., Rawat, D. B., & Rahman, A. (2022). A survey on data-driven learning for intelligent network intrusion detection systems. *Electronics (Basel)*, *11*(2), 213. DOI: 10.3390/electronics11020213

Abdullah, M. T., & Ali, N. H. M. (2024, May). Facial deepfake performance evaluation based on three detection tools: MTCNN, Dlib, and MediaPipe. In AIP Conference Proceedings (Vol. 3097, No. 1, p. 050015). AIP Publishing LLC.

Abedzadeh, N., & Jacobs, M. (2023). A Reinforcement Learning framework with Oversampling and undersampling algorithms for intrusion detection system. *Applied Sciences (Basel, Switzerland)*, *13*(20), 11275. DOI: 10.3390/app132011275

Abir, W. H.. (2023). Detecting deepfake images using deep learning techniques and explainable AI methods. *Intelligent Automation & Soft Computing*, *35*(2), 2151–2169. DOI: 10.32604/iasc.2023.029653

Achuthan, K., Ramanathan, S., Srinivas, S., & Raman, R. (2024). Advancing cybersecurity and privacy with artificial intelligence: Current trends and future research directions. *Frontiers in Big Data*, *7*, 1497535. DOI: 10.3389/fdata.2024.1497535 PMID: 39703783

Adhikari, P., Hamal, P., & Baidoo, F.Jnr. (2024). Artificial Intelligence in fraud detection: Revolutionizing financial security. *International Journal of Science and Research Archive*, *13*(1), 1457–1472. DOI: 10.30574/ijsra.2024.13.1.1860

Adijat Bello, O., Ogundipe, A., Mohammed, D., Folorunso, A., & Ayodeji Alonge, O. (2023). AI-Driven Approaches for Real-Time Fraud Detection in US Financial Transactions: Challenges and Opportunities. *European Journal of Computer Science and Information Technology*, *11*(6), 84–102. DOI: 10.37745/ejcsit.2013/vol11n684102

Adijat, F. & Onwuchekwa, J. (2023, January). A Comprehensive Framework for Strengthening USA Financial Cybersecurity : Integrating Machine Learning and AI in Fraud Detection Systems. *European Journal of Computer Science and Information Technology*, *11*. Advance online publication. DOI: 10.37745/ejcsit.2013/vol11n66283

Admass, W. S., Munaye, Y. Y., & Diro, A. A. (2024). Cyber security: State of the art, challenges and future directions. *Cyber Security and Applications*, *2*(October 2023), 100031. DOI: 10.1016/j.csa.2023.100031

Agrafiotis, I., Erola, A., Happa, J., Goldsmith, M., & Creese, S. (2016). Validating an Insider Threat Detection System: A Real Scenario Perspective. *Proceedings - 2016 IEEE Symposium on Security and Privacy Workshops, SPW 2016*, 286–295. DOI: 10.1109/SPW.2016.36

Ahmad, T. (2025, May 21). *AI-Driven Dynamic firewall optimization using reinforcement learning for anomaly detection and prevention*. arXiv.org. https://arxiv.org/abs/2506.05356 DOI: 10.36227/techrxiv.174952992.29897123/v1

Ahmad, A., Maynard, S. B., & Park, S. (2014). Information security strategies: Towards an organizational multi-strategy perspective. *Journal of Intelligent Manufacturing*, *25*(2), 357–370. DOI: 10.1007/s10845-012-0683-0

Ahmad, I., Kumar, T., Liyanage, M., Okwuibe, J., Ylianttila, M., & Gurtov, A. (2018). Overview of 5G security challenges and solutions. *IEEE Communications Standards Magazine*, *2*(1), 36–43. DOI: 10.1109/MCOMSTD.2018.1700063

Ajayi, A. M., Omokanye, A. O., Olowu, O., Adeleye, A. O., Omole, O. M., & Wada, I. U. (2024). Detecting insider threats in banking using AI-driven anomaly detection with a data science approach to cybersecurity. *World Journal of Advanced Research and Reviews, 24*(2), 123–132. DOI: 10.30574/wjarr.2024.24.2.3182

Ajoy, A., Mahindrakar, C. U., & Gowrish, D. (2021, September). DeepFake Detection using a frame based approach involving CNN. In *2021 Third International Conference on Inventive Research in Computing Applications (ICIRCA)* (pp. 1329-1333). IEEE.

Akamai Technologies. (2023). Akamai Intelligent Edge Platform. https://www .akamai.com/resources

Akamai Technologies. (2023). State of the Internet / Security report (Q4 2022 data). https://www.akamai.com/security-research/the-state-of-the-internet

Akartuna, E. A., Johnson, S. D., & Thornton, A. (2025). A Holistic Network Analysis of the Money Laundering Threat Landscape: Assessing Criminal Typologies, Resilience and Implications for Disruption. In *Journal of Quantitative Criminology* (Vol. 41, Issue 2). Springer US. DOI: 10.1007/s10940-024-09594-3

Akartuna, E. A., Johnson, S. D., & Thornton, A. E. (2023). The money laundering and terrorist financing risks of new and disruptive technologies: a futures-oriented scoping review. In *Security Journal* (Vol. 36, Issue 4). Palgrave Macmillan UK. DOI: 10.1057/s41284-022-00356-z

Akash, T. R., Sany, N. J., & Akter, L. (2025). Privacy-preserving technique in cybersecurity: Balancing data protection and user rights. Journal of Computer Science and Technology Studies. https://al-kindipublishers.org/index.php/jcsts/article/view/9495

Akintan, A., Favour, A., Ali, A., Muthanna, A., Alkhalidy, M., & Ravi, R. (2025). *Improving Detection Accuracy of Insider Threats in M2M Systems Using Adaptive Trust Models. July.*

Al Al-Fatlawi, A., Al Al-Khazaali, A. A. T., & Hasan, S. H. (2024). AI-based model for fraud detection in bank systems. *Fusion: Practice and Applications, 14*(1), 19–27. DOI: 10.54216/FPA.140102

Al Faisal, N., Nahar, J., Sultana, N., & Mintoo, A. A. (2024). Fraud Detection In Banking Leveraging Ai To Identify And Prevent Fraudulent Activities In Real-Time. *Non Human Journal, 1*(01), 181–197. DOI: 10.70008/jmldeds.v1i01.53

Alagic, G., et al. (2022). Status report on the third round of the NIST post-quantum cryptography standardization process (NIST Internal Report 8413). DOI: 10.6028/ NIST.IR.8413

Alazab, M., Awajan, A., Mesleh, A., Alazab, M., & AlQudah, M. (2022). AI-driven security analytics for threat detection. *Journal of Cybersecurity Intelligence and Cybercrime*, *5*(3), 201–218.

Ali, A., Husain, M., & Hans, P. (2025). *Real-Time Detection of Insider Threats Using Behavioral Analytics and Deep Evidential Clustering*. https://arxiv.org/abs/2505.15383

Ali, S., & Awad, A. I. (2018). Cyber security for financial sector: A framework for ensuring regulatory compliance. *Journal of Information Security and Applications*, *38*, 103–118.

Aliyu, I., Van Engelenburg, S., Mu'Azu, M. B., Kim, J., & Lim, C. G. (2022). Statistical detection of adversarial examples in blockchain-based federated forest in-vehicle network intrusion detection systems. *IEEE Access : Practical Innovations, Open Solutions*, *10*, 109366–109384. DOI: 10.1109/ACCESS.2022.3212412

Alketbi, K. S., & Mehmood, A. (2025). A Comprehensive Survey of Explainable Artificial Intelligence Techniques for Malicious Insider Threat Detection. *IEEE Access : Practical Innovations, Open Solutions*, *13*(June), 121772–121798. DOI: 10.1109/ACCESS.2025.3587114

Almars, A. M. (2021). Deepfakes detection techniques using deep learning: A survey. *Journal of Computer and Communications*, *9*(05), 20–35. DOI: 10.4236/jcc.2021.95003

Al-Mhiqani, M. N., Ahmad, R., Zainal Abidin, Z., Yassin, W., Hassan, A., Abdulkareem, K. H., Ali, N. S., & Yunos, Z. (2020). A review of insider threat detection: Classification, machine learning techniques, datasets, open challenges, and recommendations. *Applied Sciences (Basel, Switzerland)*, *10*(15), 5208. Advance online publication. DOI: 10.3390/app10155208

Alohaly, M., Balogun, O., & Takabi, D. (2022). Integrating Cyber Deception Into Attribute-Based Access Control (ABAC) for Insider Threat Detection. *IEEE Access : Practical Innovations, Open Solutions*, *10*(August), 108965–108978. DOI: 10.1109/ACCESS.2022.3213645

Alonge, E. O., Eyo-Udo, N. L., Ubanadu, B. C., Daraojimba, A. I., Balogun, E. D., & Ogunsola, K. O. (2021). Enhancing Data Security with Machine Learning: A Study on Fraud Detection Algorithms. *Journal of Frontiers in Multidisciplinary Research*, 2(1), 19–31. DOI: 10.54660/.IJFMR.2021.2.1.19-31

Alrawashdeh, K., & Purdy, C. (2020). Toward lightweight IDS for the IoT. *Journal of Internet Services and Information Security*, *10*(1), 16–27.

Alserhani, F. (2025). Intrusion Detection and Real-Time Adaptive Security in Medical IoT Using a Cyber-Physical System Design. *Sensors (Basel), 25*(15), 4720. DOI: 10.3390/s25154720 PMID: 40807889

Alzaabi, F. R., & Mehmood, A. (2024). A Review of Recent Advances, Challenges, and Opportunities in Malicious Insider Threat Detection Using Machine Learning Methods. *IEEE Access : Practical Innovations, Open Solutions, 12*(March), 30907–30927. DOI: 10.1109/ACCESS.2024.3369906

Amazon Web Services. (2021). AWS Shield threat landscape review: 2020 year-in-review. https://aws.amazon.com/blogs/security/aws-shield-threat-landscape-review-2020-year-in-review/

Aminu, M., & Akinsanya, A. (2024). Enhancing Cyber Threat Detection through Real-time Threat Intelligence and Adaptive Defense Mechanisms. *International Journal of Computer Applications Technology and Research*, (August), 10–27. DOI: 10.7753/IJCATR1308.1002

Amodei, D., Olah, C., Steinhardt, J., Christiano, P., Schulman, J., & Mané, D. (2016). *Concrete Problems in AI Safety*. 1–29. https://arxiv.org/abs/1606.06565

Anderson, B., Quist, S., Neil, D., Storlie, C., & Lane, T. (2011). Graph-based malware detection using dynamic analysis. *Journal of Computer Virology, 7*(4), 247–258. DOI: 10.1007/s11416-011-0152-x

Antonakakis, M.. (2017). Understanding the Mirai botnet. In *Proceedings of the 26th USENIX Security Symposium* (pp. 1093–1110). USENIX Association.

Aramide, O. O. (2025). Federated learning for distributed network security and threat intelligence: A privacy-preserving paradigm for scalable cyber defense. Journal of Data Analysis and Critical Management. https://jdacm.com/index.php/jdacm/article/view/47

Article, G. D. P. R. 29 Working Party. (2018). Guidelines on transparency under regulation 2016/679. European Commission.

Ashe, S. S., Application, C., Academy, S., Application, C., & Academy, S. (2024). *Exploring Machine Learning Methods for Comprehensive Literature Review on Financial Fraud Detection Gopikrishna PandaAshe, S. S., Application, C., Academy, S., Application, C., & Academy, S. (2024). Exploring Machine Learning Methods for Comprehensive Lit*. Issue Ml.

Austin-Gabriel, B., Hussain, N. Y., Ige, A. B., Adepoju, P. A., Amoo, O. O., & Afolabi, A. I. (2021). Advancing zero trust architecture with AI and data science for enterprise cybersecurity frameworks. *Open Access Research Journal of Engineering and Technology*, *1*(1), 47–55. DOI: 10.53022/oarjet.2021.1.1.0107

Axelsson, S. (2000). The base-rate fallacy and the difficulty of intrusion detection. *ACM Transactions on Information and System Security*, *3*(3), 186–205. DOI: 10.1145/357830.357849

Azuma, R., Baillot, Y., Behringer, R., Feiner, S., Julier, S., & MacIntyre, B. (2001). Recent advances in augmented reality. *IEEE Computer Graphics and Applications*, *21*(6), 34–47. DOI: 10.1109/38.963459

Bahulkar, A., Sharkey, T., & Wallace, W. (2018). *Integrative Analytics for Detecting and Disrupting Transnational Interdependent Criminal Smuggling,* .

Baldini, I.. (2017). Serverless computing: Current trends and open problems. In *Research advances in cloud computing* (pp. 1–20). Springer., DOI: 10.1007/978-981-10-5026-8_1

Bao, Y., Ke, B., Li, B., Yu, Y. J., & Zhang, J. (2020). Detecting Accounting Fraud in Publicly Traded U.S. Firms Using a Machine Learning Approach. *Journal of Accounting Research*, *58*(1), 199–235. DOI: 10.1111/1475-679X.12292

Basel Committee on Banking Supervision. (2018). *Cyber-resilience: Range of practices*. Bank for International Settlements.

Bass, L., Clements, P., & Kazman, R. (2021). *Software architecture in practice* (4th ed.). Addison-Wesley Professional.

Baum, E. B. (2022). On the capabilities of multilayer perceptrons. *Journal of Complexity*, *4*(3), 193–215. DOI: 10.1016/0885-064X(88)90020-9

Bee, S., Iram Jafry, S., Saucedo, G., Dorata, N. T., Phillips, C. R., Fico, J., Lanier, C., Kirchner, M., Grimes, N., Hilmi Elifoglu, I., Abel, I., Tasseven, Ö., Salvino, R., Tarleton, T., Kuhn, N., & Kauffman, R. (2018). Business Interdisciplinary Journal on Risk and Society Review of Accounting Conversations: A Case Study in Auditor Communications 1 Rehiring the Retired: An Examination of Double Dipping in Public School Districts 13 Corruption and Culture: Empirical Anal. *Business Interdisciplinary Journal on Risk and Society Review, 38*(2). www.stjohns.edu/ROB

Beeravalli, K. R., & Eluru, N. (n.d.). Comparison Analysis of DeepFake Detection Techniques: A Comprehensive Review.

Bell, A. J. C., Rogers, M. B., & Pearce, J. M. (2019). The insider threat: Behavioral indicators and factors influencing likelihood of intervention. *International Journal of Critical Infrastructure Protection*, *24*, 166–176. DOI: 10.1016/j.ijcip.2018.12.001

Bello, O. A., & Olufemi, K. (2024). Artificial intelligence in fraud prevention: Exploring techniques and applications challenges and opportunities. *Computer Science & IT Research Journal*, *5*(6), 1505–1520. DOI: 10.51594/csitrj.v5i6.1252

Benedek, B., & Nagy, B. Z. (2023). Traditional versus AI-Based Fraud Detection: Cost Efficiency in the Field of Automobile Insurance. *Financial and Economic Review*, *22*(2), 77–98. DOI: 10.33893/FER.22.2.77

Berente, N., Gu, B., Recker, J., & Santhanam, R. (2021). Managing Artificial Intelligence. *Management Information Systems Quarterly*, *45*(3), 1433–1450. DOI: 10.25300/MISQ/2021/16274

Berman, D. S., Buczak, A. L., Chavis, J. S., & Corbett, C. L. (2019). A survey of deep learning methods for cyber security. *Information (Basel)*, *10*(4), 122. DOI: 10.3390/info10040122

Bernstein, D. J. (2009). Introduction to post-quantum cryptography. In *Post-quantum cryptography* (pp. 1–14). Springer., DOI: 10.1007/978-3-540-88702-7_1

Bernstein, D. J., & Lange, T. (2017). Post-quantum cryptography. *Nature*, *549*(7671), 188–194. DOI: 10.1038/nature23461 PMID: 28905891

Bhuyan, M. H., Bhattacharyya, D. K., & Kalita, J. K. (2015). Network anomaly detection: Methods, systems and tools. *IEEE Communications Surveys and Tutorials*, *16*(1), 303–336. DOI: 10.1109/SURV.2013.052213.00046

Biggio, B., & Roli, F. (2018). Wild patterns: Ten years after the rise of adversarial machine learning. *Pattern Recognition*, *84*, 317–331. DOI: 10.1016/j.patcog.2018.07.023

Bilge, L., & Dumitras, T. (2012). Before we knew it: An empirical study of zero-day attacks in the real world. In *Proceedings of the ACM Conference on Computer and Communications Security* (pp. 833–844). ACM. DOI: 10.1145/2382196.2382284

Biometric Data and Privacy Laws (GDPR, CCPA/CPRA). (2021, June 16). Thales. https://www.thalesgroup.com/en/markets/digital-identity-and-security/government/biometrics/biometric-data

Blanchard, P., El Mhamdi, E. M., Guerraoui, R., & Stainer, J. (2017). Machine learning with adversaries: Byzantine tolerant gradient descent. In *Advances in Neural Information Processing Systems* (Vol. 30, pp. 119–129). Curran Associates, Inc.

Bon, A., Dittoh, F., Lô, G., Pini, M., & Bwana, R. WaiShiang, C., Kulathuramaiyer, N., & Baart, A. (2022). Decolonizing Technology and Society: A Perspective from the Global South. In *Perspectives on Digital Humanism* (pp. 61–68). Springer International Publishing. DOI: 10.1007/978-3-030-86144-5_9

Bonawitz, K., Ivanov, V., Kreuter, B., Marcedone, A., McMahan, H. B., Patel, S., Ramage, D., Segal, A., & Seth, K. (2017). Practical secure aggregation for privacy-preserving machine learning. In *Proceedings of the 2017 ACM SIGSAC Conference on Computer and Communications Security* (pp. 1175–1191). ACM. DOI: 10.1145/3133956.3133982

Bonnema, G. M., & Borches, P. D. (2021). Design with Overview – how to survive in complex organisations. *INCOSE International Symposium, 18*(1), 1120–1134. DOI: 10.1002/j.2334-5837.2008.tb00867.x

Bose, B., Avasarala, B., Tirthapura, S., Chung, Y. Y., & Steiner, D. (2017). Detecting Insider Threats Using RADISH: A System for Real-Time Anomaly Detection in Heterogeneous Data Streams. *IEEE Systems Journal, 11*(2), 471–482. DOI: 10.1109/JSYST.2016.2558507

Bouveret, A. (2018). Cyber risk for the financial sector: A framework for quantitative assessment. IMF Working Paper.

Brakerski, Z., & Vaikuntanathan, V. (2014). Efficient fully homomorphic encryption from (standard) LWE. *SIAM Journal on Computing, 43*(2), 831–871. DOI: 10.1137/120868669

Buczak, A. L., & Guven, E. (2016). A survey of data mining and machine learning methods for cybersecurity intrusion detection. *IEEE Communications Surveys and Tutorials, 18*(2), 1153–1176. DOI: 10.1109/COMST.2015.2494502

Budhwar, P., Chowdhury, S., Wood, G., Aguinis, H., Bamber, G. J., Beltran, J. R., Boselie, P., Lee Cooke, F., Decker, S., DeNisi, A., Dey, P. K., Guest, D., Knoblich, A. J., Malik, A., Paauwe, J., Papagiannidis, S., Patel, C., Pereira, V., Ren, S., & Varma, A. (2023). Human resource management in the age of generative artificial intelligence: Perspectives and research directions on ChatGPT. *Human Resource Management Journal, 33*(3), 606–659. DOI: 10.1111/1748-8583.12524

Cai, X., Wang, Y., Xu, S., Li, H., Zhang, Y., Liu, Z., & Yuan, X. (2024). LAN: Learning Adaptive Neighbors for Real-Time Insider Threat Detection. *IEEE Transactions on Information Forensics and Security, 19*, 10157–10172. DOI: 10.1109/TIFS.2024.3488527

Carrio, A. Pompeu Fabra University, Barcelona School of Management, & The IOC Olympic Studies Centre. (2023). The Ethics of AI in Sport. Taking athletes' rights and wellbeing seriously. In *Technical Report.* https://www.researchgate.net/publication/375278970

Castro, W., Oblitas, J., Santa-Cruz, R., & Avila-George, H. (2019). Multilayer perceptron architecture optimization using parallel computing techniques. *PLoS One*, *12*(12), e0189369. DOI: 10.1371/journal.pone.0189369

Cavoukian, A. (2011). *Privacy by design: The 7 foundational principles*. Information and Privacy Commissioner of Ontario.

CERT-In. (2024). *Annual report 2023–2024*. Indian Computer Emergency Response Team. https://www.cert-in.org.in

Chang, R. K. C. (2002). Defending against flooding-based distributed denial-of-service attacks: A tutorial. *IEEE Communications Magazine*, *40*(10), 42–51. DOI: 10.1109/MCOM.2002.1039856

Charmet, F., Tanuwidjaja, H. C., Ayoubi, S., Gimenez, P.-F., Han, Y., Jmila, H., Blanc, G., Takahashi, T., & Zhang, Z. (2022). Explainable artificial intelligence for cybersecurity: A literature survey. *Annales des Télécommunications*, *77*(11–12), 789–812. DOI: 10.1007/s12243-022-00926-7

Chattopadhyay, P., Wang, L., & Tan, Y. P. (2018). Scenario-based insider threat detection from cyber activities. *IEEE Transactions on Computational Social Systems*, *5*(3), 660–675. DOI: 10.1109/TCSS.2018.2857473

Chawande, S. (2024). Insider threats in highly automated cyber systems. *World Journal of Advanced Engineering Technology and Sciences*, *13*(2), 807–820. DOI: 10.30574/wjaets.2024.13.2.0642

Chawla, N. V., Bowyer, K. W., Hall, L. O., & Kegelmeyer, W. P. (2002). SMOTE: Synthetic minority over-sampling technique. *Journal of Artificial Intelligence Research*, *16*, 321–357. DOI: 10.1613/jair.953

Check Point Research. (2023). *Cyber attack trends: 2023 mid-year report*. https://research.checkpoint.com

Chen, H., Tran, N., Thumati, A. S., Bhuyan, J., & Ding, J. (2021). *Data curation and quality assurance for machine learning-based cyber intrusion detection.*

Chen, L., Ai, H., Zhuang, Z., & Shang, C. (2018). Real-Time Multiple People Tracking with Deeply Learned Candidate Selection and Person Re-Identification. *Proceedings - IEEE International Conference on Multimedia and Expo, 2018-July*. DOI: 10.1109/ICME.2018.8486597

Chen, Y., Al-Rubaye, S., Tsourdos, A., Baker, L., & Gillingham, C. (2023, May). Differentially-private federated intrusion detection via knowledge distillation in third-party IoT systems of smart airports. *ICC 2023 - IEEE International Conference On*.

Chen, J., Liu, K., & Wu, Y. (2022). Federated learning-based intrusion detection for IoT networks. *IEEE Access : Practical Innovations, Open Solutions, 10*, 34567–34578. DOI: 10.1109/ACCESS.2022.3163854

Chen, J., Xue, J., Wang, D., Luo, L., Li, H., Han, J., & Liu, J. (2022). Machine learning in cybersecurity: A survey of applications, adversarial challenges, and future research directions. *Electronics (Basel), 11*(24), 4073. Advance online publication. DOI: 10.3390/electronics11244073

Chen, L., Kuang, X., Xu, A., Suo, S., & Yang, Y. (2020). A novel network intrusion detection system based on CNN. In *2020 Eighth International Conference on Advanced Cloud and Big Data (CBD)* (pp. 243–247). IEEE. DOI: 10.1109/CBD51900.2020.00051

Chen, R., Park, J. M., & Marchany, R. (2007). A divide-and-conquer strategy for thwarting distributed denial-of-service attacks. *IEEE Transactions on Parallel and Distributed Systems, 18*(5), 577–588. DOI: 10.1109/TPDS.2007.1014

Chen, Y., Zhao, C., Xu, Y., Nie, C., & Zhang, Y. (2025). *Deep Learning in Financial Fraud Detection: Innovations, Challenges, and Applications*. Data Science and Management., DOI: 10.1016/j.dsm.2025.08.002

Cheon, J. H., Kim, A., Kim, M., & Song, Y. (2017). Homomorphic encryption for arithmetic of approximate numbers. In *International Conference on the Theory and Application of Cryptology and Information Security* (pp. 409–437). Springer. DOI: 10.1007/978-3-319-70694-8_15

Chinamanagonda, S. (2023). Automating Incident Response in DevOps - Automated incident response mechanisms in DevOps workflows. *International Journal of Novel Research and Development, 8*(10), e154–e156. https://www.ijnrd.org/papers/IJNRD2310419.pdf

Choi, E., Kim, Y., Lee, J., & Choi, J. (2021). Federated learning-based intrusion detection system for edge computing networks. *Sensors (Basel), 21*(4), 1375. PMID: 33669229

Chollet, F. (2017). Xception: Deep learning with depthwise separable convolutions. In *Proceedings of the IEEE conference on computer vision and pattern recognition* (pp. 1251-1258).

Cloudflare. (2023). DDoS attack trends for Q2 2023. Cloudflare Radar. https://radar.cloudflare.com/reports/ddos-2023-q2

Cody, T., & Beling, P. A. (2023). Towards operational resilience for AI-based cyber systems in multi-domain operations. In Solomon, L., & Schwartz, P. J. (Eds.), *Artificial Intelligence and Machine Learning for Multi-Domain Operations Applications V* (p. 68). SPIE. DOI: 10.1117/12.2675862

Cosma, S., Văleanu, M., Cosma, D., Vasilescu, D., & Moldovan, G. (2019). Efficient Data Organisation in Distributed Computer Systems using Data Warehouse. *International Journal of Computers, Communications & Control, 8*(3), 366. DOI: 10.15837/ijccc.2013.3.463

Cramer, R., Damgård, I. B., & Nielsen, J. B. (2015). *Secure multiparty computation and secret sharing*. Cambridge University Press., DOI: 10.1017/CBO9781107337756

Crankshaw, D., Wang, X., Zhou, G., Franklin, M. J., Gonzalez, J. E., & Stoica, I. (2017). Clipper: A low-latency online prediction serving system. In *Proceedings of the 14th USENIX Symposium on Networked Systems Design and Implementation* (pp. 613–627). USENIX Association.

Creswell, J. W., & Plano Clark, V. L. (2018). *Designing and conducting mixed methods research* (3rd ed.). Sage Publications.

CROWDSTRIKE 2024 THREAT HUNTING REPORT. (n.d.). https://www.googleadservices.com/pagead/aclk?sa=L&ai=DChsSEwiTn92AutWOAxW_p2YCHfRJDOQYACICCAEQABoCc20&co=1&ase=2&gclid=Cj0KCQjws4fEBhD-ARIsACC3d2-r9JyjPUGiOaumcgOT_DPDd6sOCHvCDkI6px1bBD-hFCfKQPQDwvoaAhJBEALw_wcB&ohost=www.google.com&cid=CAESVeD2jnv3zPM4NSCKCPOsA6P95dn_qB2o3i50Am1WsbGZHT2eUw64-54Ooo5CNbwS41iBRLTbgX5jMxjVrbpoFHAy2Pfro9XV1sk299VKdQQwWliwcE4&category=acrcp_v1_40&sig=AOD64_2_Ca7swzJvqlITfZMZQnNFSwdDfA&q&nis=4&adurl&ved=2ahUKEwiS-teAutWOAxX01DgGHTiUFMsQ0Qx6BAgaEAE

Cuéllar, M. F. (2023). The tenuous relationship between The fight against money laundering and the disruption of criminal finance. *SSRN, 93*(2–3), 311–466. DOI: 10.2139/ssrn.445000

Cybersecurity Ventures. (2024). *Cybercrime report 2024.* Cybersecurity Ventures Publishing.

Cypersecurity. (2020). Framework for improving critical infrastructure cybersecurity. *Framework, 535*, 9–25. file:///C:/Users/thiag/AppData/Local/Mendeley Ltd./Mendeley Desktop/Downloaded/National Institute of Standards and Technology - 2018 - Framework for improving critical infrastructure cybersecurity.pdf

Czyz, R., Kallitsis, M., Gharaibeh, M., Papadopoulos, C., Bailey, M., & Karir, M. (2015). Turtles all the way down: Exploring the cultural dimensions of the DDoS-for-hire service industry. In *Proceedings of the 24th USENIX Security Symposium* (pp. 1011–1026). USENIX Association.

Damage to brand or reputation top risk for the sports and entertainment industry. (n.d.). https://aon.co.za/insights/damage-to-brand-or-reputation-top-risk-for-the-sports-and-entertainment-industry/

Dang, T.-V., & Tran, H.-L. (2023). A Secured, Multilevel Face Recognition based on Head Pose Estimation, MTCNN and FaceNet. [JRC]. *Journal of Robotics and Control, 4*(4), 431–437. DOI: 10.18196/jrc.v4i4.18780

Darktrace. (2023). *AI-powered cybersecurity platform overview.* https://www.darktrace.com

Darmont, J., Boussaïd, O., Ralaivao, J. C., & Aouiche, K. (2020). AN ARCHITECTURE FRAMEWORK FOR COMPLEX DATA WAREHOUSES. *Proceedings of the Seventh International Conference on Enterprise Information Systems*, 370–373. DOI: 10.5220/0002538503700373

de Fuentes, J. M., González-Manzano, L., Tapiador, J., & Peris-Lopez, P. (2017). PRACIS: Privacy-preserving and aggregatable cybersecurity information sharing. *Computers & Security, 69*, 127–141. DOI: 10.1016/j.cose.2016.12.011

Deng, C., & Qiao, H. "Network security intrusion detection system based on incremental improved convolutional neural network model," *2016 International Conference on Communication and Electronics Systems (ICCES)*, Coimbatore, India, 2016, pp. 1-5, DOI: 10.1109/CESYS.2016.7889881

Denning, D. E. (1987). An intrusion-detection model. *IEEE Transactions on Software Engineering, 13*(2), 222–232. DOI: 10.1109/TSE.1987.232894

Dhanushkodi, K., & Thejas, S. (2024). AI Enabled Threat Detection: Leveraging Artificial Intelligence for Advanced Security and Cyber Threat Mitigation. *IEEE Access : Practical Innovations, Open Solutions, 12*(November), 173127–173136. DOI: 10.1109/ACCESS.2024.3493957

Dhinakaran, N., & Anto, S. (2023). Defenses for adversarial attacks in network intrusion detection system – A survey. *Int. J. Comput. Digit. Syst., 13*(1), 1287–1299. DOI: 10.12785/ijcds/1301105

Di Simone, L., & Zanardi, D. (2020). On the relationship between sport and financial performances: An empirical investigation. *Managerial Finance, 47*(6), 812–824. DOI: 10.1108/MF-09-2020-0478

Differential Privacy Team. Apple. (2017). Learning with privacy at scale. Apple Machine Learning Journal, 1(8). https://machinelearning.apple.com/research/learning-with-privacy-at-scale

Dilek, S., Cakr, H., & Aydn, M. (2015). Applications of artificial intelligence techniques to combating cyber crimes: A review. *International Journal of Artificial Intelligence & Applications, 6*(1), 21–39. DOI: 10.5121/ijaia.2015.6102

Dini, P., Elhanashi, A., Begni, A., Saponara, S., Zheng, Q., & Gasmi, K. (2023). Overview on intrusion detection systems design exploiting machine learning for networking cybersecurity. *Applied Sciences (Basel, Switzerland), 13*(13), 7507. DOI: 10.3390/app13137507

Dolhansky, B., Howes, R., Pflaum, B., Baram, N., & Ferrer, C. C. (2019). The deepfake detection challenge (dfdc) preview dataset. arXiv preprint arXiv:1910.08854.

Dommari, S. (2025). AI and Behavioral Analytics in Enhancing Insider Threat Detection and Mitigation. SSRN *Electronic Journal, 9*(1). DOI: 10.2139/ssrn.5259337

Dorigo, M., & Stützle, T. (2004). *Ant colony optimization*. MIT Press., DOI: 10.7551/mitpress/1290.001.0001

Douligeris, C., & Mitrokotsa, A. (2004). DDoS attacks and defense mechanisms: Classification and state-of-the-art. *Computer Networks, 44*(5), 643–666. DOI: 10.1016/j.comnet.2003.10.003

Duah, M. A. (2023). The disruption of money laundering in the western hemisphere as an effect on developing states – Can international customary law maintain and create a standard to improve financial regulation at an international level? *The Disruption of Money Laundering in the Western Hemisphere as an Effect on Developing States – Can International Customary Law Maintain and Create a Standard to Improve Financial Regulation at an International Level?* https://sas-space.sas.ac.uk/6849/

Dupuis, D., & Gleason, K. (2021). Money laundering with cryptocurrency: Open doors and the regulatory dialectic. *Journal of Financial Crime, 28*(1), 60–74. DOI: 10.1108/JFC-06-2020-0113

Dwork, C., & Roth, A. (2014). The algorithmic foundations of differential privacy. *Foundations and Trends in Theoretical Computer Science*, *9*(3-4), 211–407. DOI: 10.1561/0400000042

Dwork, C., Rothblum, G. N., & Vadhan, S. (2010). Boosting and differential privacy. In *Proceedings of the 2010 IEEE 51st Annual Symposium on Foundations of Computer Science* (pp. 51–60). IEEE. DOI: 10.1109/FOCS.2010.12

Eiben, A. E., & Smith, J. E. (2015). *Introduction to evolutionary computing* (2nd ed.). Springer., DOI: 10.1007/978-3-662-44874-8

Eleftheriou, I., Embury, S. M., Moden, R., Dobinson, P., & Brass, A. (2018). Data journeys: Identifying social and technical barriers to data movement in large, complex organisations. *Journal of Biomedical Informatics, 78*(April 2017), 102–122. DOI: 10.1016/j.jbi.2017.12.001

Evans, E. (2003). *Domain-driven design: Tackling complexity in the heart of software*. Addison-Wesley Professional.

Fagade, T., & Tryfonas, T. (2017). *Fagade, T ., & Tryfonas, T . (2017). Malicious Insider Threat Detection : A Conceptual Model . In Security and Protection of Information 2017 (SPI) (Security and Protection of Information). University of Defence . Advance online publication . University of Bristol – Bristol Research Portal Malicious Insider Threat Detection : A Conceptual Model. 2017.*

Fan Data: Personalized Fan Engagement | Deloitte US. (2025, July 4). Deloitte. https://www.deloitte.com/us/en/services/consulting/articles/personalized-fan-engagement.html

Foerst, A. (2023). Artificial intelligence: Walking the boundary. *Artificial Intelligence: Walking the Boundary*, *73*(i), 160–163.

Forrester Research. (2024). *The Forrester wave: Extended detection and response platforms, Q1 2024*. Forrester Research, Inc.

Francois, J., Aib, I., & Boutaba, R. (2012). FireCol: A collaborative protection network for the detection of flooding DDoS attacks. *IEEE/ACM Transactions on Networking*, *20*(6), 1828–1841. DOI: 10.1109/TNET.2012.2194508

Fredrikson, M., Jha, S., & Ristenpart, T. (2015). Model inversion attacks that exploit confidence information and basic countermeasures. In *Proceedings of the 22nd ACM SIGSAC Conference on Computer and Communications Security* (pp. 1322–1333). ACM. DOI: 10.1145/2810103.2813677

Future-Proof Your Security: Actionable Quantum-Safe Solutions for 2025 | FutureX. (2025, February 28). Futurex. https://www.googleadservices.com/pagead/aclk?sa=L&ai=DChsSEwiZ6tqVutWOAxXEo2YCHWLLCrQYACICCAEQAxoCc20&co=1&ase=2&gclid=Cj0KCQjws4fEBhD-ARIsACC3d29Qt6Amcw3IEn7rFUXgJ97XjYunH1GVl56E_p6_SYl7xeUr1DoY7oAaAsIYEALw_wcB&ohost=www.google.com&cid=CAESVeD2IPG2tckLvB3ThvHG_-PagpjXeTk_gQy3FDAjF2BSIBcb0JJjWhecgG6THHTe1h-h6WoUJFyqJ1FDvS0tJZmwMG7EF3zYk-EJolfrVcg8e1Rsj9g&category=acrcp_v1_40&sig=AOD64_1KH4QBqFejYMzpgwhOLR5df_4liw&q&nis=4&adurl&ved=2ahUKEwjo59WVutWOAxUt2DgGHex8DKoQ0Qx6BAgLEAE

Gajjar, S. R.Shraddhaben R. Gajjar. (2025). Neuro-symbolic ai for cloud intrusion detection: A hybrid intelligence approach. *GSC Adv. Res. Rev.*, *22*(2), 142–144. DOI: 10.30574/gscarr.2025.22.2.0049

Gambín, Á. F., Yazidi, A., Vasilakos, A., Haugerud, H., & Djenouri, Y. (2024). Deepfakes: Current and future trends. *Artificial Intelligence Review*, *57*(3), 64.

Garcia, A. R., Filipe, S. B., Fernandes, C., Estevão, C., & Ramos, G. (2020). *Humans, animals, machines: Blurring boundaries*. State University of New York Press.

Gartner. (2024). Market guide for security information and event management. Gartner, Inc.

Gatlan, S. (2019, December 20). Tokyo 2020 Staff warns of phishing disguised as official emails. *BleepingComputer*. https://www.bleepingcomputer.com/news/security/tokyo-2020-staff-warns-of-phishing-disguised-as-official-emails/

GeeksforGeeks. (2025, July 12). *What is DDoS(Distributed Denial of Service)?* GeeksforGeeks. https://www.geeksforgeeks.org/computer-networks/what-is-ddosdistributed-denial-of-service/

Gentry, C. (2009). Fully homomorphic encryption using ideal lattices. In *Proceedings of the 41st Annual ACM Symposium on Theory of Computing* (pp. 169–178). ACM. DOI: 10.1145/1536414.1536440

George, A. S., Baskar, T., & Srikaanth, P. B. (2024). Cyber Threats to Critical Infrastructure: Assessing Vulnerabilities Across Key Sectors. [PUIIJ]. *Partners Universal International Innovation Journal*, *2*(1), 51–75. DOI: 10.5281/zenodo.10639463

Geyer, R. C., Klein, T., & Nabi, M. (2017). Differentially private federated learning: A client-level perspective. arXiv. https://arxiv.org/abs/1712.07557

GitHub. (2018). February 28th DDoS incident report. GitHub Blog. https://github.blog/2018-03-01-ddos-incident-report

Goldreich, O. (2019). Foundations of cryptography: Volume 2, Basic applications. Cambridge University Press.

Goodall, J. R. (2008). Introduction to visualization for computer security. In *VizSEC 2007* (pp. 1–17). Springer., DOI: 10.1007/978-3-540-78243-8_1

Goodall, J. R., Lutters, W. G., Rheingans, P., & Komlodi, A. (2006). Focusing on context in network traffic analysis. *IEEE Computer Graphics and Applications, 26*(2), 72–80. DOI: 10.1109/MCG.2006.31 PMID: 16548462

Goodfellow, I., Shlens, J., & Szegedy, C. (2015). Explaining and harnessing adversarial examples. In *Proceedings of the International Conference on Learning Representations.* https://arxiv.org/abs/1412.6572

Goriparthi, R. G. (2024). *AI-Enhanced Data Mining Techniques for Large-Scale Financial Fraud Detection Rithin Gopal Goriparthi Department of Computer science, San Francisco Bay University.* Issue November.

Goswami, A. (2025). Privacy-preserving AI models in cloud-based cybersecurity. https://books.google.com/books?hl=en&lr=&id=cUZKEQAAQBAJ

Greenberg, A. (2018, February 12). "Olympic Destroyer" malware hit Pyeongchang ahead of opening ceremony. *WIRED.* https://www.wired.com/story/olympic-destroyer-malware-pyeongchang-opening-ceremony

Greenberg, A., & Excerpt. (2019, October 17). Inside Olympic Destroyer, the most deceptive hack in history. *WIRED.* https://www.wired.com/story/untold-story-2018-olympics-destroyer-cyberattack/

Gregg, B. (2013). *Systems performance: Enterprise and the cloud.* Prentice Hall.

Guarnera, L., Giudice, O., & Battiato, S. (2020). Deepfake detection by analyzing convolutional traces. In *Proceedings of the IEEE/CVF conference on computer vision and pattern recognition workshops* (pp. 666-667).

Gudepu, B. K. (2016)... *AI-Powered Anomaly Detection Systems for Insider Threat Prevention.*, *2*(2), 1–9.

Gueye, B., Ziviani, A., Crovella, M., & Fdida, S. (2006). Constraint-based geolocation of internet hosts. *IEEE/ACM Transactions on Networking, 14*(6), 1219–1232. DOI: 10.1109/TNET.2006.886332

Guo, F., Jiao, H., Zhang, X., Zhou, Y., & Feng, H. (2024). Information security network intrusion detection system based on machine learning. In *2024 International Conference on Data Science and Network Security (ICDSNS)* (pp. 1–4). IEEE. DOI: 10.1109/ICDSNS62112.2024.10691041

H. S. V. N. M., R. M. P., & E. S. G. S. R. (2023). CopulaGAN boosted random forest-based network intrusion detection system for hospital network infrastructure. In 2023 14th International Conference on Computing Communication and Networking Technologies (ICCCNT) (pp. 1–7). IEEE. DOI: 10.1109/ICCCNT56998.2023.10306951

Haddad Pajouh, H., Dehghantanha, A., Khayami, R., Choo, K. K. R., & Parizi, R. M. (2019). A survey on deep learning approaches for intrusion detection systems. *Computers & Security*, *86*, 35–56. DOI: 10.1016/j.cose.2019.05.008

Hafez, I. Y., Hafez, A. Y., Saleh, A., Abd El-Mageed, A. A., & Abohany, A. A. (2025). A systematic review of AI-enhanced techniques in credit card fraud detection. *Journal of Big Data*, *12*(1), 6. DOI: 10.1186/s40537-024-01048-8

Haidar, D., & Gaber, M. M. (2019). *Data Stream Clustering for Real-Time Anomaly Detection: An Application to Insider Threats*. 115–144. DOI: 10.1007/978-3-319-97864-2_6

Halbouni, A., Gunawan, T. S., Habaebi, M. H., Halbouni, M., Kartiwi, M., & Ahmad, R. (2022). Machine Learning and Deep Learning Approaches for CyberSecurity: A Review. *IEEE Access*, *10*(Ml), 19572–19585. DOI: 10.1109/ACCESS.2022.3151248

Hall, M., Kea, B., & Wang, R. (2019). Recognising bias in studies of diagnostic tests part 1: Patient selection. *Emergency Medicine Journal : EMJ*, *176*(3), 139–148. DOI: 10.1136/emermed-2019-208446

Hanafi, H., Pranolo, A., Mao, Y., Hariguna, T., Hernandez, L., & Kurniawan, N. F. (2023). IDSX-Attention: Intrusion detection system (IDS) based hybrid MADE-SDAE and LSTM-Attention mechanism. *Int. J. Adv. Intell. Inform.*, *9*(1), 121. DOI: 10.26555/ijain.v9i1.942

Han, S., Mao, H., & Dally, W. J. (2016). Deep compression: Compressing deep neural networks with pruning, trained quantization and Huffman coding. *International Conference on Learning Representations (ICLR)*. https://arxiv.org/abs/1510.00149

Hard, A., Rao, K., Mathews, R., Ramaswamy, S., Beaufays, F., Augenstein, S., Eichner, H., Kiddon, C., & Ramage, D. (2018). Federated learning for mobile keyboard prediction. arXiv. https://arxiv.org/abs/1811.03604

Haroon, M. S., & Ali, H. M. (2023). Ensemble adversarial training based defense against adversarial attacks for machine learning-based intrusion detection system. *Neural Network World*, *33*(5), 317–336. DOI: 10.14311/NNW.2023.33.018

Harrath, Y., Adohinzin, O., Kaabi, K., & Ka, S. (2025). Bridging domains: Advances in explainable, automated, and privacy-preserving AI for computer science and cybersecurity. *Computers*, *14*(9), 374. Advance online publication. DOI: 10.3390/computers14090374

Hashemi, S. K., Mirtaheri, S. L., & Greco, S. (2023). Fraud Detection in Banking Data by Machine Learning Techniques. *IEEE Access : Practical Innovations, Open Solutions*, *11*(January), 3034–3043. DOI: 10.1109/ACCESS.2022.3232287

Helmiawan, M. A., Julian, E., Cahyan, Y., & Saeppani, A. (2021). Experimental evaluation of security monitoring and notification on network intrusion detection system for server security. In 2021 9th International Conference on Cyber and IT Service Management (CITSM) (pp. 1–6). IEEE. DOI: 10.1109/CITSM52892.2021.9588988

Herath, H. M. M. (2025). Advancing Machine Learning for Financial Fraud Detection : A Comprehensive Review of Algorithms, Challenges, and Future Directions. *ASEAN Journal of Economic and Economic Education*, *1*(February), 49–67.

Hevner, A. R., March, S. T., Park, J., & Ram, S. (2004). Design science in information systems research. *Management Information Systems Quarterly*, *28*(1), 75–105. DOI: 10.2307/25148625

Homoliak, I., Toffalini, F., Guarnizo, J., Elovici, Y., & Ochoa, M. (2020). Insight into insiders and IT: A survey of insider threat taxonomies, analysis, modeling, and countermeasures. *ACM Computing Surveys*, *52*(2), 1–40. Advance online publication. DOI: 10.1145/3303771

How data privacy compliance strategies can mitigate cyber threats. (2024, August 5). Thomson Reuters Legal. https://legal.thomsonreuters.com/en/insights/articles/understanding-data-privacy-a-compliance-strategy-can-mitigate-cyber-threats

Huang, C., Li, J., Zhang, Y., & Wang, X. (2023). Artificial intelligence-driven cybersecurity: Emerging trends and future directions. *IEEE Access : Practical Innovations, Open Solutions*, *11*, 15432–15445. DOI: 10.1109/ACCESS.2023.3245678

Hunker, J. Jeffrey Hunker Associates LLC, Probst, C. W., & Technical University of Denmark. (n.d.). Insiders and insider threats. In *Journal of Wireless Mobile Networks, Ubiquitous Computing, and Dependable Applications* (Vols. 2–2, pp. 4–27). https://isyou.info/jowua/papers/jowua-v2n1-1.pdf

Husnaningtyas, N., & Totok Dewayanto, . (2023). FINANCIAL FRAUD DETECTION AND MACHINE LEARNING ALGORITHM (UNSUPERVISED LEARNING): SYSTEMATIC LITERATURE REVIEW. *Jurnal Riset Akuntansi Dan Bisnis Airlangga*, *8*(2), 1521–1542. DOI: 10.20473/jraba.v8i2.49927

Ibitoye, O., Abou-Khamis, R., el Shehaby, M., Matrawy, A., & Shafiq, M. O. (2019). The threat of adversarial attacks on machine learning in network security –. *Survey (London, England).*

IEEE Standards Association. (2023). *IEEE recommended practice for software requirements specifications (IEEE Std 830-1998).* IEEE.

Ifty, A. A. (2023). Introduction to the Perceptron and Its Applications. *Research Paper, December 2023.* DOI: 10.13140/RG.2.2.10439.10404

Iguodala, O. D., & Oyiborhoro, A. (2025). AI-Powered Anti-Money Laundering (AML) and fraud detection - enhancing financial security through intelligent fraud detection. *World Journal of Advanced Research and Reviews, 26*(2), 3702–3714. DOI: 10.30574/wjarr.2025.26.2.0637

Ijiga, O. M., Idoko, I. P., Ebiega, G. I., Olajide, F. I., Olatunde, T. I., & Ukaegbu, C. (2024). Harnessing adversarial machine learning for advanced threat detection: AI-driven strategies in cybersecurity risk assessment and fraud prevention. *Journal of Science and Technology, 11*(1), 1–24. DOI: 10.53022/oarjst.2024.11.1.0060

Ingle, S. (2017, November 27). Wada cyber attack: Williams sisters and Simone Biles targeted by Russian group. *The Guardian.* https://www.theguardian.com/sport/2016/sep/13/wada-russian-cyber-attack-espionage-group?utm_source=chatgpt.com

International Organization for Standardization. (2013). *Information technology — Security techniques — Information security management systems — Requirements (ISO/IEC 27001:2013).* ISO.

Islam, Z., Shil, S. K., & Buiya, R. (2024). Ai-Driven Fraud Detection in Financial Services: Enhancing Security and Building Trust in the Digital Age. *European Economic Letters, October 2023.* DOI: 10.52783/eel.v14i4.2124

Islam, T., Islam, S. M., Sarkar, A., Obaidur, A., Khan, R., Paul, R., & Bari, M. S. (2024). Artificial intelligence in fraud detection and financial risk mitigation: Future directions and business applications. *International Journal for Multidisciplinary Research, 6*(5), 1–23.

ISO/IEC 27001:2013. Information technology — Security techniques — Information security management systems — Requirements.

Isolauri, E. A., & Ameer, I. (2023). Money laundering as a transnational business phenomenon: A systematic review and future agenda. *Critical Perspectives on International Business, 19*(3), 426–468. DOI: 10.1108/cpoib-10-2021-0088

Iyamu, T. (2019). The architectures of data and information: Their confounded confusion. *South African Journal of Information Management, 21*(1), 1–9. DOI: 10.4102/sajim.v21i1.1060

Iyamu, T. (2023). The architecture of information in organisations. *South African Journal of Information Management, 13*(1). Advance online publication. DOI: 10.4102/sajim.v13i1.419

Jackson, T., Jessop, M., Fletcher, M., & Austin, J. (2023). A Virtual Organisation deployed on a Service Orientated Architecture for Distributed Data Mining applications. In *Grid-Based Problem Solving Environments* (Vol. 239, pp. 155–170). Springer US., DOI: 10.1007/978-0-387-73659-4_9

Jahan Sarna, N., Ahmed Rithen, F., Salma Jui, U., Belal, S., Amin, A., Kabir Oishee, T., & Muzahidul Islam, A. K. M. (2025). AI Driven Fraud Detection Models in Financial Networks: A Comprehensive Systematic Review. *IEEE Access : Practical Innovations, Open Solutions, 13*(August), 141204–141233. DOI: 10.1109/ACCESS.2025.3596060

Javaid, A., Niyaz, Q., Sun, W., & Alam, M. (2016). A deep learning approach for network intrusion detection system. *EAI International Conference on Bio-inspired Information and Communications Technologies*. DOI: 10.4108/eai.3-12-2015.2262516

Jayaraman, B., & Evans, D. (2019). Evaluating differentially private machine learning in practice. In *Proceedings of the 28th USENIX Security Symposium* (pp. 1895–1912). USENIX Association.

Jnguyen. (2023, June 5). *Ransomware Attack - What is it and How Does it Work?* Check Point Software. https://www.checkpoint.com/cyber-hub/threat-prevention/ransomware/

Johora, F. T., Hasan, R., Farabi, S. F., Akter, J., & Al Mahmud, M. A. (2024). AI-POWERED FRAUD DETECTION IN BANKING: SAFEGUARDING FINANCIAL TRANSACTIONS. *The American Journal of Management and Economics Innovations, 6*(6), 8–22. DOI: 10.37547/tajmei/Volume06Issue06-02

Kairouz, P., McMahan, H. B., Avent, B., Bellet, A., Bennis, M., Bhagoji, A. N., Bonawitz, K., Charles, Z., Cormode, G., Cummings, R., D'Oliveira, R. G. L., Eichner, H., El Rouayheb, S., Evans, D., Gardner, J., Garrett, Z., Gascón, A., Ghazi, B., Gibbons, P. B., & Zhao, S. (2019). Advances and open problems in federated learning. arXiv. https://arxiv.org/abs/1912.04977

Kamuangu, P. (2024). A Review on Financial Fraud Detection using AI and Machine Learning. *Journal of Economics. Finance and Accounting Studies*, *6*(1), 67–77. DOI: 10.32996/jefas.2024.6.1.7

Kamuangu, P. K. (2024). Journal of Economics, Finance and Accounting Studies A Review on Financial Fraud Detection using AI and Machine Learning. *Journal of Economics. Finance and Accounting Studies*, *6*(1), 67–77. DOI: 10.32996/jefas

Kaplan, A., & Haenlein, M. (2019). Siri, Siri, in my hand: Who's the fairest in the land? On the interpretations, illustrations, and implications of artificial intelligence. *Business Horizons*, *62*(1), 15–25. DOI: 10.1016/j.bushor.2018.08.004

Kaur, H., & Sinha, A. (2021). Machine learning-based intrusion detection systems: A comprehensive survey. *Journal of Network and Computer Applications*, *170*, 102804. DOI: 10.1016/j.jnca.2020.102804

Kavitha, R., & Amutha, S. (2022). Performance analysis of deep neural network and LSTM models for secure network intrusion detection system. In 2022 IEEE 4th International Conference on Cybernetics, Cognition and Machine Learning Applications (ICCCMLA) (pp. 390–396). IEEE. DOI: 10.1109/ICCCMLA56841.2022.9989253

Kemmerer, R. A., & Vigna, G. (2002). Intrusion detection: A brief history and overview. *Computer*, *35*(4), 27–30. DOI: 10.1109/MC.2002.1012428

Khalil, H. A., & Maged, S. A. (2021). *"Deepfakes creation and detection using deep learning." 2021 International Mobile, Intelligent, and Ubiquitous Computing Conference (MIUCC)*. IEEE.

Khamis, R. A., Shafiq, M. O., & Matrawy, A. (2020, June). Investigating Resistance of Deep Learning-based IDS against Adversaries using min-max Optimization. *ICC 2020 - 2020 IEEE International Conference on Communications (ICC).*

Khamis, R. A., & Matrawy, A. (2020, October). Evaluation of adversarial training on different types of neural networks in deep learning-based IDSs. *2020 International Symposium on Networks, Computers and Communications (ISNCC)*. DOI: 10.1109/ISNCC49221.2020.9297344

Khan, M. A., Karim, M. R., & Kim, Y. (2020). A scalable hybrid intrusion detection system based on machine learning techniques. *Journal of Information Security and Applications*, *52*, 102447. DOI: 10.1016/j.jisa.2020.102447

Khan, S. (2024).. . *ADAPTIVE CYBERSECURITY STRATEGIES FOR CLOUD-BASED REAL-TIME DATA.*, *15*(5), 414–424.

Khattak, H. A., Latif, S., & Farooq, M. (2019). Optimization models for cyber security: A review. *Computers & Security*, *85*, 398–421.

Khotanzad, A., & Chung, C. (2020). Application of multi-layer perceptron neural networks to vision problems. *Neural Computing & Applications*, *7*(3), 249–259. DOI: 10.1007/BF01414886

Kim, B., Sagduyu, Y. E., Davaslioglu, K., Erpek, T., & Ulukus, S. (2020). *How to make 5G communications ``invisible'': Adversarial machine learning for wireless privacy.*

Kim, A., Oh, J., Ryu, J., & Lee, K. (2020). A review of insider threat detection approaches with IoT perspective. *IEEE Access : Practical Innovations, Open Solutions*, *8*, 78847–78867. DOI: 10.1109/ACCESS.2020.2990195

Kim, J., Kim, J., Kang, H., & Youn, B. (2025). Ethical implications of artificial intelligence in sport: A systematic scoping review. *Journal of Sport and Health Science. Journal of Sport and Health Science*, *101047*, 101047. Advance online publication. DOI: 10.1016/j.jshs.2025.101047 PMID: 40316133

Kim, J., Park, M., Kim, H., Cho, S., & Kang, P. (2019). Insider threat detection based on user behavior modeling and anomaly detection algorithms. *Applied Sciences (Basel, Switzerland)*, *9*(19), 4018. Advance online publication. DOI: 10.3390/app9194018

Kim, J., Park, S., & Lee, H. (2021). Detecting insider threats using unsupervised machine learning in enterprise environments. *Computers & Security*, *101*, 102127. DOI: 10.1016/j.cose.2020.102127

Kiran, A., Prakash, S. W., & Kumar, B. A., Likhitha, Sameeratmaja, T., & Charan, U. S. S. R. (2023). Intrusion detection system using machine learning. In 2023 International Conference on Computer Communication and Informatics (ICCCI) (pp. 1–4). IEEE. DOI: 10.1109/ICCCI56745.2023.10128363

Kleyko, D., Rosato, A., Frady, E. P., Panella, M., & Sommer, F. T. (2024). Perceptron Theory Can Predict the Accuracy of Neural Networks. *IEEE Transactions on Neural Networks and Learning Systems*, *35*(7), 9885–9899. DOI: 10.1109/TNNLS.2023.3237381

Kohli, A., & Gupta, A. (2021). Detecting deepfake, faceswap and face2face facial forgeries using frequency cnn. *Multimedia Tools and Applications*, *80*(12), 18461–18478. DOI: 10.1007/s11042-020-10420-8

Kolias, C., Kambourakis, G., Stavrou, A., & Voas, J. (2017). DDoS in the IoT: Mirai and other botnets. *Computer*, *50*(7), 80–84. DOI: 10.1109/MC.2017.201

Koli, L., Kalra, S., Thakur, R., Saifi, A., & Singh, K. (2025). *AI-Driven IRM: Transforming insider risk management with adaptive scoring and LLM-based threat detection*. https://arxiv.org/abs/2505.03796

Korea JoongAng Daily. (2024, March 13). *Faker's League of Legends team the latest victim of DDoS attack*. https://koreajoongangdaily.joins.com/news/2024-03-13/business/industry/Fakers-League-of-Legends-team-the-latest-victim-of-DDoS-attack/2000553

Korteling, J. E., van de Boer-Visschedijk, G. C., Blankendaal, R. A. M., Boonekamp, R. C., & Eikelboom, A. R. (2021). Human- versus Artificial Intelligence. *Frontiers in Artificial Intelligence*, *4*(March), 1–13. DOI: 10.3389/frai.2021.622364

Kotb, H. M., Gaber, T., AlJanah, S., Zawbaa, H. M., & Alkhathami, M. (2025). A novel deep synthesis-based insider intrusion detection (DS-IID) model for malicious insiders and AI-generated threats. *Scientific Reports*, *15*(1), 1–14. DOI: 10.1038/s41598-024-84673-w PMID: 39747424

Koutsouvelis, V., Shiaeles, S., Ghita, B., & Bendiab, G. (2020). Detection of insider threats using artificial intelligence and visualisation. *Proceedings of the 2020 IEEE Conference on Network Softwarization: Bridging the Gap Between AI and Network Softwarization, NetSoft 2020*, 437–443. DOI: 10.1109/NetSoft48620.2020.9165337

Krebs, B. (2016). KrebsOnSecurity hit with record DDoS. KrebsOnSecurity Blog. https://krebsonsecurity.com/2016/09/krebsonsecurity-hit-with-record-ddos/

Kumar, K., Joshi, R. C., & Singh, K. (2011). A distributed approach using entropy to detect DDoS attacks in ISP domain. In *Proceedings of the International Conference on Signal Processing, Communications and Computing*. IEEE.

Kumar, R., & Singh, R. (2020). Machine learning approaches for enterprise network security: A survey. *International Journal of Computer Applications*.

Kumar, S., Doshi, R. P., Patel, B., Bharadi, B. J., Bairwa, A. K., & Kotecha, S. (2021). A comprehensive survey on distributed denial-of-service (DDoS) attacks and defense techniques in SDN environment. *Journal of Information Security and Applications*, *60*, 102855. Advance online publication. DOI: 10.1016/j.jisa.2021.102855

Kuzmanovic, A., & Knightly, E. W. (2006). Low-rate TCP-targeted denial of service attacks and counter strategies. *IEEE/ACM Transactions on Networking*, *14*(4), 683–696. DOI: 10.1109/TNET.2006.880180

Kwon, D., Kim, H., Kim, J., Suh, S. C., Kim, I., & Kim, K. J. (2022). A survey of deep learning-based network anomaly detection. *Cluster Computing*, *25*, 473–493. DOI: 10.1007/s10586-021-03474-9

KYODO NEWS. (2025, May 15). Phishing scam on Tokyo 2020 Olympics tickets spotted. *Japan Wire by KYODO NEWS*. https://english.kyodonews.net/articles/-/7784

Lai, G. (2023). Artificial Intelligence Techniques for Fraud Detection. In *Preprints*. DOI: 10.20944/preprints202312.1115.v1

Lakkaraju, K., Yurcik, W., & Lee, A. J. (2004). NVisionIP: Netflow visualizations of system state for security situational awareness. In *Proceedings of the ACM Workshop on Visualization and Data Mining for Computer Security* (pp. 65–72). ACM. DOI: 10.1145/1029208.1029219

Lee, C.-W., Fu, M.-W., Wang, C.-C., & Azis, M. I. (2025). Evaluating Machine Learning Algorithms for Financial Fraud Detection: Insights from Indonesia. *Mathematics*, *13*(4), 600. DOI: 10.3390/math13040600

Lee, S., & Kim, H. (2017). DDoS detection method using CNN-based deep learning. *KSII Transactions on Internet and Information Systems*, *11*(10), 5177–5190.

Lee, W., & Stolfo, S. J. (1998). Data mining approaches for intrusion detection. In *Proceedings of the 7th USENIX Security Symposium* (pp. 79–94). USENIX Association.

Li, J. (2022). Network intrusion detection algorithm and simulation of complex system in Internet environment. In 2022 4th International Conference on Inventive Research in Computing Applications (ICIRCA) (pp. 520–523). IEEE. DOI: 10.1109/ICIRCA54612.2022.9985720

Li, P., Liu, Q., Zhao, W., Wang, D., & Wang, S. (2018). *BEBP: An poisoning method against machine learning based IDSs*.

Li, X. (2022). Research and design of network intrusion detection system. In 2022 IEEE 2nd International Conference on Power, Electronics and Computer Applications (ICPECA) (pp. 1069–1072). IEEE. DOI: 10.1109/ICPECA53709.2022.9718920

Liang, X. (2025). Smart stadiums and the future of sports entertainment: Leveraging IoT, AI, and blockchain for enhanced fan engagement and venue management. *Applied and Computational Engineering*, *138*(1), 155–160. DOI: 10.54254/2755-2721/2025.21386

Lin, A. K. (2024). The AI Revolution in Financial Services : Emerging Methods for Fraud Detection and Prevention. *Jurnal Galaksi*, *1*(1), 43–51. DOI: 10.70103/galaksi.v1i1.5

Li, T., Sahu, A. K., Talwalkar, A., & Smith, V. (2020). Federated learning: Challenges, methods, and future directions. *IEEE Signal Processing Magazine*, *37*(3), 50–60. DOI: 10.1109/MSP.2020.2975749

Li, T., & Zhai, X. "Design and Implementation of an Initiative and Passive Network Intrusion Detection System," *2009 Second International Symposium on Information Science and Engineering*, Shanghai, China, 2009, pp. 196-198, DOI: 10.1109/ISISE.2009.29

Liu, Y., Li, S., Chen, F., Vorobeychik, E., & Chen, B. (2021). Adversarial machine learning in network intrusion detection systems. *ACM Computing Surveys*, *54*(6), 126. Advance online publication. DOI: 10.1145/3447548

Li, W., Liu, J., Meng, W., & Kwok, L. F. (2020). Enhancing collaborative intrusion detection networks against insider attacks using supervised machine learning. *Journal of Network and Computer Applications*, *143*, 127–140.

Li, X., Li, X., Jia, J., Li, L., Yuan, J., Gao, Y., & Yu, S. (2023). A High Accuracy and Adaptive Anomaly Detection Model With Dual-Domain Graph Convolutional Network for Insider Threat Detection. *IEEE Transactions on Information Forensics and Security*, *18*, 1638–1652. DOI: 10.1109/TIFS.2023.3245413

Lonare, M. B., Joshi, B. C., Tripathy, S. K., Kumar, S., & Tiwari, S. (2024). Real-time network monitoring and reporting using network intrusion detection system. In 2024 IEEE 9th International Conference for Convergence in Technology (I2CT) (pp. 1–6). IEEE. DOI: 10.1109/I2CT61223.2024.10543613

Lou, W. (2023, June). Fortifying your defenses: Techniques to thwart adversarial attacks and boost performance of machine learning-based intrusion detection systems. *Proceedings of the 2023 ACM Workshop on Wireless Security and Machine Learning*. DOI: 10.1145/3586209.3591392

Luckey, D., Stebbins, D., Orrie, R., Rebhan, E., Bhatt, S. D., & Beaghley, S. (2019). *Assessing continuous evaluation approaches for insider threats.*

Lunt, T. F. (1993). A survey of intrusion detection techniques. *Computers & Security*, *12*(4), 405–418. DOI: 10.1016/0167-4048(93)90029-5

Luo, B., Zhang, Z., Wang, Q., Ke, A., Lu, S., & He, B. (2025). AI-powered Fraud Detection in Decentralized Finance: A Project Life Cycle Perspective. *ACM Computing Surveys*, *57*(4), 1–38. DOI: 10.1145/3705296

Lu, W., Wang, D., & Yang, Q. (2020). Concept drift adaptation in deep learning-based intrusion detection systems. *Neurocomputing*, *414*, 223–233. DOI: 10.1016/j.neucom.2020.06.015

Ma, Q., & Rastogi, N. (2020). DANTE: Predicting insider threat using LSTM on system logs. *Proceedings - 2020 IEEE 19th International Conference on Trust, Security and Privacy in Computing and Communications, TrustCom 2020, December 2020*, 1151–1156. DOI: 10.1109/TrustCom50675.2020.00153

Mainul, M., Zerine, I., Rahman, M. A., Islam, M. S., & Ahmed, M. Y. (2025). AI-Driven Fraud Detection in Financial Transactions Using Machine Learning and Deep Learning to Detect Anomalies and Fraudulent Activities in Banking and E-Commerce Transactions. SSRN *Electronic Journal, 16*(5). DOI: 10.2139/ssrn.5287281

Malik, P., Shahdadpuri, P., Malviya, R., Patil, R., Badwaniya, V., & Rudra Sthapak. (2024). Biometric data analysis in Athlete Monitoring: advancements, applications, and implications. *International Journal of Innovative Research in Technology, 10*(12). https://www.researchgate.net/publication/381160736

Malone, H., Nicholl, H., & Tracey, C. (2023). Awareness and minimisation of systematic bias in research. *British Journal of Nursing (Mark Allen Publishing), 23*(5), 279–282. DOI: 10.12968/bjon.2014.23.5.279

Mamieva, D., Abdusalomov, A. B., Mukhiddinov, M., & Whangbo, T. K. (2023). Improved face detection method via learning small faces on hard images based on a deep learning approach. *Sensors (Basel), 23*(1), 502.

Marcus, G. F. (2023). Multilayer Perceptrons. In *The Algebraic Mind* (pp. 7–34). The MIT Press., DOI: 10.7551/mitpress/1187.003.0004

Mari, A.-G., Zinca, D., & Dobrota, V. (2023). Development of a machine-learning intrusion detection system and testing of its performance using a generative adversarial network. *Sensors (Basel), 23*(3), 1315. DOI: 10.3390/s23031315 PMID: 36772355

Marius-Constantin, P., Balas, V. E., Perescu-Popescu, L., & Mastorakis, N. (2025). Multilayer Perceptron (in Neural Networks). In *Machine Learning for Industrial Applications* (Vol. 8, Issue 7, pp. 51–61). Wiley. DOI: 10.1002/9781394268993.ch3

Masood, M., Nawaz, M., Malik, K. M., Javed, A., Irtaza, A., & Malik, H. (2023). Deepfakes generation and detection: State-of-the-art, open challenges, countermeasures, and way forward. *Applied Intelligence, 53*(4), 3974–4026. DOI: 10.1007/s10489-022-03766-z

Masunda, M. (2025). Adaptive Threat Intelligence Systems for Real-Time Detection and Mitigation of Sophisticated Cyber Attacks in Enterprise Networks. *International Journal of Research Publication and Reviews, 6*(7), 470–491. DOI: 10.55248/gengpi.6.0725.2433

McMahan, H. B., Moore, E., Ramage, D., Hampson, S., & Arcas, B. A. (2017). Communication-efficient learning of deep networks from decentralized data. In *Proceedings of the 20th International Conference on Artificial Intelligence and Statistics* (pp. 1273–1282). PMLR.

McMillen, J. (2021). Ransom DDoS attacks continue to evolve. *Network Security, 2021*(9), 6–8. DOI: 10.1016/S1353-4858(21)00100-7

Meng, G., Liu, Y., Zhang, J., Pokluda, A., & Boutaba, R. (2015). Collaborative security: A survey and taxonomy. *ACM Computing Surveys, 48*(1), 1–42. Advance online publication. DOI: 10.1145/2785733

Mihai, S., Yaqoob, M., Hung, D. V., Davis, W., Towakel, P., Raza, M., Karamanoglu, M., Barn, B., Shetve, D., Prasad, R. V., Venkataraman, H., Trestian, R., & Nguyen, H. X. (2022). Digital Twins: A Survey on Enabling Technologies, Challenges, Trends and Future Prospects. *IEEE Communications Surveys and Tutorials, 24*(4), 2255–2291. DOI: 10.1109/COMST.2022.3208773

Mirkovic, J., & Reiher, P. (2004). A taxonomy of DDoS attack and DDoS defense mechanisms. *Computer Communication Review, 34*(2), 39–53. DOI: 10.1145/997150.997156

Mirsky, Y., Doitshman, T., Elovici, Y., & Shabtai, A. (2020). Kitsune: An ensemble of autoencoders for online network intrusion detection. *NDSS Symposium*. https://doi.org/DOI: 10.14722/ndss.2020.23036

MITRE Corporation. (2024). MITRE ATT&CK framework version 14. https://attack.mitre.org/

Modi, C., Patel, D., Borisaniya, B., Patel, H., Patel, A., & Rajarajan, M. (2013). A survey of intrusion detection techniques in Cloud. *Journal of Network and Computer Applications, 36*(1), 42–57. DOI: 10.1016/j.jnca.2012.05.003

Mohamed, N. (2025). Artificial intelligence and machine learning in cybersecurity: A deep dive into state-of-the-art techniques and future paradigms. *Knowledge and Information Systems, 67*(8), 6969–7055. Advance online publication. DOI: 10.1007/s10115-025-02429-y

Mohammadi, B., & Sabokrou, M. (2019, October). End-to-end adversarial learning for intrusion detection in computer networks. *2019 IEEE 44th Conference on Local Computer Networks(LCN)*.

Mohammadi, M., Al-Fuqaha, A., Sorour, S., & Guizani, M. (2018). Deep learning for IoT big data and streaming analytics: A survey. *IEEE Communications Surveys and Tutorials, 20*(4), 2923–2960. DOI: 10.1109/COMST.2018.2844341

Moore, A. W., & Zuev, D. (2005). Internet traffic classification using Bayesian analysis techniques. In *Proceedings of the ACM SIGMETRICS Conference* (pp. 50–60). ACM. DOI: 10.1145/1064212.1064220

Moraes, G. S. de O., Ferreira, M. de A., Guim, A., Tabosa, J. N., Chagas, J. C. C., & Almeira, M. de P. (2019). Application of deep learning to cybersecurity: A survey. *Neurocomputing*, *221*, 133–138.

Mosca, M. (2018). Cybersecurity in an era with quantum computers: Will we be ready? *IEEE Security and Privacy*, *16*(5), 38–41. DOI: 10.1109/MSP.2018.3761723

Mothukuri, V., Parizi, R. M., Pouriyeh, S., Huang, Y., Dehghantanha, A., & Srivastava, G. (2021). A survey on security and privacy of federated learning. *Future Generation Computer Systems*, *115*, 619–640. DOI: 10.1016/j.future.2020.10.007

Mudyń, K. (2023). The expansion of artificial intelligence and the problem of values. *The Expansion of Artificial Intelligence and the Problem of Values*, *38*(2), 37–46. DOI: 10.4467/18982026SZL.23.017.18684

Mujawar, M., Gunasekaran, T., Pramono, S., & Muduli, A. (2024). Jeans Substrate Based Circularly Polarized Wearable Dielectric Resonator Antenna. *Wireless Personal Communications*, *134*(4), 1945–1957. DOI: 10.1007/s11277-024-10931-9

Mujawar, M., & Raizada, A. (2025). Enhanced Network Intrusion Detection Using Machine Learning: A Comparative Analysis of Classification Algorithms and Performance Metrics. In Rathore, V. S., Murala, S., Tuba, E., & Singh, M. M. (Eds.), *Modern Practices and Trends in Expert Applications and Security. MP-TEAS 2024. Lecture Notes in Networks and Systems* (Vol. 1379). Springer., DOI: 10.1007/978-981-96-5784-1_28

Mujawar, M., & Raizada, A. (2026). Real-Time Network Intrusion Detection System with Machine Learning. In Choudrie, J., Mahalle, P. N., Perumal, T., & Joshi, A. (Eds.), *ICT for Intelligent Systems. ICTIS 2025. Lecture Notes in Networks and Systems* (Vol. 1509). Springer., DOI: 10.1007/978-981-96-8793-0_14

Mujawar, M., Raizada, A., & Gubbi, A. (2026). AI-Powered Phishing Detection System. In Arbi, A. (Ed.), *Safe Data-Driven Control for Cyber-Physical Systems* (pp. 1–24). IGI Global Scientific Publishing., DOI: 10.4018/979-8-3373-1832-5.ch001

Mujawar, M., Sridharan, M., Kalbande, M., Aggarwal, P., Krishnaiah, N., & Genç, Y. (2024). Optimizing connectivity: A novel AI approach to assess transmission levels in optical networks. *The Journal of Supercomputing*, *80*(18), 26568–26588. DOI: 10.1007/s11227-024-06410-4

Mujawar, M., Vijaya Saradhi, D., Naz, M. A., & Muduli, A. (2022). Design and performance comparison of arrays of circular, square and hexagonal meta-material structures for wearable applications. *Journal of Magnetism and Magnetic Materials, 553*, 169235. DOI: 10.1016/j.jmmm.2022.169235

Munir, A., Aved, A., & Blasch, E. (2022). Situational Awareness: Techniques, Challenges, and Prospects. *AI, 3*(1), 55–77. DOI: 10.3390/ai3010005

Munzner, T. (2000). Interactive visualization of large graphs and networks [Doctoral dissertation, Stanford University].

Naseer, H., Maynard, S. B., & Desouza, K. C. (2021). Demystifying analytical information processing capability: The case of cybersecurity incident response. *Decision Support Systems, 143*, 0–34. DOI: 10.1016/j.dss.2020.113476

National Council of ISACs. (2024). State of information sharing report 2024. National Council of ISACs.

National Institute of Standards and Technology. (2020). *Security and privacy controls for information systems and organizations (NIST SP 800-53, Rev. 5)*. U.S. Department of Commerce., DOI: 10.6028/NIST.SP.800-53r5

National Institute of Standards and Technology. (2023). *Framework for improving critical infrastructure cybersecurity, version 1.1 (NIST Cybersecurity Framework)*. U.S. Department of Commerce., DOI: 10.6028/NIST.CSWP.04162018

Neapolitan, R. E., & Jiang, X. (2018). Neural Networks and Deep Learning. In *Artificial Intelligence* (pp. 389–411). Chapman and Hall/CRC., DOI: 10.1201/b22400-15

Neustar. (2023). Worldwide DDoS attacks and cyber insights research report. Neustar Security Report. https://www.security.neustar/resources/whitepapers

Newman, S. (2015). *Building microservices: Designing fine-grained systems*. O'Reilly Media.

Nexusgroup. (2024, September 6). *How to build a secure IoT infrastructure | Nexus Group*. https://www.nexusgroup.com/how-to-build-a-secure-iot-infrastructure/

Niek, de Vries, K. J., de Jong, M., Dosoula, N., van den Akker, B., Smith, J., Thuong, O., & Bernardi, L. (2021). Machine Learning for Fraud Detection in E-Commerce: A Research Agenda. In *Communications in Computer and Information Science: Vol. 1482 CCIS* (pp. 30–54). DOI: 10.1007/978-3-030-87839-9_2

Nirkin, Y., Wolf, L., Keller, Y., & Hassner, T. (2021). Deepfake detection based on discrepancies between faces and their context. *IEEE Transactions on Pattern Analysis and Machine Intelligence*, *44*(10), 6111–6121. DOI: 10.1109/TPAMI.2021.3093446 PMID: 34185639

NIST. (2018). *Framework for Improving Critical Infrastructure Cybersecurity, Version 1.1*. National Institute of Standards and Technology.

NIST. (2023). Post-quantum cryptography standardization. NIST Computer Security Resource Center. https://csrc.nist.gov/projects/post-quantum-cryptography

Nowostawski, M. M. P. (2021). An architecture for self-organising evolvable virtual machines.International Workshop on Engineering Self-Organising Applications. *An Architecture for Self-Organising Evolvable Virtual Machines." International Workshop on Engineering Self-Organising Applications.*

Nunamaker, J. F.Jr, Chen, M., & Purdin, T. D. (1991). Systems development in information systems research. *Journal of Management Information Systems*, *7*(3), 89–106. DOI: 10.1080/07421222.1990.11517898

NVIDIA. (2024). CUDA toolkit documentation. NVIDIA Corporation. https://docs .nvidia.com/cuda/

Ogundairo, O. Ladoke Akintola University of Technology, & Broklyn, P. (2024). Predictive analytics for cyber threat intelligence. *Journal of Cyber Security*. https:// www.researchgate.net/publication/382918018

Okafor, M. O.Maureen Oluchukwuamaka Okafor. (2024). Deep learning in cybersecurity: Enhancing threat detection and response. *World Journal of Advanced Research and Reviews*, *24*(3), 1116–1132. DOI: 10.30574/wjarr.2024.24.3.3819

OpenTelemetry Community. (2023). OpenTelemetry specification v1.18.0. https:// opentelemetry.io/docs/specs/

Padayachee, K., & Venter, H. S. (2021). Enhancing industrial IoT intrusion detection using hybrid deep learning. *Journal of Industrial Information Integration*, *22*, 100207.

Padhiar, S., & Patel, R. (2023). Outside the Closed World: On Using Machine Learning for Network Intrusion Detection. *Smart Innovation. Systems and Technologies*, *361*(May), 265–270. DOI: 10.1007/978-981-99-3982-4_23

Padmanabhan, V. N., & Subramanian, L. (2001). An investigation of geographic mapping techniques for internet hosts. In *Proceedings of the ACM SIGCOMM Conference* (pp. 173–185). ACM. DOI: 10.1145/383059.383073

Paidy, P. (2025). *AI and Machine Learning in Cyber Threat Detection*. 10–18. DOI: 10.56472/ICCSAIML25-102

Papadopoulos, P., von Essen, O., Pitropakis, N., Chrysoulas, C., Mylonas, A., & Buchanan, W. J. (2021). Launching adversarial attacks against network intrusion detection systems for IoT. *J. Cybersecur. Priv.*, *1*(2), 252–273. DOI: 10.3390/jcp1020014

Papernot, N., McDaniel, P., Sinha, A., & Wellman, M. (2018). SoK: Security and privacy in machine learning. In *Proceedings of the IEEE European Symposium on Security and Privacy* (pp. 399–414). IEEE. DOI: 10.1109/EuroSP.2018.00035

Park, J., Iwai, S., Tanaka, H., & Kurokawa, T. (2014). Analysis of slow HTTP DoS attacks. In *Proceedings of the International Conference on Information Networking* (pp. 232–237). IEEE. DOI: 10.1109/ICOIN.2014.6799694

Pashine, S., Mandiya, S., Gupta, P., & Sheikh, R. (2021). Deep fake detection: survey of facial manipulation detection solutions. arXiv preprint arXiv:2106.12605.

Patel, Y., Tanwar, S., Gupta, R., Bhattacharya, P., Davidson, I. E., Nyameko, R., Aluvala, S., & Vimal, V. (2023). Deepfake generation and detection: Case study and challenges. *IEEE Access : Practical Innovations, Open Solutions*, *11*, 143296–143323. DOI: 10.1109/ACCESS.2023.3342107

Pei, G., Zhang, J., Hu, M., Zhang, Z., Wang, C., Wu, Y., & Tao, D. (2024). Deepfake generation and detection: A benchmark and survey. *ACM Computing Surveys*.

Peng, T., Leckie, C., & Ramamohanarao, K. (2007). Survey of network-based defense mechanisms countering the DoS/DDoS problems. *ACM Computing Surveys*, *39*(1), 3. Advance online publication. DOI: 10.1145/1216370.1216373

Perez, A., Gupta, S., & Bhandari, R. (2022). Understanding IDS failure in logistics: A case-based perspective. *International Journal of Network Security & its Applications*, *14*(2), 45–57.

Perols, J. (2011). Financial Statement Fraud Detection: An Analysis of Statistical and Machine Learning Algorithms. *Auditing*, *30*(2), 19–50. DOI: 10.2308/ajpt-50009

Petrovic, V. M. (2018). Artificial Intelligence and Virtual Worlds Toward Human-Level AI Agents. *IEEE Access : Practical Innovations, Open Solutions*, *6*, 39976–39988. DOI: 10.1109/ACCESS.2018.2855970

Pickman, D. (2023). The use of virtual reality and augmented reality in enhancing the sports viewing experience. *International Journal of Arts Recreation and Sports*, *1*(2), 39–49. DOI: 10.47941/ijars.1516

Plohmann, D., Yakdan, K., Klatt, M., Bader, J., & Gerhards-Padilla, E. (2016). A comprehensive measurement study of domain generating malware. In *Proceedings of the 25th USENIX Security Symposium* (pp. 263–278). USENIX Association.

Polack, F. A. C. (2023). Self-organisation for Survival in Complex Computer Architectures. In *Lecture Notes in Computer Science (including subseries Lecture Notes in Artificial Intelligence and Lecture Notes in Bioinformatics): Vol. 6090 LNCS* (Issue May, pp. 66–83). DOI: 10.1007/978-3-642-14412-7_4

Ponemon Institute. (2023). Cost of a data breach report 2023. IBM Security. https://www.ibm.com/security/data-breach

Ponemon Institute. (2024). *The state of collaborative cybersecurity 2024*. Ponemon Institute LLC.

Pontin, J. (2018). The Limits of Artificial Intelligence and Deep Learning. *Wired, December 2024*, 1–12. DOI: 10.29086/2519-5476/2025/sp43a02

Poudel, S., & Dhungana, U. R. (2022). Artificial intelligence for energy fraud detection: A review. [IJAPE]. *International Journal of Applied Power Engineering, 11*(2), 109. DOI: 10.11591/ijape.v11.i2.pp109-119

Purdum, D. (2022, December 20). Cyberattack breaches DraftKings, FanDuel users - ESPN. *ESPN.com*. https://www.espn.com/sports-betting/story/_/id/35291945/draftkings-fanduel-breached-cyberattack

Qayyum, A., Qayyum, S., Alghamdi, M., & Alghamdi, S. (2021). A deep learning-based threat intelligence framework for enterprise systems. *IEEE Access : Practical Innovations, Open Solutions, 9*, 106131–106144.

R, A., R, A., & R, A. (2025, February 11). Fake Premiere League ticket scams (Campaign). *CyberMaterial - Security Through Data*. https://cybermaterial.com/fake-premiere-league-ticket-scams-campaign/

Radford, A., Metz, L., & Chintala, S. (2019). Unsupervised Representation Learning with Deep Convolutional Generative Adversarial Networks. *4th International Conference on Learning Representations, ICLR 2016 - Conference Track Proceedings*, 1–16. https://arxiv.org/abs/1511.06434

Raghavan, S. S. (2025). A COMPREHENSIVE STUDY OF ARTIFICIAL INTELLIGENCE APPLICATIONS IN INTRUSION DETECTION AND PREVENTION. [IJAIRD]. *International Journal of Artificial Intelligence Research and Development, 3*(1), 16–37. DOI: 10.34218/IJAIRD_03_01_002

Raghuwanshi, P. (2024). AI-Driven Identity and Financial Fraud Detection for National Security. *Journal of Artificial Intelligence General Science (JAIGS) ISSN:3006-4023, 7*(01), 38–51. DOI: 10.60087/jaigs.v7i01.294

Rahman, M. A., Asyhari, A. T., Leong, L. S., Satrya, G. B., Tao, M. H., & Zolkipli, M. F. (2020). Scalable machine learning-based intrusion detection system for IoT-enabled smart cities. *Sustainable Cities and Society, 61*, 102324. Advance online publication. DOI: 10.1016/j.scs.2020.102324

Rana, P. J. (2019). A Survey on Fraud Detection Techniques in Ecommerce. *A Survey on Fraud Detection Techniques in Ecommerce, 113*(14), 5–7.

Rana, A., Singh Rawat, A., Bijalwan, A., & Bahuguna, H. (2018). Application of Multi Layer (Perceptron) Artificial Neural Network in the Diagnosis System: A Systematic Review. *2018 International Conference on Research in Intelligent and Computing in Engineering (RICE), August*, 1–6. DOI: 10.1109/RICE.2018.8509069

Raudys, Š. (2023). Evolution and generalization of a single neurone: I. Single-layer perceptron as seven statistical classifiers. *Neural Networks, 11*(2), 283–296. DOI: 10.1016/S0893-6080(97)00135-4

Rauf, U., Mohsen, F., & Wei, Z. (2023). A Taxonomic Classification of Insider Threats: Existing Techniques, Future Directions & Recommendations. *Journal of Cyber Security and Mobility, 12*(2), 221–252. DOI: 10.13052/jcsm2245-1439.1225

Ravikumar, A. S., & Mamadiyarov, Z. (2025). Mitigating risks through AI-powered fraud detection systems in digital banking. In *Innovating Cost-Efficient and Scalable Business Models in the Digital Era* (pp. 343–376). IGI Global Scientific Publishing. DOI: 10.4018/979-8-3373-2120-2.ch011

Ravikumar, R. N., Aarthi, S., Ashirova, A., Masharipova, G., Mamadiyarov, Z., & Sang, L. T. (2025). Cyber resilient smart cities through big data and cryptography. In *Securing Smart Cities Through Modern Cryptography Technologies* (pp. 103–136). IGI Global Scientific Publishing., DOI: 10.4018/979-8-3373-3326-7.ch004

Razzaq, K. (2025). *Next-Generation Machine Learning in Healthcare Fraud Detection : Current Trends, Challenges, and Future Research Directions.*

Real-time threat detection strategies for resource-constrained devices. (n.d.). https://arxiv.org/html/2403.15078v1

Reddy, V. Y., Reddy, N. H. V., Adithya, T. J., & Ramesh, K. (2024). Intrusion Detection and Prevention System. In Hyderabad Institute of Technology and Management, *International Journal of Innovative Research in Technology* (Vol. 11, Issue 6) [Journal-article]. https://ijirt.org/publishedpaper/IJIRT169653_PAPER.pdf

Reporter, G. S. (2016, July 18). Former Cardinals scouting director jailed for hacking Astros' player database. *The Guardian*. https://www.theguardian.com/sport/2016/jul/18/st-louis-cardinals-hacking-houston-astros-jail-sentence

Rescorla, E. (2018). *The transport layer security (TLS) protocol version 1.3 (RFC 8446)*. Internet Engineering Task Force., DOI: 10.17487/RFC8446

Richards, J. (n.d.). *Market segmentation and target marketing in sport*. Sports Marketing. https://westernsydney.pressbooks.pub/sportmarketing/chapter/market-segmentation-and-target-marketing-in-sport/

Riedmiller, P. M. (2024). Multi-layer perceptrons. Computational intelligence: a methodological introduction. *Multi-Layer Perceptrons. Computational Intelligence: A Methodological Introduction, 1*.

RiftFeed. (2024, June 10). League of Legends: Riot releases statement regarding DDOS attacks. *RiftFeed*. https://riftfeed.gg/lol-news/league-of-legends-riot-releases-statement-regarding-ddos-attacks

Ring, M., Wunderlich, S., Scheuring, D., Landes, D., & Hotho, A. (2019). A survey of network-based intrusion detection data sets. *Computers & Security*, *86*, 147–167. DOI: 10.1016/j.cose.2019.06.005

Rose, S., Borchert, O., Mitchell, S., & Connelly, S. (2020). Zero trust architecture (NIST Special Publication 800-207). National Institute of Standards and Technology. DOI: 10.6028/NIST.SP.800-207

Rossler, A., Cozzolino, D., Verdoliva, L., Riess, C., Thies, J., & Nießner, M. (2019). Faceforensics++: Learning to detect manipulated facial images. In Proceedings of the IEEE/CVF international conference on computer vision (pp. 1-11).

Roughan, M., Sen, S., Spatscheck, O., & Duffield, N. (2004). Class-of-service mapping for QoS: A statistical signature-based approach to IP traffic classification. In *Proceedings of the ACM SIGCOMM Conference* (pp. 135–146). ACM. DOI: 10.1145/1028788.1028805

Roy, S., Ellis, C., Shiva, S., Dasgupta, D., & Shandilya, V. (2010). A survey of game theory as applied to network security. In *HICSS*. IEEE.

Ruck, D. W., Rogers, S. K., & Kabrisky, M. (2023). Feature Selection Using a Multilayer Perceptron. *Published in Journal of Neural Network Computing*, 2(2), 40–48.

Ruiz, P. P. (2019). *A networked perspective on the engineering design process: at the intersection of process and organisation architectures*. http://dx.doi.org/10.5281/zenodo.22785

Saadi, C., Belghiti, I. D., Atbib, S., & Radah, T. (2024). Contribution to threat management through the use of AI-based IDS. *Rev. Gest. Soc. Ambient.*, *18*(10), e09000. DOI: 10.24857/rgsa.v18n10-096

Sadeeq, S. S. (2024). Navigating the Boundaries of Human Identity and Artificial Intelligence in Contemporary Literature. *Qalaai Zanist Scientific Journal*, *9*(1), 1385–1406. DOI: 10.25212/lfu.qzj.9.1.48

Sandberg, J. (2015). *Human element of corporate espionage risk management: literature review on assessment and control of outsider and insider threats. April*, 87. https://tampub.uta.fi/bitstream/handle/10024/97116/GRADU-1432196786.pdf

Santomier, J. P. (2024). Digital transformation: the global sport industry. In *Elsevier eBooks*. DOI: 10.1016/B978-0-443-13701-3.00209-7

Sarker, I. H. (2021). AI-driven cybersecurity: An overview, security intelligence modeling and research directions. In *Preprints*.

Sarker, I. H. (2022). Machine learning for intelligent data analysis and automation in cybersecurity: Current and future prospects. *Annals of Data Science*.

Sarker, I. H., Kayes, A. S. M., Badsha, S., Alqahtani, H., Watters, P., & Ng, A. (2020). Cybersecurity data science: An overview from machine learning perspective. *Journal of Big Data*, *7*(1), 41. Advance online publication. DOI: 10.1186/s40537-020-00318-5

Scalability of ecosystem architectures. (2014, April 1). IEEE Conference Publication | IEEE Xplore. https://ieeexplore.ieee.org/document/6827099/

Scams and fraud | Own Your Online. (n.d.). Own Your Online. https://www.ownyouronline.govt.nz/personal/know-the-risks/common-risks-and-threats/scams-and-fraud/

Scarfone, K., & Mell, P. (2007). Guide to intrusion detection and prevention systems (IDPS) (NIST Special Publication 800-94). DOI: 10.6028/NIST.SP.800-94

Scheurer, F. (2020). Getting complexity organised. *Automation in Construction*, *16*(1), 78–85. DOI: 10.1016/j.autcon.2005.10.006

Scroxton, A. (2020, November 23). Manchester United praised for swift response to cyber attack. *ComputerWeekly.com*. https://www.computerweekly.com/news/252492512/Manchester-United-praised-for-swift-response-to-cyber-attack

Security, I. B. M. (2022). *Cost of a data breach report 2022*. https://www.ibm.com/reports/data-breach

Security, I. B. M. (2024). *Cost of a data breach report 2024*. IBM Corporation.

Shah, A., Clachar, S., Minimair, M., & Cook, D. (2020). Building multiclass classification baselines for anomaly-based network intrusion detection systems. In 2020 IEEE 7th International Conference on Data Science and Advanced Analytics (DSAA) (pp. 759–760). IEEE. DOI: 10.1109/DSAA49011.2020.00102

Shamir, A. (1979). How to share a secret. *Communications of the ACM*, *22*(11), 612–613. DOI: 10.1145/359168.359176

Sharafaldin, I., Lashkari, A. H., & Ghorbani, A. A. (2018). *Toward generating a new intrusion detection dataset*. ICISSP.

Sharma, H. (2021). Impact of Dspm on Insider Threat Detection : Exploring How Dspm Can Enhance the Detection and Prevention of Insider Threats By Monitoring Data Access Patterns and Flagging Anomalous Behavior. [IJCSERD]. *International Journal of Computer Science and Engineering Research and Development*, *11*(1), 1–15.

Sharma, S., Singh, D., & Chaurasia, B. K. (2020). Improving Snort with deep learning for smart homes. *Procedia Computer Science*, *171*, 650–659.

Shi, W., Cao, J., Zhang, Q., Li, Y., & Xu, L. (2016). Edge computing: Vision and challenges. *IEEE Internet of Things Journal*, *3*(5), 637–646. DOI: 10.1109/JIOT.2016.2579198

Shneiderman, B. (2020). Human-centered artificial intelligence: Reliable, safe & trustworthy. *International Journal of Human-Computer Interaction*, *2*, 1–9.

Shokri, R., Stronati, M., Song, C., & Shmatikov, V. (2017). Membership inference attacks against machine learning models. In *Proceedings of the 2017 IEEE Symposium on Security and Privacy* (pp. 3–18). IEEE. DOI: 10.1109/SP.2017.41

Shone, N., Ngoc, T. N., Phai, V. D., & Shi, Q. (2018). A deep learning approach to network intrusion detection. *IEEE Transactions on Emerging Topics in Computational Intelligence*, 2(1), 41–50. DOI: 10.1109/TETCI.2017.2772792

Shu, D., Leslie, N. O., Kamhoua, C. A., & Tucker, C. S. (2020, July). Generative adversarial attacks against intrusion detection systems using active learning. *Proceedings of the 2nd ACM Workshop on Wireless Security and Machine Learning*. DOI: 10.1145/3395352.3402618

Silowash, G., Cappelli, D., Moore, A., Trzeciak, R., Shimeall, T., & Flynn, L. (2012). Common Sense Guide to Mitigating Insider Threats, 4th Edition. *Software Engineering Institute, December*, 168. DOI: 10.21236/ADA585500

Sil, S., Datta, I., & Basu, S. (2025). Use of AI-methods over MD simulations in the sampling of conformational ensembles in IDPs. *Frontiers in Molecular Biosciences, 12*, 1542267. Advance online publication. DOI: 10.3389/fmolb.2025.1542267 PMID: 40264953

Simon, J. P. (2019). Artificial intelligence: Scope, players, markets and geography. *Digital Policy. Regulation & Governance*, *21*(3), 208–237. DOI: 10.1108/DPRG-08-2018-0039

Singh, K. P., & Sood, S. K. (2020). A decision support system for DDoS attack detection using deep learning. *Computers & Security*, *94*, 101872.

Singh, S., & Chana, I. (2016). A survey on resource scheduling in cloud computing: Issues and challenges. *Journal of Grid Computing*, *14*(2), 217–264. DOI: 10.1007/s10723-015-9359-2

Siris, V. A., & Papagalou, F. (2006). Application of anomaly detection algorithms for detecting SYN flooding attacks. *Computer Communications*, *29*(9), 1433–1442. DOI: 10.1016/j.comcom.2005.09.008

Sivakumar, N., Raza Khan, A., Umar, S., Ravikumar, R. N., Bremnavas, I., Lunagaria, M., Vaghela, K., Tejani, G. G., & Kumar Sharma, S. (2025). A hybrid brain tumor classification using FL with FedAvg and FedProx for privacy and robustness across heterogeneous data sources. *IEEE Access : Practical Innovations, Open Solutions*, *13*, 57705–57719. DOI: 10.1109/ACCESS.2025.3549440

Smith, J., & Karan, D. (2025). *AI-Driven Anomaly Detection for Insider Threat Prevention in Identity and Access Management (IAM) Systems Authors : Jordan Smith, Dash Karan. December 2023.*

Smith, L., & Lamprecht, C. (2025). *Identifying the limitations associated with machine learning techniques in performing accounting tasks* (Vol. 22, Issue 2). DOI: 10.1108/JFRA-05-2023-0280

Solans, D., Biggio, B., & Castillo, C. (2021). Poisoning attacks on algorithmic fairness. In *Lecture Notes in Computer Science* (pp. 162–177). Springer International Publishing. DOI: 10.1007/978-3-030-67658-2_10

Sommer, R., & Paxson, V. (2010). Outside the closed world: On using machine learning for network intrusion detection. *IEEE Symposium on Security and Privacy.* DOI: 10.1109/SP.2010.25

Staff, A. (2024, August 13). *Data governance in healthcare*. Arcadia. https://arcadia.io/resources/data-governance-in-healthcare

Subhani, A., Khan, I. A., & Zubair, A. (2021). Review of insider and insider threat detection in the organizations. *Journal of Advanced Research in Social Sciences and Humanities*, *6*(4), 167–174. DOI: 10.26500/JARSSH-06-2021-0402

Suganthi, S. T.. (2022). Deep learning model for deep fake face recognition and detection. *PeerJ. Computer Science*, *8*, e881. DOI: 10.7717/peerj-cs.881 PMID: 35494811

SuIP, M. T. (2016). False positive reduction techniques in network intrusion detection systems. *International Journal of Network Security*, *18*(4), 764–771.

Suliman, S. I., Abd Shukor, M. S., Kassim, M., Mohamad, R., & Shahbudin, S. (2018). Network intrusion detection system using artificial immune system (AIS). In 2018 3rd International Conference on Computer and Communication Systems (ICCCS) (pp. 178–182). IEEE. DOI: 10.1109/CCOMS.2018.8463274

Sutton, R. S., & Barto, A. G. (2018). *Reinforcement learning: An introduction* (2nd ed.). MIT Press.

Tabrizchi, H. (2020). *threats, and solutions.*

Tamke, M., & Thomsen, M. R. (2018). Complex Modelling. *International Journal of Architectural Computing*, *16*(2), 87–90. DOI: 10.1177/1478077118779432

Tang, M., Nikolaenko, M., Alrefai, A., & Kumar, A. (2025). Metaverse and digital twins in the age of AI and extended reality. *Architecture (Washington, D.C.)*, *5*(2), 36. DOI: 10.3390/architecture5020036

Tang, T. A., Mhamdi, L., McLernon, D., Zaidi, S. A. R., & Ghogho, M. (2016). Deep learning approach for network intrusion detection in software defined networking. In *Proceedings of the International Conference on Wireless Networks and Mobile Communications* (pp. 258–263). IEEE. DOI: 10.1109/WINCOM.2016.7777224

Tao, X., Liu, J., Yu, Y., Zhang, H., & Huang, Y. (2025). An insider threat detection method based on improved Test-Time Training model. *High-Confidence Computing*, *5*(1), 100283. DOI: 10.1016/j.hcc.2024.100283

Tavallaee, M., Bagheri, E., Lu, W., & Ghorbani, A. A. (2009). *A detailed analysis of the KDD Cup 99 data set*. IEEE CISDA. DOI: 10.1109/CISDA.2009.5356528

Thammareddi, . (2023). Analysis on Cybersecurity Threats in Modern Banking and Machine Learning Techniques for Fraud Detection. *The Review of Contemporary Scientific and Academic Studies*, *3*(11). Advance online publication. DOI: 10.55454/rcsas.3.11.2023.004

Thaseen, I. S., & Kumar, C. (2017). Intrusion detection model using fusion of PCA and optimized SVM. *Computers & Security*, *70*, 277–288.

Thawait, N. K.Naveen Kumar Thawait. (2024). Machine Learning in Cybersecurity : Applications, Challenges and Future Directions. *International Journal of Scientific Research in Computer Science. Engineering and Information Technology*, *10*(3), 16–27. DOI: 10.32628/CSEIT24102125

Thompson, M., & Rodriguez, A. (2021). Content delivery network security: Challenges and solutions. *IEEE Network*, *35*(3), 134–141. DOI: 10.1109/MNET.011.2000398

Timofte, E. M., Dimian, M., Graur, A., Potorac, A. D., Balan, D., Croitoru, I., Hri - can, D.-F., & Pu ca u, M. (2025). Federated learning for cybersecurity: A privacy-preserving approach. *Applied Sciences (Basel, Switzerland)*, *15*(12), 6878. Advance online publication. DOI: 10.3390/app15126878

Tripathi. (2024). Artificial Intelligence vs. Human Intelligence: Are the Boundaries Blurring? *Open Access Journal of Data Science and Artificial Intelligence*, *2*(1). DOI: 10.23880/oajda-16000156

Turner, R. M., Spiegelhalter, D. J., Smith, G. C. S., & Thompson, S. G. (2020). Bias Modelling in Evidence Synthesis. *Journal of the Royal Statistical Society. Series A, (Statistics in Society)*, *172*(1), 21–47. DOI: 10.1111/j.1467-985X.2008.00547.x

U.S. Department of Health and Human Services. (2013). HIPAA security rule (45 CFR Parts 160, 162, and 164). https://www.hhs.gov/hipaa/for-professionals/security/index.html

Ugtakhbayar, N. (2012). Classification of artificial intelligence IDS for smurf attack. *International Journal of Artificial Intelligence & Applications*, *3*(1), 47–51. DOI: 10.5121/ijaia.2012.3104

University of Oxford's Researcher Strategy Consultancy, NCC Group. Phoenix Sport & Media Group, Lewis, M., & Barnes, C. (2026). The hidden opponent: CyberTheats in sport. In *The Hidden Opponent: CyberTheats in Sport*. https://www.nccgroup.com/media/zugjppis/cyber-threats-in-sport-whitepaper_final.pdf

Vaccari, I., Carlevaro, A., Narteni, S., Cambiaso, E., & Mongelli, M. (2022). EXplainable and reliable against adversarial machine learning in data analytics. *IEEE Access : Practical Innovations, Open Solutions*, *10*, 83949–83970. DOI: 10.1109/ACCESS.2022.3197299

Vaiyyali, C. K. (2024). Technology in sports event management. In International Journal of Research Publication and Reviews [Journal-article]. *International Journal of Research Publication and Reviews*, *5*(7), 5035–5038.

Varis Abdussalam, A., & Alif Auladi, G. (2024). Pushing Boundaries: AI and Computer Science in the Era of Technological Revolution. *TechComp Innovations: Journal of Computer Science and Technology, 1*(1), 01–09. DOI: 10.70063/techcompinnovations.v1i1.22

Vasilomanolakis, E., Karuppayah, S., Mühlhäuser, M., & Fischer, M. (2015). Taxonomy and survey of collaborative intrusion detection. *ACM Computing Surveys, 47*(4), 55. Advance online publication. DOI: 10.1145/2716260

Verizon. (2024). 2024 data breach investigations report. Verizon Communications Inc.

Vinayakumar, R., & Soman, K. P. Prabaharan Poornachandran, & Akarsh, S. (2019). Application of Deep Learning Architectures for Cyber Security. In *Advanced Sciences and Technologies for Security Applications* (Issue March 2020, pp. 125–160). Springer International Publishing. DOI: 10.1007/978-3-030-16837-7_7

Vinayakumar, R., Soman, K. P., & Poornachandran, P. (2019). Evaluating deep learning approaches to characterize and classify DDoS attacks. *Neural Computing & Applications, 31*(8), 4265–4277.

Wagner, C., Dulaunoy, A., Wagener, G., & Iklody, A. (2019). MISP: The design and implementation of a collaborative threat intelligence sharing platform. In *Proceedings of the 2019 ACM SIGSAC Conference on Computer and Communications Security* (pp. 1297–1312). ACM. DOI: 10.1145/3319535.3345662

Wagner, M., Schmalstieg, D., & Billinghurst, M. (2006). Handheld AR for collaborative edutainment. In *Proceedings of the 16th International Conference on Artificial Reality and Telexistence* (pp. 85–96). IEEE. DOI: 10.1007/11941354_10

Wang, H., & Liu, C. (2020). A novel approach to detect and mitigate DDoS attacks using machine learning. *Future Generation Computer Systems, 108*, 1096–1106. DOI: 10.1016/j.future.2020.03.013

Wang, J., Wang, H., Zhang, S., & Wu, J. (2024). A survey of major cybersecurity compliance frameworks. *Journal of Information Security, 15*(1), 1–20.

Wang, P., Li, Y., Liu, H., & Bai, G. (2018). Machine learning for networking: Workflow, advances and opportunities. *IEEE Network, 32*(2), 92–99. DOI: 10.1109/MNET.2017.1700200

Wang, S., Zhang, Z., Li, W., Yin, C., Ma, Y., & Xu, W. (2024). Dynamic residual graph attention network for network intrusion detection system. In *2024 Sixth International Conference on Next Generation Data-driven Networks (NGDN)* (pp. 53–56). IEEE. DOI: 10.1109/NGDN61651.2024.10744080

Warren, M. M. (2024). *Shanitamol Sojan Gracy A global analysis of data breaches from 2004-2024 using Microsoft Power BI Anti-Plagiarism Declaration. August.*

Wasko, S., Rhodes, R. E., Goforth, M., Bos, N., Cowley, H. P., Matthews, G., Leung, A., Iyengar, S., & Kopecky, J. (2021). Using alternate reality games to find a needle in a haystack: An approach for testing insider threat detection methods. *Computers & Security, 107*, 1–54. DOI: 10.1016/j.cose.2021.102314

Wen, J., Zhang, Z., Lan, Y., Cui, Z., Cai, J., & Zhang, W. (2023). A survey on federated learning: Challenges and applications. *International Journal of Machine Learning and Cybernetics, 14*(2), 513–535. DOI: 10.1007/s13042-022-01647-y PMID: 36407495

Wenyan Wu, L. M. (2024). Is Machine Learning Really Effective in Detecting Corporate Fraud? *Is Machine Learning Really Effective in Detecting Corporate Fraud, 4*(02), 7823–7830.

West Ham supporters have data leaked by club website. (2021, March 12). IT Security Guru. https://www.itsecurityguru.org/2021/03/12/west-ham-supporters-have-data-leaked-by-club-website/

West, D. M. (2018). The future of work: Robots, AI, and automation. *The Future of Work: Robots, AI, and Automation*, 1–205.

What is a Data Breach & How to Prevent Data Leaks. (2025, February 26). /. https://www.kaspersky.com/resource-center/definitions/data-breach

What is AI bias? Causes, effects, and mitigation strategies | SAP. (n.d.). https://www.sap.com/resources/what-is-ai-bias

What is Real-Time Threat Intelligence? - Logsign. (n.d.). Logsign. https://www.logsign.com/blog/what-is-real-time-threat-intelligence/

Witten, I. H., Frank, E., Hall, M. A., & Pal, C. J. (2016). *Data mining: Practical machine learning tools and techniques* (4th ed.). Morgan Kaufmann.

Wu, . (2020). Emerging Technologies and Innovative Research (JETIR). [JETIR]. *Journal of Emerging Technologies and Innovative Research, 06*(4), 7–20.

Wu, D., & Negi, R. (2003). Effective capacity: A wireless link model for support of quality of service. *IEEE Transactions on Wireless Communications, 2*(4), 630–643. DOI: 10.1109/TWC.2003.814353

Xie, C., Koyejo, S., & Gupta, I. (2019). Asynchronous federated optimization. arXiv. https://arxiv.org/abs/1903.03934

Xing, B., & Gao, W.-J. (2021). Introduction to Computational Intelligence. In *Intelligent Systems Reference Library* (Vol. 62, pp. 3–17). DOI: 10.1007/978-3-319-03404-1_1

Yadav, M. (2020). Blurring Boundaries: Artificial Intelligence and the Transformation of Human Identity. *Blurring Boundaries: Artificial Intelligence and the Transformation of Human Identity, d*(02), 1–23.

Yadav, S. (2023). AI-Powered Fraud Detection in Financial Transactions. *International Journal on Science and Technology (IJSAT) IJSAT23041216, 14*(4), 148–156.

Yang, S., Luo, P., Loy, C. C., & Tang, X. (2016). Wider face: A face detection benchmark. In *Proceedings of the IEEE conference on computer vision and pattern recognition* (pp. 5525-5533).

Yang, Y., Zeng, P., Yang, X., & Huang, Y. (2010). Efficient intrusion detection system model in wireless mesh network. In *2010 Second International Conference on Networks Security, Wireless Communications and Trusted Computing (NSWCTC)* (pp. 393–396). IEEE. DOI: 10.1109/NSWCTC.2010.226

Yaw Agyeman, A., & Gbli Tetteh, S. (2024). Using Machine Learning Models to Detect the Increasing Threats of Financial Fraud in the Cyberspace. [IJISRT]. *International Journal of Innovative Science and Research Technology*, (August), 1551–1558. DOI: 10.38124/ijisrt/IJISRT24JUL959

Ye, X., Cui, H., Luo, F., Wang, J., Xiong, X., Zhang, W., Yu, J., & Zhao, W. (2025). Daily insider threat detection with hybrid TCN transformer architecture. *Scientific Reports*, *15*(1), 1–21. DOI: 10.1038/s41598-025-12063-x PMID: 40764628

Yilmaz, E., & Can, O. (2024). Unveiling Shadows: Harnessing Artificial Intelligence for Insider Threat Detection. *Engineering. Technology and Applied Science Research*, *14*(2), 13341–13346. DOI: 10.48084/etasr.6911

Yuan, S., & Wu, X. (2021). Deep learning for insider threat detection: Review, challenges and opportunities. *Computers & Security*, *104*, 1–30. DOI: 10.1016/j.cose.2021.102221

Yuan, X., He, P., Zhu, Q., & Li, X. (2019). Adversarial examples: Attacks and defenses for deep learning. *IEEE Transactions on Neural Networks and Learning Systems*, *30*(9), 2805–2824. DOI: 10.1109/TNNLS.2018.2886017 PMID: 30640631

Yuhertiana, I., & Hadi Amin, A. (2024). Artificial Intelligence Driven Approaches for Financial Fraud Detection: A Systematic Literature Review. *KnE Social Sciences*, *2024*, 448–468. DOI: 10.18502/kss.v9i20.16551

Yu, S., Zhou, W., Jia, W., Guo, S., Xiang, Y., & Tang, F. (2012). Discriminating DDoS attacks from flash crowds using flow correlation coefficient. *IEEE Transactions on Parallel and Distributed Systems*, *23*(6), 1073–1080. DOI: 10.1109/TPDS.2011.262

Yu, W., Wang, Y., Liu, L., An, Y., Yuan, B., & Panneerselvam, J. (2024). A Multi-perspective Fraud Detection Method for Multiparticipant E-Commerce Transactions. *IEEE Transactions on Computational Social Systems*, *11*(2), 1564–1576. DOI: 10.1109/TCSS.2022.3232619

Zangana, H. M., Mohammed, H. S., & Husain, M. M. (2025). Addressing Insider Threats: The Human Factor in Cybersecurity for Financial Institutions. [JINITA]. *Journal of Innovation Information Technology and Application*, *7*(1), 88–96. DOI: 10.35970/jinita.v7i1.2686

Zargar, S. T., Joshi, J., & Tipper, D. (2013). A survey of defense mechanisms against distributed denial of service (DDoS) flooding attacks. *IEEE Communications Surveys and Tutorials*, *15*(4), 2046–2069. DOI: 10.1109/SURV.2013.031413.00127

Zarpelão, B. B., Miani, R. S., Kawakani, C. T., & de Alvarenga, S. C. (2017). A survey of intrusion detection in Internet of Things. *Journal of Network and Computer Applications*, *84*(January), 25–37. DOI: 10.1016/j.jnca.2017.02.009

Zhang, L., & Zhou, E. (2024). Research on network intrusion detection system based on independent Q-learning. In 2024 International Applied Computational Electromagnetics Society Symposium (ACES-China) (pp. 1–3). IEEE. DOI: 10.1109/ACES-China62474.2024.10699591

Zhang, K., Zhang, Z., Li, Z., & Qiao, Y. (2016). Joint face detection and alignment using multitask cascaded convolutional networks. *IEEE Signal Processing Letters*, *23*(10), 1499–1503. DOI: 10.1109/LSP.2016.2603342

Zhang, X., Wu, L., Wang, W., & Xie, Y. (2021). Federated edge learning for distributed IoT intrusion detection. *IEEE Internet of Things Journal*.

Zhang, Y., Deng, R. H., & Liu, J. K. (2018). Efficient and privacy-preserving data aggregation in smart grid for load forecasting. *IEEE Transactions on Industrial Informatics*, *14*(6), 2602–2610.

Zhang, Z., Al Hamadi, H., Damiani, E., Yeun, C. Y., & Taher, F. (2022). Explainable artificial intelligence applications in cyber security: State-of-the-art in research. *IEEE Access : Practical Innovations, Open Solutions*, *10*, 93104–93139. DOI: 10.1109/ACCESS.2022.3204051

Zhan, S., Huang, L., Luo, G., Zheng, S., Gao, Z., & Chao, H. (2025). A review on Federated Learning Architectures for Privacy-Preserving AI: Lightweight and Secure Cloud–Edge–End Collaboration. *Electronics (Basel)*, *14*(13), 2512. DOI: 10.3390/electronics14132512

Zhao, Y., Li, M., Lai, L., Suda, N., Civin, D., & Chandra, V. (2018). Federated learning with non-IID data. arXiv. https://arxiv.org/abs/1806.00582

Zhao, Y., Wang, Z., & Li, H. (2022). Hybrid AI architectures for cloud-native IDS. *Future Generation Computer Systems.*

Zhu, G., Yuan, H., Zhuang, Y., Guo, Y., Zhang, X., & Qiu, S. (2021). Research on network intrusion detection method of power system based on random forest algorithm. In 2021 13th International Conference on Measuring Technology and Mechatronics Automation (ICMTMA) (pp. 374–379). IEEE. DOI: 10.1109/ICMTMA52658.2021.00087

About the Contributors

Yasir Abdelgadir Mohamed (Senior Member, IEEE) received the B.Sc. degree in Computer Technology and the M.Sc. degree in Network and Computer Engineering from the University of Gezira, Sudan, in 2001 and 2003, respectively, and the Ph.D. degree in Information Technology from Universiti Teknologi PETRONAS in 2010. He is an academic and researcher with extensive experience in information systems, cybersecurity, and advanced networking technologies. He previously served as the Head of Information Systems and the Head of the Statistics Department at Karary University (2012–2021), contributing to curriculum development and academic quality enhancement. He has delivered postgraduate (M.Sc.) courses, supervised numerous postgraduate students, and published in reputable journals and conferences. His research interests include network security, cloud computing, software-defined networking (SDN), the Internet of Things (IoT), and artificial intelligence applications.

Akbar Khanan earned his master's degree in computer science from Kohat University of Science and Technology in Kohat, Pakistan. He has been a dedicated full-time Faculty Member at the College of Business Administration in the Department of Management Information System, at A'Sharqiyah University in Ibra, Oman. His research domains encompass a wide range, including IoT, connected vehicles, wireless communications, networking, security issues in wireless networks, big data, cloud computing, and smart cities. Over the years, Akbar has guided numerous graduate and undergraduate students at the College of Business Administration. He has also taken an active role in organizing various workshops, seminars, and training sessions. In addition to his academic contributions, Akbar has a keen interest in quality auditing (QA) and has actively participated in numerous QA initiatives, including self-review auditing. Notably, Akbar has played a significant role in shaping the future of learning. He has been instrumental in creating new bachelor's degrees in Cybersecurity and Internet and Information

Technology, proposing an innovative program in Data Science and Data Analytics, and updating the Bachelor of Business Administration (Management Information System) program.

Aisha Hashim is currently a Professor at the Department of Electrical and Computer Engineering, Faculty of Engineering, International Islamic University Malaysia. She completed his bachelor degree studies in Electrical Engineering at the University of Gezira, Sudan. She completed her MSc and Ph.D. in Electrical and Computer Engineering from International Islamic University Malaysia. Her research interests include Wireless Networking, Network Mobility, and Cognitive Radio. He is a registered senior member of the IEEE. Professor Aisha who is actively involved in research and postgraduate programmers, has published more than 200 journal/conference papers, and supervised/co-supervised more than 40 Ph.D/Master's students. She received the Promising Researcher Award in 2009 during IIUM Quality Day. She has also received many medals/awards in different national/international research exhibitions. One of her research exhibitions won the Promising Commercial Value Award (Second Runner Up) in IRIIE 2014.

***

Ar Arunarani is the Assistant Professor, Department of Computational Intelligence, School of Computing, College of Engineering and Technology, SRM Institute of Science and Technology, Kattankulathur Campus, Chennai. Former Teaching Fellow at the faculty of Department of Computer Science and Engineering, CEG Campus, Anna University, Chennai, India. She received her B.Tech degree in Information technology from CEG Campus, Anna University, Chennai in 2008 and her M.E. degree in Computer Science and Engineering degree from Anna University, Chennai in 2011. She obtained Ph.D. degree in Information and Communication Engineering from Anna University in 2018. She has nearly 11 years of teaching experience. Her research interest's spans over Cloud Computing, Social Network Analysis, Information Retrieval, Data and Text Mining, Machine Learning, Artificial Intelligence, NLP and Big data. Dr AR Arunarani completed the SPARC-2019 project and She has published around 19 papers in international journals - SCI journals over Elsevier, Springer and reputed conferences. She is a Life Member of ISTE.

Ashish Avasthi is a Professor (Research Cadre) in the Department of Computer Science with over two decades of academic and research experience in higher education institutions across India. Currently affiliated with Poornima University, Jaipur. It must sincerely thanks Dr. Ajay Khunteta, Dr. Shikha Sharma, Dr. Udit

Mamodiya, Dr, Bhavesh Kumar Chauhan, Prof Gaurav Mishra and My family (Anamika Avasthi, Sparsh Avasthi and Madhawan Avasthi (Gopal)) for providing me support during my journey of life.

T. Balachander received the B.Tech degree in Information Technology from Madurai Kamraj University, Madurai, and the M. Tech degree in Advanced Computing from SASTRA University, Thanjavur. He was conferred Ph.D. in the area of Cognitive Radio Networkrs from SRM Institute of Science and Technology, Chennai. He has more than 20 years of teaching experience. He is currently working as Assistant professor in SRM Institute of Science and Technology, Chennai. He has published research publication in reputed National & International Journals and Conferences. His area of research includes Cognitive Radio networks, 5G, Block chain Technology, Java Programming, Python Programming, Internet Of Things (IoT) and Cyber security.

Isa Bayhan completed his primary and secondary education in Bolu. He received his bachelor's degree in Hospitality Management Education from Gazi University in Ankara and subsequently earned his master's degree in Tourism Management Education at the same university. He obtained his Ph.D. in Tourism Management from the Institute of Social Sciences at Istanbul University. In 2019, he was appointed as an assistant professor at the Faculty of Tourism, Bolu Abant İzzet Baysal University, where he continues his academic career as a faculty member.

Ulugbek Bobamuratov is a faculty member in the Department of Information Technology and Exact Sciences at Termez University of Economics and Service, Termez, Uzbekistan. He is engaged in teaching and academic activities in information technology and exact sciences, with interests in applied computing, data-driven problem solving, and technology-enhanced education. His work focuses on strengthening students' analytical and technical competencies through contemporary pedagogical approaches, and he contributes to curriculum development and academic initiatives supporting innovation and quality education in higher education.

Renuka Devi D is an Assistant Professor in the Department of Computer Science at Stella Maris College (Autonomous), Chennai, India. With extensive academic and research experience, she specializes in Data Mining, Machine Learning, Big Data Analytics, and Artificial Intelligence. She holds a Ph.D. in Computer Science from the University of Madras, where her research focused on computational intelligence. She has published widely in reputed journals and international conferences indexed by IEEE, Springer, Scopus, and Web of Science. Her innovations are protected by several granted patents in areas such as virtual network security, sentiment analysis, AI-powered applications, and assistive technologies. She is the author of the book Research Practitioner's Handbook on Big Data Analytics, published by Apple Academic Press, CRC Press, USA. Her work has earned her multiple Best Paper Awards and the Best Researcher Award. She is an active peer reviewer for high-impact journals, an editorial board member of the Journal of Advances in Management Sciences & Information Systems, and affiliated with professional bodies like ICSES and IAENG. She has also served as a technical program committee member and session chair for various international conferences. She was invited to represent India in a global academic roundtable, where she contributed insights on the role of AI in higher education. Her applied research spans AI-based intrusion detection frameworks, ensemble deep learning models for sentiment analysis, interactive AI web and voice applications, and smart assistive devices for the visually impaired, incorporating IoT and GPS technologies. She collaborates with industry experts, government agencies, and academic institutions to bridge the gap between research and real-world applications. As a passionate educator and mentor, she encourages interdisciplinary innovation and nurtures the next generation of researchers and technologists. Driven by a vision to advance knowledge and create transformative solutions through collaborative research, she welcomes academic inquiries, consulting roles, and partnerships in her fields of expertise. She can be contacted at drenukadevi@stellamariscollege.edu.in.

Nandhini Devi is an Assistant Professor at V.S.B. Engineering College, Karur, with over 16 years of experience in the field of education. Her area of specialization is Data Mining, and she is deeply committed to staying updated with emerging technologies in Information Technology. She brings a dynamic and forward-thinking approach to teaching, consistently integrating innovative practices into her academic work.

T. Eswaran earned his Ph.D. from the prestigious Thiagarajar College of Engineering, Madurai, through fulltime study. A recipient of the Rajiv Gandhi National Fellowship from the UGC for his Ph.D. and the MHRD GATE fellowship for his ME in Power Systems Engineering at Thiagarajar College, he has qualified GATE in both 2003 and 2011. Dr. Eswaran boasts an impressive academic portfolio, with 16 publications in power quality and 11 papers on COVID-19 analysis. For the past 8 years, he has been recognized as an outstanding reviewer for ISA Transactions, Elsevier. He has also received seminar grants from renowned Government Funding Agencies such as DRDO, CSIR, ICSSR, and SERB, successfully conducting six national seminars. Additionally, Dr. Eswaran secured TANSCST grants for conducting Popularization of Science activities for 2023-2024.

Abdullah Gubbi is an academician and researcher with over 30 years of teaching, research, and administrative experience in Electronics and Communication Engineering. He is currently the Head of the Department of ECE at Bearys Institute of Technology, Mangalore. His research interests include VLSI Design, Embedded Systems, Machine Learning, and Pattern Recognition, with applications in EEG-based stress detection, IoT, and intelligent computing. He has guided numerous student projects, mentored IEEE Student Branch activities, and promoted innovation through Beaspaire Student Association. With strong contributions in publications, industry collaborations, and faculty development, he continues to foster academic excellence and research growth.

Anorgul I. Ashirova is a faculty member in the Department of General Professional Sciences at Mamun University, Khiva, Uzbekistan. She is involved in teaching and academic development across general professional disciplines, contributing to foundational skill building and interdisciplinary education. Her academic interests include professional education, curriculum development, and the application of innovative instructional strategies to enhance student engagement and learning outcomes in higher education.

Namrata Jogi is an academician and researcher with 15 years of combined industry and teaching experience in Computer Science and Management. She earned her Ph.D. in Computer Management from Savitribai Phule Pune University in 2025, focusing on video data security using metamorphic cryptography. She has published four books, including works on Java Programming, Computer Networking, Advanced Web Technologies, and Cryptography & Steganography. Dr. Jogi holds four Indian patents in artificial intelligence, cryptography, and video security systems. She has presented and published more than ten research papers in national and international conferences and journals. Her research interests include cryptography, machine learning, cloud computing, blockchain, and artificial intelligence. She has been actively involved in curriculum design, faculty development programs, and academic bodies at Savitribai Phule Pune University and other institutions. Currently, she is serving as Senior Assistant Professor at JSPM University, Pune, from June 2025, after her tenure at Modern College of Arts, Science, and Commerce.

Rakesh K. Kadu is an accomplished academician and researcher with over 22 years of experience in teaching, research, and academic leadership. He is currently serving as an Assistant Professor in the Department of Information Technology & Security at Ramdeobaba University, Nagpur, Maharashtra, India. He earned his Ph.D. in Computer Science and Engineering from Rashtrasant Tukdoji Maharaj Nagpur University. Dr. Kadu's research interests span Cryptography and Network Security,

Cloud Computing, IoT, and Machine Learning. He has published extensively in International Journals and presented his work at leading international conferences, including those hosted by IEEE and Springer. His scholarly contributions include peer-reviewed publications, multiple patents (granted and published), and copyrights. Dr. Kadu also serves as a reviewer for International journals and Conferences. Dr. Kadu's academic journey is marked by a strong dedication to interdisciplinary learning, ethical technology deployment, and contributing to India's educational and technological advancement.

Trinkul Kalita is an Assistant Professor and marketing professional with over 12 years of experience spanning academia and industry. He holds an MBA in Marketing and teaches Advertising, Sales Promotion, and Retail Management to BBA students in Guwahati. His research focuses on sustainability in quick commerce and last-mile delivery operations, areas where he actively contributes to emerging scholarship. Known for blending practical insights with academic rigor, he guides students to link management theories with real-world applications. Passionate about mentoring, Trinkul encourages innovation, critical thinking, and professional growth, while working toward advancing marketing education and sustainable business practices in India.

Ashok Koujalagi is currently working as an Assistant Professor in the Department of Computer Science & Engineering at Shri Vishnu Engineering College for Women, Bhimavaram, India. He completed his M.Sc. in Computer Science from Bangalore Central University, M.E. in Computer Science and Engineering from Anna University, Chennai, and Ph.D. from the Central University of Allahabad. Additionally, he holds five Microsoft certifications. He has authored six books and published 11 Indian patents (including three design grants), six UK design patents, and two Canadian copyright patents. He has over 53 research publications in Web of Science, Scopus, and UGC-CARE journals, and has contributed 12 book chapters indexed in Scopus. Dr. Koujalagi is an active member of 21 international professional bodies and serves on 18 editorial boards, 20 peer-review boards, and five advisory boards. He has also contributed to six international conferences as an organizing committee member and has been invited as a speaker at 16 international conferences. His research interests include Cyber Security, Cloud Computing, and Software Engineering.

P. Krishnamoorthy is an Associate Professor in the Department of Computer Science and Engineering at Sasi Institute of Technology & Engineering, Andhra Pradesh, India. He has over 15 years of academic and research experience and is a ratified faculty member of JNTU Anantapur. He earned his B.E. in CSE from

Anna University, Chennai, and M.Tech in CSE from PRIST University, Thanjavur. Currently, he is pursuing his Ph.D. at SRM University, Kattankulathur. He has published more than 45 research papers in reputed journals and conferences. He is the author of 10 textbooks in Computer Science and Engineering. He has been granted 10 design patents for his innovative contributions. His research interests include Artificial Intelligence, Cloud Computing, IoT, Machine Learning, Federated Learning, and Quantum Computing.

Rajkumar M is a highly experienced academician, with distinctive knowledge in business research techniques, marketing research, organizational behavior, and human capital management. At the center of his research is a persistent interest in leadership dynamics, motivation science, and organizational citizenship—threads he has pursued through multiple publications in Scopus-indexed journals and presentations given at global conferences. Aside from mentoring students and program management, Dr. Rajkumar is a peer reviewer for a leading academic journal (ABDC). He is also the Associate Editor for . His proficiency in research methodologies, data analysis (SPSS, AMOS, SmartPLS), and structural equation modeling has been instrumental in conducting numerous workshops and faculty development programs

Swetha Margaret is an accomplished professional with a diverse background in academia, research, and industry, with expertise spanning Cyber and Network Security, Cloud Computing, Computer Networks, IoT, IIoT, Big Data, and Artificial Intelligence. She currently serves as an Assistant Professor in the Department of Computer Science at Stella Maris College, where she brings dedicated teaching experience enriched by earlier roles in the industry with IBM and Citrix. Her industry tenure involved IBM mainframe backend support, task management, and load creation, contributing to her well-rounded skill set. Dr. Margaret earned her Ph.D. in Computer Science following her role as a full-time Doctoral Research Scholar at Quaid E Millath College, Chennai. She holds international certifications from platforms such as IBM, Big Data University, and Udemy in areas like Cloud Computing and Data Science Methodology. Her leadership capabilities are further exemplified by her role as Chief Information Security Officer (CISO) at Stella Maris College, where she oversees the safeguarding of the institution's information infrastructure. Dr. Margaret's scholarly contributions include over 20 publications in respected international journals, including those indexed in Scopus, IEEE, and Springer. Her academic excellence and research contributions have earned her several prestigious recognitions, including the International Research Excellence Award presented by the International Institute of Organized Research (I2OR) in collaboration with institutions such as Western Sydney University, Green ThinkerZ, and Elsevier's Mendeley. She was honored with the International Award for Emerging Excellence in Artificial Intelligence and Youth Tech Empowerment, presented by the International Centre for Professional Studies & Cultural Exchange. Her innovative spirit is reflected in her patent portfolio, which includes an innovation patent for Un Nanban, an AI-based interactive web and voice application, a design patent for a Smart Walking Stick for visually impaired individuals, and a UK-approved design patent for an Artificial Intelligence Assisted Iris Recognition Scanner for secured passwordless access. Dr. Margaret also represented India as a panelist in the international roundtable Global Perspectives on Artificial Intelligence in Higher Education, organized by the Alamo Colleges District, San Antonio, USA, where she contributed insights into the transformative role of AI in education. She continues to be a visionary educator, researcher, and innovator dedicated to shaping the future of technology and empowering the next generation of tech leaders.

Kavita Mathad, a Gold Medallist in her post-graduation from Karnatak University, Karnataka, India, and an alumnus of Harvard Business School Online holds rich academic and research experience. She is currently the Professor and Dean of School of Business, Indira University, Pune. She has conducted several International Conferences, Business Conclaves, Webinars, and FDPs/MDPs and has actively participated in various webinars and FDPs MDPs as a resource person. To her credit, she has a good number of Scopus ABDC and Elsevier-indexed research papers and book publications, Major Research Projects, and consultancy done mainly in International Business, Digital Economy, and Sustainability. Dr Kavita Mathad has worked at the most eminent institutes and Universities Like XIME, Alliance University, IFIM Business School, CHRIST University, GIBS Business School, Presidency University, in Bangalore and Galgotias University, NCR, in various leadership positions and as a member of the core team of accreditations/rankings of NAAC, NBA and the QS Ranking. Dr. Kavita is known for her leadership acumen in building new perspectives and values in the HEIs ecosystem.

Mehaboob Mujawar is a Research Scholar in the Department of Computer Science Engineering and Applications at Mangalayatan University, Beswan, Aligarh. He is an academician and researcher specializing in Cyber security, Artificial Intelligence, and related fields. He has authored six books, published 36 papers in reputed journals and conferences, and contributed 15 book chapters with publishers including CRC Press, Springer, Wiley, and Nova Publishers. He holds 4 patents, serves as a reviewer for leading journals, and is a member of IETE, ISTE, IAENG, and INSC. He is presently working as Head of Department, Department of Artificial Intelligence and Data Science at Bearys Institute of Technology, Mangalore.

Samatha Naidu, completed MCA, MPhil computer science, MTech in Computer Science and Engineering, PhD in Computer Science, currently working as Professor and Principal Annamacharya PG College of computer studies, Rajampet since 20 years, 2 years industrial experience as network support engineer, 12 years research experience, Completed consultancy and major projects like AICTE and other IT industry.150 international Research journal papers published,100 national and international conferences are attended and presented papers.10 National And International Design Grant Patents, Utility Patents, Copy Rights, Patents Are Published. 15 Text Books are published. 20 national and international awards are recieved. 22 national and international professional bodies Life member, associate member, fellow member.

Amitava Pal is the Associate Dean at the International Institute of Sports Management (IISM), which received the prestigious President's Award in 2020. A seasoned academic and industry expert, he has guided pivotal industry reports in collaboration with organizations like FICCI, ASSOCHAM, and IMC. As Training and Research Head, he guided SOPs for the 37th National Games, Khelo India Youth Games, and Khelo India University Games. His research has been featured in leading publications, including Bonn University, Germany, and the University of California, and he received the Best Paper Award for Sustainability in Sports. Additionally, Amitava has mentored IIC fellows for the University of Chicago Harris School of Public Policy and spearheaded training, operation and implementation of the computer science curriculum researched and developed at IIT, Bombay for InOpen, SINE, IIT Bombay.

Vivekanand Pandey, Professor, Amity University has more than 26 years of experience in Academics and Academic Administration. Dr. Pandey has authored 03 textbooks, 23 edited books, 01 reference book and contributed various chapters in edited books. He has published more than 15 IPRs and is highly instrumental in ensuring student's startups. He has conducted number of workshops for government officials of Door Darshan, All India Radio, Judicial Training Center, Uttar Pradesh Police, Indian Railways, Management Development of Uttar Pradesh, etc. The prime objective of Dr. Pandey as an educationalist is to deploy knowledge towards Analysis, Synthesis and fine-tuning of the organization and task in order to suit the dictates of the environment. Academics apart, He has keen interest in conducting researches especially in the area of Entrepreneurship for Economic Upliftment of Weaker Section of Society.

Subuh Pramono was born in Indonesia. He received the B. Eng degree in Electrical Engineering from Telkom University, Indonesia in 2003, and the M. Eng degree in Electrical Engineering from Institut Teknologi Bandung (ITB), Indonesia, in 2009. He got his Ph.D from Graduate School of Science and Engineering, Chiba University, Japan in 2024. He has published three books, four book chapters, and three Indonesia patents. He has published 84 papers in the international journals and conferences. He is currently a lecturer at Department of Electrical Engineering, Faculty of Engineering, Universitas Sebelas Maret, Surakarta-Indonesia, and he is serving as reviewer in some reputable journals. He is a member of IEEE, IEEE Comsoc, and IEEE Antennas & Propagation Society. His main areas of research interests are wireless and mobile communications, antenna and propagation, wireless sensor networks, and synthetic aperture radar.

Ravikumar R. Natarajan is an experienced academician with over 12+ years of teaching and research expertise across institutions in India, the UAE, and the Maldives. He currently serves as an Assistant Professor at Marwadi University, Rajkot, specializing in Machine Learning, Recommender Systems, and AI-driven applications in healthcare and security. He holds a Ph.D. in Machine Learning and Recommender Systems from Amity University, Jaipur, a Master of Engineering in CSE from VMRF University, Salem, and a Bachelor of Engineering in CSE from Anna University. He also has a MiniMBA from the Swiss eLearning Institute. Dr. Ravikumar has authored more than 8+ multiple SCIE/Scopus-indexed journal articles, 25+ IEEE/Springer conference papers, and co-authored a book on Artificial Intelligence. He has also published 9 patents and contributed 10+ book chapters in emerging domains such as Federated Learning, Blockchain, and Digital Twins for IGI Global, Wiley and Springer publisher. He actively mentors students through initiatives like the Research Activities Club (RAC) and Student Research Internship Training (SRIT), promoting innovation and research culture.

Pankaj Rahi (MCA, M.Phil. in Computer Science, Ph.D. in Computer Applications) is an Associate Professor in the School of Computer Applications at Lovely Professional University (LPU), Punjab, India. With over 17 years of professional experience in the information technology industry and more than four years in academia and research, he brings a unique blend of practical expertise and scholarly depth to his teaching and research endeavors. His interdisciplinary research interests encompass Data Mining, Big Data Analytics, Artificial Intelligence, Machine Learning, e-Health Informatics, Internet of Medical Things (IoMT), and the development of smart e-Health systems. Dr. Rahi has made substantial contributions to the field of computer applications and digital health. He has authored 24 research publications indexed in Scopus, presented in several international conferences, and holds three international patents and twelve Indian patents, along with an edited research volume in his domains of specialization. In 2020, he received the State Commendation Award from the Hon'ble Governor of Punjab and Administrator of the Union Territory of Chandigarh, conferred by the Health Department, Chandigarh Administration. This prestigious recognition highlighted his outstanding contributions to digital health and e-governance, particularly in the areas of e-Health, m-Health, telemedicine, Health Management Information Systems (HMIS), Mother and Child Tracking System (MCTS)/Reproductive and Child Health Information System (RCH-IS), e-Governance initiatives, and the Ayushman Bharat Digital Mission including Health and Wellness Centre Information Systems. He has played a pivotal role in several national-level digital health initiatives, such as the online Aadhaar-enabled birth registration system in hospitals, Direct Benefit Transfer (DBT) schemes through the Public Financial Management System (PFMS), and the implementation of eSanjeevani, the Government of India's flagship teleconsultation platform, across Health and Wellness Centres in Chandigarh. Dr. Rahi is actively engaged with the professional community as a member of the Association for Computing Machinery (ACM) and the Institute of Electrical and Electronics Engineers (IEEE). He is also a life member of the International Institute of Engineers (IIE).

Aasheesh Raizada is an Associate Professor in the Department of Computer Science Engineering and Applications at Mangalayatan University, Beswan, Aligarh. His research primarily focuses on workload optimization using MapReduce. With more than 15 years of academic experience, he has contributed in various teaching and administrative capacities, including serving as Coordinator and Deputy Center Superintendent for examinations. His research interests include Big Data, Cloud Computing, IoT, and Energy Optimization. Dr. Raizada has authored numerous publications in reputed journals and conferences, holds a patent, and is dedicated to promoting innovation in technology-driven education and research.

Aarthi S is a dedicated Assistant Professor in Computer Science with over six years of teaching experience. She is currently pursuing her Ph.D. at Marwadi University, Gujarat, and holds an M.Phil. and MCA from Bharathiar University, Tamil Nadu. Throughout her academic career, Aarthi has specialized in programming languages such as C++, Java, and C, and contributed to research in recommender systems and AI-related data privacy. She has published journal articles, contributed to book chapters, and actively participated in technical workshops. Known for her student mentorship and engagement in academic events, Aarthi remains committed to fostering innovation and excellence in computer science education.

Bala S is the founder of Vaagai IP. He holds a Bachelor's degree in Electronics and Communication Engineering from Anna University and has seven years of experience in research and development. He specializes in authoring numerous research papers, filing multiple patents, and working as a patent analyst.

Abhishek Sharma is an Assistant Professor of Marketing at Lovely Professional University, Phagwara, Punjab, India. He earned his Ph.D. in 2022 from the same university. His research interests include Digital Marketing, Consumer Behaviour, Internet of Things (IoT), and Public Administration. He has published 8 Scopus-indexed papers, 3 ABDC-C category papers, and 2 UGC CARE papers. He holds 4 patents in areas such as AI, rural digital marketing, social media, and CRM technologies. Additionally, he has one UK design titled Robofly. He also holds a copyright on Industrial Relations Environment and Work Culture in Public and Private Sector Organizations. Overall, his academic contributions reflect a strong intersection of technology, marketing, and public policy.

Ravinder Singh is a distinguished computer scientist, currently an Assistant Professor at Lovely Professional University, Punjab, India. His career has been marked by significant contributions to AI Based Cybersecurity Mr. Singh most substantial impact lies in his extensive research work, reflected in numerous well-received publications in prestigious journals and conferences. Beyond research, he has held influential academic and administrative positions, shaping the educational landscape. Presently, at Lovely Professional University, he continues to inspire the next generation of computer scientists while pushing the boundaries of knowledge. Mr. Singh's journey is a testament to his unwavering dedication to computer science, characterized by pioneering research, leadership, and a profound impact on academia.

Somasekhar Donthu is working as an Assistant Professor in the School of Business, GITAM University, Bangalore. He completed his Ph.D. in Management from Acharya Nagarjuna University, Guntur. He has 17 years of experience in teaching and research. He was qualified in UGC-NET for Lectureship and APSET - Eligibility for Assistant Professor in September. He completed Data Science, AI Certifications from IIT Madras, ISB and Great Learning. He completed CII SCMPro (Supply Chain Management Professional) Certification and CII SCA (Supply Chain Analytics Certification) from CII (Confederation of Indian Industry). He is life member in ISTD (Indian Society for Training & Development). He published 18 research papers in various National and International Journals which are Scopus Indexed, Web of Science, ABDC and UGC CARE List. He also completed 10 NPTEL Certifications in Management discipline with special focus on Business Analytics. He also completed 4 Annual Refresher Programme in Teaching (ARPIT) Certifications from MHRD in the areas of Management and Higher Education. He has attended 15 Faculty Development Programs in the areas of Business Analytics, Data Science and MOODLE from Central Universities, NIT's and ATAL. His area of research are Data Science, Business Analytics and Human Resource Management.

Amit Subramanyam is an emerging scholar of notable academic rigor, currently pursuing his doctoral study under the guidance of Dr. Devaraju, Associate Professor, PG Department of Business Administration at Rani Channamma University, Belagavi, Karnataka. His research interests are primarily situated within the domains of general management, human resource management, and organizational behavior, with a specific emphasis on sustainable HR practices and strategic organizational development. With over five years of teaching experience across undergraduate and postgraduate programs, he brings a valuable synergy of academic and practical insight to his pedagogy. Demonstrating a strong commitment to scholarly excellence, Amit has presented a substantial body of research at both national and international conferences, garnering significant recognition, including three Best Paper Awards at high-impact global forums. His work on employee engagement, artificial intelligence in HR functions, and sustainable management practices within the framework of Industry 5.0 has earned acclaim in international academic circles, including conferences held in Cambodia, Vietnam, Bali, and Thailand, with publications also extending to Sri Lanka and Germany. His research has appeared in Scopus-indexed and UGC-CARE-listed journals, complemented by authored chapters in reputed academic volumes. Actively engaged in faculty development programs, workshops, and invited lectures, he remains committed to advancing scholarly discourse while fostering student development and community outreach. He represents a new generation of scholars committed to meaningful, interdisciplinary research aligned with the evolving needs of business and society.

Gunasekaran Thangavel received his B.E. degree in Electronics and Communication Engineering from Bharathiar University, India, in 2000, the M.E. degree in Communication Engineering from the Birla Institute of Technology and Science (BITS), Pilani, Rajasthan, India, in 2003, and the Ph.D. degree in Information and Communication Engineering from Anna University, Chennai, India, in 2013. He has 25 years of professional experience in teaching and research. He has authored and co-authored around 60 publications in reputed national and international journals and conference proceedings and holds five patents to his credit. He is currently working as a Senior Lecturer in Electronics and Communication Engineering with the Electrical, Electronics and Computer Engineering Unit, Department of Engineering, College of Engineering and Technology, University of Technology and Applied Sciences, Muscat, Sultanate of Oman. His research interests include wireless channel modeling and planning, antenna design, and bio-electromagnetics. He is a Life Member of the ISTE and a Senior Member of IEEE.

Varun Tiwari, Associate Professor at Don Bosco Institute of Technology, Delhi (affiliated with Guru Gobind Singh Indraprastha University, Delhi), is an accomplished academician and researcher with over 18+ years of experience in teaching, research, and academic administration. Holding dual doctorates (Ph.D.) in Computer Applications and Computer Science & Engineering, along with M.Phil., MCA, and BCA degrees, he specializes in programming, cybersecurity, AI, cloud computing, Internet of Things and Big Data Analytics. Dr. Varun Tiwari is the author of five patents, has reviewed academic works, published a number of research papers in reputable journals that are indexed by Web of Science, Google Scholar, Scopus, and UGC, and has written books. A recognized expert in Big Data, Software Development, and Cybersecurity, Dr. Tiwari is dedicated to advancing technology education and preparing future-ready professionals.

Bhoopathy V is a Professor at Sree Rama Engineering College. He holds a Ph.D. in Information and Communication Engineering from Anna University and has over 16 years of academic experience. Specializing in wireless sensor networks and IoT, he has published numerous research papers and holds several international patents. Dr. Bhoopathy is a recipient of prestigious awards for his contributions to education and research. His commitment to academia continues to drive innovation and excellence in the field of computer science.

Index

Symbols

A

B

C

D

U

X

www.ingramcontent.com/pod-product-compliance
Lightning Source LLC
LaVergne TN
LVHW062326300926
849161LV00007B/1586